BULLETS AND FIRE

BULLETS AND FIRE

Lynching and Authority
in Arkansas, 1840–1950

EDITED BY GUY LANCASTER

THE UNIVERSITY OF ARKANSAS PRESS | FAYETTEVILLE
2018

ISBN: 978-1-68226-044-9
eISBN: 978-1-61075-622-8

22 21 20 19 18   5 4 3 2 1

Designer: April Leidig

∞ The paper used in this publication meets the
minimum requirements of the American National
Standard for Permanence of Paper for Printed
Library Materials z39.48-1984.

Library of Congress Control Number: 2017942360

CONTENTS

ACKNOWLEDGMENTS

First and foremost, I have to thank the various contributors to this volume. All of them have been very generous with their time. For some of these authors, lynching is tangential to their larger research projects, while others are more fully immersed in the study of mob violence in the state. Either way, the reader should keep an eye out for future work by these authors. This book is by no means the final word on the subject—there is so much more to be done.

Mike Bieker and David Scott Cunningham, the director and editor-in-chief, respectively, of the University of Arkansas Press, embraced this project with great zeal and have been very supportive throughout, and it has been wonderful working with the various staff at the press. John David Smith at the University of North Carolina at Charlotte was the editor for my previous book and gave me a lot of good advice for putting this one together. Grif Stockley, probably the state's foremost expert on racial violence, has been a constant encouragement throughout my career, as have Carol O'Connor and Clyde Miller, under whom I studied in the Heritage Studies PhD program at Arkansas State University. John Kirk, now director of the Joel E. Anderson Institute on Race and Ethnicity at the University of Arkansas at Little Rock, has always been a reliable source of conversation and criticism over a few beers. My friend and colleague Michael Keckhaver contributed the image of fire that serves as part of this book's cover. Of course, the anonymous reviewers of this volume offered numerous suggestions for improvement, and I greatly appreciate their thorough analysis.

When I was young and enduring the scourge of braces, I went to an orthodontist whose whole office was decorated with clown paraphernalia. One time, under the influence of some splendid gas, I asked him, "Why do you like clowns so much?" He leaned in close and said conspiratorially, "I don't, actually. See, I had a patient once bring me some little clown picture as a gift, and, being a nice guy, I put it on the wall. Soon thereafter, another patient saw that and, thinking I was into clowns, brought me a little statuette, which I also put on display. After that, it just exploded. People thought I liked clowns and brought me more and more." I mention this because, since publishing a few articles and a book relating to racial violence, I, too, have become the recipient of many gifts of newspaper articles, scans from old volumes, and more on the subject, though, given my role here, these are much more useful to me than clown-themed kitsch. So I want to thank everyone who has passed along to me some little bit of information that helps to shed light on the darker recesses of Arkansas history.

Finally, I must thank my wife, Anna, because it is apparently habit to put those most precious to you at the end of the acknowledgments section. For someone who does not have the study of atrocity as her calling, she has not only tolerated my discussing it quite a lot but has always been patient, loving, and encouraging, challenging me to the utmost.

BULLETS AND FIRE

Introduction

"The cedar stump to which Ed Coy was burned
has been manufactured into cuff buttons."
—*Arkansas Gazette*, March 11, 1892

"Hell is empty and all the devils are here."
—William Shakespeare, *The Tempest*

While researching my previous book on racial cleansing in Arkansas, I spent many hours in front of various microfilm readers, scanning years and years of newspaper headlines hoping to catch sight of some reported event that would explain the dramatic loss of black population in the county in question between two census surveys. As weeks of state and local history flitted by my blurry eyes, I hit a number of stretches in the newspaper record wherein it seemed some new racial atrocity, or rumored race riot, was occurring on a near-daily basis. Headlines shouted the impromptu execution of yet another unfortunate individual, and the pursuit of another anticipated sacrifice by a frenzied posse, and more, and yet more. It proved difficult to pass over these many events and stay focused upon the subject at hand—specifically the expulsion of African Americans, a phenomenon that only occasionally overlapped with that of lynching and other mob activities—amid this wider ecosystem of violence. And I am not the only person who has been taken aback by sheer ubiquity of atrocity reported; as the veteran Arkansas journalist Ernie Dumas once recalled, "Some years ago, my friend Bob Lancaster and I started to work on a book that would be a collection of articles from the 172 years of the old *Arkansas Gazette* that would catch the flavor of the Gray Lady and the state's colorful history. The project ended, for my part, in grief over what the book would have to include: the great newspaper's rich accounts of lynchings, vigilantes and posses that people thought kept them safe from the uncivilized minority. The stories sometimes came almost daily and were written with verve and attention to sickening detail."[1] For example, the matter-of-fact note above regarding the aftermath of the lynching of Ed Coy in Texarkana—that cuff buttons were being manufactured from the cedar stump on which he was burned—made the front page of the *Arkansas Gazette* some twenty days after the event occurred, included in the State News column among such trivialities as "Camden's electric plant will be in operation within the next sixty days" and "Editor W. D. Rice, of the Prairie Gem, published at DeValls Bluff, says he will soon change the name of his paper."[2] Indeed, perhaps more disturbing than the big, bold headlines lustily proclaiming death and dismemberment are those occasions on which a lynching is mentioned in passing among other bits of local news. The 1882 lynching of Jim Sanders in Pulaski County, for one, was first reported on page four of the *Gazette*, deep in the column Local Paragraphs.[3] Lynching could be both the dramatic atrocity gleefully explicated under lurid headlines and the everyday occurrence that needed no further elaboration.

Much of the public interest when it comes to lynching centers upon the number of victims. While scholars are also concerned with gender and patriarchy, law and order, memory and forgetting, and much more, quantifiable numbers do help us understand the dynamics that underlie lynching both through time and across geographic regions. If more lynchings occurred in one place than another, or more in one year than another, questions arise that help people to understand the shifting nature of mob violence. In his 1999 doctoral dissertation, "Racial Violence in Arkansas: Lynchings and Mob Rule, 1860–1930," Richard Buckelew documented 318 victims of lynching in Arkansas, 231 of whom were black.[4] In the years that have passed since his dissertation, more lynchings have been discovered in Arkansas, in part due to the growing availability of resources, especially online databases and scanned newspapers. For example, the Library of Congress maintains the website Chronicling America (http://chronicling america.loc.gov/), which offers nearly two thousand completely searchable newspapers from across the United States dating from between 1836 and 1922. This tool has greatly facilitated inquiry into lynching, especially given that many lynching reports circulated nationally, and that the full runs of numerous local Arkansas newspapers have not survived to the present day. In February 2014, the Equal Justice Initiative of Montgomery, Alabama, released a new report on lynching in the American South that documented lynchings of 3,959 African Americans in the South between 1877 and 1950. Of these, 503 victims were killed in Arkansas. This number, however, is skewed by the inclusion of more than 200 who are alleged to have died during the Elaine Massacre of 1919. Not only does the death count from this event remain debated, but, depending upon the definition employed, many scholars would hesitate to call the Elaine Massacre a lynching per se, given that anecdotal evidence holds that US troops from Camp Pike also participated in the slaying of African Americans; the presence of federal authorities would make this less a vigilante action than something akin to a violent, government-sanctioned massacre, not unlike the Ludlow Massacre that occurred in Colorado five years before and also involved the suppression of organized labor.[5] The 2015 publication of *Lynched: The Victims of Southern Mob Violence* by Amy Kate Bailey and Stewart E. Tolnay coincided with the release of the online Center for Studies in Demography and Ecology's Lynching Database (http://lynching.csde.washington.edu/), which began with data collected over a period of thirty years by Tolnay and E. M. Beck and has since been expanded. The definition of lynching employed by these researchers is that developed by the National Association for the Advancement of Colored People in 1940, which many scholars use and which requires the following: there is evidence that a person was killed; the killing was illegal; at least three people were involved in killing the victim; and the killing was justified with reference to tradition, justice, or honor. This inventory currently records 317 lynching victims in Arkansas between the years 1877 and 1950—but, as noted, it is being maintained and supplemented as additional information arrives.

Of course, as partially demonstrated by the various figures given for the "body count," what constitutes a lynching remains quite open to debate, and the definition of lynching has shifted over time, as Christopher Waldrep ably documented in his 2002 book, *The Many Faces of Judge Lynch: Extralegal Violence and Punishment in America*. The word reportedly had its origin in the impromptu trials and punishment of individuals suspected of treason during the Revolutionary War but soon came to apply, by the early nineteenth century, to the whipping of "miscreants" on the ever-advancing American frontier, typically by people representing the broader community, outside the legal process. The 1835 execution of five gamblers in Vicksburg, Mississippi, solidified a view of lynching as violence endorsed by society, an expression of popular sovereignty. This connection between community support and extralegal violence often led the Ku Klux Klan, during Reconstruction, to disguise their explicitly political killings "to resemble lynchings, hoping to win community support by making it look like they already had it."[6] In fact, Republican leaders worked hard not to describe Klan violence as lynching lest they grant it the authority of the community; as Waldrep goes on to explain,

> Understanding why racial violence in the Reconstruction era was not called lynching helps explain the difference between Reconstruction and the lynching era. Reconstruction was a revolutionary time, a time when power as expressed in language was genuinely up for grabs. Once the white population seized power and rallied itself into a racial bloc, then, and only then, could they kill confident that they had the support of what they defined as the community. And they understood a community-sanctioned killing to be a lynching.[7]

After Reconstruction, lynching became much more racialized and much more heavily associated with the South. During the early twentieth century, as concern about lynching became an increasingly national phenomenon, journalists and organizations like the National Association for the Advancement of Colored People (NAACP) and the Tuskegee Institute all employed varying definitions of lynching in their attempts to study, and advocate against, mob violence; the NAACP eventually moved away from an explicit connection to community support and toward the more abstract definition cited above, in part to acknowledge the increase of secretive "committees" in carrying out racial murders.[8] For Waldrep, "There is no single behavior that can be called 'lynching.' Any attempt to impose a definition on such a diverse, subtle, and complex reality will inevitably miss the point."[9]

In his introduction to his 2014 *Genocide: A Reader*, Jens Meierhenrich called for the equivalent of the sort of "bench research" that is the foundation of the natural sciences, "research undertaken with the sole objective of increasing understanding of fundamental aspects of genocidal dynamics" without any broader policy considerations—a dire need in a field established "on the borderline between moral indignation and academic inquiry," leading to conditions in which many "advocate for solutions to the problem on the back of partial or incomplete understanding of the phenomenon."[10] Regarding racial violence in the United States, we, too, often proceed with a partial understanding of the phenomenon and a readiness to indulge in theoretical speculation on the basis of a handful of cases; the secondary literature on lynching, much of it quite excellent, is rife with attempts to tackle the "meaning" of lynching, as if we can discuss the essence of an act the definition of which is regularly (and rightly) debated, an act that lies on a continuum with other forms of violence, both vigilante and state-driven. Part of the aim of this book is to fulfill the need for such bench research by presenting some studies that might be incorporated into even larger surveys, thus adding to the richness of scholarly research on racial violence, on Arkansas, and on the South as a whole.

However, the major aim of this book is to shift our conception of lynching—away from the heat-of-the-moment passions carried out in the face of weak law enforcement that are so common in popular depictions and toward a better representation of lynching as a political act, intimately connected to state authority. A quick glance at the table of contents will reveal to the reader that the time period named in the subtitle of this book, 1840–1950, is arguably misrepresentative, for the Civil War and Reconstruction go largely unstudied herein. This is by design. As Paul Dumouchel notes at the beginning of *The Barren Sacrifice: An Essay on Political Violence*, there is a scandal that "comes from the contradiction between the official function of the state, namely, protection of its members, and policies that target the extermination of a very large number of those members."[11] The fact that violence, even of the exterminatory kind, occurs during war or states of emergency, such as military occupation, should not surprise us. We accept that law and order can break down in such circumstances, leaving behind that Hobbesian state of nature, the war of all against all. In such a power vacuum, "the distinction between violence and reason disappears. . . . Recourse to violence then looks to individuals not only like a rational option, but also, very often, eminently reasonable."[12] That is, in such circumstances, wherein the state's monopoly of violence has disappeared, individuals may be more easily motivated to act on long-standing grudges against neighbors, business competitors, and others.[13] Developments in Arkansas during the Civil War illustrate this breakdown and the concomitant emergence of armed bandits who took advantage of the chaos in order to rob and plunder. After his defeat at the Battle of Pea Ridge in northwestern Arkansas, Maj. Gen. Earl Van Dorn was transferred to the Army of Mississippi, and he took troops and supplies with him, leaving the state well-nigh defenseless. In response, Van Dorn's successor, Gen. Thomas Hindman, issued General Order No. 17, which promoted the raising of independent guerrilla companies. As historian Robert R. Mackey notes, "Hindman hoped that by permitting Arkansans to serve in their own districts and to organize as they saw fit, he could field additional men against the Northern juggernaut. In reality, he and the other Confederate leaders gave Arkansans carte blanche to fight the war without interference from the military or government and encouraged the spread of uncontrolled partisan units who owed loyalty to neither side."[14]

Moreover, racial atrocities were committed within a military context in Arkansas during the war, most notably on April 18, 1864, at the Engagement at Poison Spring in southwestern Arkansas. There, following a Union defeat, Confederate forces relentlessly murdered black Union troops, members of the First Kansas Colored Infantry, after their capture. One letter written by a Confederate soldier shortly after the massacre recounts:

> I have said Fed yes of deepest dye negroes. I think there were 10 negroes killed to one white Fed. Just as a had said before, they made the negroes go in front and if they negro was wounded, our men would shoot him dead as they were passed and what negroes that were captured have, from the best information I can obtain, since been shot. I have seen enough myself to know it is correct our men is determine not to take negro prisoners, and if all of the negroes could have seen what occured that day, they would stay at home.[15]

As Gregory J. W. Urwin notes, "The Poison Spring Massacre has gone down in history as the worst war crime ever committed on Arkansas soil."[16] However, though a war crime like this certainly exists along a continuum of racial violence with what we call lynching, to conflate the two—to dub as a lynching those atrocities that occur during a state of war or intense political instability—obscures lynching's close relationship to established political authority.

The conditions of political insecurity persisted after the surrender of Robert E. Lee at Appomattox, largely on account of a poorly planned Union occupation, one in which the jurisdiction of military versus civil authority was not firmly decided, leading to widespread ambiguity about who was in charge. As Daniel Kato writes in *Liberalizing Lynching: Building a New Racialized State*, "The 'headless' nature of the occupation not only exacerbated the confusion regarding jurisdiction, but it also contributed to the debasement of the rule of law. The initial jurisdictional incoherency and subsequent executive indecision spawned crises of inconsistency, bias, and dysfunction."[17] Much of the growth of southern extremism, as typified by the rise of the Ku Klux Klan, depended upon the desire to restore some semblance of stability: "The Ku Klux Klan was explicit about couching their actions in ways that addressed the primary concerns of white Southerners, which centered on the weakness of the federal government to administer the law effectively. Southern extremists were able to convince many white Southerners that a limited degree of extralegality was necessary to ensure a wider degree of stability."[18] As Dumouchel observes, political violence "is violence that legitimizes itself. It is violence with which those other than those who commit it identify."[19] The Klan and its sympathizers saw the restoration of white supremacy (and, ideally, the restoration of slavery, by nature if not by name) as the precondition for stability, federal Reconstruction having overturned the divine (and profitable) order of things.

Because so much of the southern white population held the same view, the same fears of "Negro rule," the Klan and other likeminded groups and individuals proved to be a legitimate insurgency in the eyes of many. Much of the violence carried out during Reconstruction would certainly fall under some definitions of lynching. Historian Randy Finley offers a brief selection of some such killings: "Jacksonport freedman James Hanover's body was discovered in December 1866, riddled with seventeen bullet holes. At about the same time in Paraclifta in southwestern Arkansas, a freedwoman and her three children were found in the woods near their home with their heads split open. In Van Buren, a black man married to a white woman was murdered in February 1868, a symbol of the sentiment many whites held toward interracial marriage."[20] However, such violence was no doubt linked to the larger political project of turning back the clock on black independence and Northern political authority over the former Confederacy. Finley documents an array of violent events in Arkansas that are part of a larger insurgent campaign: threats to kill landowners who rented to former slaves, an attack on a white citizen who voted for a black congressional candidate, the incitation of a mob to kill country registrars, the beating of a justice of the peace who fined a white man for aggravated assault against a freedman, death threats against those who taught black students, and attacks upon agents of the Bureau of Refugees, Freedmen, and Abandoned

Lands (commonly called the Freedmen's Bureau).[21] Figures such as Cullen Baker illustrate the continuity of violent conditions between the Civil War and Reconstruction. Baker was drafted by the Confederates in 1862 but eventually found himself a guerrilla soldier in Perry County, east of Little Rock, in 1864, where he gathered other Confederate sympathizers before relocating to southwestern Arkansas at war's end; there, he engaged in insurgent violence until his 1868 death: "Enlisting fifteen Rebel true-believers to join him, he robbed, whipped, and killed scores of blacks in both Arkansas and Texas. At Bright Star in Miller County, for example, he told black residents that he would kill any black who voted, a threat which kept many freedpersons away from the polls."[22]

During the period of Reconstruction, there were essentially two poles around which authority coalesced, the federal government and southern extremists, but eventually the federal government backed off and ended its Reconstruction policies. The insurgency won.

Granted, Arkansas differed somewhat from the rest of the South, largely due to the work of Powell Clayton, a Union brigadier general who served in Arkansas and was elected governor in early 1868 on the Republican ticket, following the ratification of a new state constitution that contained provisions necessary for Arkansas to rejoin the Union, such as giving African-American men the right to vote.[23] The Ku Klux Klan emerged in Arkansas that same year and began carrying out a campaign of murder and harassment, including the murder on October 22, 1868, of congressman James Hinds by George A. Clark, secretary of the Democratic Committee of Monroe County.[24] The day after the November 1868 general election, Clayton declared martial law in ten Arkansas counties, expanding this to another four soon thereafter. Some of the fighting that went on across the state rivaled the events of the Civil War. For example, Daniel Phillips Upham, who headed up the northeast military district of the state, faced off against numerous armed Klansman while fighting for the control of Augusta and was later ambushed by a hundred more such insurgents.[25] According to historian Alan W. Trelease, Powell Clayton "accomplished more than any other Southern governor in suppressing the Ku Klux conspiracy."[26] However, order was not completely restored during Reconstruction in Arkansas. For example, Pope County erupted in violence in 1872 and had to be placed under martial law, an event that seemed to presage the Brooks-Baxter War two years later.[27] In April 1874, Joseph Brooks engaged in a coup d'état, throwing out of the governor's office

Elisha Baxter, the man who had bested him in the 1872 gubernatorial campaign (and who was seen by many Republicans as too conciliatory toward former Confederates). Each man lined up armed supporters, and more than two hundred people were killed in the ensuing weeks until the intervention of Pres. Ulysses S. Grant put an end to the conflict by siding with Baxter.[28] After this, a new state constitutional convention was held, which essentially solidified Democratic power in Arkansas. This new governing document largely localized power, in part by explicitly forbidding the state government from carrying out specific activities.[29] As Carl H. Moneyhon has noted, this newly re-empowered Democratic Party "clearly represented the landed interests of the state" and was, in many ways, "an extension of the power of the antebellum elite."[30] The insurgency had effectively ended in victory for the rebels, and peace (at least, in a formal, political sense) was achieved.

Though violence resembling lynching can certainly occur in states of violent upheaval, lynching as we understand it—complete with its demands for law and order that often entail attacks upon the very representatives of law and order—only exists alongside some authority that possesses the monopoly on legitimate violence. In his 1982 short story "Burning Chrome," science fiction writer William Gibson describes a particular criminal activity as "so popular it's almost legal."[31] This description could be similarly applied to lynching. After all, the nature of crime is best determined not by the laws a state or nation has on its books but rather by the laws a state or nation, employing its monopoly on legitimate violence, can enforce and actually bothers to enforce. The premeditated murder of a person—not to mention the attacks upon law enforcement personnel or the damage to police and city property that lynching often entailed—could have been prosecuted under existing law, requiring no specific law against lynching, especially given that members of lynch mobs often carried out their deeds undisguised. That perpetrators of lynching were not regularly arrested and brought to trial (unless they were black themselves, as sometimes happened) reveals the real nature of law and law enforcement as practiced in Arkansas and the rest of the South. Only before the Civil War and after Reconstruction was there some semblance of uncontested authority in Arkansas, and lynching, for the most part, existed perfectly well alongside this authority, even as it ostensibly offered a challenge, given that private individuals were taking the law into their own hands. Indeed, lynching only increased as Arkansas slowly became less a frontier and more an integral part of the national economy, not only with the development of railroads and various extractive industries, but also a rise in manufacturing. As will be discussed, the 1890s was the peak decade of lynching in the state, and this decade, despite the Panic of 1893, ended with Arkansas on its way to becoming a modern state, with nearly 30 percent of its workers earning their primary income from nonagricultural pursuits.[32] However, such violence as occurred during this time period and afterward was rarely viewed in political terms. As Kato observes, "Reconstruction violence was understood to be highly political if only because it seemed to operate in a highly partisan fashion. Post-Reconstruction violence was characterized as apolitical—in part because it seemed to operate independently of any partisan advantage and because its modus vivendi changed from being a divisive, partisan act that stifled opposition to a unifying, social act that suppressed insubordination."[33] Klan murders during Reconstruction *were* political acts, but they were not connected intimately to the authority of the state. After all, a significant number of white Arkansans had opposed secession and even took up arms against the Confederacy during the Civil War; after the war, many of these people were involved in Republican Party politics alongside the newcomers derisively dubbed "carpetbaggers."[34] Whites in Arkansas did not form a "racial bloc" until after Reconstruction.

Of course, lynching after Reconstruction was not so apolitical: despite its ostensible challenge to authority (as exemplified by mob attacks upon police officers or courthouses), such violence, in fact, backed up the authority of a white supremacist system. As Bruce E. Baker has written,

there is a tendency to assume that "politics" as such disappears [after Reconstruction] and that while violence before that might have been overtly and directly political, violence after that dividing line was somehow less political. If African Americans and the Republican party no longer had a realistic chance of holding power at the state level, then surely things like lynchings could have little political importance, except in the most indirect kind of way. However, the period between the collapse of Reconstruction and the rewriting of state constitutions in the South so as to thoroughly disfranchise African Americans was a period of flux and uncertainty, and if we are to understand the struggles for power, for the ability to shape the circumstances in which one lived, then we need to take a broader view of what politics was and how it was conducted.[35]

In other words, such violence continued to be political—continued to exemplify the exertion of political authority—long after Reconstruction. This relationship between mob violence and authority continued in Arkansas even after the 1936 murder of Willie Kees, the last recorded lynching in the state, as can be seen clearly in the challenges to a culture that had not yet turned its back completely on lynching. For example, the Arkansas branch of the Association of Southern Women for the Prevention of Lynching (ASWPL) continued its activities for several years after 1936. A white women's organization, the ASWPL, in advocating against lynching, also took aim at a culture of chivalry that held mob violence as necessary in order to preserve the purity of white womanhood. The persistence of such a culture of chivalry even after the last recorded lynching in the state meant that lynching remained a possibility, something that could recur under the right (or wrong) circumstances. As Congress debated antilynching laws, Arkansas's representatives and senators, who played an outsized role in hindering such legislation, argued that such laws at the federal level would undermine the state's authority to govern its own citizens. As late as 1950, Rep. Boyd Tackett of Arkansas was defending his state's record on lynching before the Judiciary Committee of the House of Representatives. Lynching thus retained its ties to authority, even if its violence existed only *in potentia*. By broadening the scope of this volume beyond the body count to examine this broader relationship, we hope to illustrate that lynching was not a disease afflicting the nation but rather one of the vital organs within the body politic of white supremacy. To that end, this volume will focus upon lynching violence before the Civil War and after Reconstruction in order to illustrate better its relationship to authority. Lynching did not result from a breakdown of, or a challenge to, to law and order—it was law and order.

Kelly Houston Jones opens this volume with the first-ever study of the lynching of slaves in Arkansas—and one of but a handful of such studies published anywhere. The lynching of slaves has largely escaped the attention of scholars, who have tended to assume such lynchings were rare exceptions to the rule, given the value wrapped up in black bodies and the political power of slave owners, who would be loath to see their possessions murdered at the hands of the mob. However, as Jones makes clear, the lynching of slaves was not unknown in Arkansas. Moreover, slave patrols themselves often exhibited many of the same characteristics as lynch mobs. The fact that the standard policing of slaves occasionally resulted in the murder of human property calls into question the dividing line between official and vigilante justice, especially after 1854, when the Arkansas Supreme Court affirmed the right of any common person to subdue a suspected slave rebellion.

Next, Nancy Snell Griffith scours reports of mob lynchings in order to cast some light on what is often invisible in the study of such violence—the mob itself. The lynch mob often stalks the pages of newspapers with great anonymity, its size left vague, its members unnamed. By sifting through those newspaper reports that offer some reliable information on the makeup of the mob, Griffith works to show that, while Arkansas followed many of the patterns of other southern states on which there have been written comparative scholarly accounts of lynching (Mississippi, Georgia, Virginia, and South Carolina), there were some notable differences. Griffith also touches upon the subject of black-on-black lynching, a phenomenon deserving of more investigation.

The 1890s, Arkansas's deadliest decade, provides the subject for Randy Finley's chapter. Finley not only surveys the alleged crimes that provided the casus belli against the state's African American population, he also immerses himself into the broader culture of spectacle, paying particular attention to the sensationalistic newspaper reporting of the era. He also illuminates one particularly heinous case of mass violence, what has come to be called the Little River Race War of 1899, bringing to light some previously unrevealed documentation on the subject.

Richard Buckelew presents a particular case study rooted in the violence of the 1890s—namely, the lynching on August 9, 1898, of five African Americans in the Delta community of Clarendon. What makes this particular case stand out is, first, the inclusion of women among the victims (indeed, a mother and son were lynched together), and, second, the fact that these five were lynched for colluding with a white woman in the murder of her husband. This case complicates our view of the nature of lynching because, contrary to expectations, underlying it was a woman's violence against a man, a sure defiance of patriarchal authority during this era.

As revealed by Vincent Vinikas, Arkansas is home to what may have been the deadliest lynching in American history, which happened in Saint Charles in 1904. Here, thirteen black men were killed over the space of a few days in a violent frenzy that gripped the town of Saint Charles and the surrounding area. However, this chapter is not only an exposé of this event. Vinikas also uses the event to question how we define a lynching, as well as how we approach the discipline of history itself, because what happened in Saint Charles is only documented by a handful of newspaper sources. Reprinted from the August 1999 issue of the *Journal of Southern History* under a slightly different title, this chapter features updated references, as well as a postscript by the author on how lynching constituted a de facto denial of Fourteenth Amendment rights to African Americans.

Todd Lewis offers a survey of both lynching activity and antilynching activism efforts in the early twentieth century. By examining the motives given for lynching, the rhetoric employed to defend the practice as a necessary evil deriving from the state of race relations, and the strategies exercised to combat the scourge of mob violence, Lewis subtly explores how lynching served as a nexus for an ongoing debate over the nature of authority in Arkansas and the South as a whole. Equally important, Lewis examines a few cases of what Brent M. S. Campney has termed "lynchings in the making," which are relatively understudied in the literature despite the fact that, as Campney notes, "they generated a level of fear among blacks commensurate with that experienced during completed lynchings because the final outcomes could never be predicted."[36] His chapter, greatly expanded and updated from a piece he published in the Summer 1993 issue of the *Arkansas Historical Quarterly*, also provides a broader context for the subsequent chapters in the book.

My own contribution covers mob violence in Pulaski County prior to the 1927 lynching of John Carter. Because lynching has been so classically viewed as emblematic of a "weak state," one that lacked the resources needed to combat mob violence, I wanted to highlight the tradition of such vigilante justice within the capital county of Arkansas, where, presumably, authority would be at its strongest. One of these events, in fact, even entailed a direct attack upon the governor of the state. I also wanted to show that the lynching of John Carter, covered in the chapter that follows mine, had plenty of local precedent and did not simply erupt during a temporary season of madness. This chapter is an expanded version of an article first published in the Spring 2016 issue of the *Pulaski County Historical Review*.

Of course, the lynching of John Carter probably ranks as the state's best known case of what has come to be called "spectacle lynching." Stephanie Harp offers the most detailed analysis yet produced of this event, sifting through newspaper accounts and legal records, as well as a number of oral history interviews. What emerges is not a singular narrative of the event but an array of stories as the interpretation of what happened fractures along lines official and unofficial, white and black, male and female. Where the events at Saint Charles threaten to disappear into obscurity due to the paucity of sources, the lynching of John Carter illustrates similar challenges at arriving at some semblance of "truth" even when source material abounds.

The last two chapters of this book go beyond the violence happening in the streets and examine, more specifically than previous chapters, the broader cultural and legal debate regarding lynching. Cherisse Jones-Branch offers the first-ever account of the Arkansas council of the Association of Southern Women for the Prevention of Lynching, an organization of white women who challenged the patriarchal norms that lay behind white-on-black mob violence. Although only a handful of lynchings occurred in Arkansas during the state council's eleven-year existence, these women were remarkably effective in getting law enforcement to use all their powers to prevent vigilante murders, as well as to advance the debate on lynching in the political realm.

Wrapping up the book is an examination of the Arkansas congressional delegation's role in the fight over antilynching legislation. William H. Pruden III reveals how the state's senators and representatives continually fought for what they believed to be the interest of their constituents, and against efforts to bring the mob to justice. Even the much-admired Hattie Caraway, the first woman elected to the US Senate and a point of pride for Arkansans, took to the floor of that chamber to denounce antilynching legislation, claiming that "certain groups want to destroy the South not only as a political entity but as a business threat in competition with other sections." By tracking the continued salience of lynching within state and national political discourse, Pruden demonstrates the undiminished authority of white supremacy even beyond those days when black bodies regularly hung from trees.

"Doubtless Guilty"

Lynching and Slaves in Antebellum Arkansas

While whites moved quickly in Arkansas to shore up the institution of slavery with a detailed legal code, it was violence that ultimately upheld mastery west of the Mississippi River. As elsewhere in the South, slaves in Arkansas were often given the right to trial when suspected of crimes, but sometimes they were lynched by angry mobs. Slaves suspected of murdering masters or overseers faced the most danger of being hanged or burned by a crowd of whites. African Americans suffered lynchings under different circumstances as slaves and as free people in later periods. For example, lynchings of enslaved people created less of a public spectacle— absent the picnics and postcards of the twentieth century—probably because the lynchers' actions destroyed the property of the wealthiest class of their society. In some instances, white men acting as ad hoc slave patrols committed what should be considered lynchings. Slaveholders' interests in Arkansas's slave society overwhelmingly discouraged slave lynching, so the practice occurred rarely. Slaveholders themselves participated in the lynching of their own bondspeople even more rarely. Ultimately, lynching in Arkansas provided everyday whites in a slave society a way to enforce white supremacy and expedite their version of justice on the southern frontier, but at the expense of slaveholders. The phenomenon of slave lynching provides a unique opportunity to examine how the incentive to profit and the need to uphold white supremacy could be in conflict in a slave system. It also reminds us that enslaved people were violently policed by all parts of white society, not only masters and overseers. Yet, extraordinarily little has been written about the practice.[1] A study focused solely upon slave lynching will provide a much-needed antebellum context for the chapters that follow.

Vigilante justice assumed a central role in the antebellum South as it stretched westward. Policing of the southern margins was often impromptu and violent. In 1836, white Arkansans' willingness to limit themselves to legal justice was put to the test when an enslaved man named William reportedly murdered his master, another white man, and five fellow bondsmen while the group traveled through Arkansas in migration to Texas. Newspapers reported that William attempted to burn the bodies to destroy the evidence of his deed before traveling back to Tennessee to his previous home near Memphis. As the story went, he claimed that the party had been attacked and killed by Indians. The State of Arkansas asked for his extradition, and Tennessee officials complied. After William arrived in Hot Spring County, however, a group of whites took him from the sheriff's custody, tied him to a tree, and burned him alive. The *Arkansas Gazette* criticized the action, arguing that the evidence against William was strong enough that he should have been allowed to be prosecuted legally.[2]

As servants, African Americans held in slavery could find themselves involved in the administration of frontier justice. In 1840s Washington County, a slave helped capture John Work, "a notorious outlaw, and wholesale murderer and robber," who had gone on a spree of stealing and killing through Arkansas and Indian Territory. A "hastily summoned" group organized by the sheriff devised a plan to capture Work, enlisting help of a man owned by one Mr. Funkhauser. The man pretended to assist Work, provisioning him and advising where to steal a horse. He led Work into the trap, where "eight men, with rifle in hand, were to wait his coming." As soon as Work was close enough, "each man fired, and each ball took effect." According to the newspaper account (as well as the story told decades later in a history of northwestern Arkansas), Work tried to stab the slave but fell from his wounds and died.[3] There is no way of knowing how enthusiastic the enslaved man, caught in the crossfire, had been about his participation in the risky endeavor. Slaves might be used to help round up deviants but more often were the objects of those efforts. Historians have linked post–Civil War lynching to areas with quickly increasing black populations and to sparsely populated regions overall. Arkansas *before* the war certainly fit that description, but without more data on antebellum lynchings it is difficult to apply the postwar model there.[4]

The *Arkansas Gazette* sometimes commented on the usefulness of extralegal justice but offered scathing condemnation at others, as seen in William's case. It may not be possible to rationalize that inconsistency as editors and opinions changed over the years. Shortly before Arkansas's statehood, the *Gazette* advocated rough justice for a couple of outlaws accompanied, at least for a short time, by a runaway slave. In 1835, a man who is not named in the available account (but said to be owned by Emzy Wilson) joined two white men, Morgan Williams and Firdling G. Secrest, as they broke out of jail. It seems that he eventually parted ways with Williams and Secrest, however, because reported sightings of the men in southeastern Arkansas did not mention him. It indeed would have been prudent of Wilson's slave to distance himself from Williams and Secrest, because the newspaper called for a merciless posse to round them up, declaring that the people of Arkansas Territory should not "trouble our court or juries with them" and that, instead, "they ought to be hunted down as wild beasts and their carcasses left as food for the buzzards."[5] The denunciation of "lawless and organized banditti" by the *Gazette* included a fear of runaway slaves. As Arkansas's slave society matured in the statehood period, fugitive slaves became an increasing concern for whites, as will be discussed below.[6]

As the years passed and as Arkansas's slave society grew, the newspaper reports of justice on the margins came to include more slave lynchings. Lynching expert Christopher Waldrep has argued that slavery itself "promoted extralegal violence" because both the law *and* customs that supported slavery allowed whites to use their own judgment in the punishment of those they held in bondage. Waldrep pinpoints the issue when he writes that "whites' imagined right to 'chastise' black people outside the law, a sentiment that formed a central component of lynching, had its origins in slavery."[7] The bulk of this judgment was personal and took place on farms, plantations, and roads, in cabins, houses, and woods, and went unrecorded. But sometimes tempers flared, and groups of whites exacted punishment on slaves in public. Although it is impossible to know exactly how often, whites sometimes lynched slaves who, they believed, practiced violence against other whites. Newspaper accounts bear out historian Michael J. Pfeifer's assertion that the murder of masters constituted an especially grave threat to the slave system, making whites more likely to avenge those deaths with lynching. While the twentieth-century press was often a tool to expose and criticize the practice of lynching, lynching stories in the antebellum period primarily reinforced the norms of slavery. Sometimes the *Arkansas Gazette* encouraged vigilante violence and at other times the newspaper criticized it. Even when critical of the practice, however, the *Gazette*'s lynching reports declared the certain guilt of the slave who had been killed. White vigilante mobs acted on what they determined to be true, such was their anger and haste in seeking to make an example out of the accused.[8]

These administrations of extralegal justice did not necessarily play out publicly. In Phillips County, where the enslaved population was dense and where whites were often outnumbered, slaveholder Henry Yerby was found dead on his farm in 1849. Someone had concealed his body with a couple of logs about six hundred yards from his house. The *Liberator* ran two stories on the events that followed, relying on information from the Helena *Shield*. While whites prepared to give the dead man a proper burial, two runaway slaves who had fled Yerby's place a couple of months before emerged from the woods. Whites present quickly became suspicious of the two men as well as two other slaves. After reportedly questioning all four men separately, the party came to the conclusion that the two returned fugitives had slain Yerby. Although the pair claimed innocence, whites tied them to a tree and burned them alive. It is not known how many whites were present or exactly who they were. It is also not known if the family and friends of the lynched men were present to witness their violent end. For *any* slaves present, however, the horrific incident would have served as a reminder of the dangers inherent in running away as well as a warning of the gruesome reprisal that could result if slaves murdered their masters (or if they came under suspicion of murder). This is, of course, what the lynchers intended.[9]

The obvious problem for slaveholders in impromptu executions like what happened on the Yerby farm was their loss of property. If anyone stood to inherit Yerby's property, the lynching deprived them of two adult male slaves—the most valuable enslaved demographic. Usually, masters other than slave traders did not bother to hold insurance policies on men and women they held in slavery—except when hiring them out for potentially dangerous work, such as railroad building or labor on steamboats. Such policies often did not insure the full value of a slave, and they almost never covered them for life, only for a specified term of months or years to cover the amount of time that the slave would have been performing the high-risk work. Considering these qualifications, it is doubtful that insurance companies would have covered a slave's death by lynching. It is also unlikely that the Yerbys or other cotton planters in rural Arkansas held insurance policies on the slaves who worked their operations, much less policies that would have offered enough coverage to eliminate the financial damage inflicted by a lynching. Thus, slave lynchings occurred to the detriment of slaveholders' financial interests.[10]

Yet, however rarely, members of slaveholding families could become angry enough to disregard that economic interest. Whites at the J. W. Carpenter place outside Helena used the lynching of a slave who had killed an overseer to send a warning to other slaves on the plantation in August 1859. The slave reportedly hit Robert Bickers in the head with an axe and hid in a barn loft on the plantation for several days. When he emerged, whites hanged him from a tree on the place and left his body hanging for an entire day. J. W. Carpenter or his family must have approved of the action taken since it occurred on his property. Their desire to make an example out of the man to other bondspeople apparently outweighed their financial interest in the one individual.[11]

While we might assume that some of the party who lynched Yerby's and Carpenter's slaves must have been part of the slaveholding household, an incident on the other side of the state certainly involved the slaveholding family. Goodspeed's 1886 history of northwestern Arkansas recalls the lynching of two slaves who were hanged by a crowd in Fayetteville in 1856. According to the account, the slave men killed their master, James Boone, a physician who lived a few miles outside of town. They were assisted by a man belonging to a neighbor. The men made enough noise in the yard one night to draw Boone out of the house and then attacked, beating him to death. All three of the men confessed, according to the story, and likely gave those confessions under coercion. As a result, the slain man's sons led a group who took the two slaves who had been owned by their father from the jail in Fayetteville and hanged them. The Boone party left the third man alone. He was later tried by the circuit court and executed legally.[12]

It is significant that the man who was owned by someone other than the Boones was allowed a trial (even though all three were eventually put to death in one way or another). The events demonstrate the clash of the financial interest that encouraged slaveholders to prevent loss of slave life and slave society's need to uphold white supremacy. Although Boone's sons led the lynch mob, doing so did not amount to a profitable business decision, because they chose to take the lives of valuable property they would have inherited. But such was their anger in response to the murder of their father, fueled by like-minded whites who had been eager to assist them. Yet the brothers and their gang refrained from exacting their revenge on the man owned by another slaveholder. It seems that the men perceived a limit to their revenge. Perhaps the Boone brothers felt that leading the mob against the property of a fellow member of the slaveholding class would have been going too far. They may even have cautioned their party against it.[13]

The Boone lynching must have been on the minds of northwestern Arkansans four years later when a drama played out in Washington County that was so appalling to local whites that the *Gazette*'s informant declared that "there is a great deal of bad feeling . . . and it will require a full generation to get rid of it." Like the Boone lynching, this incident began with the murder of a master, and, like the Boone lynching, it involved a group storming a jail to thwart the legal process. In spring 1860, a slave man killed his elderly master, Jacob Mullis, in Mountain Township, toward Cane Hill. Mullis had purchased this man, his only slave, sometime between 1856 and 1859. Some whites in the community came to believe that in the intervening years, the enslaved man and Jacob's wife, Emily Mullis, engaged in a romantic affair. Emily was only around thirty-six years old in 1860, much younger than her seventy-four-year-old husband, a fact that surely fanned the flames of scandal for whites who believed that Emily and the young bondsman engaged in "intimacy as would be too revolting to mention."[14] When the man killed Jacob Mullis in 1860, some speculated that his mistress influenced him to do it. The man admitted to killing Mullis, insisting it was self-defense, and went willingly to the Fayetteville jail without a struggle. As word of the incident spread, however, an angry crowd formed and took matters into their own hands. According to the *Gazette*, white Fayetteville society became "enraged, and dreading the escape of the murderer or disliking too long a delay of justice to him, after a few hours consultation, took him from the jail and hung him to a limb." According to the *Gazette*, Emily Mullis pleaded to prevent the lynching and grieved publicly upon its conclusion. She was not harmed by the mob, but she eventually moved away.[15]

While the Mullis lynching draws parallels to the Boone lynching in that a crowd of angry whites extracted a man awaiting prosecution from Fayetteville's jail, the crowd who lynched the man owned by Mullis was not led by members of the Mullis family. Instead, local whites had decided that they could not stomach waiting for the legal process to determine the man's guilt. Rumors of a relationship between a black man and his master's young white wife, as well as whispers that the enslaved man paid exorbitant attorney's fees with his dead master's money, further fanned the flames. Allowing the man his day in court clearly affronted northwestern Arkansans' commitment to white supremacy. A raging crowd enacted their version of justice without regard to the wishes of the slaveholding family. In this way, the Mullis lynching was more typical of public slave lynchings.[16]

Whites perpetuated a similar lynching in central Arkansas in the 1850s. Toll, a man held in slavery by Samuel McMorrin in Saline County, was believed by many central Arkansas whites to have killed two white men, Jessup Molleary and John Douglas, in 1853. Reports claimed that, while the two men were deer hunting in the woods about fifteen miles outside of Little Rock, Toll crept up on the pair and shot them. The newspaper did not speculate as to Toll's motive. He was arrested and indicted by a Pulaski County grand jury in December. Because the State of Arkansas did not reimburse slaveholders when their slaves were executed for capital convictions, and perhaps because he believed in Toll's innocence, Samuel McMorrin paid for counsel to defend his valuable property in court— or, as the *Gazette* put it, McMorrin "felt it to be his duty to employ to defend his negro to use no undue or improper means in his defence; but to see that his negro had a fair trial and simple justice meted to him. If he was guilty, he did not desire him to escape, but receive the punishment due his crime. If he was innocent, as a humane and just man, he wanted his innocence to be established by a fair trial before twelve legal jurors of the country."[17]

It was in the McMorrins' interest to see the formal process through (Samuel died while the case proceeded, and his widow continued the effort), but the white public became restless as delays mounted. Toll's case was to be heard in the Pulaski County Circuit Court but was then moved to Saline County. Because an out-of-town witness caused the trial to be put off another six months (after having already suffered previous delays), some whites of central Arkansas grew impatient with the proceedings. More than a year had passed since the deaths of the two white men, and the accused slave's trial had still not yet begun. Local whites became enraged at the length of time that passed. An angry mob whom some estimated to be more than a hundred people (who were not identified by reports) overpowered the sheriff, took Toll from the Saline County jail, and hanged him in Benton. Toll proclaimed his innocence to the last.[18]

Although some of its other reports had shown support for rough justice, the *Arkansas Gazette* criticized this lynching, labeling it an "outrage." The story explained that although Toll was probably guilty, "it is only justice to say, that upon full examination of the case, there were certain points in the testimony, which might well make doubts in the mind of any jury as to whether he was really guilty or not." The editorial claimed that Toll had actually passed up an opportunity to escape the jail, preferring instead to await trial, but a lawless mob had refused to allow the legal system to work. Worse in the writer's mind was that the lynching was not undertaken in the heat of the moment, which might be otherwise excusable; instead, the "perpetrators" acted after "long, and cool well matured reflection." The paper even went as far as to call for the mob members to be arrested and damages to be paid for slave lynchings (without offering details on how such a policy would work)—not out of any "feeling in favor of the negro," the writer clarified, but out of respect for law and property.[19]

The *Gazette*'s criticism of lynchings reflected the paper's deference to Arkansas's ever-strengthening slaveholding class. By the time Toll was arrested for murdering two white men in 1853, Arkansas's slave society was one of the fastest-growing in the South. Slavery was growing more quickly in Arkansas and the Trans-Mississippi than anywhere else in the American South. When angry Arkansans hanged Toll in the name of white supremacy, Arkansas's slave population was on track to more than double its numbers by 1860 because of natural growth and the influx of new slave-holders. The lynchers acted against the wishes of the McMorrins, but the *Gazette* sided with Arkansas's ever-strengthening slaveholding class. "Law and order" in Arkansas had been constructed to protect slaveholders, the *Gazette* seemed to imply, and should be allowed to work.[20]

About ten years before the lynching of Toll, delayed judicial proceedings incensed whites in the Delta who sought revenge for the murder of an overseer, Reece Hewitt. William, a slave in Chicot County, was said to have slain Hewitt, H. F. Walworth's overseer, around 1844. As in the case of Toll, William was peacefully arrested. His first trial resulted in a hung jury, and the second in a conviction, but while the details are not clear, some sort of technicality seems to have ensured that the case would be tried again. By this time, two years had passed since Hewitt was killed and buried on the Walworth plantation. This latest delay "produced great excitement through the county, particularly among the overseers," and a crowd materialized to take action. They captured and locked up the sheriff, "battered down" the doors of the Columbia jail, and hanged William "in open daylight." Although the *Arkansas Democrat* declared William "doubtless guilty," the story it ran disparaged the mob action, passing the following judgment: "Such acts of popular violence cannot be too severely reprobated, in any community; and we hope the peaceable and law-abiding portion of our fellow-citizens of Chicot county, will use all proper and lawful means, to bring the perpetrators to punishment, and endeavor to prevent the recurrence of similar horrible acts in future." Walworth probably agreed. Because he was an incredibly wealthy, and therefore probably influential, planter of the county and region, it makes sense that other influential whites would use the chance to publicly denounce the destruction of his property. However, enslaved people already made up 70 percent of the total population of Chicot County, and outnumbered whites must have felt the need to make an example of William.[21]

In the lynchings described above, groups of whites responded in outrage to murders of whites. But Waldrep is right to suggest that historians should cast a critical eye on other ways in which groups of whites interacted with slaves—such as the formal and informal policing of slaves. Sometimes slaves were killed in altercations with white parties seeking to subdue them. Arkansas developed a slave patrol system but also relied upon hastily summoned posses to recapture runaway slaves or restrain those who lashed out against slaveholders or overseers. These altercations could turn deadly.[22]

The roots of the white paranoia that led to an expanded framework for patrols lay in the years before Arkansas had even been granted statehood. Fear rippled across the slaveholding South after Nat Turner's rebellion in Virginia in 1831, and whites in all slave territory passed laws meant to minimize the possibility of slave insurrection. Existing codes strengthened over time to provide for the capture and punishment of runaways and truants and to limit slaves' group activity. In territorial Arkansas, slaves were unable to leave the master's residence without a pass, and those caught "strolling" by the patrols could be whipped on sight. The assembly of slaves was monitored closely. Slaves caught inciting insurrection were to be punished with death.[23] The fundamental task was to provide mechanisms to prevent slave uprising. Antebellum Arkansas law evidenced real concern for the possibility of "riots, routs, affrays, fightings, and unlawful assemblies." Each township elected a constable (who appointed deputies) to put down any such incidents. Coroners, in addition to their main duties, were also directed to "quell and suppress" all riots and affrays. This arrangement of duties involved white county officials in the maintenance of the frontier slave society and helped to knit a white front against slaves' rebellion.[24]

While the law of the land encouraged any and all whites to enforce mastery, specially appointed neighborhood patrols were authorized to comb the countryside on horseback for runaways, truants, and unauthorized slave gatherings. Laws provided for patrols of a fairly fluid structure, probably because the slave population varied greatly across the state. The justice of the peace, when "three householders of his township" felt it necessary, was empowered to appoint from one to three patrol committees, each with a fixed captain, who presided over up to five underling patrollers, all of whom served terms of four months. As of an act of January 12, 1853, patrols were encouraged to ride at least once every two weeks— and more often if deemed necessary. Patrols were empowered to ride to "any place in their township where they have reason to believe that negroes will assemble unlawfully." The Arkansas Supreme Court held in 1854 that patrols should be understood as neighbors protecting their community:

> The patrol system is a police regulation, which, being kept alive upon the statute book, is a slumbering power, ready to be aroused and called into action, whenever there is an apparent necessity for it. The presumption is, that the people of each township are able to quell all ordinary disturbances occurring in it, by or among their slaves, and this can be better and more appropriately done by those who are neighbors and friends, having a common interest to protect, and a common danger to guard against, than by strangers, whose interference has not been invited.[25]

Arkansas's slave patrol system seems to have been looser and less formal than what historian Sally Hadden documented in her study of slave patrols in Virginia and the Carolinas. Doubtless this impression is due in part to the scarcity of the surviving record, but white Arkansans worked to protect mastery in a young and quickly growing slave state that may not have had the manpower or resources to support a very widespread and consistent patrol system.[26] Arkansas law provided counties the power to establish area patrols but did not require them. Slave patrols, then, were loosely structured, varied by area, and stood at the ready to be called upon when needed. It seems that much of the actual policing of slaves was carried out on an ad hoc basis, when a slaveholder called upon his or her neighbors for assistance in subduing a disobedient slave or recapturing a runaway. Indeed, in 1854, the state supreme court affirmed the right of *any* white person to subdue a slave in rebellion. Thus, whites policed and patrolled slave communities even if they did not act as formally organized "patrollers."[27]

Policing efforts heavily focused on truant or runaway slaves. When enslaved people removed themselves from their work for a short time or fled altogether, they mounted direct resistance against the system and forced whites to react. Sometimes slaves ran away after violent confrontation with masters or overseers. In those cases, groups of whites may have been more apt to use deadly force in their recapture, although whites always viewed fugitive slaves as a dangerous menace.[28] Alph of Benton County tested whites' resolve when he fled after killing his master. In fall 1849, Alph reportedly killed James Anderson while the two were on their way to Fort Smith. Because Anderson planned to sell him once they arrived, Alph was probably motivated, at least partially, by a desire to prevent separation from his wife, who remained in northwestern Arkansas. According to the report of the *Arkansas Gazette* (much of which was attributed to the *Van Buren Intelligencer*), Alph had crushed Anderson's skull and slit his throat, leaving him on the side of the road at Vache Grasse. While Anderson "welter[ed] in his own gore," Alph headed back north. When residents of Fayetteville spotted him with Anderson's horse and clothes, whites formed at least one party to pursue him. Their certainty of Alph's guilt came from conversations they claimed he had with a slave and some free blacks before and after the murder. Although the first reports claimed that if Alph was captured he would be tried in Crawford County, the news that followed made it clear that the whites of the Fayetteville area were determined to exact revenge immediately.[29]

A posse caught up with Alph outside of town and shot him twice but did not immediately capture him. The *Gazette* declared that Alph would probably die from his wounds while on the run. But Alph's story resurfaced months later in the *Liberator*, which reported his name (a detail the *Gazette* did not print) and his fate. A posse finally captured Alph. He admitted to the murder of his master to a crowd of whites. It is not clear if the confession was offered freely or if Alph had been coerced. The report also claimed that Alph had pointed to a white man in the crowd who had "instigated him to the crime." He might have been telling the truth, or his implication of a white person might have been a desperate attempt to save his life. Either way, the claim did not lessen his guilt in the eyes of his captors; Alph was hanged without trial on October 20.[30]

In a similarly deadly incident, two slave men who had fled from Thomas E. Clark's Crittenden County plantation in late 1840 fought recapture. When Clark and another white man named James Martin pursued the men, they attacked and killed Clark after he had become separated from his partner. Although the intervening time from the murder and the apprehension of the two men is not clear in the account, the *Gazette* applauded the speed with which local whites captured the men and hanged them. The *Gazette* cautiously praised the action: "We are opposed to the principle of mob or Lynch law, in all its ramifications, but in the present instance, will lay aside our opposition, and applaud the citizens of Crittenden county, for the active and speedy measures used by them, to rid the country of such desperadoes." The two had shown the lengths they would go to in order to prevent being pressed back into slavery, and so the cause of white supremacy trumped the Clark family's financial interest.[31]

The killings of Alph and the two Crittenden County men on the run were clearly lynchings, but what about instances where parties pursuing fleeing slaves used deadly force against them? In 1836, a runaway slave named Jefferson, who had been "camped" near David Trammel's home in Hot Spring County, was slain by "the company" who tried to capture him. The white men who pursued Jefferson lived to tell the story, and his side will never be known. They said that he resisted them violently, swiping at them with a knife, and claimed that he grabbed one man's gun. The gun "was discharged and its contents lodged in" Jefferson's body. He continued to resist and was shot again, dying from the wounds after being subdued. Although it might have been true, the posse's careful explanation—that the shooting was accidental and unavoidable—may have represented an attempt to avoid trouble with Abraham Speers of Mississippi, who was likely none too pleased to hear of the fate of his valuable property.[32] A group of whites in Pulaski County told a similar story after their attempt to bring in a man who had fled from Thomas Thorn ended in the slave's death. They claimed the fugitive resisted by trying to stab them. In response, one of the men, Isaac Jones, shot and killed him. Although the story in the surviving issue of the *Gazette* is

nearly illegible, it seems to suggest that Jones could expect a lawsuit from Thorn for the loss of valuable slave property.[33]

The incidents described above raise the question, when does a posse gathered for the purpose of policing slaves become a lynch mob? It may not be that these men gathered for the premeditated purpose of killing the slaves they pursued, but it is true that they were acting as a group in a police effort and were ready and willing to use lethal force. Should an incident be called a lynching if the death was not public and the slain man died fighting? Would the men taken from county jails have been any less victims of lynching if they had had the chance to stab their attackers on the way out? Would the two men burned to death on Yerby's farm have been any more victims lynching if a larger crowd had witnessed their deaths? Lynching of African Americans looked different in the antebellum period, and the circumstances usually associated with twentieth-century lynchings might not always fit the pre–Civil War period very neatly. Killings resulting from white parties' efforts at policing or recapturing should be considered lynchings, and the incidents described above should prompt historians to look more critically at white patrols overall.[34]

However rarely slave lynching may have occurred, it remains significant. As a point of comparison, most slaves never ran away — and even fewer achieved freedom that way — but flight remains crucial to the story of slavery.[35] It is probably more important to understand that masters are rarely named as participants in the lynchings of their slaves. This is partly because the master in many instances was not alive to take part (when his very murder was the catalyst for the mob), and it might also have to do with the lack of documentation — rarely is *anyone* in a lynch mob named in newspaper accounts, which are the major sources for lynching activities. But while the action of an amorphous crowd of whites does not lend itself to naming each person individually, it would be pertinent for newspaper editors to mention that a master was involved if they found that out. This would seem to be especially true for the *Arkansas Gazette* because lynching stories were always accompanied by commentary — either excusing the action or railing against it. It seems that any knowledge of the involvement of the master would certainly influence those comments. All this is to say not that masters never slayed bondspeople but that they rarely did so and even more rarely lynched them. This is important to note not to whitewash the behavior of masters but to emphasize the power of their financial interest.

In order to understand lynching under slavery, it might be helpful to ask questions about instances when lynching did not occur. Whites did not always avenge murders in that way.[36] An incident in Saint Francis County shows how the age and gender of the accused might have been factors. A housekeeper owned by James Calvert was not lynched after she killed him but was perhaps nearly lynched. She snuck up behind him and hit him over the head with a "mallet or mall that had been used for beating hominy." At first, she told the neighbors who came over to investigate that Calvert had fallen off the roof trying to fix a leak. But they suspected foul play. The dead man's brother threatened her life and extracted a confession. He "put a rope around her neck, and swung her up to a peach tree. After hanging a few minutes, she was cut down, and on being interrogated, confessed" that she had actually killed her master. Whether her extorted confession was true or not, her guilt was affirmed for whites who chose not to lynch her. It may have been because, as the *Gazette* described her, she "had been a family servant for many years, and is upwards of fifty years of age." It is not known what became of the woman afterward.[37]

As shown here, murder of a white person—especially a master—was the act that prompted slave lynchings in antebellum Arkansas, but what about rape? Rape allegations are important to examine because in the post–Civil War period they were so often the reason given for lynching African American men. This was not the case, however, in the antebellum years of the South, including Arkansas. (It is important to note, however, that murders of slaves in reaction to rape accusations may have occurred more often, but without leaving written record.) In Drew County, when whites suspected a slave man belonging to the Glascock family of raping a fourteen-year-old girl and then murdering her and her eleven-year-old brother, they burned him. Two African American men were lynched by a mob in Ashley County in 1857 after they were caught with a gang of white and black men who were believed to have both raped and murdered whites in the area, but it is unclear whether the black men were enslaved or not.[38] Legal historian Diane Miller Sommerville explains that the desire to safeguard their investments incentivized masters to protect and defend slaves who were accused of rape. She also argues that white hysteria and preoccupation with the danger of black men raping white women did not exist in the antebellum period. The circumstances discussed below support her findings.[39]

The Arkansas Supreme Court reviewed three rape trials within a decade: *Dennis, A Slave, vs. The State* in 1844, *Joe Sullivant, A Slave, vs. The State* in 1848, and *Pleasant vs. The State* in 1853.[40] In the earliest of these three cases—May 1843—Jeduthan Day, a white man, along with slaves Frank and Dennis, stood trial for the crime of rape in the Crawford County Circuit Court. Day appears in the 1842 tax records of Crawford County as having no taxable property.[41] The alleged rape was supposed to have been committed in September 1842. The records surrounding this case are sparse, but the court report shows a snapshot in the evolution of Arkansas's legal policy toward slave crime. The defense's argument included a claim that, on the day of the supposed assault, no law existed punishing slaves for the crime of rape.[42] The courts sustained objections toward the indictment of the white man, Jeduthan Day (based on technicalities), who may have then gone free, but overruled those for the slaves Frank and Dennis. Both were convicted and sentenced to death.[43] The appeal of Dennis's case to the Arkansas Supreme Court pressed the issue of the legality of punishing him with death. In February 1838, a proclamation by the governor declared that any person convicted of rape should be punished with death—with no distinction between white men and black slaves. A law passed by the end of that same year, however, made the distinction that white men convicted of rape would face jail time while slaves would suffer the death penalty. In December 1842, a new law declared that all persons convicted of rape were to be put to death. Thus, the supreme court held that the punishment of death for slaves found guilty of rape was valid and that the judge of the Crawford County court should get about the business of notifying his sheriff with a death warrant for Dennis. This case represents the initial struggles of Arkansas's legal system to deal with differing sentences between blacks and whites.[44] While the construction of prisons gave southern states something to do with white rapists besides execution, slaves who were charged with rape continued to be sentenced to death. As Sommerville explains, "What might have been a capital offense before the building of a state penitentiary later became a noncapital offense. This was the case in Arkansas, Alabama, and Texas."[45]

Five years later, the case of Joe Sullivant, a slave in Dallas County, came to the state supreme court on the request for a new trial. Joe Sullivant, owned by Eccanah Sullivant, had allegedly entered the home of Benjamin Clemens, a non-slaveholder for whom he had been hired out previously.[46]

Benjamin's wife, Emeranda Clemens, claimed that she awoke in the middle of the night and "felt some person over me in the act of committing a rape."[47] The person, whom she could not identify, ran from the room and through the cotton field. Joe was implicated because his shirt felt like the one that Clemens said she felt, and his feet fit the tracks left by the perpetrator. After being whipped by Clemens's husband, Joe confessed to the crime. He later pleaded "not guilty," stating that he had only entered the Clemens household to "steal a little."[48]

The state supreme court again reviewed a case wherein a non-slaveholder accused a slave of attempted rape two years later in the form of *Charles vs. The State*. On the night of January 23, 1850, five "school girls" came to visit overnight with the Summeron family of Hempstead County. Among them was fourteen-year-old Almyra Combs.[49] According to the census of 1850, Combs and her siblings lived with a couple that seems to have been their aunt and uncle—David and Rebecca Cocknaham.[50] Almyra Combs testified that in the early morning hours, she awoke when a "man partly undressed" attempted to turn her over and climb on top of her body in order to "do violence."[51] When Combs cried for help, the person—whom she admitted she could not identify—left the room through the door. When the Summerons rushed to the frantic girls' room, they found both the door and window open. Outside the window, according to Michael Summeron, were tracks in the mud that led to the slave cabin and bed that a slave named Charles shared with "two other negro boys, smaller than Charles."[52] It was then that the men awakened Charles, whom Summeron described as pretending to sleep, his toes caked "with mud of the same kind of that between the room and the cabin."[53]

Significantly, the accused slave, Charles, was not owned by the white man on whose farm he lived—Michael Summeron—but by a man named Jacob Standly.[54] Charles had been hired to work for Summeron, a slave-holder with a small work force.[55] Dr. Joel Conway, presumably acting on behalf of Charles's owner, Jacob Standly, arrived to the Summeron place and took Charles to town, where he repeatedly confessed that he had entered the room where the girls slept but only to wake Mr. Summeron. Dr. Conway made a point to include in his testimony that "all these confessions were made in presence of, and when interrogated by white men, and when bound." Charles was convicted by the Hempstead County Circuit Court of attempted rape and sentenced to hang.[56] But the state supreme court reversed the original decision of the lower court against Charles, mainly because of the judgment that if Charles had intended to rape Almyra Combs, he did not intend to do so by force. The report explains, "We do not think that the testimony evinced that settled purpose to use force, and to act in disregard of the will of the prosecutrix, which the law contemplates as essential to constitute the crime."[57] Put simply, because the girl was able to fight him off or scare him away, there was no real threat to Combs, and the attacker could not be guilty of attempted rape. Standly mounted what must have been a costly defense to protect a black man from the gallows despite the fact that he was believed to have sexually assaulted a white child. Standly put his investment before any desire he might have had to end Charles's life as an example to other enslaved men.

In Union County, Sophia Fulmer accused a slave man named Pleasant of attempted rape in November 1851. She claimed that Pleasant walked into the family's home, began to drink their liquor, and then "caught her by the bosom and asked for tobacco." She gave it to him, hoping he would leave, but Pleasant then grabbed her, throwing her onto the floor and then onto the bed. According to Fulmer's story, he pulled her skirts up over her head and crawled on top of her in an attempt to rape her. But when Fulmer managed to grab a gun, he fled. Like the other rape accusations, this one came from non-slaveholders. Pleasant was not owned by the Fulmers but by a man named James Milton. Sophia Fulmer was acquainted with Pleasant, testifying that they had met when he came "to the fence to ask for peaches"—a statement that suggests he lived on a neighboring farm. Pleasant was originally found guilty and sentenced to hang but was granted a new trial by the state supreme court because the original proceedings had not allowed Sophia Fulmer to answer to certain accusations of extortion from Pleasant's owner, James Milton. The delay of justice did not result in a lynch mob. Thus, accusations of rape or attempted rape, although an important trigger for later periods of the history of lynching, did not cause much mob action in antebellum Arkansas. The trials and appeals discussed here bring lynchings for murder into sharper relief by demonstrating the relatively uneventful public reaction to rape accusations. In addition, the cases reveal the time and expense that slaveholders were willing to sacrifice to prevent slave executions.[58]

In antebellum Arkansas, enslaved people were "guilty" of being black and of residing at the bottom rung of society. When they seemed to be guilty of murdering whites, they betrayed the delusion that slavery served as a civilizing institution for happy and loyal servants. This real and perceived culpability unleashed whites' willingness to enforce white supremacy violently, without waiting for legal justice. Slaves did not have the opportunity to defend themselves against accusations of murder or rape, so when they did receive their state-given right to trial, it happened at the pleasure of slaveholders who sought to preserve the lives of their chattel. Sometimes, groups policing slaves took their lives. But profit and the standing of wealthy slaveholders in a given community remained significant factors. Finally, while slave lynching worked against the individual economic interests of slaveholders, it reinforced the racial code upon which slavery depended. For Arkansas's slaveholding class, such lynchings constituted collateral damage in a system that relied upon white supremacy to justify slavery. The end of the Civil War and slavery created a turning point in extralegal violence against African Americans.[59] Willis Winn, held in slavery in Hempstead County, told an interviewer with the Works Progress Administration decades later of a chilling prediction (or threat) uttered by his master when slavery ended. Now that the institution of slavery had been destroyed, the man warned, "Some of you is going to get lynched." He was right, and Winn said he knew of a lynching that occurred only months later.[60] As some of the earlier economic and social incentives for whites to preserve black life disappeared, lynch law would become amplified.

"At the Hands of a Person or Persons Unknown"

The Nature of Lynch Mobs in Arkansas

There is a widespread popular belief that lynchings of African Americans were carried out by groups of masked white men, sometimes members of the Ku Klux Klan. Examination of lynchings in Arkansas, however, reveals that this assumption is not accurate. There were many different types of lynch mobs in the state. Many Arkansas lynchings were committed by mobs of local citizens, sometimes described as prominent men, who were totally unmasked. According to published reports, a number of these lynchings, however horrible, were orderly and caused little concern in the white community. Blacks were sometimes murdered by their white coworkers on the railroad and in lumber mills because they worked for lower wages than their white counterparts. Some were murdered in mysterious circumstances, apparently by vigilantes. While many accounts seem to indicate at least tacit participation by law enforcement, in a number of other cases, the authorities were obviously complicit. Lynch mobs were not always made up of white men. In some cases, there were all-black mobs or mobs composed of both blacks and whites.

The face of lynching in Arkansas mirrors the changes in the status of blacks in the state. Following the Civil War, Reconstruction brought political power to Arkansas's African Americans, and Gov. Powell Clayton's 1868 declaration of martial law (in response to violence from the Ku Klux Klan) ensured a measure of peace, even in Arkansas's more violent counties.[1] Even after Reconstruction ended in 1874, there was little terrorism directed toward blacks.[2] Political controversy was ameliorated by the use of fusion politics, which made a certain number of offices available to black candidates, giving African Americans a modicum of power.

During the 1870s and 1880s, African Americans began to flock to Arkansas from other southern states, drawn by the possibility of land ownership and the economic opportunities in the newly established timber and railroad industries. Between 1870 and 1890, the number of African Americans in Arkansas nearly tripled.[3] Lynching during this period was largely performed quietly by small private mobs.

Beginning in the 1880s, however, cotton prices began to drop, causing competition for jobs. By 1890, the state had developed what historian Story L. Matkin-Rawn referred to as "the violent imposition of an occupational caste system preserving the best jobs for whites."[4] In addition, the Democrat-controlled legislature began to pass laws limiting the rights of African Americans. Among these was the state's first segregation law, which separated whites and blacks on railway carriages. Other laws essentially disfranchised African Americans by imposing poll taxes and making it difficult for illiterate voters to identify the party affiliation of candidates on the ballot. This caused a steep drop in voting among blacks; in 1882, 72 percent of eligible African Americans voted, but this number had been reduced to 24 percent by 1894.[5]

These efforts to subjugate blacks resulted in a sharp increase in lynchings, which peaked in the state in the 1890s (as explored further in chapter 3). As blacks lost both civil and economic status, they became more helpless, and, as historian Terence Finnegan notes, lynching was characterized by more indiscriminate violence, which "served notice that blacks who challenged white hegemony were beyond the protection of the law."[6] It was during this time that terrorist mobs, lynchings by posses, and lynchings by huge crowds of people began to predominate. During the second two decades of the twentieth century, following the increased status and economic opportunities provided by World War I, terrorist lynchings continued in an effort to remind African Americans of their subordinate status. As the national outcry over lynching increased, however, it eventually died out not only in Arkansas but across the South.

One of the more interesting phenomena is that some private and mass mobs consisted solely of African Americans. According to Karlos Hill's study of African Americans' responses to lynching in the Arkansas and Mississippi Deltas, blacks in those plantation societies lacked faith in the white judicial system. As a result, they resorted to vigilante justice to enforce their own community morals, punishing alleged cases of incest, rape, or murder perpetrated by other African Americans.[7]

In his 1999 dissertation on racial violence in Arkansas between 1860 and 1936, historian Richard Buckelew examined primarily those lynchings reported in the *Arkansas Gazette*. Excluding the 1919 Elaine Massacre from his findings, he reported 188 lynching events targeting African Americans, for a total of 231 black victims.[8] In 2014, the Equal Justice Initiative published a report on lynching in America. They discovered 503 lynchings in Arkansas between 1877 and 1950, placing it fourth in the nation behind Georgia, Mississippi, and Louisiana. They included the Elaine Massacre in their count, which made Phillips County the leader in the nation with 243 lynchings.[9]

The data used in this study comes not only from lynchings included on Buckelew's list, but from examination of newspapers published between 1865 and 1922, available through the Chronicling America site of the Library of Congress. In 102 of these instances, there was sufficient information about the size, composition, or characteristics of the mob to warrant study. The model used to differentiate between the types of lynch mobs is that described by W. Fitzhugh Brundage in his study *Lynching in the New South: Georgia and Virginia, 1880–1930* (1993).[10] Terence Finnegan's 2013 book, *A Deed So Accursed: Lynching in Mississippi and South Carolina, 1881–1940*, will also be used to analyze some of the patterns in mob characteristics.[11]

PRIVATE MOBS

Brundage described four basic types of lynch mobs. The first two are types of small mobs, which were secretive and involved fewer than fifty participants. The first of these, the small private mob, was intended to punish various crimes, real or imagined. Often composed of only a handful of men operating in secret, they avenged such crimes as murder, rape, or attempted rape. Mob members might include friends or relatives of the victim and were sometimes masked.[12] Many historians have noted that there was no real need for this type of mob because the white judicial system was more than capable of punishing such criminals. Nevertheless, in the heat of the moment, mobs often chose to act outside of the law. They operated both undisguised and masked. Many of them were described as orderly and proceeding in quiet.

bent on intimidation were common in Arkansas. In line with Brundage's research, they were small and secretive to the point that there is very little information as to their composition. Some were intended to frighten African Americans—who were often paid less than whites—away from mills and railroads. Some punished blacks for minor offenses, or for slightly overstepping their bounds. Others were used to intimidate those who refused to work on farms for little or no pay. Still others were intended to punish prominent African Americans, and thus to discourage other successful blacks.

In 1891, in one of the earliest terrorist lynchings, a group of masked men lynched perhaps more than a dozen men for carrying out a cotton pickers' strike near Marianna in Lee County.[37] Sometimes, small mobs used lynching to warn African Americans against what might seem fairly minor offenses, including stealing hogs. There were two such cases in the late 1890s. The first was that of Presley Oats, lynched in Pope County in 1897 after supposedly stealing a ham. On May 13, a mob of masked men took Oats from his home and hanged him in a nearby swamp. Before leaving, the mob attached a sign to Oats's body reading, "A Warning to Stealers of Hog Meat."[38] The second was the case of an unidentified African American man lynched for allegedly stealing a hog near Sherrill in Jefferson County in 1898. The mob left the body lying across a dead hog's carcass bearing a card that read, "You will never tell who told you to kill this hog."[39] These incidents are reminiscent of the days of Reconstruction when freedmen, no longer fed by their former masters, were driven to find other ways to procure food, which prompted members of the Ku Klux Klan and other nightriders to take action against them.[40]

Another goal of the terroristic mob was to punish prominent African Americans, who were seen as a threat to white superiority. Such was the case in Lonoke County in June 1897, when a mob ransacked a black normal school, took Prof. D. T. Watson into the woods, and severely beat him. Despite an investigation by the Arkansas attorney general and the state superintendent of public instruction, by September Watson was dead, mysteriously killed by unknown persons. His body was found hanging from a tree bearing a note: "A warning to 'nigger' schoolteachers. We want none of this kind of people in this country, others beware."[41]

In June 1898, two other prominent blacks, this time prosperous farmer G. W. Ricks and his son Moses, who was a preacher, were lynched in southern Monroe County for an alleged assault on a white farmer's wife.

Published accounts described the elder Ricks as "one of the most prominent colored men in Monroe County," and his son was described by the *Arkansas Gazette* as a "fairly well educated" preacher and "religious exhorter, well known among the members of his race in this vicinity." After he was lynched, Moses's body "was left dangling in the air with placards printed on the clothing as a warning to other negroes."[42]

During the late 1890s, a different kind of terrorist mob, still bent on intimidation, started to appear. During this period, railroads and other industries began to hire increasing numbers of African American workers, who would work for lower wages than whites. At the same time, Arkansas was experiencing a severe economic depression. According to Matkin-Rawn, this worsening economy caused whites to band together "to force black Arkansan workers out of the railroad and timber industries. Tremendous terror and violence accompanied the restructuring of occupational segregation."[43] During the latter part of 1896, there were three separate racial incidents on job sites in and around El Dorado in Union County. The first, which occurred in mid-November, was a "race war" between white and black workers at Hawthorne Mills, twelve miles southwest of El Dorado. Apparently, the white workers, who were outnumbered by the African Americans, first warned the blacks to leave. When they got no response, several white men whipped one of the black workers, and then a mob of armed white men surrounded a makeshift camp in which the African American workers were sleeping and fired over a hundred shots into it. One woman was killed in the fusillade.[44]

In early December, in what the *St. Paul Globe* called "one of the foulest massacres of negroes that has ever blackened the record of that locality," unknown men shot five black section men working on the line of the Cotton Belt Railroad between Camden and Bearden in Ouachita County.[45] Later that month, near McNeil in Columbia County, approximately twenty blacks were shot when white men raided a sawmill.[46]

There were additional incidents in Lafayette County later in December. On December 13, African American workers in Frostville were hit by birdshot and badly wounded, a result of "the determination on the part of the whites to run the negroes out of the county and prevent them from working around the mills."[47] White workers at the Canfield lumber mill warned blacks to "leave the mill or suffer the consequences." When the black workers failed to do so, a white mob surrounded their shanties and began to fire shots into them. Those who were uninjured escaped, but the wounded were left where they fell with no attempt to get them medical attention.[48]

There was also trouble in Nevada County. According to the *New York Times*, white laborers in the county made frequent unsuccessful attempts to drive off African Americans. On May 29, 1897, at the Sayre Lumber Company, white employees set fire to a cabin where ten of the company's African American workers were sleeping. The black laborers remained in the cabin until the roof began to cave in and then attempted to flee. Members of the mob fired on them, wounding four. The other six escaped. Newspaper reports indicated that the arsonists were not county residents but were transient laborers who had been roaming the district attempting to intimidate African Americans in local lumber mills. In contrast to the other incidents, following a two-month investigation instigated by local residents, four members of the gang were indicted (though they were later cleared of the charges against them).[49]

In 1896, black workers on the Kansas City, Pittsburg and Gulf Railway in Polk County encountered racial animus from the local population. On August 10, a group of local residents—accompanied by Italian, Swedish, and Hungarian immigrant workers—raided the black workers' camp. Three African Americans were killed and eight wounded. The *Salt Lake Herald* had noted earlier that "the hardy old mountaineers of that section have not allowed any negroes to stop in that section for two years." As the railroad contractors persisted in hiring black labor, "the natives have served notice that Sambo must move on, as it is against their religion to permit them to desecrate their soil with pick and shovel or otherwise."[50]

In 1918, in an incident intended to intimidate a farm laborer, a mob lynched Elton Mitchell near Earle in Crittenden County for allegedly wounding the wife of W. M. Langston, a prominent local planter. The *Chicago Defender* reported that Mitchell's real crime was refusing to work for Langston for no pay—to punish him, prominent citizens carved him with knives and hanged his remains from a tree.[51] Clyde Ellison, lynched at Star City in Lincoln County on June 13, 1919, suffered a similar fate. According to the *Arkansas Gazette*, Ellison assaulted Iselle Bennett, the daughter of farmer David Bennett. After Ellison was captured, a mob took him to a nearby bridge, put a rope around his neck, and forced him to jump off. As is sometimes the case, other accounts of these events were very different. According to Robert Thomas Kerlin, quoting the July 5 *Colorado Statesman* (Denver), Ellison was actually lynched because he refused to

work in David Bennett's cotton field for eighty-five cents a day. In an effort to frighten him into working, Bennett invented the story of the assault and instructed his daughter to cooperate in the deception. The mob carried Ellison to the bridge and gave him one more chance to work on Bennett's terms. When he refused, they stripped him naked and burned his body with flat irons. They then left his corpse hanging from the bridge carrying a sign that stated, "This is how we treat lazy niggers."[52]

While it involves murder by a single individual rather than a lynch mob, the 1920 death of Prof. J. W. Gibson in Helena in Phillips County also fits this mold. Gibson was well known among African Americans in Helena. According to the *Dallas Express*, he was "identified with everything for the advancement of the community and for the race, and stood high in all kinds of lodges being a Mason with all of the degrees from the first to the thirty-third." On December 23, carrying an unloaded shotgun, Gibson left his farm near Cotton Plant to return to Helena. As he stood on the corner of Cherry and Missouri streets waiting for the streetcar, a night watchman approached him and asked him to turn over his shotgun. Gibson replied that he was carrying no shells for it. The watchman asked him why, and Gibson said that he felt no need to carry any. The watchman then asked to search his "hand bag" but found only books and papers. At this point, he asked Gibson, "What kind of nigger is you?" Gibson reportedly replied "that he was a man the same as the night watchman was." Thereupon, the watchman allegedly struck Gibson across the face before taking the shotgun and hitting him with it. He then marched him up Cherry Street to the jail. When a prominent African American druggist, Dr. J. W. Jennings, later called the jail to inquire about Gibson, the night watchman replied, "I have just killed that d—— Nigger."[53]

An African American did not need to be prominent or prosperous to draw attention. In some instances, blacks who had slightly overstepped their bounds were summarily punished. This was particularly true after World War I, when African Americans who had served or had gotten better-paying jobs during the war began demanding their rights. In September 1919, newly discharged soldier Clinton Briggs was walking down a sidewalk in Star City in Lincoln County when a white couple approached. Briggs moved aside to let them pass, but he did not step down from the sidewalk. The woman brushed against him and informed him that "Niggers get off the sidewalk down here." When Briggs replied, "This is a free man's country," the woman's escort seized him until others came

with an automobile and carried Briggs outside of town. Unable to find a rope to hang him with, the mob took the automobile chains, tied Briggs to a tree, and riddled his body with bullets.[54] In 1922, a mob killed laborer John West near Guernsey in Hempstead County for what the *Arkansas Gazette* described as "impudence." He apparently drank from a shared cup while working on a mixed-race paving gang, asserting that he was "as good as any white man."[55]

In his study of lynching in Virginia and Georgia, Brundage found that between 1880 and 1930, terrorist mobs were responsible for 12.8 percent of lynchings in Georgia and only 3.5 percent in Virginia. He attributes this discrepancy to the fact that Georgia had a tradition of extralegal violence while Virginia did not.[56] In this study, 18 of 102 lynchings (17.6 percent) were terrorist. The higher number may be a result of the fact that Arkansas, too, because of its frontier nature, was more prone to terroristic violence. The fact that it was sparsely settled meant that law enforcement was sometimes not available, and many decisions were left up to justices of the peace. Eleven of the state's terroristic lynchings (61.1 percent) involved either workplace intimidation or wage disputes. Three of the remaining incidents involved prominent African Americans, two of the victims had "overstepped their bounds" (both after 1910), and two were lynched for theft. Eleven of the eighteen terrorist mobs (61.1 percent) were in counties with African American populations of over 50 percent.[57] It may be that whites, who were outnumbered, were more fearful of African Americans than residents of other counties with lower black populations. The number of terrorist mobs increased greatly in the 1890s when economic pressures and the large number of new black settlers combined to put increasing pressure on the African American population.

POSSES

The third type of mob described by Brundage is the posse. Like the groups of patrollers who roamed the roads during the time of slavery (described in chapter 1), these groups could be officially organized or composed more loosely of like-minded men. As Karlos Hill notes, posses were quasi-legal and "operated with near impunity. In most communities, posses were respected and viewed as heroes. . . . Often they had the support of local elected officials including the sheriff and mayor as well as community leaders."[58] Such posses could include any number of people, from a handful

to hundreds. While posses, like slave patrols, were organized to apprehend offenders, they sometimes overstepped their bounds and meted out justice themselves.[59] There were also lynchings in which authorities were openly involved, complicit, or negligent, and because these are related to actions by law enforcement, they are included in this category. Because posse mobs could involve any number of participants, there is some overlap here with both small private mobs and mass mobs.

There are some Arkansas cases where posse members were clearly involved in lynchings. During prolonged racial strife in Hampton in Calhoun County in 1892, posse members fired into an old house where African Americans had gathered, killing two or three men and wounding several more.[60] There were many other incidents in which law enforcement officials, while not openly involved, were negligent or complicit. In numerous cases, prisoners were moved, supposedly for their own protection, late at night and with very few guards. After being bound over for the grand jury in 1892, Julius Mosely was put under the care of a single constable, who was apparently keeping him overnight in his home when a large mob removed him from custody and hanged him.[61]

That same year, law enforcement officials seemed to leave a prisoner to the mercy of the mob intentionally. When a mob gathered outside the penitentiary in Little Rock demanding prisoner Henry James, penitentiary manager Col. S. M. Apperson sent the guards to their quarters and chose to meet the mob on his own. He then informed the mob that James would be moved back to the county jail the following morning and that they should take him then rather than attacking the penitentiary, thus effectively advising them on the best time for the lynching. Despite Apperson's appeal, the mob removed James from custody. The *Appeal*, an African-American newspaper published in Saint Paul, Minnesota, subsequently inquired: "Does any fair-minded person suppose there was any actual desire on the part of the authorities to prevent the mob at Little Rock, Ark., from breaking into the penitentiary and taking therefrom Henry James the Afro-American accused of outraging the little white girl last week?" The paper further noted that the penitentiary guards "could have kept a mob of ten thousand at bay for an indefinite period."[62] (See chapter 7 for more on this lynching.)

There are several Arkansas lynchings in which law enforcement officials were openly involved. When a mob lynched Henry Phillips for allegedly murdering Tom McClanahan in Mississippi County in 1897, the apparent

involvement of local sheriff Charles Bowen sparked a controversy between Bowen and local newspaper editor Leon Roussan. According to a story published by Roussan on November 20, Bowen had announced publicly that Phillips would be lynched, and reports of his statements had run in the Memphis, Tennessee, newspapers. Roussan was outraged: "When we see those who are our friends and whom the people at large have elevated to positions of honor and trust . . . fall short and fail in the discharge of a public duty, we feel like throwing away our pencil and bowing our head in shame and pitying silence. . . . What do we pay taxes for and build Courthouses and jails and elect officers to carry out and execute the laws? Surely not to engender and fester the mob spirit in our free American land, where every man is deemed innocent until declared guilty by a jury of his peers."[63]

In another posse lynching in early January 1898, two African Americans named Devoe and Huntley (no first names given) were lynched by posses near Bearden in Ouachita County for allegedly attempting to assault an elderly woman, one Mrs. Paine, there a year earlier. When Huntley was discovered working on the Cotton Belt Railroad, the posse that went to apprehend him returned empty-handed, saying he could not be found. According to the *New York Times*, however, the posse had actually captured him and lynched him on their way back to Bearden. Authorities arrested Devoe and took him under guard to be identified by his alleged victim. Although his guards maintained that he escaped while they were returning him to Bearden, the *Arkansas Gazette* speculated that he was lynched in a "necktie party" somewhere along the road home. The *Sacramento Daily Union* reported that Devoe could not have escaped, as some said, because he was escorted by a heavy guard and was in fact chained to the wagon. The *Daily Union* speculated that after the posse left Mrs. Paine's house, they stopped, put a rope around Devoe's neck, made him stand up in the wagon, and drove the wagon out from under him. Mob members then fired several bullets into the body, left it, and returned to town, saying he had escaped.[64] Almost two decades later, a mob hanged James Smith (also referred to as Roy Anderson) from a telephone pole near Proctor in Crittenden County. According to the *Washington Herald*, his body "bore mute testimony . . . to the fact that a posse which had been seeking him since last Monday for the murder of Fred W. Hicks, a special deputy sheriff, had found him."[65]

In 1921, Gov. Thomas C. McRae accused authorities of negligence following the lynching of Henry Lowery. He questioned why the officers bring-

ing the prisoner back to Arkansas took such a circuitous route when he had specifically asked them to bring Lowery directly to the state penitentiary in Little Rock. Newspaper reports quoted McRae as saying "officers apparently turned him over to a mob in Mississippi with lamb-like docility and permitted his transportation into Arkansas and his burning at the stake without any effort to prevent his execution."[66] The Lowery lynching prompted McRae to "recommend to the legislature the enactment of a law which will place the responsibility directly upon the officers having custody of prisoners, and will recommend some act by which a sheriff who permits, or does not prevent, the lynching of a prisoner in his charge be removed from office."[67]

When John Carter was captured near Little Rock on May 14, 1927, for allegedly attacking a white woman and her daughter, not only was he lynched by the posse, but law enforcement officials declined to stop the rioting that followed. According to the *Arkansas Gazette*, a posse apprehended Carter and lynched him in the Hopson-Sachs addition. They subsequently dragged his body through the streets of Little Rock and brought it to the heart of the city's African American community. Gov. John Martineau eventually sent National Guard troops to the scene to stop the rioting. According to the *Gazette*, however, until the Guard appeared "there was no attempt on the part of the police, the sheriff's department or any other official to quell the riot, or to check the indiscriminate firing of weapons, of which there were thousands in evidence." The report indicated that "neither Mayor Moyer nor Chief Rotenberry was at home or at the city hall during the trouble. . . . Assistant Chief Crow said that the police were helpless to cope with the mob, and he made no effort to interfere with the parade to Ninth street and Broadway or to prevent the burning of the body. Informed that several officers were engaged in a card game in the basement of the city hall during the rioting, Crow said he was not aware of that." An editorial printed on the front page of the *Gazette* on May 5 proclaimed: "Our peace officers, city and county, let a riddled corpse be brought to town for a Saturnalia of savagery. . . . Little Rock and Pulaski county must demand an accounting of the officers who have failed us."[68] (See chapter 8 for a detailed account of this event.)

The lynching of Owen Flemming also involved a posse, and the sheriff himself was complicit. In 1927, a posse of five hundred people surrounded the tent where Flemming was hiding after allegedly murdering overseer J. H. Woods near Mellwood in Phillips County. When Flemming

surrendered, they shot him. Before shooting him, however, mob members first asked Sheriff J. D. Mays of Helena to take Flemming into custody, but Mays supposedly replied, "I'm busy. Just go ahead and lynch him." The *Pittsburgh Courier* responded: "Along with other phrases, this will go down in history as one of the most notable ever delivered, for it conveyed into the hands of a white mob of five hundred people the living form of Owen Flemming . . . and made of him one more sacrifice upon the bloody altar of the reign of this country's uncrowned sovereign—'King Lynch 'Em.'"[69]

That same year, there was a case where law enforcement officials seemed to leave their prisoner to the mercy of the mob intentionally. After Sheriff John C. Riley arrested Winston Pounds in 1927, he took him into Wilmot in Ashley County and left him unattended in his car while "discussing with his deputies and several business men plans for getting Pounds out of town to avert mob violence." Several men jumped into the car and drove out of town followed by several other cars full of men. The mob then hanged Pounds from a tree limb.[70]

Brundage's research indicated that there was only one posse lynching in Virginia, perhaps because the legal system there was more organized, producing less extralegal violence. In contrast, 51 of the 460 Georgia lynchings (11.1 percent) studied by Brundage involved posses.[71] Such mobs were rare in Georgia before 1910 but became more numerous in the 1910s and 1920s.[72] Of the one hundred two Arkansas lynchings in this sample, seven (6.9 percent) definitely involved posses. Of these, three occurred in the 1890s, with the other three taking place after 1900. Another three lynchings seemed to originate with posses, which would bring the total to ten, or 9.8 percent. Law enforcement officials were openly involved in two other lynchings and were negligent in seven more. Of these latter incidents, three occurred in the 1890s, one in the 1910s, and three more in the 1920s. The total number of lynchings involving law enforcement was nineteen, or .18.6 percent of the total. Perhaps, as W. Fitzhugh Brundage contended, in less-developed societies like the frontier society of Arkansas, posses reflected "the weakness of law enforcement."[73]

MASS MOBS

Brundage's fourth type of mob is the mass mob composed of more than fifty members. At times, these mobs were huge, numbering in the thousands. They operated in public, and such lynchings were often spectacles which

involved great ceremony and ferocity.[74] According to Terence Finnegan, "as whites struggled to justify the imposition of the color line, so called 'spectacle lynchings' which 'conjured whiteness' . . . occurred more frequently."[75] As Grace Hale and Amy Louise Wood noted, such lynchings served not only as punishments but also as amusements, replacements for the cultural and entertainment opportunities missing in the rural South. According to Wood, they were a result of a changing society where even small towns were being urbanized, and where the social fabric was being undermined. The mobs were dominated by members of the new middle class who were determined to differentiate themselves from blacks and other lower-class citizens by asserting their dominance. Hale concurs, asserting that such spectacles emphasized the alien and separate nature of blackness. Most of the time, the alleged crimes being punished were serious, involving murder and sexual crimes against whites.[76]

As Hale asserted, and as is the case here, these mobs sometimes included prominent members of the community. This may be because many of these mobs were assembled to avenge crimes against prominent people, and as Brundage notes, since the victim's friends and family were often members of the mob, the status of the perpetrators may mirror the status of the victims.[77] As theologian and Arkansas native James H. Cone observed, newspapers always protected the names of these prominent people: "Strange . . . that the men who constitute these [mobs] can never be identified by . . . governors or the law officers, but newspapers know all about them."[78] The references to prominent participants may have been used to indicate broad public approval or to indicate to those who did not live in the South that not all mobs were savage and irrational.

Despite their large size, newspapers often described mass mobs as quiet and orderly. This, too, may have been done purposely to lessen the perception that all mobs were savage and chaotic. Because of the extreme brutality of many of these lynchings and the widespread publicity they garnered, mass mobs attracted the most media attention, and there is substantial information about them.

The earliest mass mob in this study, and one of only three that occurred before 1890, gathered in 1881 for the lynching of four African American men accused of murdering Martha "Mattie" Ismael, the daughter of a prominent planter, near Jonesboro in Craighead County. Green Harris (sometimes referred to as Hawes), Giles Peck, John Woods (sometimes referred to as Jud Woods), and Burt Hoskins (sometimes referred to as

Haskins) were arrested for the murder, appeared before local magistrates, and were bound over to the grand jury. Authorities decided to hold the prisoners overnight in a church under a strong guard. Around midnight, two to three hundred masked men surrounded the church, overpowered the guards, and broke in the doors and windows. They dragged the four men outside and hanged them from a tree. The mob left their bodies "dangling in the air and presenting a horrible spectacle in the moonlight."[79]

Some mass lynchings in Arkansas were extremely brutal. On February 20, 1892, Edward Coy was burned at the stake in Texarkana in Miller County before a crowd of approximately one thousand people. Coy reportedly went to the home of Henry Jewell to sell him some hogs. When he found that Jewell was not at home, he allegedly raped Jewell's wife, Julia. Some newspaper accounts, however, indicate that Coy and Julia Jewell had been engaged in a year-long relationship. Coy was eventually captured on a nearby farm, and a posse took him back to Texarkana, where Jewell identified him. That afternoon, a mob of one thousand people marched Coy to the Iron Mountain roundhouse, where he was tied to a stake, doused with coal oil, and burned alive.[80]

As noted before, there are a number of accounts of prominent citizens being involved in mass lynchings in Arkansas. In 1892, after John Kelley allegedly murdered W. T. McAdams, "one of Pine Bluff's most highly respected citizens," the police arrested him at Rison and brought him back to Pine Bluff on the train. A mob of two hundred armed men met them, and as they led Kelley up the main street toward the courthouse, the mob swelled, eventually numbering around one thousand people. They lynched Kelley from a telephone pole across from the courthouse and then riddled his body with bullets. According to the *Arkansas Gazette*, "the mob was composed of some of our best citizens, and no masks were used, and everything transpiring could be seen by the bright lights and the moon."[81] In 1895, Wiley Dunn and two accomplices, brothers Jim and Jack Ware, allegedly murdered Allen Martin in Hampton in Calhoun County. Dunn escaped, and despite scant evidence that the Wares were actually involved in the crime, a mob of between fifty and seventy men, some of them prominent citizens, removed the brothers from jail and lynched them.[82]

On June 3, 1898, a mob lynched Bud Hayden in Miller County for an alleged assault on twelve-year-old Jessie Scott, the daughter of late circuit clerk J. V. Scott. Local citizens were outraged, and on the night of June 2, "hundreds of Texarkana's leading citizens" stood guard outside the jail. By the following morning, the crowd was estimated to be in the thousands, and the *Arkansas Gazette* noted that "a cooler headed mob never collected." Seven of "the best men in the city" took Hayden to the Scott home, where Jessie identified him as her assailant. They then brought Hayden back to the jail where, in front of the mob, "numerous speeches were made in which the case and as to what should be done was freely discussed." Having decided to hang Hayden, members of the mob put a rope around his neck and dragged him through the crowd, "and everybody struck him as he passed." They then took him to a tree near the Iron Mountain Railroad crossing, where they hanged him and riddled his body with bullets.[83]

Like the mob who lynched Hayden, the mob who lynched five people in Monroe County in 1898 was also described as quiet and orderly. Manse Castle, Will Sanders, Lorilla Weaver, Dennis Ricord, and Susie Jacobs were lynched in Clarendon for their alleged complicity in the murder of merchant John T. Orr. The *Wichita Daily Eagle* described the mob as "a most orderly one, not a word being unnecessarily spoken, and not a shot being fired."[84] (See chapter 4 for a detailed account.) In Faulkner County in 1905, authorities accused Frank Brown of attacking the widow Arlena Lawrence, killing her eldest son and wounding the younger one. Authorities eventually arrested him for the crime and jailed him in Conway. A mob of more than a hundred men went to the jail, removed Brown, "put him in a buggy, carried him to the Lawrence house and strung him to a tree in the yard." According to the *Arkansas Gazette*, "the work of the mob was accomplished so quietly that many residents of the town knew nothing of what was transpiring."[85]

Mass lynchings continued into the twentieth century. In 1912, a mob of five hundred men lynched Sanford Lewis in Sebastian County for allegedly killing deputy constable Andrew Carr.[86] In June 1913, in an extremely brutal spectacle lynching, an African American named Will Norman, accused of assaulting a young white girl in Hot Springs, was captured in the mountains in Garland County. Thirty minutes later, a mob of "several thousand citizens" took him and hanged him from a telephone pole "on a prominent business corner of the city."[87] The *Salt Lake Tribune* reported that "Norman's body, stripped of its clothing and punctured by hundreds of bullets, was left hanging under an arc light for more than an hour, after which it was cut down and burned."[88]

In 1915, Loy Haley, accused of killing a young planter near Lewisville in Lafayette County, was taken from Sheriff Ruff Boyette by a mob of over fifty men and hanged.[89] In December of that year, a mob of at least a hundred men took alleged murderer William Patrick from the Forrest City jail in Saint Francis County and lynched him.[90] In October 1916, three hundred men removed Frank Dodd, accused of annoying a white woman, from the jail in DeWitt in Arkansas County and hanged him from a tree outside of town.[91]

Mass lynchings continued into the 1920s. The spectacle lynching of Henry Lowery in Nodena in Mississippi County on January 26, 1921, was one of the most horrific in Arkansas history. Lowery allegedly murdered planter O. T. Craig and his daughter Mary on Christmas Day of 1920. He escaped, but authorities arrested him in El Paso, Texas, in late January. The officers sent to retrieve Lowery took a circuitous route, and sixteen men met and disarmed them at the station in Sardis, Mississippi. They then took Lowery to a spot near the Craigs' home in Nodena. Although the *Arkansas Gazette* reported that Lowery was lynched by a mob of only forty people, William Pickens, writing for the *Nation*, noted that the "six hundred lynchers and sightseers" had come from "all the surrounding communities."[92] They chained Lowery to a log and surrounded him with leaves soaked in gasoline. They set the leaves on fire, adding fresh ones as the fire died down. According to the *Dallas Express*, "once or twice he attempted to pick up the hot ashes in his hands and thrust them into his mouth in order to hasten death. Each time the ashes were kicked out of his reach by a member of the mob."[93] A Missouri newspaper reported on February 3: "It was forty minutes before the last death agony relaxed . . . repeatedly he had to be turned over and more oil poured on the flames to hasten the burning. . . . It is reported that several hundred people had gathered at the scene of the crime . . . and that most of the spectators remained until the victim's body was a charred mass and life was extinct."[94]

Prominent citizens were involved once again in the lynching of Wade Thomas (nicknamed "Boll Weevil") on December 26, 1920, in Craighead County for the alleged murder of a Jonesboro police officer. Authorities arrested Thomas, who appeared before a hastily called coroner's jury and was put in jail to await the next session of the circuit court. At five o'clock that afternoon, a mob of around five hundred men arrived at the jail. Ignoring pleas by circuit court judges R. E. Lee Johnson and R. H. Dudley, they took the keys from the jailor and approached the cellblock. Jonesboro mayor Gordon Frierson and police chief Gus Craig, armed with shotguns, had barricaded themselves inside but offered no resistance. Mayor Frierson later told his nephew that he and Craig failed to defend Thomas because "when the mob opened the door, the first half-a-dozen men standing there were leading citizens—businessmen, leaders of their churches and the community."[95]

On March 15, 1921, a mob lynched twenty-eight-year-old Browning Tuggle, driver of a jitney (vehicle for hire), at Hope in Hempstead County for allegedly attacking a white woman. Following Tuggle's arrest, a mob of between one hundred and five hundred men broke down the door of the jail and took him from his cell. They hanged him from a water tank tower and then riddled his body with bullets. His body was left hanging there overnight, and the *Arkansas Gazette* reported that over two thousand people viewed it before it was cut down.[96] In 1922, authorities accused Gilbert Harris of murdering Maurice Connelly, a prominent young Garland County businessman. On August 1, a mob of approximately five hundred people removed Harris from the jail in Hot Springs, and despite assurances by local officials that he would be tried and convicted, they took Harris to the intersection of Central and Ouachita Avenues, in front of the Como Hotel, and hanged him.[97]

There were also mass mobs composed of both blacks and whites. In 1894, African Americans in Desha County participated in the mixed-race mob that hanged Luke Washington, Richard Washington, and Henry C. Robinson for the alleged murder of local merchant H. C. Patton. The mob took the prisoners from the sheriff and hanged them from telephone poles near the crime scene. Their bodies were then riddled with bullets.[98] Frank Livingston, a former US soldier, was accused of murdering his employer and his wife near El Dorado in Union County in 1919. A mob of both whites and African Americans numbering between 150 and 200 people tied Livingston to a tree and set him on fire.[99]

There were also several mass mobs in Arkansas that consisted entirely of African Americans. In December 1874, a mob of sixty armed African Americans removed Isaac Ruffin, accused of "a brutal outrage and attempted murder," from the Marion jail in Crittenden County and shot him.[100] In 1882, Charles Branch was hanged in Lincoln County by a mob of one hundred African Americans for allegedly raping a nine-year-old African American girl.[101]

On June 30, 1892, a mob of three hundred African Americans lynched Robert Donnelly in Lee County for repeatedly assaulting a twelve-year-old black girl. Donnelly was found guilty at a preliminary trial and was held in the city jail until he could be moved to nearby Marianna. The crowd surrounded the jail, took Donnelly, and hanged him from a nearby tree, breaking his neck.[102] Just twelve days later, a mob of one hundred African Americans hanged Julius Mosely, accused of raping his stepdaughter, from a gin house near Halley in Desha County.[103]

That same year, in another extremely brutal lynching, a Jackson County mob turned on a preacher named G. P. F. Lightfoot, who had fraudulently collected money from them for passage to Liberia. After they told him to return their money, they shot him as he ran off.[104] The *Arkansas Gazette* reported: "The frenzied mob continued shooting until his body was riddled with bullets. Not satisfied, some jumped upon the prostrate and blood-smeared body, from which the vital sport had not yet departed, while others hacked his face [and] throat."[105]

In his research on lynching, Brundage found that mass mobs accounted for 34 percent of all lynchings in Georgia and 40 percent in Virginia.[106] The number seems to be slightly lower in Arkansas. Of the one hundred two lynchings in this sample, thirty-two (31.4 percent) were committed by mass mobs. Serious crimes, mostly rape and murder, were the reason for twenty-nine mass lynchings (93.5 percent). The only exceptions were the lynchings of Reverend Lightfoot for fraud in 1892, Charles Richardson and Robert Austin for abetting a jailbreak in 1910, and Frank Dodd for arson in 1916. Mass lynchings began in the 1870s, but there were only three before 1890. During the 1890s, the number spiked considerably, with twelve mass lynchings occurring in that decade alone. There were two in the first decade of the twentieth century, followed by seven each in the two succeeding decades.

CONCLUSION

The study of lynchings in Arkansas reveals both similarities and differences between Arkansas lynchings and those in other parts of the South. Terence Finnegan concluded that lynchings in South Carolina and Mississippi peaked during the 1890s and then spiked again around 1900 and 1920.[107] In Arkansas, the peak was also in the 1890s, with forty-seven lynchings (46.1 percent) occurring in that decade alone. There were ten lynchings between 1900 and 1909, sixteen during the teens, and twelve between 1920 and 1929. The fact that Arkansas had a higher number of lynchings between 1910 and 1919 may be due to the fact that the state was slower to develop than the states studied by Brundage and Finnegan.

There seem to be fewer private mobs in Arkansas than there were in South Carolina or Mississippi. According to Finnegan, 40 percent of all lynch mobs in Mississippi contained less than fifty people; in South Carolina, the number was 52.4 percent.[108] The situation in Arkansas is much more like that in Georgia, where Brundage found that 30 percent of the mobs were private mobs.[109] The number is virtually identical in Arkansas, with thirty-two mobs consisting of fewer than fifty people. In Arkansas, twenty-one of the thirty-two private mobs formed before 1900, with eight in the 1880s and nine in the 1890s. Only twelve occurred after 1900. As in Georgia, the majority of lynchings in Arkansas (60.8 percent) were perpetrated by private or mass mobs. Terrorist mobs seem to be more prevalent in Arkansas than they were in other states, accounting for 17.6 percent of all mob violence, as opposed to 12.8 percent in Georgia and 3.5 percent in Virginia.[110]

Terence Finnegan correlated the size of lynch mobs with the seriousness of the alleged crime, concluding, "If mob size was an indication of community sanction, then alleged rape and other crimes that involved women and murder or attempted murder were seen as the greatest threats to white solidarity."[111] This was also true in Arkansas. Twenty-nine of the thirty-two mass mobs in this study were formed to redress serious crimes. Brundage added that "the composition of the mob principally reflected the status of the victim of the alleged crime."[112] In the Arkansas sample, alleged crimes against prominent people were also more likely to be redressed by mass mobs. There were eighteen mobs formed to avenge crimes against prominent people. Seven of these (38.9 percent) were private mobs, and eleven (61.1 percent) were mass mobs.

It is also interesting to compare the information on African American mobs with other studies. Brundage's research indicates that there were few black lynch mobs because white residents would take their activities as a symptom of a general uprising, especially in counties with large African American populations.[113] In Arkansas, however, African Americans organized 16.7 percent of lynch mobs, and nine of the seventeen lynchings conducted by black mobs occurred in counties where African Americans were in the majority. As in other studies, the majority of such mobs (70.6 percent) were assembled to punish the crimes of murder, rape, and incest. Terence Finnegan determined that African Americans preferred hanging to shooting by a ratio of two to one.[114] The method was specified in thirteen of the Arkansas lynchings perpetrated by African American mobs. Hanging and other methods were also more common in Arkansas, but the figures were slightly different, with only 54 percent of victims being hanged or killed by other means.

The earliest African American mob in this sample was organized in 1885. Karlos Hill asserts that "by the 1890s, lynching had become a racialized phenomenon in which blacks were the primary targets of white lynch mob violence. In addition, the emergent black beast rapist discourse rationalized white-on-black lynching as a moral duty to protect white womanhood. These developments likely compelled blacks to increasingly abstain from lynching after the 1880s because black extralegal violence might have implied black support for white-on-black lynching and the racist discourses that rationalized it."[115] Interestingly, that was not the case in this sample. As with other types of mobs, African American mobs were most prevalent in the 1890s, with ten of the seventeen occurring during that decade. Only one, the lynching of John Barnett in 1905, occurred in the twentieth century.

It is evident that lynch mobs in Arkansas adhered to the main types that existed across the South. As in other states, lynching reached its peak there between 1890 and 1900. When compared with earlier studies on Virginia, Georgia, Mississippi, and South Carolina, however, there are some differences in the prevalence of the different types of mobs, the years they were most numerous, and their distribution across the state. A mere analysis of the statistics leaves many questions unanswered. Why, when Terence Finnegan determined that private mobs were most evident in counties with large African American populations, did only one third of private mobs in Arkansas operate in such counties? Why were there fewer private mobs after 1900? Why do there seem to be more terrorist mobs in Arkansas?

It seems that more research on African American mobs is also warranted. Why were there more African American private mobs in Arkansas? Why, if Karlos Hill asserts that lynchings by African Americans declined after the 1880s, did this sample indicate that they peaked in the 1890s? Why, if Brundage found that there were few African American mobs in Virginia and Georgia, were almost 17 percent of the mobs in Arkansas composed of African Americans? Similarly, Brundage asserted that because of fears of black insurrection, these mobs were less evident in counties with large African American populations. Why then did more than half of the black mobs in Arkansas operate in majority-black counties?

Questions like these should provide fertile ground for future research, especially into the nature of African American mobs.

A Lynching State

Arkansas in the 1890s

Bearden native, African American theologian, and Union Theological Seminary professor James H. Cone recalls: "I was born in Arkansas, a lynching state. . . . By the 1890s, lynching fever gripped the South, spreading like cholera, as white communities made blacks their primary targets, and torture their force. . . . Lynching became a white media spectacle." Malcolm Argyle, a black preacher from Arkansas, testified to the horrors unfolding in Arkansas in the 1890s to a friend in Philadelphia, Pennsylvania: "All over the state, blacks were being murdered by whites: some being strung up to telephone poles, other burned at the stake; and still others being shot like dogs. In the last thirty days there have not been less than eight colored persons lynched in this state." Historian Grif Stockley called the 1890s "open season on Arkansas blacks."[1]

Richard Buckelew, historian of Arkansas lynching, gives us the statistical foundations of lynching in Arkansas. In the 1890s, more lynching occurred in the summer and winter (thirty in the summer and twenty-eight in the winter) and fewer in the spring and fall (twenty in the planting time of spring and twenty-three in the harvest time of autumn). Until the 1880s, more whites than blacks were lynched. Before the 1890s, forty-one blacks (31 percent) and ninety-two whites (69 percent) were lynched. In the 1890s, however, the tide turned racially. In that decade, eighty blacks (78 percent) and twenty-two whites (22 percent) were lynched. This volteface in racial composition of lynching victims clearly revealed something fundamental happened in how the dominant white power structure defined justice, honor, manhood, and acceptable behavior. Something seriously

Table 3.1. Reported causes for lynching in each decade

Motive for lynching	1860s	1870s	1880s	1890s	Total
Sexual offenses	1	3	18	19	41
Assault	1	2	3	6	12
Murder	2	16	32	55	105
Property crimes	0	14	7	28	49
Politics	1	0	1	3	5

disturbed white Arkansans in the late 1880s and 1890s that spawned this shift in who was lynched.[2]

In each decade of the latter half of the nineteenth century, murder was the leading motivation underlying acts of lynching. Undoubtedly, property crimes and sexual offenses often culminated in murder. Table 3.1 reveals the reported causes for lynching in each decade.

If the murder involved feuds or moments of uncontrolled anger, the community often let the usual channels of justice unfold. If, however, the violence outraged a community norm, or some thought the judicial system would miscarry justice, lynching more likely occurred.[3]

What is also intriguing about the alleged causes of lynching is the significant increase in sexual offenses. Four lynchings occurred in the 1860s and 1870s after rape, attempted rape, or "assault of a white girl." But the numbers of reported sexual crimes leading to lynching increased dramatically in the 1880s and 1890s. Ninety percent of all blacks and whites lynched for sexual offenses from 1860 to 1900 were lynched in the 1880s and 1890s. Clearly, deep concerns about sexuality or gender roles and norms erupted in the fin-de-siècle South.

Of course, the motives given for lynching, especially as presented in newspaper reports, may not necessarily reflect the reality of the circumstances in which these murders occurred. As Ida B. Wells-Barnett argued in her 1895 pamphlet, "The Red Record: Tabulated Statistics and Alleged Causes of Lynching in the United States," lynching did not necessarily function as an expression of criminal justice; for example, many interracial relationships were recast as rape by those who sought to justify the lynching.[4] With this in mind, newspaper reporting such as that offered in the

Arkansas Gazette does not constitute an irrefutable source of information regarding the motives behind "rough justice" in the state. However, such reports can help us to understand the sequence of events surrounding individual lynchings. Moreover, these accounts shed light on the public narratives of lynching during the 1890s—the scripts into which murderous events were written as white Arkansans fashioned the stories they told themselves, and the wider world, about lynching.

Many fundamental changes rocked the United States, the South, and Arkansas in the 1890s. "The deepest roots of mob murder," historian Robert W. Thurston insists, "lies in crisis." Whites tried to remaster and renegotiate white hegemony. "The rural South," historian Amy Louise Wood argues, "was undergoing an uncertain and troubled transformation into modern, urban societies." Raymond Arsenault points out that Arkansas in the late 1800s was "a metropolitan economy but not a metropolitan society." People moving to the city tried to maintain their rural perspectives and folkways while living in cities. Rural values often clashed with newer, urban ways. As Bruce Baker observes, it was a time of "new people dealing with new situations and testing the limits under changing rules."[5]

Economic upheavals spawned anxieties that dramatically increased lynching in the 1890s. Most Arkansans lived and worked on the land, ever attuned to the fickleness of markets and weather. The Panic of 1893 rocked the global economy and heightened white Arkansans' anxieties and fears. The *Arkansas Gazette* often echoed the economic unrest Arkansans suffered, worrying in 1895 that the "market closed very nervous and much depends on market at Liverpool," and lamenting in 1897 "the low price of cotton, almost the lowest on record."[6]

Politics, always a key to power and identity, grew more contentious in the last years of the nineteenth century in the United States and in Arkansas. The Populists, a powerful third party with its power base among western and southern farmers, favored a stronger, more interventionist and activist federal government, including governmental control of railroads and banks. They championed currency reform to ease the difficulty of trade, as well as a subtreasury plan that loaned farmers money at harvest time when crop prices bottomed out and helped them wait until a more lucrative price for their crops could be obtained. Most importantly, the Populists taught its members to examine the issues of the day through the lens of class and not myopically focus on race. Populist membership in Arkansas soared to over seventy-five thousand in 1888, leading many historians to believe that their gubernatorial candidate in Arkansas actually won in 1888 but that the Democrats stole the election.[7]

In 1892, the Arkansas Populist platform denounced lynching and demanded that criminals be punished only by courts of law. Arkansas whites wrestled with racial identity and what it meant to be a true white man through lynching. Political allegiance was now tainted with charges of betrayal of the white race, especially the domestic ideal of white womanhood. The *Nashville News* (Nashville, Arkansas) asserted that "the white men . . . are not going into league . . . with the nigger to control the offices of this county." The *Southern Standard* was reminded of the "dark days of Reconstruction," and the *Arkadelphia Siftings* proclaimed, "No one can make us believe that the plain, practical farmers who have been raised in the South . . . have suddenly become negro lovers, or defenders of negro rapists and criminals." With the constant drumbeat of media emphasis on race over class, Populist support in each subsequent election dwindled between 1888 and 1896.[8]

To stabilize control over the state by the white Democratic Party, the Democratic-controlled legislature and governor pushed for "electoral reform" as a response to the political challenges birthed by Populism. The legislature established a "secret ballot" in 1891 and the one-dollar poll tax the following year. The processes burdened the voter: one might forget to pay the poll tax, or the secret ballot might prove too complex for many voters (especially those who were illiterate) to master. The new laws drastically reduced black voter participation. In the Black Belt, voter participation fell from 74 percent in 1888, to 44 percent in 1894, to 33 percent in 1900. Although African American voting declined in the 1890s, black voters still paid their poll taxes more than their white counterparts in Lafayette, Chicot, Jefferson, Phillips, and Saint Francis Counties and competed numerically with their white peers in Little River, Columbia, and Hempstead Counties. Political agitation in the late 1880s and 1890s exacerbated the uneasiness and anxiety that led to lynching and racial violence.[9]

The blurring of boundaries between civilized and uncivilized behavior troubled thoughtful Arkansans. Just what was a human being? What did a civilized, educated, Christian man or woman do and not do? The lines fluctuated and seemed unclear. Some undoubtedly had been exposed to Charles Darwin's *Origin of Species* (1859) and *Descent of Man* (1874) and clung even more firmly to their view of divine creation as laid out in the first chapters of Genesis; but a new, literal reading of that old, old story made some wonder what was correct. "Human life is altogether too cheap at Texarkana," the *Arkansas Gazette* editorialized as the deputy sheriff and a local postmaster were murdered "wantonly and without provocation." Violence and blood lust made one reconsider if one were human or animal. "Much Blood Flows at Horatio Arkansas," another *Gazette* headline broadcast. "Five Men Shot to Death; Pandemonium at Hot Springs, Terrible Street Duel," the *Arkansas Gazette* headline blared, causing many Arkansans to wonder just how low Darwin's man had descended. The western border with Indian Territory, which was in the process of becoming Oklahoma, seemed especially barbarous and violence-ridden, as in 1898 when the Seminoles went to war against each other, culminating in an Arkansas mob of three hundred burning two Seminole leaders to death. Governor Daniel Webster Jones even worried about events at the University of Arkansas when a football game between students and citizens of Fort Smith seemed "out of harmony with a proper educational system." "The higher civilization," he extolled, "which we profess is entirely inconsistent with the toleration of such a game."[10]

As often happened in the South, racial attitudes reflected racial anxieties. "This is a white man's country, and white men are going to rule it," the *Arkadelphia Siftings* editor reassured himself and his readers in 1892. Racism danced a strange line before the Civil War under chattel slavery and in the early days of Reconstruction when freedom reached Arkansas's former slaves. Blacks constantly negotiated, even under slavery, what they could and could not do. But Jim Crow laws ossified in the late nineteenth century, as evidenced by the 1891 Separate Coach Law (and an amendment prohibiting black nurses from riding in the same car as their white charges) passing the legislature in 1891. Violence against African Americans erupted across the state, ranging from full-fledged riots like that in Forrest City in 1889 to smaller cases of harassment, including attempted expulsions of black residents from Lonoke County in 1892 and Mena in 1897. In 1898, Gov. Daniel Webster Jones offered fifty dollars for the arrest of whites who used intimidation to get blacks to leave Monroe County. In many other locales, blacks knew to be out of town before sundown to ensure their safety. The US Supreme Court upheld the doctrine of "separate but equal" in its 1896 *Plessy v. Ferguson* ruling. Jim Crow hardened everywhere.[11]

In the study of lynching in the 1890s, the problems of language are critical. Historian Trudier Harris insists that students of lynching underestimate the importance of language. Michael Ayers Trotti agrees and warns that "historians have sound reasons to avoid a preoccupation with the numbers and trends of lynching." "Why was lynching," he continues, "deployed as a tool of terror in the history of the South?" Numbers and historical context help us understand what happened during a lynching and, to some degree, why it happened. But the words that described what happened during a lynching critically shaped the event's meanings. After the corpse had been buried, what had the lynching meant? How did description of the lynching mold the consciousness of Arkansans—blacks and whites, leaders and led, men and women, well-to-do and poor—who tried to fathom the event and make it somewhat understandable?[12]

Arkansans of the 1890s tried to explain, sometimes in cold and objective language, sometimes in rhetoric as red hot as the flames that consumed the lynched victim, what occurred in a lynching. How did this lynching happen? What really happened? Think of the blacks and whites who either participated in the event or who heard various descriptions of the event in its aftermath and how, at night in bed and when working in the fields, they replayed and reconstructed the actual event and the meanings of the lynching. They probed causes and meanings. For days and then years after the lynching, they tried to make sense of the moment. What always clouded the attempts to verbalize a momentous event in an individual's life and in the communal musings of a village or town in Arkansas is that, as Richard Buckelew reminds us, "considerable diversity existed with regards to time, place, and the prevailing local conditions." People found and used words shaped with cultural baggage from the past to describe, to understand, to fashion, to control. But the words almost always failed because they could never quite arrive at the dialectic between the rational and the irrational concerning what went on before, during, and after a lynching. The deeply irrational elements fractured normal discourse and left one unsatisfied and troubled and do so now. They pretended and we pretend to fathom the unfathomable. It is important to try and do so; but we are never sure we see it clearly or have it right.[13]

Newspapers of the era shaped individual and community consciousness and understandings of lynching in the context of race, class, and gender. Lynching was not a dirty southern family secret ensconced deeply in the back room closet; rather, the local, state, regional, national, and international press openly and publically reported it in the late 1800s. "THEY BURNED HIM," the *Arkansas Gazette* blared to its readers, and no one doubted what the headline meant. The headline "Another Lynching" frequently appeared and confirmed to Arkansans that lynching was the new norm of the day. Using the telegraph lines that crisscrossed the state and tapping into a long-distance telephone line installed in 1897, the *Arkansas Gazette* struggled to be the paper of record for the state and received and sent information throughout the United States. Sometimes the *Gazette* placed a story in small capitals on page 1 with no description, story, or explanation of the headline, as in the jarring note "Two Men Reported to Have Been Hanged in Van Buren County," which appeared on the front page on February 10, 1894. The reader scavenged the paper to see if other information appeared in later pages and bought future editions of the paper, this tease of a headline whetting their appetite to find out the rest of the story. Such newspaper accounts, Bruce Baker observes, provide the narrative and context of lynchings that create community memory, so critical in understanding, fomenting, or preventing future lynchings. Lisa Arellano agrees and contends that narratives constructed before a lynching from other lynching narratives "were essential to making the violence meaningful." Richard Perloff notes that "newspaper stories may also have persuaded readers that large majorities favored lynching, thereby providing a kind of social proof that lynching was an appropriate mechanism for social control."[14]

Reports of lynching in other southern states and throughout the Union constantly appeared in the *Arkansas Gazette* in the 1890s. It was as if the paper wanted to reassure its readers that lynching was not just an Arkansas phenomenon but a regional and a national issue. One editorial noted that "Alabama is now the most unenviable state in the Union. It is seriously affected with epidemics of lynching and smallpox." A story headlined with "In Ohio, Too!" described a northern lynching, reassuring Arkansans (and their fellow southerners) that they were not alone in taking the law into their own hands. A quadruple lynching detailed from California confirmed to Arkansans that others agreed that sometimes justice must transcend formal legal mechanisms. Occasionally, the legal professionals sanctioned lynching, as when lawyers in Doyline, Louisiana, addressed a mob, "warning the crowd of negroes present that such crimes would not be tolerated in a civilized community." The mob then took ten minutes to burn the accused at the stake. Perhaps the *Gazette* encouraged the Arkansas legal community to embrace extralegal bounds themselves when necessary, or perhaps it championed in the subtext the idea that educated lawyers of Arkansas should unite to make sure this does not happen here. One senses the *Gazette* comforting its readers that lynching could even happen in France, as when "a howling mob" attempted to lynch Emile Zola in 1898. Newspaper accounts documented and often legitimized lynching as a fact of life in the 1890s.[15]

Other states used Arkansas as an example of the new barbarism the South sunk to in the 1890s. In Mississippi, the *Choctaw Plain Dealer* chillingly reported in 1893 that "a Negro murdered a white man in Arkansas last week. There followed: a crowd—a rope—a limb—a dead nigger." The unthinkable and horrendous became the everyday in other state's perceptions of Arkansas. The *London Times* in 1899 deemed Arkansas one of the worst southern states for the commission of racial outrages. Northern Republican newspapers, in a new twist to waving the bloody shirt, reminded its readers that the meanings of the Civil War were still being contested in the North and South and used lynching reports to solidify Republican power in the North. The *New York Advertizer* observed that "the rude, barbaric sense of justice and vengeance is as strong in Orange County, New York, as in Miller County, Arkansas." That the New York editor thought his readers could identify a small southwestern Arkansas county tells a lot about the perception the nation held of Arkansas lynching.[16]

Lynching became so inevitable and acceptable that the *Arkansas Gazette* predicted lynchings before they happened. "If the negro is caught nothing can save him from being lynched," the *Gazette* prophesied. When a brother and sister were found dead and the sister decapitated, the *Gazette* knew that "no power in the state can stay a session of Judge Lynch's Court." "More lynchings may occur," words describing a riot in Rison, Arkansas, in 1897, ignited more self-righteousness in the lynchers. Phrases such as "a lynching is hourly expected" or "another lynching is a strong probability" occurred frequently in newspapers of the 1890s. Such prediction legitimized for many people the acceptability of lynching and the improbability of just a few people preventing the murder. Even if it was barbaric and wrong, what could one newspaper reader do to prevent the crime? Might they not be lynched, too?[17]

Use of the word *lynching* helped people rationalize their actions with precedents and, from their viewpoint, moral grounding. Although Christopher Waldrep uses as his reference point a definition of lynching as being an "act of violence sanctioned, endorsed, or carried on by the neighborhood or community outside the law," he also convincingly argues that *lynching* and *lynchers* cannot be defined and "function as rhetoric."[18]

Newspapers occasionally resorted to euphemism in their accounts of a lynching. The *Arkansas Gazette* used "a general clean up of the area," "a necktie party," or "swinging into eternity" to divert people's attention from what really transpired. Larger circulation newspapers such as the *New York Times* or the *Atlanta Constitution* openly criticized the South for its lynching carnivals of the 1890s and, at times, jolted their readers by calling the lynching a "bee"—like a quilting or spelling bee. The *Atlanta Constitution* described a "lynching bee" in Arkansas in 1897, and the *New York Times* in 1890 reported that "the murderer was taken to Searcy to prevent a lynching bee." The *New York Times* also wrote, "a demonstration there [Arkansas] last night and a lynching bee may yet be the climax," the use of the word *bee* almost suggesting that the brutal realities of lynching had been incorporated comfortably into scenes of domesticity.[19]

The word of choice for Arkansas and southern newspapers was *lynching*. Just the single word: lynching. In the *Arkansas Gazette* in the first half of 1898, fifteen significant and lengthy stories dealt with lynching, and in each case the reporter had no trouble deciding the event described was a lynching. Occasionally, the newspaper attempted to camouflage the lynching in legal jargon like "Judge Lynch" or "mob vengeance," rendering the usurpation of the law by the mob pseudolegal and acceptable. Mass lynchings or feared mass lynchings were sometimes viewed as a "race war," a historical allusion to the Haitian revolt of 1791. The use of "race war" to describe a lynching appeared more frequently in the context of the Spanish-American War (1898) when readers obsessed over war.[20]

Arkansas lynching included hanging, burning at the stake, massive volleys of bullets, or a combination of these three modes of execution. Mobs ranged from twelve members to more than five hundred, with three executions being mass public executions witnessed by thousands of onlookers. Tree limbs, railroad trestles, bridges, and telephone poles served as places to hoist the noose and lynch. Some executions seemed purposefully vindictive and sadistic, as when George Corvett, accused of rape and murder in February 1890, was dragged to the scene of the crime where his "arms, legs, and head" were cut off and he was cremated. Fifty well-armed masked men stormed the Clinton jail and almost entirely blew off the head of murderer W. H. Hardin in April 1899. Whether in a surrounded burning house or while hanging lifeless from a tree limb, corpses were often strafed with bullets. Although most of the organizers of the 1891 Lee County cotton pickers' strike were murdered in a thicket, perhaps to defuse the situation, in Texarkana there were two cases of ritual executions witnessed by crowds numbering in the thousands: Edward Coy in 1892 and Bud Hayden in 1898. Walking through the mob, participants struck Hayden as he passed by on his way to the railroad crossing where he would die, almost at the same spot where Coy died earlier. Participants who fired their bullets into the bodies of the lynched felt they contributed to the restoration of justice in their community. The hanging body reminded them of a deer, cow, or pig hanging from a tree while being processed. In lynchings, participants believed they brought subhuman whites and blacks to their real state of animal inhumanity, mutilated and degraded, where they received their just reward.[21]

Some lynchings received meticulous forethought and planning by mobs. An 1890 Camden group of vigilantes finished within thirty minutes, with the local newspaper assessing their work as "planned well." Some lynchers wore masks to protect their identities, as in Dermott in 1891 and in Clinton in 1899, while in Pine Bluff in 1892, no masks were worn. The Pine Bluff reporter observed that "the mob was comprised of some of our best citizens and no masks were used, and everything transpiring could be seen by the bright lights and the moon."[22]

Lynchers demonized all the humans they executed illegally, but they grew especially livid about reports of rape or sexual misconduct or improprieties. To get to the point of saturating a man's body with kerosene, burning it, and then relighting it to burn the man some more, one needed to anesthetize the mind and spirit. Words helped Arkansas lynchers void their consciousness, jettison their conscience, and believe that these were not humans they dealt with. The terms of choice used by the *Arkansas Gazette* to describe those lynched for sexual crimes were *ravager*, *fiend*, and *brute*. The *Gazette* described a "Negro ravager" burned to death in Alabama in 1897 and strangely included the fact in the very brief article (on page 6) that the lynched man "can't read." It was as if the newspaper wanted to reassure its readers that they, as literate and concerned citizens, could never fall to the depravity of a ravager, someone devoured by passion and fleshly appetite.[23]

Fiend and *brute* appear far more frequently to describe those who transgressed southern and community norms. From December 1897 to June

1898, the *Arkansas Gazette* described the rapists as fiends. Four black men were lynched near Bearden in January 1898, and two were called "rape fiends." Two Indian Territory rapists, called "red fiends," met a horrible death: roasting alive. In a Mississippi lynching case reported prominently in the *Gazette*, Charlie Lewis, picked out of a lineup by the young girl supposedly sexually assaulted, was "the fiend" who denied his guilt. The young girl's father, a state senator, and a Methodist preacher reasoned with the mob to cool them down to prevent a lynching. The father worried that his young daughter could have misidentified the attacker. Charlie Lewis's lynching rope broke and he was "hung—twice." The mob deemed him a fiend, and one did not compromise and wait for judicial proceedings when dealing with a fiend, with all the religious implications of that word.[24]

When a lynched victim was called a brute, he was clearly degraded into animalistic lawlessness and bestiality. Jim Beaver, a "black brute" in Bradley County, was lynched and his body fired into fifty or sixty times for the "outrage of a school girl." A mob of five hundred murdered James Bailey, Beebe's "black brute," in 1891 after he allegedly "brutally outraged the person of a lady quite prominent in church and social circles." A fire was prepared in Hope in 1899 to "roast the brute" who committed "an outrageous crime." By calling those accused and lynched "brutes," the "responsible" citizens of a community, now murderers, rationalized their behavior.[25]

Nothing worked up a mob more than the hint of sexual impropriety and misconduct, but the language used to describe the sexual transgression had to protect the southern lady already abused, as well as all southern womanhood, the community's morals, and the children who might be listening or reading the newspaper. Arkansas lynchers thus dealt circumspectly in their language regarding the often taboo topic (at least, they did so in the published reports of their actions). When people were expected to control and limit their sexual behavior to prescribed and acceptable behavior, the language used to describe the violation of a person and of the community's norms had to be muted and strictly controlled, just as it is today. As Daniel Singal observes, white middle-class sons of the New South depended on clear boundaries between savagery and civilization. They often feared both blacks and poor whites as sources of animalistic barbarism and sub-humanity.[26] Seeing potential "ravagers" everywhere, white men bound in the 1890s to Victorian propriety perhaps found some psychological relief in lynching. Uneasy with their own bodies, whites envied how black men and women seemed much more at ease with their sexuality. "Black men were lynched," Joel Williamson argues, "for having achieved, seemingly, a sexual liberation that white men wanted but could not achieve without great feelings of guilt." Gail Bederman agrees and notes that, by 1890, "a number of social, economic and cultural changes were converging to make the ongoing gender process especially active for the American middle class." White male middle-class Arkansans could reassure themselves of their masculinity by getting rid of black men who might be conceived of as more manly. Arkansas in the 1890s may not have possessed a robust middle class, the majority of its citizens being of more modest means, but the fact that lynching reports regularly describe some of the community's "best citizens" participating in—or even leading—these mobs seems to indicate at least some middle-class participation in lynching.[27]

Morris Christopher, a black seventeen-year-old Hope drayman, was "terribly whipped" but not lynched for "a crime peculiarly atrocious and revolting and . . . different from any case on record." The *Gazette* could not bring itself to name his crime—just an act atrocious and revolting. Readers filled in the blanks from their own imaginings. But usually the *Gazette* used veiled and euphemistic language that adult readers grasped. *Outrage* was the most frequently used term for a rape or a sexual assault, as in Monroe County in 1898 in "the outrage of a respectable farmer's wife." In Beebe in 1891, James Bailey allegedly seized and threw Mrs. Folsom to the ground and "brutally outraged her person." The crowd in this instance grew "indignant and outraged" at his behavior. The white southern lady, pedestaled on the illusory ideals of innocence and purity, demanded protection. Outside Monticello in 1897, the alleged black rapist of a black woman was shot and burned in his house. Outrageous behavior could only be responded to by the community with equivalent passion and fervor for justice.[28]

Words like *assaulted*, *ruined*, and *ravished* signaled to the reader there was more here than could be openly discussed. But sometimes what really happened perplexed southerners. The *Arkansas Gazette* on October 6, 1895, referred to rape openly in its headline—"Rapist in Custody"—and graphically described the female victim as "considerably bruised on her head and breast before she succumbed to the brute." The alleged rapist, John Carter (not to be confused with the John Carter who was lynched in Little Rock in 1927), was arrested and charged with rape, but the populace was "somewhat infuriated," and the *Gazette* hoped "wise counsel may prevail and the law be allowed to take its course." It is unclear why the language of the *Gazette* is so tentative: "somewhat infuriated." Two days later, the *Gazette* reported that Carter had escaped from the Conway jail and there "was little chance of apprehension." "Some had thought lynching needed," the *Gazette* reported, but what the others thought remained unstated and unclear.[29]

Desecration of the corpse was the last ritualistic scene in the lynching and would often be necessary, the lynchers thought, to remind community members that this happened when the horrendous and unspeakable took place. The *Arkansas Gazette* assured readers in June 1894 that the "miserable carcass" of a Columbia County man who attempted to enter the bedroom of three different young ladies "is dangling from a limb." The lynched man became not a corpse but a carcass, not even human in death. Hangings took place sometimes in "a neighboring swamp" or in a thicket of a swamp, perhaps to find a place away from settlement and people where there would be less chance of interference from the legal authorities. Or perhaps justice was meted out in the area close to town that still was wild, in the area where the bears, panthers, alligators, and water moccasins still thrived, the animalistic human dying in his real habitat: the wilderness, the place lacking in all civility and decorum. Or perhaps those who lynched knew deep down what they did was animalistic and should take place far away from the light of civilization.[30]

One wonders just what was put in the coffin of a man whose body had been punctured by fifty to sixty bullets shot into it by a mob. Who prepared his body for the grave? How? In 1897, Charlie Lewis's hanged body "was left hanging by the roadside." This was the ultimate desecration, the ultimate disdain. Often, the dangling corpses served as symbols or warnings to the citizens of the area that this is what happened to one who crossed certain boundaries. Bud Hayden's "black body swung from the limb several hours and was viewed by thousands of people." Thousands in Little Rock viewed the "swinging body" of Henry James at Main and Fifth Streets in 1892. In Monroe County, Moses Ricks's body, "perforated with Winchester bullets, dangled in the air with placards printed on the clothing as a warning to other negroes."[31]

Mobs worked out their ideas of justice through noose, pyre, and bullet—but even in the lynching, public narratives of propriety and control reigned. The ideal mob should not resort to some kind of uncontrollable Dionysian orgy of hatred and bloodlust. Instead, participants, according to many newspaper reports, went about their business almost puppet-like—controlled and controlling. In a lynching near Bearden in 1898, the lynching ideal was achieved, so that "little, if any, excitement prevailed." In the planning, execution, and aftermath, control had to be maintained. It was like a play with clearly demarcated actors, acts, and scenes.[32]

Such false order and delusions of control confronted the fierce criticisms southern lynchings engendered in the 1890s in the North. The *New York Times* led the way in condemning southern acts of horror and inhumanity. In an 1892 editorial, the *Times* insisted that lynchings were an "act of a barbarous country." "The next step," said an editorial responding to an 1895 Arkansas lynching, "will naturally be to declare all laws of every kind definitely off, close all Court Houses, and return to utter barbarism." Even the renowned Arkansas "hanging judge," Isaac Parker, condemned the lynchings, calling the rule of the mob the "most revolting and disgusting acts of savagery ever displayed on uncivilized and brutal people. This condition of barbarism and brutality and savagery which manifest [*sic*] itself in a mob violence must be suppressed." However, southerners desperately clung to "civilization" even as they committed acts of barbarity— or perhaps saw such acts as the only way to cling to civilization.[33]

Southerners thought they needed to react as they did to bring about their version of justice, but they knew their audience expanded far beyond Little River and Izard Counties. A murder or an assault that resulted in a lynching usually ignited a mob at its inception with "great excitement." "Excitement in and around Anderson is at a fever heat, and more trouble is expected," a dispatch from Pine Bluff noted. Leaders made sure that excessive violence and lawlessness did not get out of hand, and this was very tricky business indeed. One made sure that the anger and rage that many southern men seethed with but kept hidden did not erupt into other areas. In Beebe, an assault at half past nine in the evening resulted in great excitement. By a little after midnight, the alleged culprit had been found and hanged, and the reporter observed that "everything is now quiet and there is no noise or interference of any kind." A similar decorum occurred during the lynching in Louisiana, where "with no ceremony Jack Davis was hung." Arkansans followed suit when townsmen methodically beat Morris Christopher: "The citizens who punished the culprit were orderly and did their work very quickly."[34]

Citizens quickly created a facade, going back to their regular routines as if nothing had happened. In Camden, the reporter observed that "everything is perfectly quiet. No further trouble is anticipated." "There is no excitement over the matter here in town [DeWitt] and business is going on as if nothing unusual had happened," another report asserts. Such denial is akin to how many white southerners ignored or blocked out the violence and horrors of antebellum slavery. If such a return to tranquility really occurred, white southerners were more deadened than historians have ever imagined. More likely, this was a rationalization, a false consciousness through which white southerners explained to themselves that this nightmarish deed had been a requirement for the protection of their family, values, and way of life.[35]

Most Arkansans never actually saw or experienced a lynching in their lifetimes. They talked of lynchings to their friends and neighbors and perhaps mulled them over in their minds, but they never actually saw bodies dangling from tree limbs. They therefore reconstructed what a lynching would be like in their imaginations. Newspapers contributed to their mental images, but many newspaper articles describing a lynching were terse—fewer than two inches of newspaper print. One lynching occurred on the streets of Little Rock in 1892 that a reporter actually witnessed. His uniquely written story resembles a morality play or a drama. The language, vivid and poetic, helps the reader see and feel what went on. Concrete details fill the story, and specific locations are mentioned. If white supremacists used the fear of lynching to control blacks—or if some whites hoped to liberalize racial norms, with denunciations of such behavior as disgusting and barbaric—then the account of the 1892 lynching of Henry James in Little Rock created the necessary pictures in people's minds. After all, this was the age of yellow journalism. National newspapers beat their sensationalistic war drums to help sell newspapers and to prepare for the Spanish-American War of 1898. *Arkansas Gazette* reporter Fred W. Allsopp learned in 1890 that one treaded carefully with one's reporting when he criticized a popular Christian evangelist, Sam Jones, calling him "merely an entertainer . . . a demagogue with a flap-jack mouth and . . . an oily tongue." The paper, Allsopp noted, lost subscribers "by wholesale." But the report of this 1892 lynching sold scores of newspapers.[36]

The story opens with one word: "Midnight!" Already, the reader has traversed into the land of Edgar Allan Poe. "It is the hour when graveyards yawn and hell breathes contagion to the world," the reporter paints his word mural. Henry James, a "copper-colored devil," allegedly "outraged little Maggie Doxie." After his arrest, a mob of five hundred went to the city jail, and when they discovered that he was not there, they then went to the state penitentiary, where guards at first steadfastly refused to give him up. However, the mob broke into the penitentiary and took James from it. Blood dripped from James's body as the crowd dragged him through the streets of Little Rock to Main and Fifth Streets, where he was hanged. His body was "perforated" with bullets. "Infuriated bystanders" knocked around Gov. James Philip Eagle, who was coming home from Memphis, Tennessee, on a Little Rock streetcar, when he tried to stop the mayhem. "He's Gone," the *Gazette* headline screamed. "No Longer Will the Lecherous Beast Indulge His Lust Upon Earth. Crowd Takes Him." Thousands visited James's swinging corpse in the next few hours, dangling "under the shadow of a building where the words 'Friendship, Charity, and Benevolence'" had been engraved. The images and details of the story were seared into the consciousness of Arkansans.[37] (See chapter 7 for more on this particular event.)

Earlier that year, the *Arkansas Gazette* graphically detailed one of the most heinous lynchings of the era, the burning at the stake of Edward Coy in Texarkana. Identified by the supposed rape victim, Coy was marched by a mob of a thousand men through the streets of the city and fastened to a stake. They saturated his clothes with kerosene, and the victim applied the first match to the pyre. "You are the rascal that assaulted me," she proclaimed. The burning took seven minutes, and the "agony was excruciating." Here, the verbiage is more terse and controlled, but readers in Arkansas and then throughout the nation read it and shuddered.[38]

Six years later, the *Arkansas Gazette* spent about as much space detailing the infamous hanging of Bud Hayden, the alleged rapist of a twelve-year-old, again in Texarkana. "Hang Him Shouted an Angry Mob at Texarkana," the headline began. "And They Hung Him. Negro Committed a Fiendish Crime," the story continued. The assailant allegedly assaulted a young girl "while [she was] picking berries." The father of the victim at first tried to keep the violence unreported, but he eventually changed his mind and told authorities. Word spread quickly throughout the town, and the woods were "scoured in every direction." Eventually, Hayden was found and arrested, and "hundreds of excited people" ringed the county jail. "Hundreds of Texarkana's leading citizens" guarded the jail on the night of June 3. "A cooler headed mob never collected," the *Gazette* assured its readers. The next day, the crowd swelled to the thousands. One speaker harangued the crowd, saying, "in the walls of that jail is a brute that has assaulted a twelve-year old child of one of our departed citizens." Hayden was handed over to the mob, and a noose was placed around his neck. The crowd struck him as he passed by to the lynching place—the Iron Mountain Railroad crossing—where Ed Coy had been burned to death in 1892. He was hanged and his body "riddled by bullets." His hanging body remained there for several hours and "was viewed by thousands of people." Again, the imagery is so vivid, the reader readily pictures the young child in the blackberry patch or the crowd striking, cursing, and spitting on Hayden as he marched to his death. But the *Gazette* printed this story on page 3 in 1898. Perhaps it was just a matter of not being able to redo page 1, but perhaps the *Gazette* had joined those more troubled than happy over lynchings.[39]

In an age of stories, both oral and written, these three descriptions lingered in the consciousness and memories of people throughout the state. Although they happened in three discrete places and at three discrete times, they warned blacks who heard about them to be aware, be circumspect, be careful—for years, even generations, afterward. The disseminated accounts of such lynchings powerfully deterred and shaped behavior, solidifying white supremacy.

The lynching of so many people in the 1890s concerned many "respectable" citizens in Arkansas. Over time, the *Arkansas Gazette* and the small but growing urban middle class began to abhor lynching and speak up against it as a prelude to Progressive reform of the early twentieth century (explored more fully in chapter 6). The *Arkansas Gazette* editorialized that "irreparable justice" resulted from a lynching. "Lynching," they insisted, "is a failure, and some other remedy should be tried." They also insisted that "lynch law is nothing more nor less than lawlessness." Responding to an 1891 lynching in the Ashley County community of Portland in which the victim was "shot from head to foot," the *Gazette* exhorted that "these violent and lawless lynchings ought to be stopped. . . . The good and order loving citizens condemn this lynching in strong terms. . . . [Lynching] is a blow to material prosperity and the county and a reproach to Christian civilization." Through its editorial voice, the *Arkansas Gazette* hoped to awaken Arkansans to the barbarism and corruption that lynching unleashed.[40]

In 1899, the *New York Times* asked several southern governors to explain what could be done about the epidemic of lynchings erupting in the South. Arkansas governor Daniel Webster Jones asserted that rape or attempted rape usually caused the lynching to occur, "especially when the assault has been made by a negro upon a white woman." "This crime is so heinous and revolting that all the laws in the world, no matter how severe the punishment or speedy its infliction, cannot in my judgment prevent lynching when the accused falls into the hands of an enraged mob," he insisted. The *Little Rock Democrat* disagreed with the governor's assessment and insisted that murder was the leading cause of lynching and used statistics to prove their case. It argued that "the reign of the mob is anarchy pure and simple" and should be resisted even when "the honor of a woman was in question." Lynching, the paper insisted, "undermines the pillars upon which society rests."[41]

Newspaper editors occasionally suffered more than community disdain for speaking out against lynching. The *Osceola Times* editor scathingly castigated the sheriff of Mississippi County for "having been a party" to an 1897 lynching. The sheriff demanded that the editor retract the statement or "he would kill him on sight." The journalist left the state rather than "chew his words." White political and religious leaders also spoke out, although in small numbers and often in muted voice. For example, at Mountain Home, legislator Jerry South and Baxter County sheriff W. E. Eaton tried to reason with a mob and deter a lynching in 1894, but they also failed. These speakers feared for their own personal safety at that moment; and later, when safe, they worried about how such activism might cost them elections, parishioners, or money.[42]

At times, local county sheriffs and law enforcement officials used more than just words to prevent lynching; they often stood in between the mob and the accused, risking their own death to preserve the rule of law. A mob of more than 250 overpowered ten guards and the Baxter County sheriff to get to the two men they wanted to lynch. Local constables and their supporters "heavily protected" the accused, Sims Gage, to prevent his lynching. A mob of 250 failed to get the keys from a jailer named Wilson at Monticello and broke into the jail to get their man. In Hope, the sheriff and twenty-five guards surrounded the jail and saved the life of a black defendant for whom the mob had already prepared a fire "to roast the brute."[43]

Most courageously, Little River County sheriff Hiram Sanderson prevented a "necktie party" in 1898 by outwitting the mob of fifty that "scoured the county" to find the alleged murderer, Ned Aiken, whom they wanted to lynch. With the *Arkansas Gazette* predicting "a lynching is hourly expected" and "lynching is almost sure to follow," Sanderson and Aiken spent the night in the woods Sanderson knew well, crossed the Red River in the dead of night, and arrived safely at Texarkana later that morning. The mob cooled down, and Aiken safely returned to Richmond to await trial. Occasionally, elected officials, too, risked their lives to avert a lynching, if only to preserve the good reputation of the city they managed. In Pine Bluff in February 1892, the mayor, following two lynchings that had already occurred, managed to save a third victim from hanging by talking the mob down. The county judge of Monroe County likewise addressed a mob in August 1898, preventing a lynching by promising them a quick settlement of the case but one legal and unsullied by mob rule.[44]

Officials used more than words to try to deter lynching. Some tried rewards to bring members of the mob to justice. A $25,000 reward was offered to help identify those involved in the burning at the stake of two Native Americans near Fort Smith in 1898. An $850 reward was offered for information about the 1895 lynching near Vilonia. In response to a scathing criticism of Arkansas lynching and lawlessness from an antilynching committee across the sea in England, Gov. William Meade Fishback in 1894 offered state rewards for information that helped identify the leaders of a mob. In an editorial entitled "The Lynching Problem," the *Arkansas Gazette* puzzled over the wisdom of the proposal by Gov. James A. Mount of Indiana to make lynching a civil crime, which would empower the next of kin to someone lynched to sue the county where the lynching occurred. As the 1890s closed with its record number of lynchings, thoughtful Arkansans hoped to end the reign of terror in their state.[45]

Black Arkansans walked a tightrope as they reacted to the lynchings taking place in the 1890s. "The social, economic, and political upheavals that marked the Nineteenth century's last decade hit black southerners especially hard," Kidada E. Williams notes. "If press accounts can be trusted," Christopher Waldrep notes, "black outrage and whites' violence escalated around 1891." Black preachers—Baptists, Campbellites, Methodists, and Presbyterians—met in Little Rock in 1892 and enacted a resolution that took the middle road of denouncing lynchers while also chastising sexual offenders. The Philadelphia *Christian Recorder* commented on the "conspicuous absence of some of our leading pastors." The statewide black Baptist convention met in Hot Springs in 1897 and condemned "inhuman wretches" and "fiends" lynched after a rape. They stayed strangely silent about the actual lynchings.[46]

The *Arkansas Gazette* reported on the back pages of its enlarged Sunday edition articles from "moderate" African American thinkers regarding lynching. Rev. J. E. Gilbert of Washington, DC, insisted that "any man, black or white, who enrages a woman, deserves to die," but the death penalty should be inflicted "by due process of law." The *Gazette* deemed this "sensible." They also applauded the moderate counsel of Charles Stewart, a black assistant postmaster who described lynching as a "disgrace to our civilization." He reassured Arkansas whites that what overheated rhetoric termed "race wars" could never happen since in his mind "it was impossible for the negro to engage in battle with the white people of any community." High-powered modern rifles, gunpowder, and dynamite were beyond the reach of most black Arkansans, voiding any successful "race war."[47]

Regardless of the advice of religious leaders or race spokesmen, ordinary black citizens decided what to do when a lynching occurred at or near their homes. Desha County blacks in the summer of 1892 lynched a black father for allegedly raping his seventeen-year-old daughter. In December 1892, Jackson County blacks lynched G. P. F. Lightfoot, a black Baptist preacher, for committing a "stupendous fraud" upon the black population. Black Arkansans sometimes joined white bystanders to form integrated lynching parties at Dermott and Clarendon. In the 1894 lynching at McGehee, the mob of three hundred was comprised of more "Negroes than white men." An old "gray headed negro" insisted to the *Gazette* reporter that if the murderers could be properly identified, "negroes would not give white people an opportunity of avenging the murder but would gladly do so themselves." In Varner in 1893, the lynching party consisted totally of African Americans. "A Negro Murdered and His Body Burned by a Mob of His Race," the *Arkansas Gazette* headlined from Lincoln County. In 1899 in Monticello, a lynching occurred after two black girls, eight and twelve years old, were reportedly assaulted. "All parties concerned are negroes, and the girls' friends are very indignant over their outrage," the *Arkansas Gazette* reporter noted. Arkansas whites seemed reassured that blacks upheld the same moral code as they: commit certain transgressions, and lynching followed.[48]

Some blacks took to the road to protect themselves and their families. Rev. E. Malcolm Argyle documented that "five hundred people are hovering, upon wharves of Pine Bluff, awaiting the steamers to take them up the Arkansas River to Oklahoma." He also observed that the *Arkansas Gazette* reported twelve hundred more passed "through the upper country enroute to Oklahoma." An African Colonization Society reporter observed in 1892 that a thousand families readied to leave Arkansas due to the heightened racial violence. Robert Davis, an African American from Lonoke County, insisted that "we are anxious to leave this state now. . . . We are going Bake in slavery every day." When return to Africa proved unfeasible, scores opted to move to Oklahoma to seek a safer and better life.[49]

Most blacks, just like their white counterparts, never actively partici-pated in lynchings. Although protestors' opposition to lynching always endangered them and their families, some blacks stood up against the vig-ilante justice of the 1890s. In Monroe County in 1898, great excitement among African Americans over a double lynching resulted in "some of them getting out of the neighborhood in terror," while others "showed an ugly temper that portend[ed] further trouble." White lynchers always feared that maybe this time they had gone too far; maybe this time they had driven out their cotton pickers forever or sparked a racial confrontation that could prove bloody and costly. The historical record controlled by whites mutes much public black protest against lynching; but one leading scholar of lynching, W. Fitzhugh Brundage, insists that black defiance was often "heavily disguised by what Michel de Certeau called the guerilla warfare of everyday life."[50]

In 1891 and 1899, at the eastern and then at the western edge of the state, blacks rebelled against their economic and racial yokes, spawn-ing mass lynchings as the white elites regained power and hegemony. In 1891 in Lee County, as part of the Colored Farmers' Alliance movement, blacks balked at collusion among Delta planters who were determined not to pay cotton pickers more than fifty cents per one hundred pounds. Just as cotton-picking season began in September, Ben Patterson, strike organizer, journeyed from Memphis, Tennessee, to the canebrakes of Lee County and, for three weeks, exhorted black workers to stand up for their rights and demand higher wages. The strike began on September 20, 1891, but never gained a large following of local African American workers. On September 25, two pickers were killed by black organizers who detested the refusal of African Americans to join the strike. "Men, women, and children . . . armed with hoes, sticks, knives, and revolvers" drove the strike leaders away. On September 28, strike organizers murdered a plan-tation overseer, "rifling his body and crushing his skull." Leaders fled to Cat Island in the Mississippi River, where a white posse surrounded them.

In the end, the white vigilantes murdered a total of fifteen, according to some sources, while six others were imprisoned. The strike ended, and things in the Delta stayed the same.[51]

"The Negro should be made to understand that they cannot commit these outrages with impunity," the Memphis *Appeal-Avalanche* exhorted; while the Kansas City *American Citizen*, a black newspaper, insisted that "the ordinary fire and brimstone of hell will not be enough for these white devils." The *Arkansas Gazette* asserted, "Lee County Trouble Settled With Rope." It assured Arkansas planters throughout the state that most of the strike leaders were outside agitators from Memphis and that the Colored Farmers' Alliance had nothing to do with the disturbance whatsoever—again, an attempt to pacify worried white planters. The language the white elite used with the help of the *Arkansas Gazette* was ambiguous. The alliance had not backed this particular strike, but they clearly saw that the pay of cotton pickers was subhuman and that something needed to be done to improve their plight. The *Gazette* and planters knowingly blurred the issue to maintain their power. And although history and humans can never be reduced to the cash nexus, to a simplistic tale of economic determinism, if one jeopardizes another's economic standing, one challenges the whole tangled web of how one creates and recreates one's identity and livelihood. A serious threat to the southern cotton economy demanded a serious and deadly response from the white elite.[52]

A "race war" in southwestern Little River County in 1899 also resulted in quick and severe reprisals by local whites to maintain their economic and racial grip on the area. Unlike the Lee County incident, which began as cotton season ended, the Little River County imbroglio began in March as cotton planting season commenced. The event is shrouded in rumor, innuendo, and false information, and no one living a century or more after the event can know what really happened. "Negro Brutally Murders a Wealthy Little River County Planter," the *Arkansas Gazette* informed what would ultimately become a national audience. James Stockton, a wealthy Little River County planter with land in three counties, had threatened General Duckett, an African American, in an effort to settle a debt. A Stockton relative possesses a written family account wherein the debt is claimed to be forty dollars. Stockton threatened to take Duckett's horse or kill Duckett with a knife if he did not pay up. Duckett fled, went home, obtained a double-barreled shotgun, and shot Stockton in the chest, killing him. The

Arkansas Gazette reported Stockton's head had been "blown off with a shotgun through the crack of a house."[53]

For four days, white mobs searched the Red River bottoms trying to find the evasive Duckett. He lived off food brought by a friend's wife to a secret rendezvous until surrendering on March 21. Taken to the scene of the murder of Stockton near Rocky Comfort, he confessed to local sheriff John Johnson, and while he was on his way back to jail at Richmond, a mob overpowered the sheriff, hanged Duckett from a tree, and riddled his body with bullets. So far, this was arguably a typical story for Arkansas in the 1890s—the murder of a powerful white man followed by the lynching of the alleged black perpetrator.[54]

But then rumors began to fly. Duckett was accused of plotting a "race war" in Little River County. The *Arkansas Gazette*, on March 23, 1899, announced to its readers that Duckett had been stirring up blacks to wage war on whites. The next day, the Little Rock newspaper insisted the "wildest excitement prevails in Little River County" as "Blacks Plot Race War." Thirty-three blacks had been implicated in the conspiracy to kill whites, and by March 24, seven had been hanged by white mobs. They included Edwin Goodwin; Joe, Ben, and Mose Jones; Adam King; General Duckett; and an unknown party. "News of a severe race war is looked for hourly," the *Arkansas Gazette* predicted. Some black locals trembled at this unexpected reign of terror. Three wagonloads of "greatly frightened" African Americans reportedly escaped to Texarkana, crossing the Red River at Index in the night. The next day's report lowered the wagonloads to two but still insisted the people were badly frightened.[55]

National newspapers took up the story as reported by the *Arkansas Gazette* and exaggerated and distorted it. The *Nebraska State Journal* claimed twenty-three to thirty-three African Americans were involved in a plot to kill leading whites and were being systematically rounded up by white mobs and hanged. "Tried to Stir up Trouble: Duckett Wanted a General Assassination of Whites," the *Houston Daily Post* proclaimed. The *New York Times* informed its readers that "a race war is on in Little River County, and during the last forty-eight hours a number of negroes have met their deaths at the hands of the white population. Seven are known to have been lynched, and the mob is not yet done." The story spread nationally and was reported in Saint Louis, San Francisco, and Chicago. Closest to the scene, the *Texarkana Gazette* insisted statewide and national coverage of the "race war" had been blown all out of proportion. They reported that the Texarkana mortuary received a call from Ashdown on March 18 that the undertaker would be needed to prepare Stockton's body for burial. Their paper's death count is three: Duckett (murderer of Stockton), Joe King (hanged on same tree with Duckett), and Mose Jones. The coroner declared Ed Goodwin died of natural causes, although the *Arkansas Gazette* claimed his neck "showed signs of encirclement by a rope." "There is no likelihood of any race war," the *Texarkana Gazette* emphatically stated, adding, "From reading the reports [in other newspapers] one would think that every tree in Red River bottoms had a negro hanging on it." The *Arkansas Democrat* admitted that "when the truth is known it will probably be found that the story of the lynching of seven negroes is very much exaggerated." "There is some strange news coming over the grape vine into the city," the *Texarkana Gazette* insisted. "The vine should be cut and stop the food for northern fanatics to harp on as to the barbarity of the South."[56]

"When the truth is known," the *Arkansas Democrat* intoned. But that would, of course, be never. Arkansas student of lynching Richard Buckelew includes four names of the lynched in this "race war" in 1899. The media of the day inflated the numbers, perhaps in an attempt to increase the guilt of southerners, or perhaps in an attempt to sell newspapers. Perhaps it was the old story of the rest of the nation demonizing the South to more easily overlook its own prejudice and racism. To call the event a "race war" devalues the language and makes subsequent readers jaded and reluctant to believe anything reported — as if race relations were not troubled enough, hyperbole and distortion only made more difficult the plight of those who wanted to end the real barbarism of lynching.[57]

What seems to be going on in Arkansas in the 1890s is the use of retaliatory, random, and capricious terror to maintain white supremacy. As Michael Trotti asserts, "Would it not be more sound to assume that terror is one of many elements of our past that is simply resistant to quantification?" Neither blacks nor whites ever really knew if or when a lynching might erupt in their community. Once it started, would a real race war follow? Whites and blacks in the land of Jim Crow Arkansas in the 1890s contested understandings of race and identities. The shadow of the noose and mob haunted Arkansans, the United States, and the world in the 1890s. And that shadow hangs over the work of historians today. "Lynching was always entangled in lies," Bruce E. Baker perceptively laments. Although historians can never know with certainty why what happened in the past occurred, they diligently try to unravel and decipher meanings. They demand that each lynching be analyzed in its uniqueness and contingency. They refuse to make history a morality play that distorts the past with a presentist liberal or conservative agenda, and they avoid overreliance on sociological patterns or trends; but they do feel burdened to expose barbarism and inhumanity when they discover them. And they sadly confess that such barbarism and inhumanity are not just relics of the past—while they are ignored and at times distorted, they are not really past.[58]

The Clarendon Lynching of 1898

The Intersection of Race, Class, and Gender

The town of Clarendon is located in the Arkansas Delta on the White River at the mouth of the Cache River. In 1898, Clarendon boasted a population of just over one thousand residents, having doubled since 1880. This peaceful, wholesome community benefitted from economic diversity and enjoyed prosperity with barely a whisper of scandal. That would forever change on Saturday, July 30, 1898, with the murder of local businessman John Orr. Saturday nights for John and Mabel Orr were routinely devoted to choir practice at the Methodist church, where John was a member of the choir and Mabel the organist. On this rainy Saturday, John was forced to go alone as Mabel remained at home sick with their four-year-old daughter, Geneva. John returned home from choir practice shortly after nine o'clock and quietly entered the kitchen to make a glass of lemonade, as was his usual routine after choir practice. As he stood at the kitchen sink, a shotgun blast came through the open window, striking him in the head. He clung to life for several hours but died Sunday afternoon.[1]

The murder of John Orr shocked and frightened the residents of Clarendon as they wondered who would do such a thing and why. By all appearances, the Orr family had it all—a happy marriage, a young daughter, a successful hardware business, and a large home staffed by servants. Appearances can often be deceiving, however, and over the next week this picture would quickly unravel, exposing an unhappy marriage marked by abuse and a wife who was desperate to escape the situation. This case illustrates how late nineteenth-century attitudes about race, class, and gender could directly contribute to a course of events that led to a murder, a mass lynching, and a suicide.[2]

Born in 1867, John Orr grew up on the family farm in Reading, Kansas, the middle child of three siblings. John was a star in high school, both as an athlete who ran the one-hundred-yard dash in just ten seconds and as a leading actor in school plays. He loved acting so much that he left Kansas to pursue his dreams in the theater and ended up touring the country as a comedian and actor for a few years before marrying sixteen-year-old Verda Willis in Columbus, Ohio, in 1887. They divorced just two years later amid allegations of abuse and mistreatment.[3]

John relocated to Chippewa Falls, Wisconsin, thereafter, establishing a hardware business and resuming his career on the stage. A year later, while performing at a Fourth of July show with his theater troupe in Iron River, Wisconsin, he met sixteen-year-old Erneze Mabel Barker. Despite strong protests from Mabel's family, John and Mabel quickly eloped and were married in Chippewa Falls on July 23, 1890.[4]

Born in 1874, in Mauston, Wisconsin, Mabel Barker was still attending school when she first met John Orr. Life had not been easy for young Mabel since her mother had passed away a few years earlier. Her father, Walter Barker, was a logger who struggled to raise her alone because his job required him to travel between the major rivers throughout northern Wisconsin. He established a residence at the Southern Hotel so that Mabel would not be left entirely alone while he was out of town. Did the loss and loneliness make her desperate for attention and a way to escape her circumstances? She was reportedly completely smitten when she met John Orr, a handsome, charismatic actor. He was apparently equally smitten with young Mabel, and they began a whirlwind romance. Through her relationship with John, she found the love and attention she so desperately craved, and the added thrill of joining his theater troupe meant she could travel and see other parts of the country. Living such an adventurous life must have seemed like a dream come true for Mabel, making it easy to disregard or minimize warning signs of potential relationship issues.

For the first few years of their marriage, John and Mabel lived in Chippewa Falls, where he maintained his hardware business and managed the local theater where they often performed. John's business afforded the couple a comfortable lifestyle, and they enjoyed the excitement of touring the country as actors when the opportunity arose. Their theater troupe was actually one of the first to perform in Clarendon's new opera house, which opened in 1893, and they became enamored with the town. When Mabel became pregnant near the end of 1893, John decided to abandon the theater and instead settle down in a wholesome environment to raise their child, and he chose Clarendon, remembering how much they loved the city.

At first glance, it may have seemed odd, in 1894, for John to move an established business from a city of over eight thousand residents to a town with just over one thousand, but here we get a glimpse at John Orr's business acumen. He knew from his earlier visit that this area was economically diverse and experiencing a relative boom. The Cotton Belt Railroad had just connected Clarendon and towns further south to Saint Louis, Missouri, providing a vital transportation link to wider markets. This stimulated development of the timber industry, which exploited the rich forests of the area and brought more laborers to the region. By the early 1890s, the town also developed an industrial port and became an important cotton center. More importantly, this rich agricultural region specializing in cotton meant that John prospered not only by selling supplies but also by financing area farmers.[5]

As it turned out, John's decision made it possible to reestablish his hardware business in Clarendon, purchase a large house, and hire an entire staff of black servants to take care of the household. As his hardware business began to prosper, the handsome young couple was soon welcomed into the finest homes. To the citizens of Clarendon, the Orrs were the type of residents they hoped to attract—young, stable, family-oriented, and prosperous.

Over the next four years, the Orrs would become firmly established in Clarendon society. A daughter, Geneva Louise Orr, was born on July 6, 1894, and they cemented firm ties within the community. They joined the Methodist church, where John sang in the choir and Mabel played the organ. Mabel was also involved in charity work through the church. John joined the Knights of Pythias and the Maccabees, and Mabel likely served in the ladies' auxiliaries of these fraternal organizations.[6]

John Orr still exhibited athleticism as an avid bicyclist who became the reigning county champion by winning races throughout Arkansas. By all accounts, John and Mabel were popular and well respected throughout the town, especially for their church-related work. Their friends and acquaintances viewed them as an ideal couple in a happy, loving marriage. Unfortunately, that was not the case.[7]

The Orrs were decidedly unhappy and fought incessantly over John's expectations for Mabel to obey him without question and conform to the traditional Victorian role of wife and mother. Mabel, however, proved unwilling to be cast in that role, instead wanting to return to a life in the theater. John's frustration caused him to try to force her into submission by tightly controlling the purse strings. Regarding his efforts to control Mabel, Lorilla Weaver, their African American cook, later testified in the coroner's inquest that John was mean and mistreated Mabel, refusing to even buy her adequate clothing. In fact, the situation reached the point that Mabel often resorted to wearing Weaver's underwear. During one of their many fights, Weaver allegedly witnessed John strike his wife. Mabel's small concessions to John only reinforced her refusal to accept the subservient, limited role he demanded of her as wife and mother, even though she put forward that facade for a number of years.[8]

Mabel played the role of the dutiful wife and mother, attending social functions on the arm of her husband and displaying the outward appearance of a happy marriage, but this was merely a show. Desperate letters to her father and stepmother back home in Wisconsin received no replies. She later learned that her husband had been intercepting her mail, and from then on she only corresponded using the name of her cook, Lorilla Weaver. Once she was able to send and receive mail successfully, she wrote a letter to her father and stepmother describing her situation:

> You ask me to come home. I have begged and pleaded to come home, but I might as well plead to a stove. I shall try to come home in the fall. I must get away from this place, and that at once, or I shall never be able to come. I weigh ninety-four pounds and you can imagine what I am going through when you see my gray-hair. As soon as I can earn enough money by giving music lessons I shall come. I have reached the end of endurance. I cannot get any money except what I scrape and dig for. . . . Not even to you, my dearest ones, could I tell the misery and suffering I endure and have gone through for the last four years. I feel much better with such a comforter and I am happy in that I have not been deserted by those who are nearest and, dearest to me.
>
> Lovingly yours,
> May Erneze Orr[9]

These appear to be the words of an abused yet ambitious woman who is trapped in a bad situation, lonely, and defeated. The powerlessness of her reality stands in stark and sobering contrast to her glory days on the stage, when she received audience applause and adulation.

Mabel had no one other than her servants to confide in until she met seventeen-year-old Rachael Morris, a local girl who longed for a life beyond Clarendon. Rachael found in Mabel an interesting and supportive friend. Their relationship blossomed, and before long she moved into the Orr home, where the two shared their hopes, dreams, and frustrations.

Mabel regaled young Rachael with stories about her travels and life on the stage. Mabel longed to escape small-town life and move to New York City, to start her own theater group and return to the stage. Sharing the dreams of life beyond Clarendon, Rachael seemingly became enamored of Mabel's exotic descriptions. Rachael, as friend and confidant, was well aware of the Orrs' marital problems and emboldened Mabel to believe that she deserved better. Mabel finally accepted the fact that her marriage was irretrievably broken and that she needed a way to escape her situation. Together, the women decided to pursue a new life in the theater and resolved to find a way to make their dream a reality. The two women apparently began to concoct a detailed plan that would allow Mabel to leave her husband but keep his money.[10]

Social mores based on Victorian values made the prospect of leaving her husband extremely difficult. The expectation that her sphere would be characterized by an emphasis on "piety, purity, submissiveness, and domesticity" was anathema to her.[11] She did not enjoy rights that might afford women control in issues of property and child custody, as these rights were by no means universal. Under the circumstances, Mabel realized that if she did try to leave her wealthy husband, she would likely be left disgraced and destitute. She became determined to come up with a better alternative.

One alternative was to find another wealthy husband with perhaps a more enlightened outlook or adventurous spirit. She began using matrimonial services to find a suitable wealthy bachelor for marriage. While we may never know exactly what type of information Mabel used in her profile, we do know that she portrayed herself as a single woman, once again using the name of her cook, Lorilla Weaver.

Mabel needed a substantial amount of money to have any chance of realizing her dreams. John controlled the family finances with an iron fist.

Forced to do without some necessities, Mabel did earn a modest income by giving music lessons, but hardly enough money for her goals. Mabel and Rachael became desperate, realizing that there were no legal means of raising the money they needed. Perhaps they could get life insurance on John, have him killed, and then collect on the policy—a far more dangerous plan. John's death would preclude the need for divorce, and as a widow, she would get all of John's assets. With this goal firmly in mind, Mabel somehow encouraged her husband to purchase a $5,000 life insurance policy through one of his fraternal organizations, either the Maccabees or the Knights of Pythias. Now all that remained was to plan his death.[12]

Neither woman wanted to be linked to the actual murder, and they pondered multiple methods of killing John. Rachael suggested feeding John ground glass, reasoning that "it works on dogs," but they decided it would be much too easy to detect. Mabel remembered Lorilla talking about a local "hoodoo doctor and conjurer" named Dennis Ricord (whose name is also given in reports as Record or Rikard), and she asked Lorilla to see if he would help.[13] Most of the black residents feared Ricord, but Lorilla put her fear aside and spoke to him on Mabel's behalf. Ricord allegedly agreed to help by providing dead scorpions and snake heads with instructions to boil them and put the concoction in a drink—the brew ostensibly contained lethal toxins that would poison whoever drank it. On July 4, 1898, Mabel instructed Lorilla to pour the concoction into John's coffee, which he drank. He promptly vomited but made a full recovery. Weaver remarked wryly that it seemed to make Orr "healthier," while Ricord explained the failure, stating that Orr "had too much silver in his skin."[14] Disheartened over her failure, Mabel blurted in front of her servants how she would give $200 dollars for someone to kill her husband, and thus the chain of events that led to John Orr's murder was set in motion.

In 1898, the mention of the huge sum of $200 certainly would have caught the attention of the black servants in the Orr household. Knowing the servants were limited to low-paying jobs, Mabel initially asked Manse Castle if he would kill her husband. He was reluctant at first, but after Mabel got him sufficiently drunk, he finally agreed to obtain a gun and promise to kill her husband in exchange for some of the insurance money. Castle managed to borrow a shotgun from a friend and hid it in the servants' house behind the Orr home, but then he had second thoughts and convinced Dennis Ricord to take the job. Mabel met with Ricord, explaining that all he had to do was show up when the time came and follow her instructions for the murder. Ricord was promised the same deal she had offered Castle.[15]

Mabel chose a Saturday evening because it coincided with choir practice at the Methodist church, which allowed her to predict his movement and location accurately. On Saturday, July 30, she set her plan in motion. Dennis Ricord and Will Sanders, Weaver's son and a porter in the Orr household, were to hide in a room adjoining the kitchen and shoot John Orr as he left for choir practice. Mabel feigned illness, and John urged her to stay home with Geneva and rest up so that she could play the organ at a funeral the next day. She readily agreed and stayed in their room waiting for the sound of the gunshot. She rushed to the dining room to see what happened after hearing her husband leave without a gunshot. Ricord explained that he was unfamiliar with the gun and could not figure out how to make it fire. Thoroughly annoyed, Mabel retrieved her husband's own shotgun from a closet and showed both Ricord and Sanders how it worked. Sanders said he knew how to use the gun and would carry out the murder. Forced to improvise, Mabel told Sanders that upon her husband's return home around half past nine, he would invariably stand at the kitchen sink while making a glass of lemonade. She told Sanders to position himself outside the kitchen window and, once Orr appeared, to shoot him. Opening the screened window and pinning the curtain with a hairpin, she ensured a clear line of sight for the hired killer. Now, they had only to wait.[16]

As expected, John Orr returned home from choir practice about 9:20 p.m. to a dark house and kept to his habit of making a glass of lemonade. A single shotgun blast came through the window as he stood at the kitchen sink, knocking him to the floor. A single pellet of buckshot entered directly above his right eye. Deputy sheriff Patrick Milwee arrived on the scene as Orr regained consciousness, and he asked Orr who was responsible. A bewildered Orr said he had no clue why anyone would want to harm him. Orr lost consciousness before answering any further questions. He lapsed into a coma overnight but clung to life until the next afternoon. Local residents reacted to the news with shock and fear.[17]

The news of John Orr's murder circulated quickly throughout Clarendon, and the stunned citizens demanded prompt action. Deputy Milwee immediately issued a general alert and then sent a telegram to Pine Bluff for bloodhounds to aid the investigation. Milwee also summoned Sheriff T. H. Jackson to return from Brinkley, where he was visiting friends.

Sheriff Jackson returned early Sunday morning to lead the investigation, but he and his deputies were unable to uncover any clues. Intermittent rain Saturday evening and Sunday hindered the bloodhounds, who were useless in tracking the assailant. Because physical evidence was lacking and the rain helped the murderer cover his tracks, Sheriff Jackson suspected that this was a well-planned murder.[18]

The investigation continued for several days with no new leads, and it appeared as though Mabel's plan might succeed, until the coroner's inquest began on Thursday, August 4.[19] During the inquest, a prominent local man reportedly came forward, under conditions of anonymity, stating that Mabel had passed him a note several months earlier asking if he would agree to kill her husband. He remarked that it had caught him completely off guard and that he could not believe Mabel Orr would think he was capable of committing or willing to commit murder. After discussing the note with a close friend (who also chose to remain anonymous), they had agreed that, because of her status, it was best not to respond but rather simply let the matter rest. He had all but forgotten the matter until hearing news of the murder, and thus his testimony provided key evidence that helped break the case.[20]

When Rachael Morris took the stand, she sensed that the plan was beginning to unravel and sought to save herself by testifying that Mabel had long been "trying to get someone to kill her husband."[21] After learning of Rachael's testimony, Mabel relayed to the jury how Rachael had constantly formulated different ways to kill her husband and continually encouraged her to follow through on the murder. Mabel even described one conversation in which Rachael suggested feeding John Orr ground glass, reasoning that it "worked on dogs."[22] As soon as the two women turned on one another, the outcome of the inquest was all but certain. After two full days of testimony, the inquest ruled that Mabel Orr instigated the murder for hire and charged Rachael Morris, Dennis Ricord, and each of the Orrs' servants — Manse Castle, Will Sanders, Lorilla Weaver, and Susie Jacobs — as co-conspirators.

Manse Castle, accused of firing the fatal shot, was the first to be arrested on Sunday August 7, nine days after the murder. A mob of outraged citizens assembled at the jail to lynch Castle, but Judge James S. Thomas arrived and persuaded the mob to trust the legal process, promising to call a special grand jury at once. On Monday, authorities arrested Mabel and her remaining co-conspirators, all except for Rachael Morris, who mysteriously disappeared after the inquest.[23]

Castle was eager to set the record straight, explaining how Mabel Orr had offered him $200 to kill her husband and that he had initially agreed but had second thoughts and convinced Ricord to take his place. Meanwhile, Mabel admitted to offering $200 to anyone who would kill her husband but swore that she only uttered those words out of frustration. She explained that they fought incessantly and that her husband had even struck her.[24]

Watching and listening to her accomplices begin to break under interrogation, Mabel Orr realized that she had no chance of escaping justice. Boldly, she decided to issue a full confession along with a statement to family friend S. W. Boardman, leaving instructions about how to dispose of her assets and what provisions were to be arranged for her daughter.

I want my baby, Neva, to stay with Mr. Faifer, with his children, while I live; then Mr. Graham to have full control of her until my father comes for her, which I want him to do. I want my father to have all of my personal effects. My body is to be shipped to my father and be buried where he resides. I want to say to Steve Boardman, Wallace Graham, Mr. Morehead and Mr. Faifer that for the kind manner in which they have treated me, I hope that God will bless them for me. I hope God will forgive Rachael (Miss Morris) for the way she has treated me. I want all of my property and home to go to my baby, Neva, and I hope that his favorite lodge, Knights of Pythias, will see that this, my last will, is carried out. I want papa to help Wallace all he can. This statement completed at 6:30 p.m., Monday, August 8, 1898.[25]

Her statement complete, she swallowed a fatal dose of poison and lost consciousness. For his part, Boardman followed Mabel's instructions and refused to disclose the contents of her statement until she died.[26]

News spread quickly through Clarendon that Mabel Orr had poisoned herself but was still clinging to life. Citizens worried that she might escape justice and announced that, if she did die, they would immediately lynch the other suspects. It was no surprise that an angry lynch mob crowded around the jail entrance, ready to drag out the prisoners. Sheriff Jackson managed to disperse the mob only after repeated assurances of a speedy trial and no change of venue, which many people feared. Later that morning, however, Sheriff Jackson left his deputy to guard the prisoners. Jackson was ill and had returned home to Brinkley.

By ten thirty on Tuesday night, an even larger and more determined mob of two to three hundred had gathered outside the jail once again, this time demanding that the prisoners be turned over immediately. With Sheriff Jackson now out sick, Deputy Milwee tried and failed to reason with the vigilantes, who quickly overpowered and disarmed him. Cells were opened, and the mob first approached Mabel lying on her cot, but when they realized she was already at death's door, they raced toward the other prisoners.[27]

As the suspects were taken from their respective cells, their hands were bound behind their backs, and nooses were placed around their necks. Eager to get the exact details of the crime, the mob reportedly gave each of the suspects an opportunity to make a statement. Manse Castle expressed remorse, stating that he deserved to die even though he had not actually fired the fatal shot. He explained how Mabel had plied him with liquor and the promise of $200 in exchange for killing her husband, admitting that he had initially agreed but later refused because he considered John Orr a friend and simply could not kill him. He admitted his culpability and added that he and his co-conspirators deserved their fate.

Lorilla Weaver denied knowing who actually shot John Orr but knew that Mabel wanted him dead. Weaver defiantly stated that she had assisted Mabel in her attempts to kill him for over a year, including the failed attempt to poison him. She reiterated that he was mean and cruel to Mabel, explaining how he refused to let her buy underwear. Weaver's son, Will Sanders, claimed that his involvement was limited to looking for someone willing to help Mabel Orr. Dennis Ricord admitted that he had supplied the scorpions and snakeheads in order to poison John Orr, but that this was the limit of his involvement. There was no statement recorded for Susie Jacobs, and none of the suspects would admit to having fired the shot that killed John Orr.[28]

The kangaroo court concluded, the suspects were hustled out of the jail by the mob and marched tooward the Halpern Sawmill. Then, just two hundred yards from the jail, the prisoners were allowed to stop and pray. The mob then systematically lynched each of the suspects from nearby tree limbs and placed a sign on the bodies stating, "This is the penalty for murder and rape," a notice that these were the offenses that warranted lynching in Clarendon (though the reference to rape in this case does not actually apply).[29] Interestingly, the mob included a significant number of black residents who allegedly expressed their outrage over the murder and supported the lynching, expressing particular relief about the lynching of Ricord, who had threatened and intimidated the black community for years by playing on their superstitions through his knowledge of hoodoo.[30]

There were conflicting reports about the number of people lynched; some newspapers reported that Susie Jacobs was a fugitive. However, eyewitness testimony from the telegraph operator working at the Cotton Belt Railroad office confirmed that there were, indeed, five bodies and that the fifth victim was located in a tree a short distance from the others. The bodies of the lynching victims remained hanging until Wednesday morning when Sheriff Jackson, now recovered from his illness, arrived and had them taken across the river for burial in the "bottoms."[31]

This lynching became national news, prompting criticism and controversy over how best to stop lynching. Gov. Daniel Webster Jones offered a $200 reward for each member of the lynch mob who was brought to justice. This was roundly criticized by James Mitchell, editor of the *Arkansas Democrat*. Mitchell characterized Governor Jones's reward as a "mockery," arguing that the reluctance to offer large rewards proved that the state was not serious about ending lynching. He acknowledged that citizens have to trust the law and regard lynching as murder but urged the state legislature to take decisive action to end lynching.[32]

Mabel Orr's grand scheme was further revealed after the lynching when a love letter addressed to Lorilla Weaver arrived from twenty-three-year old Arthur O. Archer, Ohio's youngest mayor and rising political star. The letter contained a photo with the inscription, "Trusting you will be pleased with Ohio's real kid mayor, I am still yours," proving that the two had been corresponding for some time and demonstrating that he planned on coming to Clarendon in two months.[33] When Sheriff Jackson notified Archer about Weaver's death and questioned him, Archer was shocked and confused to hear that Weaver was a black woman who was lynched as the result of a murder conspiracy and initially denied any knowledge of the case. After speaking further with Sheriff Jackson, Archer realized he had been duped by Mabel Orr and agreed to cooperate. He was cleared of any knowledge about the murder. More importantly, he helped uncover new details about Mabel's plan.

Archer revealed that he had answered an advertisement placed in a matrimonial bureau by a rich, unmarried French woman who claimed to be Lorilla Weaver. This information led authorities to search for and locate a large cache of love letters from several wealthy bachelors Mabel was corresponding with throughout the country in an attempt to start a new life. Archer apparently managed to avoid any lasting effects from this scandal—just six years later, Pres. Theodore Roosevelt appointed him assistant United States attorney of the Dawes Commission to the Five Civilized Tribes of Muskogee, Indian Territory.[34]

Mabel Orr passed away on Wednesday, having never regained consciousness after administering herself poison. Her body was prepared for burial by friends of the family, but the citizens were so suspicious that she might have escaped justice that authorities decided to place her open casket on display in the courthouse in order to remove any doubt. Hundreds came to gawk at her body. Her father, Walter A. Barker, was extremely distraught about his daughter but was unable to make the trip to retrieve her body. According to newspaper reports, Mabel was buried beside her husband in the Shady Grove Cemetery in Clarendon but may have been moved at a later date.

The Orrs' four-year-old daughter, Geneva Louise Orr, remained in the care of family friend W. A. Faifer until September because of a custody dispute between John's and Mabel's families. Both sides ultimately agreed that John's sister and brother-in-law were best suited to raise her because they had a nice home and a young son. Her uncle Joseph picked her up in September and brought her home to Duck Creek, Kansas, where she spent her childhood. Despite the early tragedies in her life, Geneva found both stability and happiness. She married Ralph Lambert in 1916, had a daughter named Edith in 1918, and remained in Kansas, where she lived until the age of eighty-four.[35]

Rachael Morris remained at large. There were conflicting reports regarding her whereabouts. There were alleged sightings of Rachael in Augusta, just north of Clarendon in Woodruff County, and also in Wynne, to the northeast in Cross County, but neither were confirmed. Residents in Pine Bluff reported seeing a young woman matching Rachael's description in the Pine Bluff jail charged with murder. Adding to the intrigue, authorities in Pine Bluff restricted admission to the jail for several days, but her presence was never confirmed. In fact, there were many rumors and alleged sightings, but none were ever confirmed. Her father indicated soon after her disappearance that he knew where she was and reportedly told the sheriff that he would turn her over once she was out of danger.

The whereabouts of Rachael Morris remain a mystery, but it would not have been very difficult for a young woman to change her identity in 1898. Considering the consequences, that would have been a wise course of action.[36]

Seven people lost their lives, and the lives of countless others were forever changed, as a result of Mabel Orr's desperate attempt to escape an unhappy marriage and pursue the life she desired. This compelling story captured national attention when newspapers reported the lurid details of the case nationwide. Was Mabel Orr a cold-blooded killer who pursued her own selfish desires at the expense of everyone around her, or was she a woman trapped in a bad marriage, a sympathetic victim of abuse who made a poor choice out of desperation? Late nineteenth-century attitudes about race, class, and gender provide a context for explaining this tragic course of events.

Clarendon in the late nineteenth-century was part of the Jim Crow South, where race relations were characterized by discrimination and segregation and based on a traditional belief in black inferiority rooted in, and shaped by, the system of slavery. Black behavior was based on a system of racial etiquette that dictated subservient behavior in the presence of whites, and any violation could result in violence. In such a system, African Americans had limited opportunities for economic advancement, and many black people were obliged to work as domestics in the homes of wealthy whites.

The Orr family employed four black servants: two women for cooking and cleaning and two men who functioned as porters. They lived in a separate house behind the Orr residence but spent countless hours around the family cooking and doing household chores. The servants were keenly aware of the Orrs' marital problems and witnessed incidents of cruelty and abuse. They developed empathy for Mabel, and she, in need of a champion, confided in her servants. By choosing to take sides, they placed themselves in a vulnerable position once they agreed to help Mabel kill her husband. Why would these servants put their own lives in jeopardy to help Mabel Orr? Mabel's decision to confide in her servants resonated with them. The promise of $200 was also a huge motivation. That was a substantial sum of money, and they could have used it to improve their situation dramatically.

For the servants, the involvement of Mabel's new confidant, Rachael Morris, proved to seal their fate. Sensing that her servants were having second thoughts, Mabel took advantage of their vulnerability and manipulated

Manse Castle by using alcohol to obtain his promise to kill her husband. Conspiring to commit murder was an extremely perilous path, but because they had chosen sides, they were already vulnerable, and even without their direct involvement in the murder, they would almost certainly be considered guilty and hanged. They had little choice but to help Mabel carry out her plan.

The decision to bypass the legal system and lynch all of the servants demonstrates the degree to which the local population embraced their own power to exercise summary justice. This power was an honor-bound tradition that was jealously guarded by local citizens who accepted racial superiority, distrusted the legal system, and preferred a more immediate and satisfying method of maintaining community standards. While it might seem unusual and particularly barbaric to lynch the two black women involved, the fact that they were involved in poisoning their employer touched a nerve in the white community. The fear of poisoning by black servants was a long-held fear of whites who employed them. According to historian Crystal Feimster, there were forty-two black women lynched during the 1890s, twelve of whom were accused of poisoning whites, indicating how the increasing fear of black criminality negatively impacted the once trusted view of black women.[37] This was also the peak decade for lynching in the South, with over eight hundred victims lynched throughout the southern states and ninety-nine in Arkansas alone. Blacks represented 83 percent of those lynched in the South during this period and 83 percent of those in Arkansas. The proclivity for lynching blacks during this period essentially guaranteed that Mabel's collaborators would be killed. Denied a trial, they were all lynched as a group without regard for their degree of involvement. Susie Jacobs was never accused of playing any part in the plan but was rather deemed guilty by association on the presumption that she knew of the murder conspiracy.[38]

Southern attitudes about social class also figure prominently into this case. John Orr was welcomed into the elite social circles of Clarendon because he was a successful, churchgoing merchant who had escaped the stigma of being an actor. As a man of means who accordingly limited his wife's independence, he embraced the attitudes befitting a man of his stature and thus sowed the seeds of Mabel's discontent and his own doom. Neither John nor Mabel came from old money, and so it was particularly important that they keep up the appearance of respectability. Mabel struggled to fulfill the social expectations placed upon her by virtue of her status. Victorian ideals dictated that she accept her situation and suffer quietly. Indeed, the highest measure of conformity within her social class was to acquiesce meekly to her husband's demands. The fact that she conspired with her servants to murder her husband was a betrayal to her social class. She was viewed not as a sympathetic figure but rather as a debased woman and a social pariah. Mabel's betrayal sparked such outrage that she, too, would have been lynched had she not committed suicide in jail.

Mabel Orr did not just betray her social class—she also betrayed the societal standards of gender. She lived in a society based on Victorian ideals in which the woman's sphere was in the home. Women were expected to exhibit the characteristics of "piety, purity, submissiveness and domesticity," and they were judged by how well they reflected these attributes. This was a patriarchal society in which women were deemed inferior to men, with obedience and submissiveness expected. Mabel Orr chafed under these restrictions.[39]

Mabel was not the type of woman John thought he married. She had grown since they married and was no longer a wide-eyed teenager desperate to escape her boring life. She was now a young woman, with a confidence and outlook developed from years of traveling and appearing on the stage. Like most women her age, she was influenced by the women's movement and was attracted to promoting increased independence for women. Magazines like *Godey's Ladies Book* even provided images of this new woman in the form of the Gibson girls, drawn by Charles Dana Gibson. His images of women dressed in a simple black skirt and white shirtwaist with an upswept hairdo imparted independence, confidence, and competence. If this appealed to the average young woman, there is no doubt that it appealed to Mabel Orr. She did not marry John to become a housewife. In fact, had she not become pregnant, she would have happily continued her career in the theater.[40]

Mabel Orr had more options available to her than we might imagine. She could have left her husband and possibly retained custody of her daughter. After the Civil War, a series of legal reforms made it easier for women to obtain a divorce and possibly even retain custody of their children. Instead, she resorted to murder, apparently without a thought as to what would happen to her daughter, while simultaneously planning to marry another wealthy man in order to finance her life on the stage. Mabel Orr put her dreams and desires above everyone around her—and for that, they paid with their lives.[41]

Thirteen Dead at Saint Charles

Arkansas's Most Lethal Lynching and the Abrogation of Equal Protection

I n the cotton country of eastern Arkansas, the port town of Saint Charles perches upon a bluff above the flood plain of the White River. It is the first town upstream from the confluence of the White, Arkansas, and Mississippi Rivers, and that point of access to the larger world puts Saint Charles on the map—although just barely. In 1890, as many as thirty-five hundred bales of cotton moved across its wharves and were loaded onto barges for the trip downstream. Folks passed through this rural outpost because of the ferry that crossed the river at Saint Charles, or they came and went because of the docks on the waterfront, but the town itself was quite small—at the turn of the twentieth century, only five hundred people lived there.[1]

On March 27, 1904, all across the state, Sunday readers of the Little Rock *Arkansas Gazette* learned that the town of Saint Charles was once again "quiet" following four days of lynching that had begun on the previous Wednesday. The calamity was front-page news. On the previous Wednesday, a few miles out of town, three men had been murdered. On Thursday, six more people were shot dead, one of them "riddled with bullets." On Friday, another corpse was found in the woods. Saturday added yet another murdered victim to the body count. Four days, eleven dead. One might guess that terror stalked the tiny town, but the *Arkansas Gazette* article that described the four days of horror reassured readers that "no further trouble is looked for."[2]

What was the nature of the "trouble"? According to the newspaper, it was "Defiance by the Negroes." Their apparently collective "threatening attitude" caused white citizens to be "alarmed." There was "no attempt," the article intoned, "to make war on peaceable and inoffensive negroes." As for the rest, however, "the most dangerous negroes have been slain."[3] Although the *Arkansas Gazette* did not mention it, the newspaper was chronicling what, in terms of the number of victims, may have been the deadliest lynching in American history. What happened in Saint Charles? What precipitated the homicidal frenzy? Who were the killers? What did they hope to achieve?

Unfortunately for historians, participants buried this episode in their past and thereby guaranteed that it would remain there obscured. Circumstances surrounding this event are untraceable in the public record, and, apart from the facts conveyed in a very limited number of sources, the available material provides only a few other clues for historians. The evidence is so flawed and scanty that it is hard to reconstruct a sequence of events: questions of who, what, when, and how are virtually unanswerable, and any suggestion of why is wild conjecture.

This event seems to have had no significance for the white people in the society in which it occurred—it simply did not matter much. It went essentially unnoticed, perhaps as just another example of behavior that, by the turn of the century, was construed as a cultural cliché. However, the search for the truth regarding the Saint Charles killings is ultimately rewarding for historians in several respects. First of all, coming to terms with this variety of murder is central to understanding the history of race relations in the United States. For several decades in the late nineteenth and early twentieth centuries, lynchings—these gruesome public homicides—were a commonplace of American life, and the victims were most often black.[4] Just as most African Americans lived in the South until the latter half of the twentieth century, so too did most lynchings occur there. Yet even in New England in the early years of the twentieth century, the practice of lynching was known well enough for the concept to have entered the vernacular. In 1914, for instance, lexicographer George Allan England compiled a glossary of the current vernacular, "Rural Locutions of Maine and Northern New Hampshire." Among the idioms that he cited as commonly expressed there was to be *death to niggers* on a given subject. In the folk tongue of the region, this slang expression was widely understood to mean *down on anything or body*, in the manner that someone of that era could be, say, *death to niggers on the automobile* or *woman suffrage* or *Teddy Roosevelt*.[5]

Examining the term *lynch* requires care with regard to vocabulary. In the effort to recapture the past and convey its meanings, the historian is obliged to eschew jargon because code words and colloquialisms cloud rather than clarify the human experience. Yet historians cannot avoid the use of terms that identify the patterns, episodes, and other assortments of noumena that students of the past encounter. Terms like *war, revolution,* and *revival* are, in a sense, tools of the trade that allow scholars to isolate evidence and to clump data into comprehensible classifications. Other terms like *white* and *black*, when referring to racial characteristics of people, are really nothing more than handy generalizations that facilitate the exchange of ideas. At the same time, however, historians are trained to appreciate that any generalization is by its nature too facile.

The word *lynch* is seriously flawed. When the term is employed to denote a specific category of human experience, it is not only imprecise, as one soon discovers; it is also what the distinguished historian James G. Randall might have characterized as too clean. In his presidential address to the Mississippi Valley Historical Association in 1940, Randall grapples with the hideous and horrific in writing the history of the Civil War and discusses how efforts to convey gruesome aspects of our past distort their essence—what he designates as their reality.[6]

Details of "blood and filth, of mutilated flesh" are repugnant and grotesque, and the extremity of the heinous behavior of lynch mobs sometimes forced contemporaries to confront the boundaries of their tolerance for human suffering. Early in 1904, at about the same time as the Saint Charles mayhem, a camp of United Confederate Veterans in Grenada, Mississippi, passed resolutions that opposed lynching. The veterans considered it unnecessary "save, perhaps, for the one unmentionable crime." The organization felt obliged to condemn specifically the increasingly frequent but "inhuman and ungodly" fashion of burning, roasting, and torching black people to death. It is impossible fully to capture these events with words, to speak of the unspeakable, because, as Randall puts it with reference to the horrors of the Civil War, "The human mind will not stand for it."[7]

Just as problematic for the student of the past, says Randall, is the manner in which the historical method imposes protocols that can distort the understanding of an event. Perhaps, like the word *war*, the term *lynch* serves a linguistic function but fails to convey full meaning. Studying an explosively irrational occurrence in order to posit the working assumption that it is amenable to reasonable explanation is perhaps to miss its significance altogether. When analyzing the actions of people who are seized by homicidal urgings, acting out a psychopathic rampage, one must instead assume that "diagnosis fails," as Randall writes in another context, to explain it. Accordingly, attempting to translate lynching into something that is understandable or predictable or conveyable is, no matter how skilled the scholar, ultimately unavailing.[8]

A historian searching for causal patterns in this sort of episode must confront a body of evidence that cannot answer key questions, a corpus of materials that will not explain basic motivations. In mapping historical causation, one must isolate factors that initiate an action and factors that sustain it. This requires that historians identify the forces acting upon the participants—in this case, the lynchers of Saint Charles. What did they intend? What combinations of forces fed their collective frenzy? These lines of inquiry place insuperable demands upon the evidence, asking it to reveal more about mixes of motive than participants themselves could possibly record. In the instance at hand, the historian can identify only the victims—not the actors, much less their specific motives. There are few clues to the particular psychopathology that compelled an individual to become a killer in Saint Charles, or to the sociopathology of the group that sustained their bloody excess. In this fundamental respect, both methodological and human boundaries limit the search for complete understanding. Ignoring the limitations imposed by the dictates of the discipline and human sensibility, one risks confabulating history that is "foggy" at best, or as Randall warns in a word, "bogus."[9]

Reconstructing bygone realities is difficult, not least because the past is captive to the coverage it received by contemporaries. For this reason, among others, the study of lynching offers peculiar challenges.[10] If contemporaries do not deem an event to be noteworthy, they do not leave a record that allows scholars to easily recover a meaningful occurrence. This bias in the data too often surfaces in the history that is subsequently written for a state like Arkansas, which, in the number of victims, actually ranks quite high among the states where residents committed lynchings. Scholars have tabulated hundreds of victims for the state.[11] The Arkansas past is distinguished by its volume of this type of brutality.

Posting alarm in 1892, a black preacher in Arkansas decried what was happening "all over the State." Blacks were dying in a storm of human atrocity, "some being strung up to telephone poles, others burnt at the stake and still others being shot like dogs. In the last thirty days there have been not less than eight colored persons lynched in this State." What might have been shocking in 1892, however, soon became an old tale. One of the factors that most troubled this minister in 1892 was the lack of attention the carnage received. "The white press of the South seems to be subsidized by this lawless element, the white pulpits seem to condone lynching," he lamented. "The Northern press seems to care little about the condition of the Negroes [of the] South. The pulpits of the North are passive." He asked for prayers for an end to the horror, but the terror against blacks continued.[12]

After more than a decade, by the time of the Saint Charles killings in 1904, lynching in Arkansas was routine, an almost monthly event, and the survivors of its raw terror were numbed by its unremitting repetition. The state ranked fourth among the eighteen states studied in the incidence of lynchings per capita in 1900, according to James Elbert Cutler, whose findings were published in *Lynch-Law*, one of the first scholarly investigations of this type of killing. With some two hundred victims for the period from 1882 to 1903, as Cutler calculated them, Arkansas was sixth in the nation in terms of a cumulative body count.[13] The fatalities continued to accumulate. In 1929, when Walter White published his study *Rope and Faggot: A Biography of Judge Lynch*, sixth-placed Arkansas ranked third in terms of the female death toll from this variant of murder. According to Robert L. Zangrando's compilation of the cumulative death toll, the state retained sixth place from 1882 through 1968.[14]

By the early twentieth century, the lynching of African Americans was as common as it was catastrophic throughout the American South. There were almost twenty-five hundred black fatalities in the forty-eight years from 1882 to 1930 in the ten southern states that Stewart Tolnay and E. M. Beck study in *A Festival of Violence*, a sociological analysis of these phenomena, and more recent research has only increased the numbers of documented victims. For the states they examined, Tolnay and Beck conclude, "The scale of this carnage means that, on the average, a black man, woman, or child was murdered nearly once a week, every week, between 1882 and 1930 by a hate-driven white mob."[15]

Since calculations in the scholarly record of lynchings are culled from articles in leading newspapers, the tally includes only the newsworthy— an evidentiary trap that ensnares the historian. When acts went unreported, they were also unrecorded. One investigator explained why the death toll in official tabulations of this sort of terrorism might best be considered to be the tip of an iceberg: "Countless Negroes are lynched yearly, but their disappearance is shrouded in mystery, for they are dispatched quietly and without general knowledge." Those missing altogether from the records are inaccessible to historical inquiry. For that reason, many lynchings belong to a secret and irrecoverable past.[16]

The description of a coroner's inquest in Mena, Arkansas, almost two hundred miles west of Saint Charles, published in 1904, portrays derision by whites as they officiate over determining the cause of death of a black woman:

> The old Judge summoned me one day on a Jury. He got a dozen of us down to his office and told us he wanted us to hold an inquest over a dead nigger. Now, we didn't like the job very well but he didn't consult our wishes but swore us in and told us where we would find the remains. We went over there and found them. It was a large fleshy black woman that would have weighed about two hundred and seventy five pounds. She was lying on the bed all covered up, except her face. She looked natural and as though she was asleep. Some of us went into the house, and some only looked in at the door. The question arose whether she was dead or not. We were all afraid to touch her for if she had moved we would have gone out the door like sheep over a fence. Finally, I suggested that we get a young chicken and fry it nicely and hold it up before her and if she didn't reach for it, she was dead. I knew that much about a nigger. She didn't reach for it, so we pronounced her dead, but the question was how did she come to her death. She lived alone and she was dead when her friends found her. There might have been a dozen bullet holes through her, but we didn't want to uncover her to see, so we decided she died with heart failure. That is, her heart failed to beat, but we never knew why it stopped beating. There were very few niggers in that part of Arkansaw and what few there were occasionally found themselves dead of a morning, but they were like all other niggers. When they won't reach for a piece of fried chicken you can prepare for a funeral.

This callous passage, which dismisses the significance of the life and death—and presumably the lynching—of black people, was meant to amuse readers of an autobiography of misadventures down in Dixie.[17]

As distinct from underreporting by contemporaries, calculation by historians is complicated by the difficulties of retrieving the statistics. Because investigators must count victims mentioned in newspaper articles, and the collection of newspapers that are culled cannot be completely inclusive, a definitive accounting of the incidence and victims of lynchings in the United States is impossible. One reference to the Saint Charles massacre in the *New York Times*, for instance, is a seven-line article that mentions only nine dead "Negroes." If that were the source employed to quantify this affair, rather than the subsequent article in the *Arkansas Gazette* that tallied eleven dead or later published counts that cited thirteen bodies, the count of the murders by lynchers in Arkansas in 1904 would be diminished by as many as four.[18]

The methodological uncertainties that confront the student of these occurrences are prodigious. Apart from the convolutions of accounting, even trying to give the word *lynch* a working definition—just attempting to make the usage operational—seems to raise more questions. What is a lynching? Simple interracial homicides do not count in this calculus because the distinction between lynching and murder, though hazy, bears on the nature of the event. As James Weldon Johnson insisted, "it is safe to say that lynching is not simply murder; that it is murder plus something else. It is murder plus revolution and anarchy." As Albert Bushnell Hart, another student of the subject, characterized it, "the process is not simply extra-legal but anti-legal." In this sense of *lynch*, the term *lynch law* is oxymoronic.[19] Without three or more assailants, the act of lynching would be indistinguishable from more mundane varieties of interracial murder. A lynching thus requires a minimum party of four—at least three perpetrators and a victim. Whether or not a part of the public record, a lynching is by definition a public event.[20]

According to the definition of lynching in various federal antilynching bills—which was adopted in order to narrow the concept and to minimize its applicability—some of the murders in Saint Charles might not qualify because the victims might not have been officially charged with or convicted of a crime. Absent those legal proceedings, the actions of the mob were not intended to forestall the due process of law; and in each case covered by that qualification, if a scholar chooses to accept it, a lynching did not occur.[21]

Yet even those reservations cannot suffice in the effort to define, to isolate, and to calculate the incidence of activities of this sort. Regardless of its definition, when violence turns into a killing spree—as occurred in Saint Charles over the course of several days in the spring of 1904— isolating and defining the discrete historical event is difficult but statistically significant. Does the rampage count as one incident or several? In his groundbreaking study of lynching, James Elbert Cutler grappled with this methodology. He determined that "ordinarily, if one whole day intervened between the lynching of one person and the lynching of another person, sufficient time had elapsed for the excitement over the lynching of the first person to abate somewhat and that the lynching of the second person in such a case could not rightfully be considered a part of the preceding act of mob violence." Cutler explained further, "Using this as a criterion, all cases in which persons were lynched on two succeeding days at or near the same place have been classified as one lynching, but all cases in which at least a day intervened in the lynching of two or more persons at or near the same place have been classified as two or more lynchings."[22]

So how should one classify the series of killings in Saint Charles? Was it one lynching with multiple homicides or more? Although the corpses accumulated over the course of several days, no single killing took place more than twenty-four hours before the next. Using Cutler's definition would minimize this chain of events, in one respect, by reducing a week-long campaign of terror to one solitary outburst of butchery. On the other hand, to the degree that Cutler's parameters provide a reliable reckoning, this same calculation makes the Saint Charles atrocity the deadliest single lynching in American history.

In its painstaking effort in 1919 to record the toll from lynching in America, the National Association for the Advancement of Colored People (NAACP) listed "Persons Lynched in United States, 1889 to 1918, inclusive, arranged by States." Victims are cited by name, state in which the lynchers operated, county, alleged offense of the victim, and date when he or she was burned, shot, hanged, chopped, or otherwise lynched. Of the thousands of incidents they cite, the event in Saint Charles is the longest single entry on the necrology.[23]

In discussing the NAACP's figures on lynching, Richard Maxwell Brown, in *Strain of Violence*, speculated that "lynchings may well have constituted an index of black opposition to oppressive white regimes in certain small towns and rural areas." He placed the Saint Charles massacre in a list of five "mass lynchings," which he asserts may have been a form of "crushing retaliation . . . aimed at obliterating the spirit of black resistance." Brown did not, however, offer the documentary basis for such a claim.[24] The Saint Charles massacre did not make the list of "Five Worst" lynchings that Tolnay and Beck compiled in 1995. Despite or because of their attempt to provide the most authoritative calculations, Saint Charles did not qualify for their count.[25] In two studies of race relations concerning postbellum and early-twentieth-century Arkansas, published in the 1990s, the Saint Charles affair goes unmentioned. In John William Graves's book, *Town and Country: Race Relations in an Urban-Rural Context, Arkansas, 1865–1905*, lynching certainly occupies a place in the dynamics he explores, but this particular event does not. More recently, in Fon Louise Gordon's study, *Caste and Class: The Black Experience in Arkansas, 1880–1920*, the Saint Charles killings are not recounted. A 1961 master's thesis titled "The History Highlights of Saint Charles, Arkansas" examined the locale of the lynching, but except for between "Rebs and Yanks," there is little word of trouble. Of the "highlights" the author studied, mass murder by mob was not among them.[26]

Among the major limitations placed on historians when they attempt to reconstruct the past is the nature of evidence: it is shaped by the biases of contemporaries who composed it. Just below the seven-line article on Saint Charles in the *New York Times* is another article that describes a mob action in Missouri. A "man" accused of highway robbery was taken from jail by a group of masked assailants who then whipped the accused "nearly to death" before releasing him. Although only one person was victimized and there were no fatalities, this article consumes sixteen lines—more than twice the coverage accorded the dead of Saint Charles. The "man" who was beaten in Missouri, Winn Davis, seemed worth mentioning by name in the *New York Times*. The dead in Saint Charles, as they appeared in print, were anonymous, merely "nine negroes." There is no indication that they, too, were "men." As reported on page one of the *Times*, their fate was apparently of little consequence.[27]

Whatever their limitations, newspaper accounts are the most useful sources at the modern historian's disposal. In his inquiry into lynchings in Georgia and Virginia, *Lynching in the New South: Georgia and Virginia, 1880–1930*, historian W. Fitzhugh Brundage advised that "there simply is no other foundation" upon which to base an investigation. For the regions he examined, Brundage discovered that "newspapers typically provide a wealth of information on the event that precipitated each lynching, the size and actions of the mob, the manner of execution, and the community response to the lynching." Contrary to this conclusion, in an article on Saint Charles in the *New York Times*, the report began by cautioning, "As is usual in crimes of this nature, it was impossible to get from the scene of the crime any adequate story of what really happened, what started the wholesale murders[,] and what blame, if any, attached to the black man" in "this wholesale butchery, the greatest in the South."[28] Although Brundage's characterization of newspaper coverage may hold for lynchings in Georgia and Virginia, it is not true for the events that unfolded in east Arkansas in 1904. These lynchings did not garner much attention. There is little more than the article in the Sunday *Arkansas Gazette* to offer illumination, and the sketchiness of the printed record makes reconstructing events in Saint Charles difficult.

Writing in June 1904, Mary Church Terrell testified, "Hanging, shooting and burning black men, women and children in the United States have become so common that such occurrences create but little sensation and evoke but slight comment now." In the case of the Saint Charles killings, even major black newspapers of the day failed to report the carnage.[29] For African Americans at the turn of the twentieth century, the prospect of sudden violent death had become a feature of everyday life. The paucity of source materials attests to its inveteracy as perceived by contemporaries and hides this aspect of the past from subsequent view.

Newspaper coverage of the paroxysm in Saint Charles was not merely minimal; it was also riddled with inaccuracy, inconsistency, omission, and contradiction. The veneer of prejudices that informed the fragmentary body of evidence renders the historical reality underneath even more impenetrable. The article from the Sunday issue of the *Arkansas Gazette* is instructive. "Two more negroes have been put to death," it reads, "making eleven negroes that have been killed as the result of the riot incited by them last Monday."[30]

Various word choices in the text are revelatory of a time and place when lynchings were culturally commonplace. When a person is "put to death," the usage usually relates to a function of the state acting in its official capacity as executioner. In the absence of a prior sentence of death imposed through due process of law, one more accurately refers to people who have been murdered, killed, assassinated, or indeed lynched. Otherwise, the reference is to sick animals. The words used by the *Arkansas Gazette* reduce the human aspect of this tale at the same time that they intimate an activity with some semblance of official approval.

The article from the Sunday *Arkansas Gazette* that describes the shootings at Saint Charles may further obscure the humanity of dead black men by using an impersonal relative pronoun to describe their fate: these were "negroes that" were killed, not "negroes who." Both the reporter who penned this piece and the editor who published it probably used *that* inadvertently, fully recognizing that when people are at issue, *who* is the correct usage. The writer's consistent use of the passive voice may also be revealing. There are no perpetrators specified in this first paragraph, save the dead men themselves, and the "riot incited by them last Monday." The objects have become the actors. The fifth paragraph of the *Arkansas Gazette* article reports on an altercation of the previous Monday that seemingly precipitated the storm of carnage. Henry Griffin and Walker Griffin, "two negroes," attacked "a white man over a trivial matter." They knocked down "the white man" and gave "similar treatment" to a deputy sheriff who tried to arrest them. That is the only concrete information regarding events on Monday that the article provided.[31]

The distinguishing characteristic of the target of the two black men is not the name of the individual in question but only his race. He is identified nowhere in this text except as a "white man." Nor do we learn of the "trivial matter" that triggered the Griffins' hostility towards him. Like his individual identity, the white man's behavior is apparently irrelevant to the causal chain of events that ended with the murder of thirteen black men.

Lynching did bear the approbation of officialdom in Arkansas. The governor of the state during these years, Jeff Davis, was an ardent exponent of murder by mob. The most notable expression of his advocacy came in a speech of greeting delivered before an audience of thousands, on the occasion of Pres. Theodore Roosevelt's visit to Little Rock in October 1905, a year and a half after the killings in Saint Charles. Although the governor's address was brief, a significant portion of his remarks concerned "the brutal criminals" of "an inferior race."[32]

Addressing President Roosevelt and throngs of listeners, Davis proclaimed that, independent of geographic location, when confronted by the circumstances faced by white southerners, lynchers would operate wherever "true manhood has a representative or virtue a worshipper."[33] To both the crowds who heard him and to those who read his speech in the papers the following day, it was obvious that the governor of Arkansas believed that neither due process of law nor "true manhood" extended to members of what he called "an inferior race." Placing Davis's remarks within the context of the whole of his public pronouncements on race relations, Willard B. Gatewood has characterized them as "relatively restrained." Raymond Arsenault, Davis's biographer, has observed that Arkansas politicians had sung this score "countless times before." Yet Davis added an unparalleled virulence to the public discussion of race relations while building an extraordinary political career in Arkansas. In 1904, he first won an unprecedented third term as governor; he then won a seat in the US Senate in 1906 and again in 1912.[34]

Although race-baiting was not new to Arkansans by the time Jeff Davis occupied the governorship in the first years of the twentieth century, historian Fon Louise Gordon argues that Davis was primarily responsible for "the injection of racial hatred, not merely exclusion, into political rhetoric." This shift in emphasis, notes Gordon, was "subtle but significant."[35] Out on the stump, it became difficult for political opponents to outdo each other in their efforts to degrade African Americans, and explicitly advocating lynching became a staple of political discourse.

On the campaign trail in 1903, responding to charges that he had pardoned a black man, Davis admitted it. The governor explained this lapse by explicating and endorsing a rationale of mob rule that made the fate of the pardoned black man exceptional: "In our country when we have no doubt about a negro's guilt we do not give him a trial; we mob him, and that ends it; . . . the mere fact that this negro got a trial is evidence that there was some doubt of his guilt." By the same logic, those who were lynched in Arkansas were, by virtue of their antilegal execution, deserving of a vicious death.[36]

By 1904, lynchings were essentially state-sanctioned events. Governor Davis, on the stump for reelection in 1904, insisted "that 'nigger' dominion will never prevail in this beautiful Southland of ours, as long as shotguns and rifles lie around loose, and we are able to pull the trigger." The racial excess of Davis's rhetoric accommodated a fundamental alteration in the structure of Arkansas politics. At the turn of the twentieth century, the old convention system of selecting political candidates was replaced by primary elections. This change caused a transformation in political campaigns in Arkansas. Richard L. Niswonger, in a study of Davis's demagoguery, asserted that, under the former method of selecting candidates to run for public office, "it seemed unnecessary to spend time campaigning among the people." With the primary in place instead, political success was tied to "appealing directly to the masses." With each new campaign, Davis crisscrossed the state, visiting "the hamlet, the crossroads, and the solitary farmer on the hillside."[37]

Davis learned that a declamation urging virulent racism transformed constituents into political supporters. Davis excoriated not just blacks but also the black vote, calling the extension of the franchise during Reconstruction "the most cruel blow that was ever struck a helpless and defenseless people." He reserved particular enmity for African American voters. A black Arkansan with a vote was, said Davis, an "ever present eating, cankerous sore" on the body politic. At the time of the lynching in Saint Charles, the primary election season was in full swing. Although the killings under consideration were committed during the last week of a heated primary campaign, it is impossible to isolate the manner in which this incendiary polemic fed the homicidal furor there.[38]

Manuscript sources suggest the nature of the incident that triggered the killing spree at Saint Charles. One recollection was penned by J. M. Henderson Jr., who was born in Saint Charles in 1880. He later became an attorney, county superintendent of schools, and editor and owner of a newspaper for the nearby town of DeWitt, the *Enterprise*. As Henderson put it in his recollection of this week of life and death in an Arkansas town, "there was a class of white men there as tough as the negroes. They would drink, shoot craps, and gamble with the negroes. Then when trouble arose, they were the first to want to excite prejudice and hard action against the negroes. Most trouble between the races has come about through these elements."[39]

According to Henderson, two men down at the docks on a riverboat were drinking and gaming when they started to argue and soon came to blows. Armed with a jug, or perhaps a table leg, the black man, named Griffin, hit the white man, Jim Searcy, a serious knock to the head. When Griffin was arrested for the assault, the police officer "possibly said things that frightened the negro and made him think he might be hung." Griffin, in turn, caught the officer off guard, struck him with his fist, grabbed his gun, and fled for his life. The black man found refuge, but he must have anticipated a reckoning.[40] The *Arkansas Gazette* reported that the killings began on Wednesday, two days after the altercation occurred. This time lag was intrinsic to the ritualized character of a lynching. Lynchings were by their nature premeditated. Richard Maxwell Brown, in his scholarly description of the stylized aspects of this sort of group violence, noted that it sometimes required "ample notice of a day or two so that whites from neighboring areas" could join in the excitement.[41]

On Wednesday, five men led by a deputy sheriff departed the county seat of DeWitt, some fifteen miles away, "to protect the town" of Saint Charles. On their way, "a few miles" from their destination, the vigilantes encountered three armed blacks. When the black men were asked the whereabouts of the Griffins, according to the *Arkansas Gazette*, they "defied the posse" and were shot dead.[42]

The article does not reveal where the black men were headed when they were gunned down or why they were armed. Other sources suggest that their possession of weapons was not unusual. In discussing early-twentieth-century race relations in *An American Dilemma*, Gunnar Myrdal noted that in the South, "the custom of going armed continually" was quite common. He confessed to being "astonished" at the degree to which lower-class whites and blacks carried weapons as a matter of course. He reported that the practice was most prevalent "in the Negro community, where personal security is most lacking."[43]

As a black man, arming oneself in rural Arkansas may have been a wise precaution since it was apparently accurate to say that lynching was "a rural and small town custom." Myrdal explained that "the isolation, the dullness of everyday life and the general boredom of rural and small town life in the South" was in itself a primary cause of this form of mayhem. It was sport. In Walter White's assessment, "The Mind of the Lyncher," he quoted H. L. Mencken's observation that "lynching often takes the place of the merry-go-round, the theatre, the symphony orchestra, and other diversions common to larger communities." It alleviated the tedium of rural existence.[44]

A few weeks earlier, across the river in Mississippi, a mob had tied up a black man to force him to watch while they cut off his wife's ears, nose, and fingers. They repeatedly plunged a corkscrew into the woman's flesh. The killers then torched their victims. Richard Hofstadter and Michael Wallace, in their investigation of this form of American violence, reported on "spectacles of sadism" that drew crowds of up to ten thousand spectators who came on special excursion trains. When sociologists Tolnay and Beck published their statistical analyses of lynchings in America, they titled their subject *A Festival of Violence*.[45] The proper study of this activity acknowledges its varied ethnographic functions and its properties as a folk celebration, albeit with a genocidal twist.

Word "spread rapidly," reported the article from the Sunday *Arkansas Gazette*, that "negroes were organizing to defy law and order." Whites quickly organized. On Thursday, sixteen more "resolute men" left DeWitt for "the scene of the trouble." Meanwhile, five blacks were in jail and under guard in Saint Charles, although the article does not specify the charges leveled against them. "A number of towns," having learned of the drama unfolding, sent more marauders gunning for action. The *Arkansas Gazette* described them as "Reinforcements to the Front," seemingly invoking the sanction of race war.[46]

As already noted, the *Arkansas Gazette* explicitly assured readers that there was no effort "to make war on peaceable and inoffensive negroes," but the mobs descending on Saint Charles were "determined" to hunt down "the ringleaders in Monday's riot, and their active aiders and abettors." In what the paper called an "engagement" that Thursday, a black man was "ferreted out and killed." But the real excitement came that night when an "indignant populace," composed of what the article described as "infuriated citizens," went to the jail, "overpowered the guards," took the five black men, and "shot them to death."[47]

One might wonder how valiantly the officers defended the inmates before they were "overpowered." Given the holes in the coverage, what transpired in this specific instance is unknown. Scholars do know something, however, of the pattern typified by officers of the peace who encountered a lynch mob. In 1907, Cutler cited numerous examples that "evidenced a criminal neglect of even ordinary duty on the part of sheriffs and constables." Writing in 1933, Arthur Raper noted that "in most cases the sheriff and his deputies merely stood by while the mob did its work, and later reported that the mob had taken them by surprise, or that, though aware of the impending danger, they were unwilling to shoot into the crowd lest they kill innocent men, women and children." One sheriff asked, "Do you think I'm going to risk my life protecting a nigger?"[48]

It may be that the recent death of the sheriff of Arkansas County contributed to local unrest. Sheriff M. A. Baker had passed away, and a successor had yet to be appointed. One can only speculate on how this sequence of events might have unfolded had the law been on hand.[49] As it was, more human remains were discovered in the aftermath of mass murder. On

Friday, the corpse of "another negro" was found "in the woods." Then, on Saturday morning, "the last of the gang of negroes that caused the trouble" was "put to death." After a week of terror, eleven black men were dead.[50]

The *Arkansas Gazette* provided its readers with a "Complete List of Dead Negroes," identifying those "who met death on account of Monday's riot." The necrology consisted of "Aaron Hinton, Randall Flood, Will Baldwin, Will Madison, Jim Smith, Charley Smith, Mack Baldwin, Abe Bailey, Garrett Flood, Kellis Johnson and Perry Carter." They were, said the article, "the most dangerous negroes." The careful reader might have noted that none of the dead were directly involved in the altercation of the previous Monday. As for Henry Griffin and Walker Griffin, the black men whose apparent incitement to "riot" seemed to require revenge, there is not a word of their fate in this article.[51] Apparently, the Griffins were killed later, but the circumstances of their slayings were not reported in the extant newspaper coverage of events in eastern Arkansas in 1904. Perhaps their murders were anticlimactic, the details unnecessary to the sort of society that regarded lynchings as fairly routine. Both of the statewide newspapers had publicly anticipated the Griffins' killings since the altercation of the previous Monday was first reported in the press. Another regional newspaper, the *Memphis Commercial Appeal*, actually insisted that they "invited instant death." Death visited them regardless. The casual nature of the coverage of their killings reflects the ordinariness of the affair to its contemporaries and renders the actual train of events irretrievable.[52]

The *Arkansas Gazette* article gave no indication that any effort would be made to apprehend or prosecute the murderers. In this instance, the absence of reference to the machinery of justice was not an odd omission. Instead, it signified the nature of the proceedings. Writing twenty-five years after the slaughter in Saint Charles, Walter White explained, "Until very recent times, and in most of the South, even today, no lyncher has ever needed to feel the slightest apprehension regarding punishment or even the annoyance of an investigation."[53] The sure knowledge that whites could attack blacks with impunity encouraged the continuing depredations. Myrdal concluded, "Any white man can strike or beat a Negro, steal or destroy his property, cheat him in a transaction and even take his life, without much fear of legal reprisal." He related that even those southern whites who opposed lynchings also opposed apprehending or prosecuting the terrorists who committed them. "Above all," according to this perception of race relations, "Negroes must not have the satisfaction of seeing the whites divided or their assailants punished." That the *Arkansas Gazette* omitted any suggestion of legal reprisal against the terrorists was thus unremarkable. The imperative of white supremacy in the South apparently transcended the rule of law.[54]

The fact that lynchings went unpunished held significance for whites in the community along with those in the mob. In *Revolt against Chivalry*, Jacqueline Dowd Hall reveals how the dynamic served to socialize whites as well as blacks. "Aimed ostensibly at blacks," she explains, "this process also operated as a means of indoctrination and social control over whites. It served the essential educational function" of reiterating the predominant public perception that blacks were inherently inferior.[55]

Lynchings were proof that black Americans existed beyond the protection of the law. For their part, as Hall notes, constant fear of being victimized by officially encouraged but ultimately invisible brutality dampened the inclination among blacks "to reach out for the symbols of dignity and equality in a white world." When African Americans neglected to observe behavioral nuances appropriate to their subordination, or if they forgot to follow the cultural protocol of their presumed inferiority, or when a particular group of whites thought that they might forget, their lynchings reminded their survivors.[56]

That was the case in Saint Charles, according to the recollections that Boyd Johnson made public fifty-nine years after the affair. During the roundup that preceded Thursday night's bloodbath, as Johnson remembered it, "some of the older Negroes refused to walk fast or trot while being brought in. Frank Parker, a young negro was chided by the older Negroes for cooperating with the whites. When asked why, he replied; 'I trotted because I thought it was trot[t]in' time.'" Parker was not listed among the fatalities.[57]

Lynchings were symptomatic of a fundamental change in the status of African Americans. As barbarities against blacks continued year after year, then decade after decade, whites could observe firsthand that blacks had far less protection under the law as citizens than they had enjoyed as chattel slaves. In his fascinating and complex history, "Slavery and the Arkansas Supreme Court," L. Scott Stafford explores the considerable legal protections that shielded slaves in Arkansas before the Civil War. Emancipation had the ironic effect of freeing blacks from the antebellum laws that, by virtue of the property interests of their owners, accorded slaves a measure of worth and human dignity in the eyes of the law (as explored in chapter 1).[58] With each unpunished killing, with every unprosecuted outrage, whites learned that, as citizens, blacks could be treated with complete contempt.

Lynchings had another effect on white Americans. To rationalize and to justify the perpetuation of "the incredible cruelty and barbarity of lynching," as George M. Fredrickson described it in *The Black Image in the White Mind*, whites had to develop a perception of blacks that made this sort of treatment seem reasonable. What resulted, according to Fredrickson, was "the most extreme defamation of the Negro character" in the tortured history of American race relations. To be able to accept the routinization of mob rule and mass murder in their society, whites had to come to view blacks as the vicious and beast-like predators that they were portrayed to be in the racist literature of the day. As a result, "even the most oppressed and rigidly subordinated black sharecropper could serve as a symbol of terror for the white- supremacist imagination."[59]

That whites around Saint Charles had whipped themselves into a state of high anxiety seems evident in what transpired there. Suspicions that blacks must be "planning an uprising," according to the reminiscences of Johnson and Henderson, ran rampant through the countryside. Those fears were fed by news of the apparent need, early that Wednesday, to kill those three black men on the road. Whites of Saint Charles gathered their families together in order to guard them and issued calls to outlying areas for armed assistance; as Henderson put it in his memoir, "a large number came." By nightfall on Wednesday, whites had posted a picket line of defenders around the town to protect themselves from blacks. Tensions ran so high that when one of the white men walked beyond his beat in the night, he was shot and wounded by a comrade in arms. The wounding of a white man in the frenzy garnered newspaper attention and aggravated the animosity that led to more bloodshed in the following days.[60]

The arrival of Sunday may have contributed to a cessation of the carnage, because the perpetrators may well have been in church. In his statistical investigation of lynchings that occurred between 1882 and 1927, White testified to an "astonishing revelation": the more Baptists and Methodists there were in a given state as a percentage of its "total church population," the greater the incidence of this type of mob murder. White claimed to have found an "almost exactly parallel" correspondence. Arkansas, fifth in the nation in terms of the concentration of Baptists and Methodists among its churchgoing population, also ranked sixth in the number of victims of lynchers.[61] In fact, the tabular data White provides does not back up this claim. Part of the reason he may have been misled is that he compared percentage of church membership to raw totals for lynching victims, not a per capita listing. Of course, the historian must avoid confusing a statistical correlation with historical causation, but even more important, data must be fairly and correctly interpreted. One cannot assume from the data actually presented that Baptists and Methodists were more likely to be either the murderers or the victims in these common communal violations of the biblical injunction "Thou shalt not kill."

When attempting to convey the collective mentality of the lynch mob, however, students of the subject have suggested a characteristic mindset amenable to this sort of bloody outburst that cannot be detached from a discussion of religion. In his analysis of the "psychopathology of lynching," Myrdal cites a "narrow-minded and intolerant" evangelical Protestantism. White insists that an emotional appetite favorable to lynching was fed by "a relentlessly vitriolic and ignorant ministry." Raper asserts that "the most common view expressed by ministers was that the lynching, though unfortunate, was inevitable. The ministers, and especially the Southern Methodists and Southern Baptists, usually felt that they would be faced with a serious division among their membership" if they actively called for the prosecution of the lynchers in their midst.[62]

Such sentiments were not confined to Methodists and Baptists. The Episcopal bishop of Arkansas proclaimed similar views at the time of the catastrophe at Saint Charles. In February 1904, just a month before the killing spree in eastern Arkansas, Bishop William Montgomery Brown traveled to the North on a speaking tour. He created such a stir in Massachusetts for his testimony on behalf of lynching that the commotion made the newspapers and precipitated public "indignation meetings" to protest his position. Bishop Brown later explained, "I have never advocated lynching, but only extenuated the offence," although his northern listeners, both white and black, clearly missed this distinction. As Brown had earlier expostulated to his flock in Arkansas, "I am a northern man, and used to look with horror on lynching, but since I have been south my eyes have been opened." Religious exculpation of the antilegal execution of African Americans by mob, if not its advocacy, was ecumenical in Arkansas.[63]

Massachusetts's unwelcoming reception of Bishop Brown's exoneration of lynchers occurred just a few weeks before the Saint Charles outburst and may well have affected the news coverage that the mayhem received.

When the killings in Saint Charles had finally come to an end, an editorial in the *Arkansas Gazette* explicitly expressed relief "for the sake of the good name of the state of Arkansas." It did not object to the extralegal executions or to the death toll per se, which the editorial regarded as "inevitable." But, it continued, "it should be remembered that a race war in which thirteen men are killed on one side is a perfect feast for the big newspapers all over the United States, especially for certain ones north of the Mason and Dixon line that seem to delight to feature something that paints Southern life in a bad way." Instead, it is a picture of southern death that the *Arkansas Gazette* had withheld from full public view.[64]

A brief survey of the contradictory "facts" from the few published details of the terror in Saint Charles suggests the banality of brutality against blacks to a society inured to accounts of yet more lynched "negroes." In the public record, even the geographic location of the scene of five of the murders is at issue. The *New York Times*, concurring with the *Arkansas Gazette's* account, reported that the Thursday night spree occurred when the mob took five blacks "from the guards at St. Charles" and shot them dead. In one of the few existing state newspapers to mention the massacre, the *Atkins Chronicle* flatly contradicted this rendition. In the total of the twenty-seven lines that it devoted to the entire episode, the *Chronicle* insisted that "several negroes were arrested and taken to De Witt" where "a crowd of about fifty people gathered and took the prisoners from the officers and shot them to death." Even though this placement of events disputes other accounts that place the Thursday night lynching of five at Saint Charles, this article is intriguing because it provides at least an estimate of the size of the Thursday night mob.[65]

The assassinations of the previous day, when three men were gunned down on the road outside Saint Charles, are also reported differently in the *Atkins Chronicle*. In this version, "a posse of officers . . . were fired upon by a crowd of negroes concealed in a thicket" before those "officers" shot three dead. An account of these same slayings in the *Arkansas Democrat* claimed that black men "were ambushed and fired on the white men," who returned fire, killing three of them. A subsequent report in the *Arkansas Democrat* states that a posse met three black men, "and asked them if they knew the whereabouts of the two Griffins. The negroes replied that they did, but that they would not tell any white man." The fight that ensued left them dead. The *Arkansas Gazette's* coverage of the incident is patently inconsistent. In the article that describes deaths on the road as cited in the text above, the killers were led by deputy sheriff P. A. Douglass. In an earlier article, these same killers were led by a constable, L. C. McNeeley. The reportage of the ostensible details of this particular string of deaths is representative of coverage of the entire week of rampage; many of the so-called facts are debatable by virtue of contradictions elsewhere in the record.[66]

Additional distortions in the printed record flavor this stew of discrepancies. It is seasoned with numerical and temporal conundrums. According to the *Memphis Commercial Appeal*, the three black men were assassinated on Tuesday afternoon rather than Wednesday. After that, "a large number were arrested and penned in a house." On Wednesday, six more blacks perished when they tried to free those in custody. What is reported elsewhere as the Thursday night incident unfolds on Wednesday in this rendition. In the *Commercial Appeal* account, the fatalities from this particular episode during the week of mayhem number six rather than five. The victims were not taken out and murdered, they were shot while trying to break in to abet their accomplices in a race war.[67]

In addition to correcting the errors of those who composed the public record of this event, historians must also contend with errors of omission and seek details that reporters overlooked, felt to be inconsequential, or otherwise decided to leave untold. News accounts of the killings make little mention of the mass arrests that preceded the Thursday night massacre. Only memoirs offer details. White riders on horseback swept across the countryside, stalking and apprehending black captives on sight. Before nightfall, Johnson recalled, the predators "rounded up the Negro men and some women and children." They seized between sixty and seventy hostages, marched them to town, and forced them into an old store building to await their fate at the hands of the mob. Rampaging outside the building, wrote Henderson, manic whites were "ready to exterminate the negro race." Some, according to Johnson, insisted that the building be torched so as to exterminate all sixty or seventy black people imprisoned inside it. They "wanted to kill the whole outfit. It was with difficulty," as Henderson expressed it, that wholesale annihilation was averted.[68]

Speakers addressing the mob began to demand restraint. "One by one," according to Johnson's memoir, they "began interceding for special Negroes." Sometime after midnight, a semblance of order restored, the crowd disbanded. It was brief respite, however, for the scores of blacks still caged within. Around three in the morning, another mob stormed the building. They wrenched away six of the captives, paraded them "to a high point" on the DeWitt–Saint Charles Highway, "stood them in a line and shot them."[69] Five of them perished in the gunfire. The sixth, shot in the leg, "played O'possum." When the crowd dispersed from the scene of the killings, he crawled into the woods. On Friday morning, he was found and shot dead, the tenth victim. Three more deaths followed in the next few days. The specific circumstances of the slayings were not recorded, just as the high adventure of chase and mass captivity was not reported by newspapers.[70]

The most conspicuous distortion in the data is the omission of the identity of the perpetrators. The two witnesses who penned reminiscences of this episode did not reveal the lynchers' names, and reporters either suppressed or failed to pursue crucial details about the identity of assassins. The anonymity of the actors in this drama makes it impossible to find their motives. As a consequence, a search for the causes of this week of rage must forever be inconclusive. Of the murderers, who they were, what they hoped to achieve, whether the dimensions of their class, age, gender, ethnicity, religion, or residence had any impact on this turn of events, the record bears mute witness.

Assigning responsibility for the massacre to the mob bears the analytical precision of blaming it on society. The behavior of lynch mobs does possess a high degree of explanatory significance, as Brundage demonstrates in his intriguing typology of mob actions in Virginia and Georgia. The meanings that he isolates among patterns of mob actions become blurred, however, in the morass of murders that occurred in Saint Charles. On Wednesday afternoon, one witnesses a posse at work; Thursday afternoon's murder, akin to that which transpired on Friday morning, might follow the pattern of what Brundage defines as a private mob; the wholesale sweep and subsequent detention of several dozens of African Americans on Thursday, culminating in the killings on the high ground that night, might characterize the initial workings of a mass mob followed by those of a terrorist mob. In some ways, in keeping with the extraordinarily varied and contradictory nature of the episodes that Brundage tracked, his thoughtful taxonomy of hundreds of lynchings can be, in Saint Charles, telescoped into one.[71]

Assignment of blame to the mob does not provide information on the individualities of those who pulled triggers or distinguish them from those who urged them on, or those who stood by as accessories to murder. All that is known of the ranks of these mobs is that they were almost certainly whites. Mob membership was legion, regardless of its operating size, if one includes in its roster all who knew or could have determined the identities of the murderers but who tacitly conspired to hide them forever. What is obvious is that, in eastern Arkansas in 1904, no one needed to wear a hood.

Looking for causal patterns, the historian runs the serious risk of seeking an explanation by turning to the behavior of the only people who are identified in the record—the victims. Thus it is that, in the literature on lynching, one finds analyses that group the phenomena by the "alleged offense" of the dead. Such a perspective warps not only understanding of the past, but it also denies the essential truth of this reign of dread. The horror of lynching inhered in its unpredictability. In their analysis of thousands of deaths, Tolnay and Beck discovered that the utter uncertainty over what might "trigger" a bloodbath was intrinsic to this form of terror. "Many African-Americans," they aver, "lived at the discretion of the white community and its whims."[72]

The lynchers in Saint Charles left a trail that cannot be mapped in even its basic directions. Because of the magnitude of inconsistency, error, and omission in the evidentiary base upon which researchers must rely, when or where or why particular killings occurred can only be deduced, inferred, or guessed. The path of the terror is lost in time and space.

If one looks for the word *lynching* in the published accounts of more than a dozen dead in Saint Charles, it is not used in every account. The *New York Times* used the word in reporting the Saint Charles massacre. Being writers, some of the reporters from the *Arkansas Gazette*, the *Arkansas Democrat*, the *Atkins Chronicle*, and the *Memphis Commercial Appeal* also must have been acquainted with the usage as both gerund and verb, yet none chose to employ the verb *lynch* or any of its variants when characterizing this chain of events.[73] According to most of the authors of the memoirs and newspaper accounts at a historian's disposal, there were neither thirteen lynchings in east Arkansas in March 1904 nor a single one waiting for the record books, because the construct itself was not part of the public discourse. Instead, according to the *Arkansas Gazette*, these were "negroes who met death."[74]

The historical record of probably the deadliest lynching in American history is incomplete. Evidentiary anomalies conceal a secret past. A detailed reporting of the facts did not matter to the white public, because the episode was seen by whites as a relatively trivial occurrence, a commonplace event. For black survivors of Saint Charles, however, a legacy of the terror must have haunted their days and nights. Over the course of a week, a town with a total population of five hundred people lost thirteen of its adult males. A brawl on Monday precipitated a pogrom.[75]

The *Arkansas Gazette* concluded its account of a week of life and death in an Arkansas town with the calming prediction that "no further trouble is looked for." The other statewide newspaper reassured readers that, "as the most dangerous negroes have been killed[,] it is thought that the others can be held in check." Quiet had returned to Saint Charles.[76]

POSTSCRIPT

After the Emancipation Proclamation, revision in the ritual expression of white supremacy eviscerated the structural changes that constitutional amendments had insinuated into southern race relations. In response to Reconstruction, the de facto denial of the Fourteenth Amendment (granting equal protection of the law to everyone born in the United States) required a more complicated cultural construction than the abrogation of the abolition authorized by the Thirteenth Amendment, or the disfranchisement that nullified the Fifteenth Amendment. Former slaves, finding themselves liberated in a world where everything, just as they had been, was owned, soon found that their labor was still locked to the land, the force of contract law as binding as a bill-of-sale in extracting from them their toil. That the freedom to pay bills, to incur debt, was extended to former slaves also—and immediately—guaranteed their continued subjugation. Wage slavery, debt peonage, and convict leasing replaced the legal foundations of chattel slavery.[77] Sabotaging the Fifteenth Amendment was equally amenable to legal fixes, in measures like the poll tax, literacy tests, the grandfather clause, the property requirement, and the "understandings" test.[78] Such fully lawful exclusions to the innovations imposed by constitutional fiat quickly neutered the impact of amendments that contravened centuries of life in the South and that contradicted cultural practices that would not be abandoned simply by imperial edicts announcing their end.

Subverting the equal protection of the law, however, and nullifying the due process of law, was far more complicated than negating the Thirteenth and Fifteenth amendments. White southerners could not depend upon the force of law to deny the rule of law. To convey that all blacks within their society (not just the lawbreakers among them) now existed beyond the protection of the law, a new twist on an old social practice became a fad and the fashion in the New South. This revision in the ritual expression of southern culture manifested in an uninterrupted wave of thousands of lynchings that informed both blacks and whites across the decades when blacks lived only at the whim of their collective overlords. After former slave owners lost any material interest in black well-being as a consequence of abolition, brutality no longer came armed with an overseer's whip, threatening pain. After emancipation, instead, marauders stalked with rope, axes, cork screws, guns and rifles, gasoline and a match— terrorizing all blacks (and their sympathizers) with the prospect of the most heinous forms of murder.

This sort of lynching suited the cultural imperative of white supremacy first by mocking due process. This invalidation of new constitutional guarantees was grafted onto an existing historical tradition, the vigilante lynchings that had occurred in frontier communities absent the formal agencies of a speedy trial. Although those situations demanded rough justice with only a pretext of due process, southern lynchers of blacks, by contrast, were engaged in objectively verifiable community efforts to negate or otherwise abort due process altogether.[79] If western lynchings indicated the absence of law, southern lynchings demonstrated the defiance of law, proved its invalidity, through a communal refusal to acknowledge the extension of presumed protections that law might otherwise provide to parties who could not be accepted cognitively by white southerners as equals. These sorts of lynchings were not merely extralegal, such as one might encounter in the absence of recognized judicial authority. These communal homicidal outbursts instead were antilegal, nullifying the pretenses of equal protection that seemed to mobs to be viscerally outrageous, imposed by illegitimate federal authority.[80]

Another significant attribute distinguished lynchers of the New South from vigilantes of the Old West. The southern strain of mob murder was not just antilegal, it was often acausal as well. That was the essence of its terror. To argue that a southern lynching was predictable—the logical outcome of perceived transgression—is to miss the essential didactic message of the phenomenon in maintaining white supremacy.[81] That conclusion is also, historically, inaccurate. In their statistical analyses of thousands of lynchings in the New South, Tolnay and Beck were forced to conclude that causality of the kind that can be tracked cannot be found in the evidence at hand: instead, anything and nothing could trigger a bloodbath against blacks. Southern blacks and whites understood at the time that the phenomenon had little to do with the rape of white women. Blaming the victim, however specious the allegation, could rationalize a human barbeque.[82] Tolnay and Beck provide an inventory of putative improprieties by black victims that were cited in the record as leading to their lynching. Though murder, rape, and robbery make the list, so too did "acting suspiciously," "arguing with white man," "being obnoxious," "demanding respect," "disorderly conduct," "gambling," "indolence," "inflammatory language," "insulting white man," "insulting white woman," "mistaken identity," "quarreling," "race hatred," "race troubles," "resisting mob," "suing white man," "testifying against white man," "trying to vote," "unpopularity," "unruly remarks," "using obscene language," "vagrancy," "voodooism," and "voting for the wrong party."[83] It is folly to pretend to find pattern in this medley of supposed motives for mob murders.

Historical causation cannot be ascribed because the killers themselves, with the complicity of their communities, remained unknown parties—and still remain that way today. The absence of the identity of actors in the database guarantees that scholars will never identify their individual motives for participating in murder either. To argue that the collective behavior of lynchers would be amenable to rational explanation, or that the intent of a single participant in these mobs would seem logical, were such evidence available, is rank speculation. The Saint Charles incident informs our understanding of this dimension of the victimization of blacks in the New South. When the black man Griffin hit white Jim Searcy that Monday night because of a poker game down at the docks, his immediate future might have been predictable—the arresting officer actually told the black man that he might be lynched, precipitating Griffin's assault on the deputy and his subsequent flight. It would require the most tendentious logic, however, to infer therefrom that mobs would murder forthwith a dozen more men for the perceived misbehavior of one.

This definitional dimension of southern lynching constituted sure proof that any black man or black woman or black child could be and might be mobbed on a whim in the most hideous fashion with total impunity by white perpetrators whatever their pretext. These thousands of public homicides committed by mobs—year after year then decade after decade unpunished, unprosecuted, often even unworthy of minimally accurate newspaper coverage—offered concrete evidence to whites and blacks, old and young, male and female alike, not just that the due process of law that was promised by the Fourteenth Amendment was fraudulent, but that the idea of equal protection of the law for black folks was entirely fatuous. Just to suggest the notion was grounds for a lynching. This revision in the folk rituals of southern life guaranteed that de jure equality would not befall the New South through military defeat, congressional edicts, court rulings, or constitutional amendments. To white southerners, confronting the cultural instabilities and cognitive disruptions of seemingly unacceptable change that accompanied the conquest of their Confederacy, lynching made sense because it made no sense save to celebrate unconditional white supremacy.

"Through Death, Hell and the Grave"

Lynching and Antilynching Efforts in Arkansas, 1901–1939

At midnight on February 20–21, 1901, a "crowd" of eight white men took a black man, Perry Berryman, out of the Mena jail and hanged him. The lynch mob's victim had been arrested earlier in the day for the offense of kicking a twelve-year-old white girl during a dispute over building a fence. Injuries to the girl were "serious," which "created a strong feeling" against Berryman. In addition, the black man had a bad reputation about town; a month before the lynching, he had allegedly "attacked an engineer with an ax and nearly killed him." Described as wearing masks, the lynching party accosted the night officer, Al Jones, and demanded that he surrender the keys to the prison. With guns pointed in his face, Jones obeyed, and the mob removed Berryman from the jail. Shortly after dawn on February 21, law officers cut down Berryman's body. A jury appointed by the local coroner reported that the lynchers could not be identified. As a result, no one was punished for the incident.[1]

Some twenty-six years after the Berryman lynching, John Carter, an African American, was accused of attacking two white women during an altercation on a rural road near Little Rock. A posse of white men assembled and apprehended Carter. But with the suspect in custody, the posse devolved into a mob and took Carter from officers. He was hanged and riddled with bullets, and his body was dragged behind a car into the black business section of Little Rock. In the city, spectators swelled the ranks of the mob, which grew to number in the thousands. A racist fury

was unleashed as the mob rioted for more than three hours without intervention of local law enforcement. Police officers allegedly stood by and
played cards as the carnage continued. Carter's body was burned in front
of the Mosaic Templars' hall, a building which, for more than a decade,
had both served the African American community as meeting house and
provided offices for some of the most successful black businessmen in the
city. Boards from a nearby church were reportedly used to fuel the fire as
the rioters destroyed property owned by African Americans. Ultimately,
Gov. John E. Martineau dispatched the state guard, which dispersed the
mob and brought the chaotic situation to an end.[2] Despite an investigation,
the rioters remained unidentified, and no one was punished. In the wake
of the riot, a large number of Africans Americans reportedly left Little
Rock for good. (See chapter 8 for a more detailed account of the Carter
lynching.)

The two lynchings—Berryman in 1901 and Carter in 1927—bore
many similarities. Notably, whites comprised the lynch mobs, while their
victims were African Americans. Both lynchings followed in the wake of
incidents involving a black man and one or more white women. But also
notable is the fact that in neither case was there any evidence of sexual
assault. In both incidents, officers of the law either could not or would
not do anything to prevent the mob violence. Both victims were hanged,
though numerous methods, including shooting and burning the victim
alive, were not uncommon means by which lynch mobs executed people.[3]
Subsequent inquests yielded no results, and no one was punished in either
incident. And the perpetrators of both incidents chose extralegal solutions
rather than allowing legal procedures to play out.

The two lynchings also featured several significant differences. Most
notably, the Berryman lynching was a secretive affair. The lynchers wore
masks, conducted their business late at night, and were reported to have
spoken very little. By contrast, the Carter lynching was a very public
affair ultimately witnessed by thousands of rioters and spectators.[4] After
Berryman was hanged, nothing further was done to the body. However,
the Carter lynching was highly ritualized. The body was mutilated—by
first being riddled by bullets, then dragged behind a car, and ultimately
burned.[5] The small size of the lynch mob in the Berryman case suggests
a very personal execution of mob justice; once the victim was dead, the
incident was over. By contrast, Carter's hanging was only the beginning of
an attack on the greater African American community in Little Rock. The

riot demonstrated a deep-seated hatred harbored by whites for blacks and revealed that this hatred had long been waiting for some incident to set it loose. And just because the Berryman lynching appears to have been a private affair, the importance of the event as a racial phenomenon should not be underestimated. Given the larger context of race relations in Arkansas, and in the South in general, it was one of thousands of extralegal executions of African Americans by white mobs.[6]

As revealed by the Berryman and Carter hangings, lynching was a complex phenomenon. This chapter will examine both the phenomenon of lynching and antilynching efforts in Arkansas during the period 1901–39. The antilynching efforts of African American activists and their non-southern white allies and the fight for the Dyer antilynching bill, as well resistance to lynching by indigenous southern blacks, have understandably garnered enormous attention from scholars.[7] But the resulting historical interpretation pitting civil rights activists against racist whites generally ignores the fact that white southerners were not united in their attitudes towards mob justice, although they were by and large committed to the racist order. In particular, this essay will investigate a conservative anti-lynching effort uniting white and black southerners.[8] Despite the friction between these two groups, their combined efforts against mob violence must be recognized as integral to the decline of lynching in Arkansas and the South.

The lynchings of Berryman and Carter were not the only incidents of mob justice in turn-of-the-century Arkansas, and Arkansas was not the only state plagued by incidents of lynching. Most states in the union had suffered lynchings, but statistics compiled by interested parties demonstrated that the lynch mobs constituted a particular problem for the South. Those keeping track of incidents of mob justice included the *Chicago Tribune* and the Tuskegee Institute, along with the National Association for the Advancement of Colored People (NAACP), which produced the book *Thirty Years of Lynching in the United States*.[9] This work revealed that 3,224 people were victims of lynching mobs in the period 1889–1918. Of these, 2,868 were lynched in southern states, including the eleven states of the Confederacy as well as the border states of Oklahoma, Kentucky, and Missouri. Furthermore, of those lynched, 2,422 were black men and women. Arkansas's own lynching record resembled the general southern record; of 215 lynchings reported by the NAACP in 1889–1918, 172 were black and only 33 were white. Of those lynched after 1900, only 8 were white.[10] The Tuskegee Institute recorded 284 Arkansans murdered by lynch mobs in the state during the period 1883–1936, ranking it among the six states with the worst lynching records.[11]

But if lynching remained a problem in the South during the twentieth century, it was one in decline. In the decade 1889–98, according to the NAACP, the traditional South averaged 137.0 lynchings per year; in 1899–1908, 84.5; and in 1909–18, 65.3. Arkansas's lynching pattern was a similar one of decline. In 1889–98, 111 persons were lynched in Arkansas, 11.1 per year; in 1899–1908, 6 persons were lynched, 6.6 per year; and in 1909–18, 30 persons were lynched, or 3.0 per year.[12] If lynching declined in frequency, this decline was never steady; any year, the number of lynchings could explode. For instance, the NAACP recorded one lynching in Arkansas in 1908. The following year, the state suffered four lynchings.[13] Then, in 1910, lynch mobs claimed the lives of nine people in Arkansas. However, the next eight years—until after the end of World War I— was a period of relatively few lynchings. In 1911–18, a total of seventeen men, all black, became victims of mob justice in Arkansas, an average of two per year. The year 1917 featured four lynchings, and two other years, 1912 and 1916, had three lynchings each, for a total of ten lynchings from 1911 to 1918; the years 1913, 1914, and 1918 each had only one lynching. In 1919, the number of lynchings increased to five, with only one lynching the following year (a figure that does not include those who were killed during the Elaine Massacre, for reasons touched upon in the introduction to this volume). The state suffered only one lynching in 1920, but in 1921, seven people died at the hands of lynch mobs, including Henry Lowery. In 1922, another six men were lynched. Afterwards, successful lynchings showed a marked decline, with only two victims in 1923, none in 1924, and one in 1925. However, 1926 and 1927 witnessed three lynchings each, including the notorious lynching of John Carter.[14] For several years after 1927, no lynchings occurred in the state. Only two lynchings, both of African American men, are known to have occurred in the 1930s, that of Frank Tucker in Crossett in Ashley County on September 15, 1932, and that of Willie Kees in Lepanto in Pointsett County in 1936, which is believed to be the last lynching in Arkansas.[15] Mob justice in Arkansas was overwhelmingly an affair of racial hierarchy. In all but eleven cases during the twentieth century, the victims were Africans Americans; only one white man, E. C. Gregor in Boone County, was lynched after 1920.[16] Also, in only a handful of incidents were the mobs not exclusively made up of whites.

While lynching was the most prominent form of extralegal violence in Arkansas during the period from 1901 to 1936, other forms were also used to terrorize and control African Americans. One of these was "night-riding," also known as "whitecapping," which employed threats of lynching and actual violence to intimidate and terrorize victims. Incidents generally occurred at night, and violence generally was limited to floggings. But nightriders also committed more serious forms of violence, including the burning of homes, dynamiting, and perhaps lynching.[17] Another form of extralegal violence, the large-scale riot, was intimately linked to lynching. Riots in the South during the late nineteenth century and first half of the twentieth century typically involved assaults on local black communities by masses of whites who attacked both people and property. A large number of lynchings included riots featuring mobs in the hundreds and even thousands.[18]

Racial violence in its various forms created an atmosphere of terror, a sense of fear that, at any moment, one could be murdered or seriously injured. This fear served to enforce the color line that prevailed throughout the South and placed African Americans in an inferior position to whites. In Arkansas, this position was sanctified by the state in 1891 when the Arkansas General Assembly passed a separate coach measure that was subsequently signed by the governor. The measure not only set a precedent for de jure segregation of public facilities but also served as a statement that African Americans would, by law, occupy a subordinate position in the state. Soon afterwards, with the adoption of a poll tax and the whites-only Democratic primary, the state essentially disfranchised of the majority of African Americans living there; after 1893, no black Arkansans served in the General Assembly again until 1973. These measures reinforced the already existing white-over-black caste system, which featured segregated schools, anti-miscegenation laws, benign neglect of educational facilities, and the prevalence of debt peonage in the state's Delta region. These conditions were exacerbated by a record number of lynchings in the late 1880s and 1890s.[19] But if at the dawn of the twentieth century, black Arkansans found themselves living under increasingly virulent conditions, their embattled community possessed one strength that endured and resisted the onslaught—a small but wealthy black middle class.

This middle class owed its existence to intrepid individuals who had taken advantages of opportunities during Reconstruction and afterwards. The results included black-owned businesses, farms, and plantations.

Black Arkansans formed their own churches and joined all-black denominations that emerged in the post–Civil War period. These denominations, in turn, founded several institutions of higher learning, such as Arkansas Baptist College and Philander Smith College in Little Rock and Shorter College in North Little Rock. Unlike Branch Normal College in Pine Bluff (now the University of Arkansas at Pine Bluff), which was founded in 1874 and was dependent upon funds approved by the legislature, these institutions were entirely controlled by African Americans. These institutions and businesses were a source of pride and independence and served as a testimony to what could be accomplished through self-reliance, hard work, and determination in the face of the worst odds. For leaders of the black middle class, these principles informed a combined strategy by which they could improve the horrendous impoverishment experienced by so many members of their community, improve race relations, and diminish racial oppression.[20]

In 1907, the *Blue Book of Little Rock and Argenta, Arkansas* publicized the accomplishments of the black community of Pulaski County.[21] Beyond serving as a social register and list of community resources, the *Blue Book* contained several essays by leading citizens. Topics included industrial education, finances, and personal hygiene. Several essays addressed race relations, including one by businessman John E. Bush, founder of the Mosaic Templars fraternal organization and one of the most prominent black Republicans in the state. He had also organized a chapter of Booker T. Washington's National Negro Business League.[22] He characterized local African Americans as "industrious, thrifty, and hardworkers," who had "the fullest confidence of their white neighbors." He claimed that these whites "as a whole, take pride in encouraging and uplifting their brother in black, both by advice, their counsel and money." Such good relations were the result of "the Negro attending strictly to his own business, his love of school and church, his industrious and sober habits."[23]

Undoubtedly, Bush wrote his comments well aware that whites would read the *Blue Book*. But that, in part, was the purpose of the book—to make whites aware of the incredible achievements made by African Americans in the short time since emancipation. They were good, hardworking citizens determined to make positive contributions to the welfare of the local community and thus deserved better treatment. As testimony to these achievements, Bush pointed out that African Americans in Little Rock owned

$2.5 million in real estate and personal property. He also listed a wide range of black-owned businesses, including jewelry stores, restaurants, blacksmith shops, and even a bank.[24] More subtly, his comments recognized the cold reality of white economic, political, and social power. Under such conditions, African Americans benefited most from the goodwill of the white community. Implicitly, he frowned upon activities that would undermine the attempt to build a bridge between communities.

In his essay on race relations, Joseph A. Booker, president of Arkansas Baptist College, defined the issue with two questions: "What would the Negro be willing and able to do for himself?" and its corollary, "What will the white man allow the Negro to do for himself?" He believed that the answer to the second question depended "upon the temperament of the [black] community—the public sentiment in favor of the Negro's progress." This sentiment, asserted Booker, "depends largely on the Negroes themselves."[25] He stressed the need for a "strict religious culture and strict moral training" along with "industrial and intellectual training."[26]

J. M. Cox, president of Philander Smith College, a Methodist institution, proclaimed the need for whites to deal with African Americans as individuals, not "one class." Essentially, each person should be judged according to that person's character, not by negative stereotypes. He claimed the key to better race relations was to "live in harmony with Bible principles, and make the Golden Rule the basis of treatment to one of the other."[27]

J. L. Wilson, pastor of Wesley Chapel, likewise called for the application of the Golden Rule as a solution to "the race problem." But he also noted in particular the role of "inflammatory newspapers" in creating racial tensions. Such papers appealed to "that element in both black and white, which is ever ready to disregard law and order."[28]

In general, the essayists all agreed that, to a large extent, African Americans bore the responsibility for bettering race relations. Such betterment depended upon their development as industrious, moral citizens. They emphasized an avoidance of tensions, implicitly rejecting the bold confrontations entered into by advocates of civil rights. Nevertheless, their essays also included subtle indictments of the role played by whites in creating poor race relations. Vital to Booker's essay was the notion that whites created obstacles to black advancement. Cox called the practice of whites to "seek a remedy suited to each and every" African American "unwise."[29] Implicitly, he alluded to the injustices endured by black Arkansans. Wilson openly pointed out the hypocrisy of the white-dominated justice system. He called for the "punishment for the [white] lyncher as well as the [black] rapist."[30]

Attorney Nelson H. Nichols was boldest of the *Blue Book* essayists. His contribution, "Necessity of the Negro Lawyer to His Race," stated the facts of the black experience. He characterized race relations in strongly pessimistic terms. He stated that the United States was "greedy, grasping and tight fisted in [its] denial of political rights" to African Americans.[31] In particular, he cited the justice system, which "by a color policy" denied African Americans the right to "sit on the jury or be represented in the halls of legislation."[32]

In the course of his essay, Nichols addressed the hypocrisy of those whites who opposed lynching. He conceded that not every white would "engage in a lynching bee, or burn alive an innocent and defenseless person." However, those same people had no "compunction of conscience at denying and using every indirection to deprive the Negro of every vestige of political right."[33] His cogent observation prophetically exposed a central problem in future efforts in interracial cooperation. While many whites were concerned with extralegal threats to African Americans such as mob justice, they remained committed to the racist color line. These whites were either unable or unwilling to acknowledge the malignant nature of the racial caste system. This fact would undermine future efforts to heal the racial divide.

In the first decade of the twentieth century, most leading black Arkansans, especially John E. Bush, had adopted the ideas of Booker T. Washington, the head of the Tuskegee Institute in Alabama.[34] Washington had risen to prominence in the mid-1890s after his speech at the Atlanta Exposition in 1895. In the speech, he assured whites that blacks did not seek social equality but rather sought to improve themselves materially through hard work. He urged his fellow black Americans to "cast down your bucket where you are."[35] He set forth ideas which could guide the black community in a time of intensified hostility, a period plagued by increased disfranchisement, segregation, riots, and lynchings. Washington was the single most prominent and powerful black leader in the South during the first fifteen years of the twentieth century. His influence in white circles led many black Arkansans, who likewise had been born slaves and struggled over decades to emerge as successful entrepreneurs, to embrace his movement. Elias Camp Morris of Helena, president of the National Baptist Convention, the largest organization of African American Baptists in the world, was among the black Arkansans who responded to the "Wizard of Tuskegee."[36] In 1906, the Baptist leader addressed the crowd at the twenty-fifth anniversary celebration of the Tuskegee Institute; in return, Washington addressed the National Baptist Convention in 1907.[37] In September 1908, Morris visited Republican presidential candidate William Howard Taft on behalf of Washington, and in October 1908 he hosted a session of Washington's National Negro Business League in Helena.[38] Morris was also among dignitaries who accompanied Washington in his tour of Texas in 1911.[39] However, at the turn of the century, Washington garnered only hostility from most white Arkansans.

Jeff Davis, governor of Arkansas from 1901 to 1906, was particularly hostile towards Washington. During the visit of Pres. Theodore Roosevelt to Little Rock in 1905, Davis took the opportunity to defend the white southern acquiescence to lynching. The president had previously earned a reputation of being supportive of African Americans and critical of southern race relations; most notably, he had entertained Booker T. Washington at the White House in 1901.[40] In a speech before the president, Davis, a Democrat with the deserved reputation of being a racist and demagogue, gave a rambling speech defending those who lynched. He proclaims that "in no section of the country" is "the love of law and order more characteristic of the inhabitants." Southern white men exemplify "chivalrous manhood," while southern white women "make the best mothers on earth" and are "tender and lovely as flowers." However, with "frankness," he asserts that certain "sporadic troubles"—lynchings—are caused by "the vicious element of an inferior race amongst us." The "better class of negroes," claims the governor, "all concur in the belief that the Southern whites," who are "the real friends of the negro . . . should be unhindered in their wise and their resolute purpose to solve vexing problems . . . for the best interests of both races." The governor acknowledges that "the brutal criminal element of the race" is a minority among African Americans. But when such criminals lay "unholy hands upon our fair daughters," asserts Davis, "nature is . . . riven and shocked." When "the father, the husband, the brother" sees "the fresh marks of the brutal clutch" on "the tender flesh" and hears the "agonizing story of the frenzied victim," nothing can prevent the inevitable. In that situation, it is "vain to plead for abstract justice or talk philosophically of the orderly vindication of the law."[41] The governor assigns blame for lynching squarely on the shoulders of its victims.

Though not proclaiming mob justice a "good" thing, he nevertheless refuses to accept any responsibility to prevent such incidents.

With the specters of Jeff Davis and racial violence looming, John E. Bush hosted a national meeting of Washington's National Negro Business League in 1905. In correspondence to Washington's secretary, Emmett J. Scott, Bush assures Scott that Washington will be safe from "bodily harm." Bush writes that "the white press will not be as liberal . . . as under ordinary circumstances" and that Washington's "coming [will] not be hailed [with the] sound of trumpet." He adds, "But . . . what Negro on earth can at all time please the white man. Are we not to fight our way to manhood through death, hell and the grave?"[42] In Little Rock, Washington was snubbed by Governor Davis, who in general was hostile to anything connected to him or the Tuskegee Institute.

Davis's attitude to lynching was one of acquiescence, and it was the attitude of the majority of white Arkansans. His term as governor was marred by the worst incident of lynching in Arkansas to date. On March 21, 1904, in Saint Charles in Arkansas County, a dispute between a white man named Jim Searcy and an African American man named Griffin devolved into a fight. When a policeman tried to arrest Griffin for assault, he fled and went into hiding. For several days, a white posse, including men from several nearby towns, searched for the accused man. The situation turned desperate as the posse failed to find Griffin; its members took out their anger by killing several other black men. Conditions were so bad that, at one point, between sixty and seventy African Americans — men, women, and children — were rounded up and held in a warehouse. Whatever order the whites had maintained among themselves dissolved, and a mob assembled demanding that the warehouse be burned to the ground with all the people in it. Fortunately, cooler heads prevailed, and a large-scale massacre was prevented. Nevertheless, six men were taken from the warehouse and shot. By March 28, the violence had ended. A total of thirteen black men, including Henry and Walker Griffin, died during this "lynching bee," the worst incident of mob justice in Arkansas to date.[43] (See chapter 5 for a more detailed account of the Saint Charles event.)

In an editorial, the *Arkansas Gazette* gave an interpretation of the Saint Charles incident that echoed Governor Davis's remarks on lynching. Dubbing the events a "race war," the *Gazette* proclaimed that, when Griffin resisted arrest and the black community refused to aid in his apprehension, "the negroes threw down the gauntlet," and "the whites promptly took it up." Under such conditions, "a conflict between the two races [was] inevitable." In effect, African Americans had provoked the white community and were thereby responsible for the events in Arkansas County. The newspaper also feared for the "good name of the state." It proclaimed that the incident provided "a feast" for "the big newspapers all over the United States, especially for certain ones north of the Mason and Dixon line." Such newspapers "delight[ed] to feature something that paints Southern life in a bad way."[44]

On April 3, 1904, the *Gazette*'s concerns were confirmed as the *Chicago Tribune*, which had a record of showcasing the abysmal condition of race relations in the South, printed a detailed account of the events in Arkansas County. Headlines included "HOW THIRTEEN NEGROES WERE MURDERED" and "ARE SHOT DOWN LIKE DOGS." The article also included illustrations, and a critique of not only racial violence but also the Jim Crow system.[45] A subsequent editorial by the *Gazette* described the *Tribune*'s account as "lurid and biased." It accused the Chicago paper of "perversity of imagination" done for the "evilest purposes."[46]

The *Arkansas Gazette*'s response to the *Chicago Tribune* was representative of the strong sensitivity white southerners felt towards criticism of their racial system from sources outside of the South. White southerners claimed that these "outside agitators," who did not live with large numbers of African Americans, were ignorant. The southerners took the position that they "understood the Negro" better than their critics, and that the southern racial system, especially segregation and disfranchisement, was in the best interest of blacks. These ideas persisted among most, if not all, white southerners from 1901 to 1936. They underlay southern resistance to federal intervention, especially antilynching laws, and were expressed in the *Arkansas Gazette* and other white Arkansas newspapers. However, the *Gazette*'s position on the inevitability of lynching was one that changed over the years—it came to see lynching as something that could be prevented. This change occurred as Progressivism emerged as the dominant force in Arkansas politics.

Probably the majority of white southerners accepted lynching as an integral part of the existing racial order. But in the early twentieth century, a group of powerful and influential whites regarded lynching as barbaric and sought to bring about its end. They tended to be conservative and paternalistic on matters of race. Members of this movement in general were deeply religious, well-educated members of the Democratic Party elite who supported the Progressive movement. They desired better race relations, and when African Americans sympathetic to Booker T. Washington reached out to them, they embraced the conservative program of industrial education and racial accommodation promoted by the "Wizard of Tuskegee." Under the banner of interracial cooperation, these white and black southerners collaborated to battle poverty, inadequate education, poor sanitary conditions, and other conditions that afflicted African Americans in southern states. The movement especially sought to bring an end to lynching. However, the movement's whites remained committed to the racist order, and consequently the conservative antilynching effort was deeply flawed. Involved African Americans found their white allies' failure to realize the broader implications of the "benign" aspects of the racist system to be stifling and problematic. Nevertheless, despite the friction, their combined efforts against mob violence must be recognized as integral to the decline and later extinction of lynching in Arkansas and the South.

The election of George W. Donaghey as governor of Arkansas in 1908 marked the triumph of Progressivism in his state. It also introduced a changed official policy in race relations. Donaghey's inaugural address in January 1909 included a section on law enforcement in which he set a tone on lynching very different from that of Governor Davis. Rather than accepting mob justice as an inevitable result of an enraged populace, Donaghey believed the determined efforts of government and law officials could prevent lynchings. He proclaimed, "The laws will be enforced when an aroused public sentiment demands their enforcement." He outlined a program in which circuit judges would take responsibility in quelling public fury. However, to be successful, they required the support of the local population. The governor asserted that "however earnestly the judges may seek to do their duty, they are helpless unless sustained by the sentiment of the people demanding that the laws shall be enforced." He hoped a "growth of sentiment" supporting the "demand [that] the laws shall be enforced" would prove to "be a significant milestone along the state's pathway of both material and moral progress."[47]

The state legislature followed the governor's lead, introducing measures against both lynching and nightriding following Donaghey's speech. On April 7, 1909, the Arkansas Senate passed Senate bill 88 with a vote of twenty-one to four.[48] Proposed by H. K. Toney of Pine Bluff, the bill provided for the immediate trial of alleged perpetrators of "the crime of rape, attempt to commit rape, murder, or any other crime calculated to arouse the passions of the people." A sheriff who failed to carry out his duties could be fined up to $1,000. However, the measure included no provision to remove a sheriff derelict in his duty from office.[49] On May 12, the state House of Representatives passed the measure, fifty-four to twenty-four; the governor immediately signed it into law.[50] The bill against night-riding was likewise approved by the Arkansas General Assembly and signed into law. When the legislature adjourned in early May, it had created the machinery necessary to suppress violence that terrorized the state's African American citizens. However, in application, it proved far less effective than Donaghey and like-minded persons had hoped.

An incident that occurred while the state legislature considered the measures against mob violence confirmed Donaghey's belief that a strong stand by Arkansas officials could prevent lynching. On March 29, 1909, a group of seventy-five white men left Hampton in Calhoun County intending to lynch the Pickett brothers, who were being held in the jail in El Dorado in Union County. The men from Hampton sought to avenge the death of Charles Abbott, a local planter, and the shooting of his brother, F. M. Abbott, the county treasurer, which had occurred the previous December. Following the incident, the alleged perpetrators, brothers Henry and Wilson Pickett, African Americans, had fled to Monroe, Louisiana, only to be arrested and returned to Arkansas.[51] But news of the lynching party reached Union County before the mob, prompting local sheriff John W. Harmon, county judge A. P. McMahon, and one Judge Hayes to contact Governor Donaghey and ask for help. In turn, the governor dispatched twenty members of the state guard to El Dorado. With the troops posted around the jail, members of the mob "stood about the streets until early in the evening" before ultimately returning home; by midnight, reports indicated that the "situation was well in hand and no trouble [was] expected."[52] A few days later, the Pickett brothers were tried for the murder and shooting, resulting in a sentence of twenty-one years in the penitentiary for both men. To prevent the further possibility of mob violence, the men were taken first to Little Rock and then to Collinston, Louisiana, escorted by an official identified as Captain Crawford and three deputies.[53]

The El Dorado incident shone as an example that local and state officials could prevent lynching if they made a determined effort. But an incident that occurred only a few days after the adoption of Senate bill 88 demonstrated the weakness of the new law. Ironically, that incident occurred in Senator Toney's own district. At midnight on May 23, a "well organized mob" of white men appeared before the jail in Pine Bluff with the intention of lynching Lovett Davis, an African American accused of attacking a sixteen-year-old white girl.[54] Brandishing a pistol, Jefferson County sheriff C. M. Philpot challenged the mob at the jail entrance. Soon, circuit judge A. B. Grace arrived on the scene. The mob paused to hear the judge make "a most impassioned speech" in which he promised that a special grand jury would immediately investigate the crime. But mob members responded with cries of "Let's get him" and "Let's string him up!" In response, Grace proclaimed that the lynchers would be punished.[55] Despite the judge's appeals and threats, the mob overran Philpot, taking Lovett to be hanged. Within days of the Davis lynching, a grand jury began an inquiry into the affair. Judge Grace testified that he had "recognized many" of the perpetrators.[56] Officers of the law interviewed by the jury refused to give the names of the lynchers.[57] The *Arkansas Gazette* reported, "Sentiment here [is] in favor of the participants." The jury made no indictments, and no one was held responsible for the lynching.[58] Arkansas's antivigilante law was nullified almost as soon as the ink dried on the document.

The grand jury's failure to make indictments following the Davis lynching made clear the weakness of Progressive antilynching efforts: without cooperation of the local population, no one would be punished for his actions. This deprived the state's law of its strength. Most egregious in the Davis case was the refusal of law enforcement officers to cooperate in the identification of mob leaders. In general, sentiment among white Arkansans remained local and tribal. After all, the failure to identify mob members maintained the stability of the community, given that the lynchers probably included family and friends of the officers, as well as business associates vital to the community. Moreover, race remained the primary way the local community was structured as whites proved unwilling to sacrifice family, friends, and productive members of their community in order to satisfy a kind of justice that seemed to them to benefit only African Americans. In the end, acquiescence was preferable to preventing lynching.

The events of March–May 1909 reveal several key features of the phenomenon of lynching in Arkansas. First, lynching was a weapon used to enforce the color line. In both of these incidents, white mobs attempted to lynch black men who allegedly violated the color line. Apologists for mob justice claimed that sexual assaults by black men on white women caused lynching. However, the case of the Pickett brothers, who allegedly shot the Abbott brothers, clearly reveals that violations of the color line provoked lynchings; no white women were involved in the incident. Mob justice thus served as a means to enforce the racial order using terror and fear to intimidate would-be violators. Furthermore, whites were not united in their support for lynching. A powerful class of whites opposed the use of mob violence against African Americans, though they did not oppose elements of the racial order such as segregation or disfranchisement. Indeed, lynching could be prevented when officials took strong measures against mob justice. But weaker measures that relied upon the support of local whites, as illustrated in the lynching of Lovett Davis, were certain to fail.

The reaction of leading whites to Washington's visit to Little Rock in 1911 was very different from that of 1905. In contrast to Jeff Davis's snubbing, Washington received a hearty greeting from Governor Donaghey, who spoke before the National Negro Business League. He was also welcomed by the mayor of the Little Rock. Washington's visit concluded with a visit to the plantation of Scott Bond, who was also a former slave, at Madison in Saint Francis County, though this event was marred by a lynching across the river in Mississippi.[59] Two years later, Washington returned to Little Rock to attend the dedication of the Mosaic Templars' hall.[60]

Efforts by southern Progressives to end lynching were not limited to the passage of laws. Academics formed organizations using interracial cooperation and education as means to end mob justice once and for all. One such organization was the University Commission on Southern Race Questions. Consisting of eleven men from different southern universities, it was formed in May 1912 upon the initiative of James H. Dillard, a professor from Tulane University in New Orleans. The members selected University of Arkansas professor of economics and sociology Charles H. Brough to be its chairman. The commission sought "to foster a scientific approach to the study of the race question in the South." Specifically, its members envisioned that it "should consult with leading men in both races" and "keep informed" regarding "the relations existing between the races." It modus operandi was "to influence Southern College men to approach the subject with intelligent information and with sympathetic interest."[61] The commission's efforts to bridge the gulf between whites and African Americans included sessions held at the Hampton Institute in Richmond, Virginia, on December 18, 1913, and the Tuskegee Institute on May 6, 1915. Booker T. Washington was one of several African American speakers at these sessions.[62]

The commission outlined its platform at its meeting in December 1912. It established areas of interest, including the condition of African Americans with regards to education, economics, health, religion, and "courts of justice." Also included was the issue of lynching, for which the commission sought a way to improve conditions. Curiously, the commission stated the effect of lynching upon whites was "worse" than that on African Americans.[63]

The commission's efforts against mob justice included an open letter to the "College Men of the South." Issued on January 5, 1916, it called lynching a "crime" that "rob[bed] its victims of their constitutional rights and their lives." But lynching impacted more than those directly involved. It "lynches law and justice, and outrages all the finer human sentiments and feelings." The letter read, "Civilization rests on obedience to law, which means the substitution of reason and deliberation for impulse, instinct, and passion." It asserted that society had "a right" to expect educated men to take a leadership role against mob justice. Such men possessed a "right and duty" to exercise that leadership in "crusades against crime and mob rule." They should speak out "boldly."[64] The letter also noted that—contrary to the claims of lynching apologists who cited the rape of white women by black men as the cause of lynching—only seven of fifty-two cases of lynching in 1914 involved that crime. Of these seven men lynched, only five had been black; the other two were white.[65]

By the beginning of 1916, Brough, who had decided to run for governor of his state, had been replaced on the commission by University of Arkansas history professor David Y. Thomas. His actions included responding to a letter that had been written to a newspaper by a "committee" claiming responsibility for the lynching of an unidentified black man in Stuttgart in Arkansas County on August 9, 1916. The members of the lynching committee remained anonymous, signing their letter, "Yours for the proper and unfailing enforcement of the law." An outraged Thomas replied that "if the law was enforced now you would be on the way to the gallows." The lynchers had "lynched" the law when they "robbed" their victim of "the right of trial in open court." Claiming that he had no "obvious reasons" for withholding his name, he signed his letter, "'Yours for the proper and unfailing enforcement of the law,' including the suppression of lynching."[66]

By creating a dialogue, the commission sought to create a bridge between the southern white and black communities. However, the endeavor was deeply flawed because its members remained committed to the southern racial system minus its violent extralegal aspects. A speech by Brough before Pres. Woodrow Wilson during the December 1914 commission meeting in Washington, DC, revealed the underlying racist assumptions of white Progressives.[67] Brough exhibited an attitude that combined beneficence with the racist beliefs common to whites in his day. Notably, he claimed that the enslavement had been good for Africans because in America the "Negro" had drifted "away from the immediate, passionate, and unreflective life of the African savage." Slavery had exposed them to a social order that was "rational rather than emotional or instinctive." Antebellum slave society provided Africans with "intimate and personal contact" with whites, which allowed "the imitative absorption of white culture by the negro."[68] Brough also considered it "unquestionably true" that the "Negro" had "a harder fight to master sexual lust than the Caucasian."[69] He believed that the "sex-instinct" was a "race instinct."[70] As evidence of his contentions, he cited higher rates of venereal disease and illegitimacy among blacks than whites.[71] He also emphasized that he and other white southerners were "unalterably opposed to the miscegenation of the races" because "fundamental incompatibilities of racial temperament and tradition" doomed intimate relationships between blacks and whites. He viewed such relationships as signs of decadence, claiming that people "who do enter upon these unions" usually "belong to the criminal or anti-social elements" of both races. He claimed that the "better elements of both races" condemned such unions.[72]

As a scholar of his day, Brough relied upon pseudoscientific evidence to support his contention that blacks and whites should remain socially separate. Echoing the racist theorists of the time, he claimed that "the great contributors to culture and human progress" had always been of racially pure descent. According to the theorists, societies produced cultures that reflected the temper inherent in the members of each different race. He thus believed that "the antipathy of the South to anything savoring of social equality between the races and particularly to race miscegenation" was something "entirely rational" because it merely expressed "the group instinct of self-preservation." A social mixing of the races would lead to miscegenation, creating a race of mulattos and a corruption of the white temper; the achievements of whites, such as Christianity and democracy, would be swept away as white society crumbled. Therefore, a "control of marriage relations" was not a restriction on personal freedom but rather the surest measure to protect white civilization.[73]

Despite such comments, Brough's involvement with the commission earned him the goodwill of leading black Arkansans. For instance, during his campaign for governor, he received congratulatory notes from Elias Camp Morris and Scipio Jones, a prominent Little Rock attorney and Republican who served as the legal counsel for the Mosaic Templars.[74] Morris wrote Brough following his win in the Democratic state primary, calling his election "a triumph for clean politics, and a rebuke to mud-slinging tactics of those who attempted to array the white Democrats against you by holding up the Negro as a bug-bear."[75] Jones had long been a leading member of the state's black community. However, because he resided in Little Rock, he occupied a secondary role to John E. Bush. The death of Bush in 1916 allowed Jones to come into his own. Following the general election in November, Jones cited the newly elected governor's work "with conferences looking to the betterment of our nation and humanity." It "convince[ed] my people that in you they will have a governor who will sympathize with their struggles" and help them "to make of themselves industrious, law-abiding, worthy citizens of our State and Republic."[76]

Undoubtedly, Jones and Morris held reservations with regards to Governor Brough. Both of these men were prominent leaders of Arkansas's small but thriving black middle class. Furthermore, they were both very active in state Republican politics and were engaged in a struggle for their right to participate in the party; most of the party's white members had aggressively embraced the Lily White movement.[77] To Jones and Morris, the future governor's interest in improving at least some conditions for African Americans was preferable to the hostilities of their former white allies.

When Brough became governor in 1917, leading members of the state's African American community were optimistic. As the United States entered World War I, they sought to do their part in the war effort, heading drives for the purchase of war bonds. Large numbers of young black men volunteered for service in the armed forces. In turn, African Americans hoped that whites would finally appreciate their value as citizens of the United States and grant them greater consideration.

In terms of lynching, 1917 remained a bad year; four black men were lynched. The year 1918 was different—for eleven months, there were no lynchings. But on December 18, Willis Robinson was lynched in Newport in Jackson County for the alleged murder of a police officer. The year 1919 proved to be even worse, as five black men were lynched; that same year, Arkansas's fledgling interracial cooperation program was to face its greatest test.[78]

In late September, violence erupted near Elaine in Phillips County. Over the next several days, whites from nearby locations joined the local posse in what became known as the Elaine Massacre.[79] Although evidence suggests that whites initially met with armed resistance by African Americans, the situation quickly devolved into a case of mass murder. The number of blacks killed ranged from twenty-five to more than two hundred (though these deaths did not factor into statistics maintained by the NAACP and the Tuskegee Institute). By October 2, the white press was reporting that African Americans had intended an "insurrection" with the goal of killing large numbers of whites. In reality, African Americans, under the leadership of Robert Hill, were organizing a branch of the Progressive Farmers and Household Union of America, which had formed in April 1919 to aid tenant farmers receive just resolutions from exploitive white planters and merchants. Ultimately, Governor Brough summoned troops from Camp Pike to the scene to restore order. A large number of Africans Americans either sought safety in Helena or were rounded up and sent there; the presence of the guard prevented additional mob violence, including lynchings (though some anecdotal evidence holds that the troops also participated in the killing). The governor also went to Phillips County to see for himself what had happened.

In Helena, Governor Brough put the conservative program against extralegal racial violence into action. He appointed the Committee of Seven, comprised of leading white men of Phillips County, to investigate the matter. Predictably, it reported that what had happened was indeed an insurrection. In what was perhaps the biggest episode of legal lynching in American history, trials of dozens of black men followed. With trials and deliberations lasting only a few minutes, more seventy men were found guilty of charges ranging from nightriding and manslaughter to first-degree murder.[80] Twelve men were sentenced to death. Such circumstances led the NAACP to denounce the trials as mockeries of justice, and the organization appealed the cases. Scipio Jones was joined by Ulysses S. Bratton, one of the few white Arkansas Republicans who rejected the growing Lily White movement in the state party, to serve as attorneys. Fearing possible retribution, possibly even a lynching, those concerned kept the involvement of Jones a secret until the cases went to the US Supreme

Court. The NAACP challenge of the twelve death penalty cases was heard as two different court cases each treating six men, *Hicks v. State* and *Moore et al. v. Dempsey*. Because of the efforts of Jones, Bratton, and the NAACP, all of the men sentenced to death were free by 1925.[81] Governor Brough, meanwhile, had also sought the extradition of Robert Hill, who been arrested in Kansas. However, appeals by the NAACP's Walter White and others resulted in Gov. Henry J. Allen of Kansas refusing to comply.[82]

The NAACP's intervention in the Elaine trial cases caused their resolution to be dragged on for several years; such slow proceedings of legal cases were commonly blamed by vigilante apologists—as well as opponents of lynching—as a major source of provocation that could lead to mob violence. For instance, according to a paper in Fayetteville in northwestern Arkansas, "lynching is generally resorted to because of the uncertainty and delay of legal procedure."[83] Despite this argument, lynch mobs in reality were not in the habit of giving legal procedures a chance. Of the 164 lynchings recorded nationally by the Tuskegee Institute from 1922 to 1927, 95 featured mobs taking prisoners from jail or from officers' custody. Law enforcement officials prevented another 263 lynchings during this period.[84] Of the 29 lynchings in Arkansas in the postwar decade, 8 featured mobs taking victims from officers. In another 7 of the 29 lynchings, mobs took victims from the jail, often battering the jail doors down.[85]

White Arkansans believed that they had handled the Elaine trouble in an exemplary fashion; they claimed that there had been no lynchings. The *Arkansas Democrat* warned that a lynching "would have made the Phillips county tragedy ten times more horrible."[86] White Arkansans were proud that they had used the instruments of the local and state governments in a "lawful" manner. Indeed, they believed that the absence of any incidents of "mob justice" was a cause for rejoicing. For instance, the *Arkansas Democrat* proclaimed that "Arkansas handled a negro insurrection . . . without the killing of a negro who was not actually menacing the lives of . . . white men." The *Democrat* lauded (inaccurately) the "fact" that Phillips County had never had a lynching, and it proclaimed that the Phillips County record should become the "record of the state." Furthermore, the *Democrat* believed that "the outside world ought to be informed, frequently and forcefully, that Arkansas stands with Phillips County" on the issue of mob justice.[87]

The Elaine affair garnered national attention and caused several investigations. The one by Memphis-based black activist Ida B. Wells-Barnett resulted in the publication of a pamphlet that denounced the "white" version of events and suggested that the true story was one of racial oppression.[88] Walter White of the NAACP also investigated the Elaine affair, resulting in short exposés in the *Nation* and the NAACP publication *Crisis*.[89] According to White, his trip to Phillips County ended with his catching a train out of Helena just ahead of a lynch mob. Two members of the governor's interracial commission, David Y. Thomas and Alexander Copeland Millar, also investigated the matter. Millar's report corroborated the account of the Committee of Seven. However, taking into account the testimony of black and white witnesses, Thomas argued that what really happened was essentially unknowable.

In contrast to the bloody record of 1919, Arkansas almost passed through 1920 without a single lynching. However, in Jonesboro on December 26, a mob avenged the death of a white police office by lynching his alleged murderer. Wade "Boll Weevil" Thomas was dragged from jail and paraded down the main street; the mob ignored the pleas of the town's mayor and a local judge to not lynch him. The mob hanged Thomas beside a highway on the edge of the town.[90]

The year 1921 again proved to be a year in which the number of lynchings exploded. Its first lynching, that of Henry Lowery in January 1921, was one of the most notorious in the state's history. In Mississippi County, Christmas Day of 1920 turned into horror on a plantation near Wilson. Henry Lowery (or Lowry), a black tenant farmer, went to the house of white planter O. T. Craig, demanding a settlement on his crops. When Craig refused to hear him, shooting erupted, leaving Craig and his daughter, Mary Bell Williamson, dead and two of Craig's sons wounded. Lowery fled, eluding a huge posse that threatened to lynch him.[91] He reached El Paso, Texas, but white authorities in Mississippi County intercepted a letter from Lowery to a friend. El Paso law officials were notified, and Lowery was arrested and extradited. Escorted by two Mississippi County deputy sheriffs, he was placed on a train bound for Arkansas via New Orleans and Memphis; the roundabout route was allegedly intended to thwart would-be lynchers poised along a Texarkana–Little Rock route.[92] But these efforts proved to be futile.

In the early morning of January 26, 1921, sixteen "grim and determined-looking men" in "five or six muddy and traveled-stained automobiles" entered Sardis, Mississippi, and parked near the train the depot. There, they took Lowery off the train and returned with him to Wilson.[93] On the Arkansas side of the Mississippi River, "a great crowd [had] gathered. Every able bodied [white] man from Wilson, a crowd from Blytheville and surrounding towns" awaited "the coming of the murderer."[94] A crowd of at least five hundred demanded that Lowery should be lynched immediately.

Mob leaders chained their hapless victim to a log, placing leaves soaked with gasoline around his feet. After granting his requests that he be allowed to eat something and see his wife and children, the mob applied the torch. "Inch by inch the negro was fairly cooked to death," related *Memphis Press* reporter Ralph Roddy, who witnessed the horror. "Every few minutes fresh leaves were tossed on the funeral pyre until the blaze had passed the negro's waist. As the flames were eating away his abdomen, a member of the mob stepped forward and saturated the body with gasoline. It was then only a few minutes until the negro had been reduced to ashes." Lowery bore an agony lasting half an hour nobly; "not once did he beg for mercy," reported Roddy. However, the dying Lowery did try to end his torment, reaching for hot ashes to eat, but members of the cruel mob kicked them out of his reach.[95] Subsequent efforts by the lynchers to lay their hands on two black prisoners held in Osceola and Blytheville, men who had helped Lowery to escape, were beaten back by cold, nasty weather and a determined stand by Mississippi County sheriff Dwight H. Blackwood, backed by American Legionnaires.[96]

The Lowery lynching provoked outrage both in Arkansas and across the nation. The NAACP conducted a special investigation, resulting in an account of the lynching published in the *Nation* as well as a pamphlet distributed to congressmen during the debate over the Dyer antilynching bill in 1922.[97] In Arkansas, prominent white newspapers like the *Arkansas Gazette*, the *Arkansas Democrat*, and the *Arkansas Methodist* editorialized on the evils of mob justice.[98] Arkansas governor Thomas C. McRae called the lynching "most disgraceful and inexcusable" and urged the adoption of a strong state antilynching law that would remove negligent law officers from office.[99] David Y. Thomas wrote the US Department of Justice requesting action. However, Asst. Atty. Gen. R. P. Stewart replied that the matter was a not federal matter. Rather, the state should handle the issue.[100]

Two months after the Lowery lynching, the specter of mob justice threatened the peace in Little Rock. Around midnight, on March 12, 1921, a white woman was brutally raped in the downtown area, reportedly by two black men. As the press learned of the event, news leaked that the preceding night another white woman had been propositioned by a black man near the site of the alleged rape.[101] An extensive manhunt began, which entailed rounding up almost twenty black men and eventually arresting three. On March 17, one of these men, Emmanuel West, was "positively identified" as the perpetrator. That night, Little Rock's white community decided to avenge the crimes. A mob of at least five hundred and perhaps as many as two thousand gathered before the Little Rock jail and demanded that the men be turned over to them. But police chief Burl C. Rotenberry had taken precautions; the three men had been hidden elsewhere in the city with plans to send them to Fort Smith. When the mob first assembled, Rotenberry was absent. The jailer allowed eight men, including the rape victim's brother, to enter the jail and search for the three black men held for the crimes. While their leaders searched the jail, the mob outside grew restless. Rotenberry arrived and ordered the mob to disperse. The mob responded with shouts of "to Hell with the law." A battle ensued. Policemen fired shots, though no one was apparently injured. Then soldiers dispatched by Governor McRae finally arrived, breaking the will of the mob, which dispersed, frustrated in the attempt to carry out the justice of "Judge Lynch."[102] Afterwards, the all-white M. M. Eberts Post No. 1 of the American Legion in Little Rock selected fifty "slow-on-the-trigger" men to patrol the streets at night as auxiliary policemen, while a hundred others remained on call in case of an emergency.[103] Little Rock's black community, led by Scipio Jones, issued a letter thanking city and county officials for preventing a lynching, guaranteeing support of law and order, and promising aid in bringing the guilty to justice.[104] Finally, Chief Rotenberry attacked what he believed to be the cause of the assaults—idle vagrants. A series of "vag" raids aimed at men "accustomed to sleep all morning and loaf all afternoon and night" netted at least sixty-nine black men and thirty white men.[105]

The failed attempt to lynch Emmanuel West in March 1921 provided the *Arkansas Gazette* with an opportunity to attack mob justice. The newspaper noted that "public resentment over this crime is so deep and so general" that "every man in Little Rock [believed that] he should be . . . the avenger of the young woman who was the victim of the brutal attack. But the real avenging," the paper exclaimed, was "avenging by the law. The real punishment is not the summary snuffing out of a brute's life." The *Gazette* proclaimed, "It is for the law to seize him, solemnly condemn him, lock him in a death cell to spend [time] with his fate always before his eyes, and finally to lead him forth and put him to death."[106]

Like the Elaine affair, the trial of Emmanuel West placed the conservative faith in law and order on trial. In early April 1921, a jury that included several prominent businessmen was assembled. Also on the jury were Alexander C. Millar and Hay Watson Smith, the theologically liberal pastor of Second Presbyterian Church in Little Rock. The antilynching white press believed that the trial would demonstrate that the legal system worked. The *Arkansas Gazette* commented, "This community will vindicate itself as a community of law and order by awaiting the orderly procedure of the courts in this case . . . and by accepting as . . . justice whatever result shall finally be reached."[107] With regards to the jury, the *Arkansas Democrat* proclaimed, "Isn't that a pretty remarkable aggregation of citizens." It queried, "If you had been charged with a similar crime and you knew in your heart how utterly false the charge was . . . wouldn't you be glad to rest your case with such a jury? And if you were guilty . . . wouldn't you hate to face that sort of a group of citizens?" The *Democrat* lauded, "And the next time somebody expresses doubt about the negro race getting justice in Arkansas, show them this jury . . . and ask them if they ever saw so much care taken in the choice of jury to try a white man."[108]

The defense asserted that, during the night of the crime at ten o'clock, West was at a real estate office in North Little Rock, far from where the crime occurred; "a score or more" of black witnesses testified that he was in church by eleven o'clock. The prosecution countered that even if the witnesses' claims were true, West could have gone to downtown Little Rock between ten and eleven o'clock and committed the crime.[109] The jury debated for almost twenty-four hours, but jurors were divided on a verdict of guilty with the penalty of death. A compromise verdict of eleven to one was returned with the penalty of life imprisonment.[110] A later retrial resulted likewise in life imprisonment for West.[111] In retrospect, given the testimony as to the accused man's whereabouts and the difficult timeline for the crime, the proposition that justice was served seems dubious. Like the Elaine trials, the West trial was in effect a legal lynching; the antilynching conservatives' faith in the legal system proved to be misplaced.

By the end of 1921, Arkansas lynch mobs had murdered seven African American men. In 1922, another six black men became lynching victims. But then Arkansas witnessed a rapid decline in the number of lynching victims; in contrast to the six men lynched in 1922, only two were lynched in 1923. On January 16, 1923, a Harrison mob executed the only white Arkansan to be lynched during the postwar decade, Ed C. Gregor, who allegedly had burned a railroad bridge.[112] Then, in Union County on August 11, 1923, a Murphyville mob lynched Ed Brock, a black man who was accused of insulting a white woman.[113] No one was lynched in 1924. In 1925, only one Arkansan, a black oil field worker known as George fell victim to mob justice; he was lynched on May 29 near Camden for an alleged assault on a white woman.[114] But this decline in lynchings proved short-lived because three black men died in lynchings in 1926.

The decline in lynchings may have been due, at least in part, to the debate over the Dyer antilynching bill in Congress. The number of lynchings nationally dropped dramatically, from fifty-seven in 1922 to thirty-three in 1923 and sixteen in 1924.[115] The NAACP strongly supported the effort to pass the Dyer bill.[116]

The Dyer bill was proposed in 1918 by Leonidas Dyer of Missouri, a Republican congressman from Saint Louis. The bill would discourage lynching by imposing a fine of $10,000 on county governments in which a lynching occurred. Members of the NAACP, especially James Weldon Johnson and Walter White, pushed for the passage of the Dyer bill. Johnson had become the NAACP's first black executive secretary in December 1920. During the second session of the Sixty-Seventh Congress, the House voted 231 to 119 for the Dyer bill on January 26, 1922. The strongest opposition against the measure came from southern Democratic members of Congress; a filibuster by senators prevailed, ending the bill's chances to pass.[117] In December 1922, Republican senators decided to postpone discussion of the bill, effectively killing it.[118]

Arkansas's congressmen joined in the southern effort to prevent the passage of the Dyer bill. Two Arkansans serving in the House of Representatives, John M. Tillman of Fayetteville and Osceola resident William J. Driver, made particularly strong assaults on the Dyer bill. In addition, Arkansas's senators also contributed to the effort against the Dyer bill. Before the Ohio Bar Association, senator Joseph T. Robinson argued that additional laws to prevent lynching were unnecessary because other laws addressed the problem.[119] His counterpart, Thaddeus Caraway, was one of several southern senators who actively participated in the filibuster.[120]

Tillman represented the state's Third Congressional District and was author of Arkansas's Separate Coach Law of 1891. Speaking before the House of Representatives on January 10, 1922, he characterized the Dyer bill as "a measure . . . radical, revolutionary, and sinister . . . in its scope and purpose." He asserted that the bill threatened to "impair, if not destroy . . .

local self-government and State sovereignty" and that its fine of $10,000 "would mean . . . immediate bankruptcy . . . to [their] taxpayers."[121] He further claimed that the Dyer bill was the product of a historical enmity for the solid Democratic South held by the Republican Party; the measure "precipitate[d] sectional bitterness and strife." Tillman cited Reconstruction, asserting that the radical Republicans disfranchised the "intelligent southern white man" and gave the "ignorant southern negro" the right to vote. The Republican Party was "blinded by party passion and obsessed by a pitiless lust for punishing" the South.[122] The Arkansas congressman also evoked the specter of the rape of white women by black men. He claimed that he did not seek to justify lynching and indeed went on record as "opposed to the abominable cult of mob murder," which he considered "barbarous" and "indefensible." Still, the fact remained, claimed Tillman, that "girls and women in many sections of the South where criminal Negroes live [were] in constant danger" of being raped, a "fate" he considered "a thousand times worse than death."[123]

Representing Arkansas's First Congressional District, Driver spoke before the House on January 25, 1922. In substance, his argument differed little from that of Tillman. Driver considered the Dyer bill "unconstitutional and unwarranted by the facts, dangerous in precedent," and almost certainly "inimical to the peace and tranquility of our people."[124] Like the Congressman from Fayetteville, Driver emphasized the threat that marauding blacks allegedly posed to the white community; "the inability to distinguish the one brute out of the mass before his savage proclivities [were] viciously asserted" remained a "danger confronting every community in which the Negro lives to-day."[125] He considered the antilynching bill "not a question of civil rights" but rather "one exclusively of political expediency." He charged that Republicans had decided to "agitate this racial question" because of the influence of northern "Negro organizations" and "Negro-phile supporters" who held "unyielding animosity for and prejudice against" the South.[126] The actions of these Republicans who supported the Dyer bill, asserted Driver, posed "a threat to the home of every man residing in a community with a Negro population."[127]

On November 29, 1922, Sen. Thaddeus Caraway attributed the Dyer bill to particularly sinister motives. He charged that a "society known as the society for the protection of the rights of colored people" had authored the bill with "one idea in view:" "to make rape permissible, and to allow the guilty to go unpunished if that rape should be committed by a negro on a white woman in the South." The bill allowed "a negro to believe that the strong arm of the Federal Government" would "thrust down into the Southern States in order to protect him and save him from punishment, however infamous his crime might be."[128] (For more on the Arkansas congressional delegation's efforts to thwart antilynching legislation, see chapter 10.)

Arkansas newspapers likewise joined the assault on the Dyer bill. The *Arkansas Gazette* in particular waged a long editorial campaign against the measure.[129] It warned that the Dyer bill would "arous[e] animosities that may increase lynching."[130] The *Gazette* considered the measure an assault on the South; it would create "sectional enmity," making it difficult for "those enlightened forces" that were "earnestly" trying to end "this barbarous practice."[131] The *Gazette* viewed the bill as hypocritical, citing other forms of violence in places like East Saint Louis, Chicago, and Washington, DC. In these places, "local authorities" had not "stopped bomb throwing, bank robbery, pay roll robbery and murder" which claimed many more lives than lynching did in the South. But northern representatives proposed no federal bills to end these problems.[132] The *Gazette* noted that Kansas had an anti-mob law similar to the one proposed in the Dyer bill; but sentiment was "growing throughout Kansas that no city is safe" from the excessive fines imposed by the law.[133] Rather than federal intervention via an act of Congress, the *Gazette* proposed an alternative way to prevent mob justice: lynching could "be eradicated only by the creation of a public sentiment"—respect for law and order—that would "not tolerate it." It argued that "quick and sure punishment for crime is the best way" to create that sentiment. And it was up to the "people of the South," not northern Congressmen, to generate that sentiment and to "stop this atrocious crime."[134]

As pointed out by one historian, southern opposition to the Dyer antilynching bill was consistent with the long tradition of southern states' rights ideology, which translated into opposition to federal interference in state racial policy.[135] By opposing the bill, white Arkansans assured the continued state control of race relations. This, in turn, preserved white supremacy in their state.

In the early 1920s, a battle over lynching continued in Arkansas's white newspapers.[136] There, the issue became not whether lynchings should occur—even "Judge Lynch's" apologists admitted that lynchings were "bad"—but what should be done to prevent them. Arkansas's most stalwart defender of lynchers during the 1920s was the *Pine Bluff Daily Graphic*. In response to antilynching commentary in the wake of several lynchings in March 1921, the *Daily Graphic* claimed that emphasis was misplaced. The discussion featured "too much about the terrible crime of lynching and . . . too little about the terrible crimes which provoke lynchings." While lynching was "a terrible crime," asserted the *Daily Graphic*, "the crime which provokes lynching was much more terrible." Indeed, lynching was a form of upholding honor, it implied, as "the white man will not tolerate any desecration of his women."[137] In effect, the *Daily Graphic* argued that lynchings occurred because black men raped white women. Lynchings would stop only when black men were controlled, when blacks remained in their correct place.[138]

The white opponents of lynching appealed to the consciences of good citizens and stressed the need for law and order. In the wake of the Omaha, Nebraska, riot in late September 1919, *Arkansas Methodist* editor Alexander C. Millar forcefully put forth the law-and-order position. Writing in the midst of the Red Scare, the *Methodist* asserted that the "madmen" who composed the Omaha mob were "the most dangerous of all criminals." Their actions were "subversive of law and liberty." In contrast to the *Daily Graphic*, which proclaimed in March 1921 that the rape of a white woman by a black man was worse than a lynching, the *Methodist* asserted that "lynching and burning and defiance of officers are worse" crimes. It considered "such orgies" a threat to democracy itself because they "destroy respect for the government which cannot prevent them." The *Methodist* asserted, "Those who love democracy and believe in it must try to make it safe for the world." Warning that "unbridled democracy" was "rapidly destroying itself," it called for restraint: "It is time for all the people to consider whether democracy means license or liberty."[139]

In contrast to the *Daily Graphic*, the law-and-order papers preferred to define the lynching problem not as one of race but rather one of values. They applauded successful antilynching efforts and decried the shame of unprevented lynchings. Of these papers, the *Arkansas Gazette* made the greatest efforts to discourage lynchings, seldom failing to give lynchings front-page coverage, editorializing against mob justice, and regularly publishing the Tuskegee Institute's annual lynching statistics.[140] The *Gazette* considered lynching to be "an atrocious and cowardly crime" which "ha[d] been proven to be a crime breeder instead of a crime deterrent." Moreover, lynching "disgrace[d] the entire country."[141]

Following the John Carter lynching, both the *Arkansas Gazette* and *Arkansas Democrat* called for the punishment of responsible city and county officials.[142] These papers were joined by the Ministerial Alliance of Little Rock and North Little Rock, the local chapter of the American Red Cross, and several businesses and community organizations in their cries to punish those responsible.[143] Judge Abner McGehee appointed a grand jury to investigate the matter. But after more than thirty witnesses had been interviewed, the jury remained unwilling to take action against city or county officials.[144] Those who could have prevented or curtailed the riot went unpunished.

By 1919, the interracial cooperation movement had reached maturity as interested parties created a committee with representatives from the majority of southern states. This Committee on After-War Cooperation became the Commission on Interracial Cooperation, which would remain the primary body by which both white conservatives and prominent black leaders engaged in a dialogue on matters of concern. John Hugh Reynolds of Hendrix College was appointed Arkansas's national representative.[145] In 1920, he was joined by a second white man, John L. Hunter of Central YMCA in Little Rock, and an African American, S. L. Green of Shorter College, who served as the Arkansas chapter's state secretary.[146] These men organized a state committee that, by November 1920, included twenty-two white members and twenty-one black members. African American members represented more than ten counties. Among these representatives were *Blue Book* contributors Joseph Albert Booker and J. M. Cox; Methodist bishop J. M. Connor; Elias Camp Morris of Helena; and wealthy planter Scott Bond from Madison. Among the whites was Governor Brough, who served as an "ex-officio" member.[147]

In addition to the national commission and its state committees, Arkansans in 1919 took the initiative to form two other interracial cooperation committees. The first was the Governor's Commission, appointed by Brough. It was composed of eight white and eight African American members. Its white members included Reynolds, while its black members included Connor, Booker, Cox, Green, Morris, and Bond. In addition to the Governor's Commission, the State Teacher's Association established a committee based on a model put forth by the Southern Sociological Congress. It consisted of seven white members, including David Y. Thomas and Alexander C. Millar.[148] The interracial cooperation movement was met with great enthusiasm in Arkansas. In June 1920, S. L. Green reported that a congress called by the governor was attended by eight hundred people, though only two hundred invitations had been issued.[149]

Arkansas's interracial committees were created during a time of crisis in race relations in the state. The horrible violence and injustice of the Elaine trials had just occurred. However, also on the minds of black Arkansans were the shenanigans of white Republicans who were attempting to create a "Lily White" state party. African Americans were further disillusioned following World War I when, despite their loyal service as both civilians and members of the military, race relations remained essentially unchanged. In December 1919, Alexander C. Millar reported that "nearly all of the negro [newspaper] editors" were "writing things that [were] calculated to stir their readers to anger and revenge." Millar noted that, at a recent event in Hot Springs, a black speaker spoke "about freedom," which "greatly stirred" the crowd. In his remarks, the white Methodist appealed to "duty and Christian discipleship" but "got no response" from the audience.[150] Similarly, in 1920, John Hugh Reynolds commented that "the situation in Arkansas is very trying." He found that black Arkansans "really feel an injustice has been done them."[151]

African Americans used the interracial meetings as means to express their discontent. In November 1919, David Y. Thomas informed Reynolds that African Americans expressed concerns beyond those associated with lynching, education, and economics, the topics addressed by the university commission. They asserted, with regards to Jim Crow laws, that "whites do not observe the law, but encroach on the space allotted to" African Americans. Also, they complained about the injustice of disfranchisement and the "inability to get justice in the courts." Finally, they also brought up the "insecurity of negro women from white rakes."[152] In 1921, Thomas S. Staples of Hendrix College reported that African American representatives at the women's interracial conference in Memphis made similar assertions about disfranchisement and the status of black women. They also spoke out against the "attitude of the white press," the "inadequacy of protection for negro home life," the lack of "equality of opportunity to earn equal wages," and "race purity and integrity." With regard to segregation, they proclaimed that it was "coupled by neglect" and that "the decent negro traveling public" received "inadequate care." Finally, they asserted that white employers failed "to provide [a] proper environment" for domestic servants.[153] While African Americans used the meetings of the interracial committees to speak out, such outspokenness was not always welcomed. For instance, in December 1919, Alexander C. Millar reported that Elias Camp Morris had spoken against Jim Crow laws. The *Arkansas Methodist* editor claimed that Morris had "somewhat discredited himself [with whites] by clamoring for the repeal of [the] separate coach law."[154]

While some white members of the interracial committees were uncomfortable with the increased assertiveness of African Americans, the national commission exhibited more tolerance to the expression of legitimate grievances. For instance, Isaac Fisher, who had managed to find secure employment at Fisk University in Nashville, Tennessee, after leaving Branch Normal College in Pine Bluff, coedited an official commission publication in which he repeated the assertions of injustice against African Americans. He noted that laws were "made without due reference to the Negro's welfare" and that they were "enforced without due reference" to their welfare or "racial pride." Segregation and other "Southern customs" were "unnecessarily and needlessly humiliating."[155] Indeed, Fisher claimed, African Americans had "no redress, no white people who seemed to understand the feelings of the colored people, or who are willing to hear him state his case." Nevertheless, he assured other African Americans that the interracial committees provided hope that the situation would change. With regard to lynching, he asserted that "no Negro's life is safe from the mob." However, through cooperation between the races, county interracial committees could aid in the suppression of mob justice. He asserted that "wherever there is reason to suspect that a mob is likely," black committee members should alert white members, who in turn would see that law enforcement officials dispersed or otherwise foiled the mob.[156] An analysis of the decline of lynching by the national commission in the mid-1930s suggested the success of Fisher's plan. It noted that three factors interacted to prevent acts of mob justice. They were the determined actions of local law officials, the efforts of local white leadership, and the appeals of local African Americans for protection against lynchers.[157]

While publications of the Commission on Interracial Cooperation provided examples of Fisher's plan in action, they did not include examples of it in Arkansas. Nevertheless, the plan explained how local interracial committees could thwart mob justice—and probably accounted for some prevented lynchings. Perhaps the most important activity of the interracial committees was to educate the public. In 1920 or 1921, "Law and Order Day" was instituted in Arkansas. The purpose of the day was to stress "respect for law and the duty of officers." The goal was to observe the day

. in every white and black church, Sunday school, college, and high school in Arkansas.[158]

The Commission on Interracial Cooperation did not limit its members to men. It also included an outspoken women's auxiliary branch. Its organizational meeting occurred in Memphis in 1920 and was attended by four black women, including Booker T. Washington's widow, Margaret. Its Arkansas chapter commented that "the lack of respect and protection of negro womanhood" was one of the "underlying causes" of lynching and other racial problems. It asserted that "an effort to emphasize a single standard was needed for both men and women that racial integrity may be assured, not to one race, but to both."[159] In 1930–1931, the commission's longtime director of women's work, Jessie Daniel Ames, founded the Association of Southern Women for the Prevention of Lynching (ASWPL). The organization's purpose was to educate the public about the problem of lynching, with a special focus on refuting the argument that mob violence was a means of preserving the honor of southern women. An Arkansas chapter was formed in 1931. (See chapter 9 for more information.) In 1933, it reported that, because of ASWPL's campaign, Arkansas State Teachers College had instituted a "carefully planned program of race relations education" with eight hundred students involved.[160] Then, in correspondence with Ames in 1936, Arkansas ASWPL member Erle Chambers discussed strategies of disseminating flyers. She suggested that they could be inserted into library books and that the parent-teacher association should also circulate them. She also suggested that "each Federation group" could have "one program on the subject."[161]

The Arkansas chapter of the ASWPL did not restrict itself to educational efforts. In February 1931, it put forth a petition claiming that a cause of lynchings was "the failure of courts and officers of the law to deal adequately with crime," which in turn had "produced a growth of lawlessness." The petition called for women's groups to contact the Arkansas Bar Association and encourage its members to revise "the criminal code of our state so as to abolish delays in criminal trials on account of technicalities."[162] Ironically, the ASWPL's pronouncement was essentially identical to the claim of lynching apologists that lynchings occurred because of the slow justice system. The reality was that lynch mobs seldom allowed the justice system to act. Typically, their victims were seized either before or immediately after officers gained custody of alleged perpetrators of crimes.

Table 6.1. Lynchings and lynchings prevented, 1915–34

Year	Lynchings	Lynchings prevented	Ratio of lynchings to lynchings prevented
1915	67	25	2.68
1916	54	25	2.16
1917	38	23	1.65
1918	64	19	3.37
1919	83	43	1.93
1920	61	84	0.72
1921	64	108	0.59
1922	57	114	0.55
1923	35	56	0.59
1924	16	61	0.26
1925	17	53	0.32
1926	30	40	0.75
1927	16	68	0.24
1928	11	40	0.28
1929	10	34	0.29
1930	21	60	0.35
1931	13	91	0.14
1932	8	43	0.19
1933	28	48	0.58
1934	15	74	0.20

Source: Tuskegee Institute, *Negro Year Book, 1937–1938*

The actions of officers proved to be the most direct cause of the decline of lynchings witnessed in the nation and Arkansas in the 1920s. Significantly, the shift in the ratio of actual lynchings to those prevented occurred more than a year before the Dyer bill debate, in 1919–1920. Before 1920, lynchings per year outnumbered lynchings prevented. But after 1920, lynchings prevented outnumbered successful lynchings annually (see table 6.1).[163]

What motivated officers to take stronger stands against lynching remains unclear, though several factors possibly played a role. One statistician

suggests that pressures outside the South influenced southern leaders—
desiring economic development and investment in their region—to oppose
lynching. Specifically, the negative press coverage in reaction to incidents
of mob justice caused southern leaders to pressure local officials to stop
lynchings.[164] Contemporaries such as NAACP officers Walter White and
James Weldon Johnson agreed with this assessment, claiming their organization's antilynching crusade, especially the Dyer antilynching bill, caused
a decline in lynching.[165]

However, as this article shows, there was very strong antilynching sentiment among leading racially conservative white southerners long before
the Dyer bill was even considered and long before black migration from
the South had created a shortage of labor. This sentiment dated back to
when the NAACP had just been formed, and it existed more than twenty
years before the ASWPL existed. These whites, generally Democrats and
Progressives, had the most direct control over law enforcement officials,
and this chapter provides several examples of the exertion of this control.
These whites were vested in the racial caste system. They subscribed to the
notion of the New South, and as racial violence was bound to alienate northern investors, it needed to be suppressed. These whites also tended to be
more concerned about how lynching affected "white civilization" than how
it affected the black community. But this does not negate the fact that they
recognized the humanitarian nature of the crisis facing African Americans.
Issues central to the interracial cooperation movement included concerns
about how disease, poverty, unclean living conditions, and poor education
afflicted many African Americans. This humanitarianism stemmed to a
large extent from the fact that both black and white southerners involved
in the interracial cooperation movement were almost all devout Christians.
Notably, George Donaghey was known for his commitment as a Methodist
layman, and Charles Brough was a dedicated Baptist who, after his term as
governor, became president of Central Baptist College in Conway. Their
religious commitments allowed these whites to bridge the racial divide with
African Americans who were also devout Christians. The southern interracial cooperation movement was, in a real sense, a Christian endeavor. The
Christian aspect of the movement becomes clear when one examines both
the black and white individuals involved, as well as organizations supporting the movement, the rhetoric used, and literary texts. Given the commitment of white conservatives to the racial caste system and the negative
impact of racial violence on business concerns, it is easy to regard their

motives in a cynical fashion. However, to do so would be to ignore the importance of the religiously motivated humanitarianism that pervaded the interracial cooperation movement.

In the end, it is superfluous to ask whether the actions of civil rights activists or those of southerners involved in the interracial cooperation movement were more important in bringing about an end to lynching in Arkansas and the South. The impact on lynching of the efforts by these groups is unmeasurable. But if the efforts of conservative southern whites played an important role in ending lynching, the basic racist assumptions of these whites prevented other important reforms. Notably, they considered segregation, limited African American participation in politics, and the existing justice system to be proper solutions to the "race problem." They did not acknowledge problems such as exploitative planters or legal lynchings. They discouraged higher education and supported only industrial education for African Americans. They believed that whites constituted the superior race and that their special mission was to "civilize" a race of "children." Though their error seems to have been less motivated by animosity than ignorance and arrogance, it nevertheless had dire consequences for African Americans. Moreover, these whites refused to accept that their "benign" solutions to racial problems were just as repressive to African Americans as the extralegal racial violence they so abhorred.

Despite the combined efforts of white and black southerners, as well as activists living outside the South, even in the late 1930s mob violence had not been completely eradicated. Although the lynching of Willie Kees in 1936 is considered to be Arkansas's last lynching, the NAACP reported that Walter Frasier (or Frazier), an African American, had been lynched in February 1939. He was "alleged to have molested a white couple at Eldorado [*sic*]." The incident did not appear in Tuskegee Institute reports, and some sources hold that he was shot in the course of an attempted robbery (see chapter 9).[166]

Events in Pine Bluff in May 1939 revealed that the lynching spirit was still strong.[167] Sylvester Williams, an African American, was arrested for the "murder-assault" of a nineteen-year-old white woman, Irene Taylor. On two occasions, May 5 and May 19, mobs assembled before the Jefferson County jail. On the first occasion, the mob dispersed following a tour of the jail revealing that Williams was not present; actually, he was well hidden by Sheriff Garland Brewer. On the second occasion, a mob of around three hundred led by Allen Taylor, the deceased girl's brother, was met by officers armed with automatic rifles, submachine guns, and tear gas bombs. Sheriff Brewer fired two shots in the air, warning the mob that any attempt to storm the jail would result in "about fifty" of the lynchers being killed. The standoff ended with two mob members touring the jail, again not finding Williams.

In preparation for Williams's trial, Brewer and county judge M. V. Bailey petitioned Gov. Carl E. Bailey to have Arkansas National Guard troops present. As a result, a unit of three officers and sixty men was mobilized in Dardanelle and sent to Pine Bluff; they were joined by thirty more Jefferson County guardsmen. The trial itself was largely a sham. Upon "ascertaining certain facts," court-appointed defense attorneys J. M. Shaw and Arnold Fink advised their client to plead guilty. In a statement, Shaw proclaimed that they considered it "their duty . . . to see that the defendant received a fair trial." However, "the defense called no witnesses," nor did it "attempt to question the witnesses called by the state." The jury condemned Williams to death in the electric chair.[168] This, arguably, represents the new state of "legal lynching." After all, the disavowal of mob violence was not a rejection of the doctrine of white supremacy; as Michael J. Pfeifer argues, white Americans, with the decline of lynching, "fashioned instead a legal order that eschewed the social chaos and unseemliness of lynching but nonetheless perpetuated its symbolic functions of ritualistic lethal retribution and the enactment of white supremacy in the punishment of crime."[169]

In May 1940, Jessie Daniel Ames sent packets of antilynching literature to the sheriffs of Arkansas. In her letter she assured the recipients that the ASWPL did "not support anti-lynching legislation." Rather, it "carr[ied] on a program of education." She noted that the state had suffered no lynchings in the previous twelve months and proclaimed that the state's sheriffs were "to be especially commended for their efforts to prevent mob violence, which have brought such splendid results."[170]

Before John Carter

Lynching and Mob Violence
in Pulaski County, 1882–1906

The 1927 lynching of John Carter (see chapter 8) exhibited a brutality that shocks the conscience even today, featuring a full-scale riot in the heart of Little Rock's black commercial and cultural district, with a white mob in the thousands robbing a local church of its pews to serve as fuel for the fire upon which Carter's body was ceremoniously burned.[1] In fact, the lynching of Carter remains a staple of local black historical consciousness, a touchstone for oral history that could not be erased even by the much more nationally prominent conflict surrounding the desegregation of Central High School some thirty years later.[2] However, the prominent place of the 1927 lynching in both local culture and historical studies on the phenomenon of lynching—especially historian Amy Louise Wood's notable work on "spectacle lynching"[3]—has obscured the broader history of mob violence in Arkansas's capital city and the county in which it is located. In his 1999 dissertation on racial violence in Arkansas, historian Richard Buckelew enumerated three separate cases of lynching in Pulaski County preceding that of John Carter, claiming a total of six victims.[4] One of these cases was the 1892 lynching of Henry James, which mirrors the 1927 case by dint of its ostensible cause lying in the assault of a young white girl, while the Argenta Race Riot of 1906 sprawled across several days and entailed numerous ambushes and cases of arson. However, other sources have documented more lynchings in Arkansas's central county, making for a higher death toll.[5]

While later lynching reports often dominated headlines, the first of these cases, which occurred in the Parker community south of Little Rock, shows up at the very bottom of the Local Paragraphs column on the fourth page of the *Arkansas Gazette* of May 30, 1882. In fact, the whole report is so brief that it can be quoted here in full:

> While sweeping out Parker's school house in Union township last Saturday evening, Miss Nancie Carr was indecently attacked by a colored youth named Jim Sanders. She screamed, and her cries were heard by Wm. Pinson, who rushed into the building and picking up Sanders' double-barreled shot-gun, fired at the latter while he was escaping. Sanders was arrested Sunday, and sent back for identification. That night the guard in charge of him was overpowered, and enough buckshot to kill a score of men were lodged in his body. The coroner went down to hold an inquest yesterday, but had not returned late last night. Comments on the case are properly reserved until the evidence is known.[6]

This brief account leaves a lot unsaid, especially with its passive construction, which avoids identifying in any way the identity of the person or persons who put so much buckshot into Sanders's body. However, national reports did fill in the blanks somewhat. For instance, the *Ottawa Free Trader*, published in Illinois, reported that Sanders was not held in a jail but was rather "placed in a frame building, preparatory to the preliminary examination," while the *Rock Island Argus*, also of Illinois, holds that Sanders was interned in a jail. According to the Ottawa newspaper, Sanders was killed by a mob composed entirely of masked men. It also reported: "The matter has created intense feeling in the neighborhood, and when the inquest was held next day threats were made of further trouble. A great many colored people live in the vicinity, nearly all of whom are very bitter regarding the shooting of Sanders."[7] Apparently, knowledge of this understandable bitterness created some trepidation on the part of local whites, for the *Gazette* reported, a week later, that "white people, at and near Wrightsville and Sweet Home, heard that the colored people were arming to slaughter them, and actually took their children and wives to the woods and secreted them." However, black residents had also heard rumors that a number of their own had been "seized and murdered" while at worship in a church. The county sheriff, in response to these rumors, sent Frank

Botsford, the police chief of Little Rock, down to investigate. Botsford's conclusion was that no one had any intention for disorder: "Some fool or knave said just enough to create a scare, and that is all."[8]

The *Gazette* reported on June 9 that the "prisoners from Union township charged with complicity in the killing of young Sanders" had been discharged the previous day on account of "no discriminatory evidence being found against them."[9] Apparently, rumors about the complicity of sheriff W. S. Oliver had been circulating, for the *Little Rock Republican* printed—and the *Arkansas Gazette* republished and endorsed—a column recounting an official investigation into reports that the sheriff had handed Sanders over to the mob. According to this report, Oliver never had actual custody of Sanders, a fact that might substantiate accounts that Sanders was never placed formally in a jail.[10]

Very little is known about the next victim of lynching in Pulaski County. A man known only as Smith was murdered on August 23, 1882. Nothing was reported of the event in the *Arkansas Gazette*, and most reports circulated nationally fall along the lines of this bare-bones report published in the *Highland Weekly News* of Highland County, Ohio: "Smith, who assaulted a white lady near Little Rock, Arkansas, was lynched by a disguised party who shot him to death."[11] The *National Republican* of Washington, DC, managed to add a little more information, specifically describing Smith as "colored" and his crime as an attempt "to outrage a white lady."[12]

The next of these cases of mob violence was also reported in brief nationally, though not in the *Arkansas Gazette*. On Saturday, December 14, 1889, Henry Wright, described as a "well-to-do farmer," was on his way to Fletcher's store in Big Maumelle when he was waylaid by four highwaymen, who pulled pistols on him and demanded his money. Not believing that he was without cash, the robbers beat Wright. The unfortunate farmer was found the following morning by neighbors who had gone in search of him, and, "although fatally injured, [Wright] rallied sufficiently to describe his attackers." The report ended succinctly: "A vigilance committee was at once organized, and the murderers were caught and lynched."[13] Wright's attackers are never identified by name or even race, though the assumption is that they were white, given that it would have been noted otherwise.

Historian W. Fitzhugh Brundage divides lynch mobs into four different categories depending upon the size, organization, and motivation of the mob, as well as their use of ritual:

Small mobs, numbering fewer than fifty participants, may be separated into two types. They were either terrorist mobs that made no pretense of upholding the law or private mobs that exacted vengeance for a wide variety of alleged offenses. Posses, the third type, which ranged in size from a few to hundreds of participants, often overstepped their quasi-legal function and were themselves responsible for mob violence. Finally, mass mobs, numbering from more than fifty to hundreds and even thousands of members, punished alleged criminals with extraordinary ferocity and, on occasion, great ceremony.[14]

So far, then, the lynchings that occurred in Pulaski County fall under Brundage's category of the small, private mob. At least, the reports in circulation give little indication that a large number of people were present at the scene of each murder. Moreover, these were not terrorist mobs (often called nightriders or whitecappers) but were ostensibly motivated by the punishment of very specific crimes. However, the next incident of lynching marked the emergence of mass mob violence in Pulaski County.

"In the South it is the unwritten law that the man who commits the most atrocious of crimes of which a woman can be made the victim will die. It was in obedience to this inexorable law that the monster Henry James, the negro who so fiendishly assaulted little Maggie Doxey, was hanged to a telephone pole early Saturday morning by an infuriated mob, and riddled with bullets." So opined the *Arkansas Gazette* on May 15, 1892, regarding the lynching of Henry James the previous day in Little Rock. Acknowledging that the courts were perfectly capable of dealing with the crime in question and that James's fate was indeed certain—"the gallows would have claimed and found its own"—the editorial writer insisted that there were times "when human passion becomes a law unto itself," when a "higher law . . . discards all legal forms."[15] As Brundage notes, "a degree of community approval and complicity, whether expressed in popular acclaim for the mob's actions or in the failure of law enforcement either to prevent lynching or to prosecute lynchers, was present in most lynchings."[16] The *Gazette*'s open endorsement of mob violence signifies perhaps the highest level of community support for the murder.

Henry James, described in various accounts as a twenty-two-year-old "mulatto," was lynched for the reported crime of raping five-year-old Maggie Doxey on Tuesday, May 10, 1892. Doxey was the adopted daughter of Charles R. Johnson, a former night clerk at the Capital Hotel, and his wife, who lived at the corner of Nineteenth and Gaines Streets with Mrs. Johnson's mother, Mrs. Pennington. James later told police that he originally hailed from Augusta, Missouri, and had been working as a waiter in a Hot Springs hotel (or, according to a later report, Gleason's Hotel in Little Rock) for several months but had been employed by the Johnsons as a "general utility man" for about two weeks prior to the incident. According to the *Gazette*, Charles Johnson had been away in Hot Springs on business for a few weeks, and his wife joined him there on Sunday, May 8. While Mrs. Pennington was in the front room of the house, preoccupied with writing a letter that Tuesday morning around eight o'clock, Henry James and Maggie Doxey were in the kitchen. There, he reportedly raped her, muffling her to avoid attracting attention and then threatening her with death in order to keep her quiet until he could flee the scene. Mrs. Pennington, later learning of what happened, sent a telegraph to Mrs. Johnson, who returned by the afternoon train and subsequently alerted mayor Henry Lewis Fletcher, who put detectives on the case. Meanwhile, Dr. G. M. D. Cantrell was called in to examine the young girl and found her injuries to be serious. James eluded capture until the detectives employed a ruse, letting it be known abroad that if James would but return to the Johnson household, the family would re-employ him. The ruse worked, and James returned to the Johnson home at around eight o'clock in the morning on May 13, where he was seized by detective Dave Adams and officer Mike Eagan and immediately conveyed to jail. The mayor, apparently fearing mob action against James, and not wanting his own jail torn down, ordered the prisoner's transfer to the county jail. But at least the mayor was still in town. The *Gazette* reporter managed to interview deputy sheriff Jesse Heard after he had just locked up James in a secure cell on the second floor of the jail, and the deputy acknowledged that the sheriff, Anderson Mills, and the chief deputy sheriff, Horace Booker, were both absent, leaving him in charge of a situation rapidly spiraling out of control — in fact, the deputy had just received word that "a mob of a thousand men would attempt to lynch James tonight."[17]

The *Gazette* published two articles on the lynching of James on May 14, the second of which picks up after James had been murdered, and which was written in a decidedly dramatic fashion, opening with: "Midnight! It is the hour when graveyards yawn, and hell breathes contagion to the world. It was about the hour when Henry James' guilty soul took its flight from his polluted body." As the story goes, a mob did arrive at the county jail and managed to discover that James was nowhere inside (having been transferred in secret to the state penitentiary at nine o'clock by Deputy Heard). Disappointed members of the mob therefore congregated in front of the Allis building to discuss options. The majority returned quietly to their homes, while some few wandered over to the state penitentiary to see if they could discover whether James was concealed there. Col. S. M. Apperson, described as "Secretary and Manager of the lesees," ordered the penitentiary guards to retire to their own rooms. Apperson met the crowd around eleven o'clock the night of May 13. The mob had first accosted the driver of a hack, believing it likely that the driver had just transferred James over. According to the *Gazette*, "The spokesman of the crowd said that when Charlie Martin read the statement of the little girl who had been so brutally treated there was not a dry eye in the crowd, and they had resolved on getting their man." Apperson acknowledged that James was present and stated that James would remain there until eight o'clock the following morning, at which point he would be handed back to the sheriff. "At this," the story continues, "the crowd appointed a committee to wait until this morning and see that their man was not spirited away. But about the time the committee had been decided upon, the word had been sent back to town that the fiend had been located at the Penitentiary had begun to work and reinforcements were arriving by the dozen."

As the mob grew, various people took turns giving speeches, no doubt riling up the mass of folk for what would come. Apperson refused, again and again, to hand his prisoner over and reminded the mob that breaking into the penitentiary would constitute a crime, but he appeared to throw a bone their way when he reminded them that the prisoner was sched-uled to be handed over to the sheriff in the morning—"and then they could get him." A proposal was raised among the mob to go to the sheriff directly (perhaps they knew where he was) and warn him that the peni-tentiary was in danger of being attacked, but the mob quickly took up the cry of "Break down the gates!" A man named Pangburn, "a physical giant, who was formerly on the police force," battered at the gates with a sledge-hammer, bringing them down with a few blows at approximately a quarter past midnight. The mob rushed in, and a committee of six went in search of the condemned man, including three who had volunteered to identify James. However, the excitement was contagious, and the mob swarmed into the jail. It took them thirty minutes to break into the cell house, but they found Henry James in the very first cell. After he was dragged outside, some of the mob began yelling for rope, but an apparent leader cried out: "No rope yet! We want to try and convict him. We want to be sure."[18] As Amy Louise Wood observes, lynchings often followed the pattern of public executions, which often included public admission of the crime committed by the condemned: "These testimonials ensured that the condemned understood his crime and punishment, an understanding that was necessary to ratify the execution as divinely sanctioned. . . . Confessions lent lynchings the trappings of lawful punishment and served to justify the mob's violence as rightful and warranted, despite that confessions were forced and were often obtained after the lynching was underway and not likely to be aborted."[19]

Apparently in the interests of providing a quasi-judicial ritual, the mob marched Henry James through the streets of Little Rock and over to the home of his victim. However, what happened fell far short of that. Instead, Charles Johnson, by this point now in Little Rock, having been alerted by couriers that the mob was bringing James over to his residence, met the mass of people outside and, upon spying his former handyman, cried out: "That is the man!" The mob decided that this was enough and determined to string up James, though debate ensued as to the best place for such a deed: "But after consultation, it was decided to take the culprit to the corner of Main and Markham streets, or to the State House yard and there mete out the swift and terrible punishment he had brought upon himself." At the corner of Eighteenth Street, someone spied a tree half a block west, "where the mob turned in to wreak their vengeance there, but this tree was not available." (This goes unexplained — perhaps it was not easily accessible, or its owner balked at the idea of so many people on his property.) So the march continued through the city, the mob growing as it traveled, until it numbered some five hundred people, "not one of whom made any effort to conceal his features." At the corner of Fifth and Main Streets, where stood Citizens Bank and a proper telegraph pole, the mob stopped, now apparently less boisterous and more focused upon carrying out the deed at hand. One person prepared a rope on the pole, and James was presented with a chance to confess his alleged crimes. James refused to cooperate for a long time, and apparently while waiting on him, the mob again decided to change the location of his execution to the corner upon which the Pythian Hall was located. There, they slung a rope over a telephone pole before he arrived. James finally said to the mob, "I guess I am guilty," and was urged to confess by a "friend of the prisoner," who was perhaps not satisfied with the less than total admission James had provided. After being allowed to spend some time in prayer, James was conveyed to his place of execution. The noose was placed around his neck, and he was soon swinging. Before he had even been raised above the heads of the assembled crowd, someone fired a shot into James, and a fusillade of bullets, estimated at more than one hundred, tore into his body; loose shots destroyed some of the windows in the Pythian Hall, leading the *Gazette* reporter to comment (with no trace of irony): "It was almost miraculous that some one was not hurt in this miscellaneous fusillade."

Gov. James Philip Eagle and his wife, Mary, having just returned to Little Rock from a trip to Memphis, Tennessee, were on a streetcar then nearing the corner of Fifth and Main Streets. The governor, seeing the large crowd, was informed that a lynching was to take place and so jumped off the streetcar just as the shooting began. He managed to take hold of the man who fired the last shot, dragging him "thirty or forty yards back to Main street" before the mob rushed upon him and freed his solitary prisoner. The governor was knocked about a bit and succeeded in punching one person during the struggle. Mary Eagle was escorted to a doorway along the road, and after her husband joined her, they hailed a carriage and were driven home. The *Gazette* described this rough treatment of the governor as "an indignity . . . that every man will resent and for which the perpetrators should be severely punished." The body of Henry James was left hanging at press time, four o'clock in the morning, though the newspaper indicated that it was to be cut down later that day. Meanwhile, thousands of people reportedly had visited the corner, where they "exchanged their opinions about the work of the mob, nearly everyone justifying what had been done."[20]

The lynching was reportedly "the all-absorbing topic of conversation" in the city the following day, as "groups of spectators, having heard through the columns of THE GAZETTE of the lynching, came to see the victim before he should be cut down." According to the newspaper, most of the sightseers were African Americans, and more than half of those were women. One black man was heard to ask, "Why did they not serve the German that way?" (This reference is not explained.) According to the *Gazette*'s reporting, other black visitors to the spot expressed approval of what occurred, but there were also reports of "incendiary" speeches given by some groups of "lawless" African Americans, while the *Democrat* reportedly received a letter warning that twenty-five black men had sent to Chicago to purchase dynamite for purposes of blowing up some large assembly of white people—a threat the *Gazette* labeled "senseless," given that "such a course would result in the speedy extermination of the colored race in this city." A photographer given only the name of Davies showed up around six o'clock to start taking photographs of the body. However, the early morning weather turned stormy at around seven. The body of James was tossed about in the wind, and Davies was forced to seek shelter momentarily. The coroner arrived around quarter past eight, at which time James was finally cut down for conveyance to the undertaker and, from there, to the potter's field of Oakland Cemetery. Meanwhile, as was common with regard to lynchings across the United States, members of the public began to take souvenirs from the night's event, starting with the rope, which was described at the newspaper as 1¼ inches in diameter and 125 feet long: "Within twenty minutes, the last vestige of the rope disappeared and no evidences of the exciting scenes of the night before were to be seen after nine o'clock, though the street was haunted by the numerous morbidly curious people, who seemed irresistibly drawn to the spot." Someone carved the name "Henry James" onto the telephone pole where he was executed.

The next day's issue of the newspaper contains some information from eyewitnesses to the mob activity. The coroner summoned a jury and began taking statements. W. G. Noble, who resided at Tenth and Main Streets, claimed to have heard Henry James confess to the crime in the company of two black men whom the witness understood to be preachers. Another witness was Julius Mackey, who worked at the Gleason Hotel on West Markham Street (possibly the previous employer of James). According to him, James was never accompanied by any friends or preachers. The inquest was concluded with determination, so common in lynching cases, that James met his death "at the hand of some person or persons to the jury unknown." The *Gazette* also included a clarification from Dr. G. W. Hudspeth, mentioned in previous reporting as one of the men who volunteered to identify James. Hudspeth insisted that, while he had been at the county jail, he was not at the penitentiary and did not take part in the mob activity later in the evening.

Reportedly, a handful of people attended the lynching dressed as if for some society occasion, including a "ladylike little woman, who occupied a seat in a carriage on one of the corners of Fifth and Main," as well as "quite a number of gentlemen in full evening dress" who hovered on the outskirts of the crowd. Finally, the *Gazette* reported upon the condition of Governor Eagle, who was said to have suffered a dislocated thumb on his left hand but was otherwise unaffected by the rough treatment at the hands of the mob. He was reported to have said that, even if he had been unable to prevent the violence, he would at least have "attempted, if the mob would hang the negro, not to have it done on the principle street of the Capital City."[21]

National newspapers picked up on the story of the Henry James lynching, adding their own details about the matter. The *Wichita Daily Eagle* reported, on May 15, that an "indignation meeting was held by the more vicious and lawless element of the negroes tonight. The better class, however, agree with the whites that only justice was meted out."[22] Various national newspapers reported that same day that Maggie Doxey had died of her injuries just one hour after the hanging of James, but the *Arkansas Democrat* reported upon just such a rumor being spread locally and checked in with the coroner, who was able to confirm that the rumor was unfounded.[23] An African American newspaper, the *Appeal* of Saint Paul, Minnesota, used the lynching of James to interrogate the broader system of white supremacy in the United States, asking these questions:

> Does any fair-minded person suppose there was any actual desire on the part of the authorities to prevent the mob at Little Rock, Ark., from breaking into the penitentiary and taking therefrom Henry James the Afro-American accused of outraging the little white girl last week? The guards in that penitentiary could have kept a mob of ten thousand at bay for an indefinite period.
>
> Does any fair-minded person believe that had Henry James been white and Maggie Doxey black and the circumstances otherwise exactly the same that there would have been any such exhibition in the defence of outraged virtue by the "superior race"?
>
> Would a black Maggie Doxey at five years of age been any less pure than a white one?
>
> Would an assault on a black virgin five years old by a letcherous white brute been any less aggravating than if the colors were reversed?
>
> Did anybody ever hear of a white mob lynching a white man for outraging a black virgin?

Why cannot a black man be tried in the legal courts? If there is any doubt of his innocense [*sic*] he will get the benefit of the doubt.

Would it not be following the first law of nature if the constantly outraged Afro-Americans take "Lex talionis" as their motto all over the South, and act in accordance with the motto?

If an insurrection a thousand-fold greater than the Nat Turner insurrection should break out in the South who would be to blame?[24]

The *Gazette* writer tried to offer some justification for the murder of James by noting that, while conviction for the crime of rape comes with a sentence of death, the "victim is of an age upon which the crime of rape the statutes of Arkansas declare is impossible to be committed."[25] However, Deputy Heard had previously said, in expressing his determination to protect James from the mob, "I am going to pull the lever that hangs James himself," apparently believing that his crime would entail the legal punishment of death.[26] In fact, it appears that the *Gazette*'s claim that James could escape death due to the youth of his victim was, at best, misinformed. The 1874 Arkansas Supreme Court case of *Dawson v. State* confirmed that someone could be tried for the crime of rape even if the victim had not yet reached puberty.[27] In 1887, the court similarly ruled in *Coates v. State* that carnal knowledge of a girl under twelve years of age, "if against her will, or she is incapable, from her tender years, or want of mental and physical development, of exercising a will, with reference to the act, it is rape, and the punishment is death."[28] Chapter 58 of the 1894 Arkansas Digest of Statutes, "Rape and Carnal Abuse," maintains the death penalty for the crime of rape but also mandates a period of imprisonment "not less than five nor more than twenty-five years" for "carnally knowing, or abusing unlawfully any female person under the age of sixteen years"—a crime different from rape, which is defined in section 1862 as "carnal knowledge of a female forcibly and against her will," a definition that deals with age not at all.[29]

While the lynching of Henry James certainly attracted its share of attention, being covered in great detail, the two subsequent acts of such violence in Pulaski County were not as well reported, even though the first entailed the only female victim in the county. On March 11, 1894, a group of African Americans discovered the body of a "mulatto" woman, who was never identified but was estimated at thirty years old, hanging from a tree about halfway between Little Rock and Marche. The body, according to reports, appeared to have been there for several days (the *Arkansas Gazette* even described the corpse as "decayed"), and around her neck was a placard reading, "If any body cuts this body down, they will share the same fate." No motive for the murder was discernible.[30] The following year, both the *Hutchinson Gazette* out of Kansas and the *Indianapolis Journal* carried this brief report in late December: "Barnett Brown, a negro, was lynched by negroes near Wrightsville, Ark., for living with another man's wife."[31] Both the lynching of women and black-on-black lynching were relatively rare, but there was no elaboration upon either of these events.

The lynching of Henry James was certainly a large-scale affair, but it does not quite rise to the level of a full-fledged race riot, especially given that the focus remained upon one person rather than a collective. Ann V. Collins defines race riots as "rational, extralegal, relatively short eruptions of white-on-black violence aimed at influencing social change."[32] Collins identifies three conditions that must be met to spur violent white mobilization: "certain *structural factors*—primarily demographic, economic, labor, political, legal, social, and institutional features; *cultural framing*, or actions and discourse by both whites and blacks to further their own causes; and a *precipitating event*, the immediate spark that ignites the violence."[33] These conditions certainly apply to the 1927 lynching of John Carter that is one of Little Rock's most infamous cases of racial violence, but they also apply to a lesser known event that happened just across the river in Argenta (later renamed North Little Rock) in October 1906. As will be seen below, however, the Argenta riot also bears more than a passing resemblance to the phenomenon of the feud, defined by Larry LeMasters as "a long-running argument or period of animosity, especially between families or clans. Feuds usually begin over a perceived injustice or insult. The feud cycle is fueled by a long-running cycle of retaliatory violence that often escalates into a 'blood feud,' in which the cycle of violence involves the relatives of someone who has been killed or dishonored seeking vengeance by killing the culprits or their relatives."[34]

The apparent genesis of the riot lay in the murder of Wiley Shelby, an African American, the previous month by Robert R. McDonald, a white man. According to the *Arkansas Gazette*, Shelby was a "Negro musician employed by the Argenta Liquor Company" on Main Street, while McDonald was "a freight conductor on the Memphis division of the Iron Mountain." The *Gazette* managed to interview McDonald at the jail following the September 12 killing of Shelby, and the jailed man related his story in full. McDonald was reportedly in the back part of the saloon, eating and drinking with a black woman named Emmie Wright (or Emily White, Minnie Wright, or Amy Wright, as she is variously named in newspaper accounts). McDonald was approached by Shelby, who soon became abusive, objecting to McDonald's being in company with this woman. His abuse of the pair increased, and soon Wiley Shelby's brother Pete also entered the bar. At this point, McDonald claimed that Wiley Shelby "reached to his rear pocket as if to draw a knife," and thus did McDonald strike first with a penknife in his possession, slashing the black man's throat. "Shelby ran from the saloon into Main street and died in the middle of the street, about fifteen feet south of the saloon," but McDonald and Wright were apparently unaware that the blow was fatal and went down the road to Adler's saloon, where McDonald was later arrested.[35]

The inquest, convened by coroner S. Paul Vaughter, began the following day at half past eleven at Colum Brothers Funeral Home on East Washington Avenue. Reportedly, a large group of African Americans had gathered at the site, and extra deputy constables were summoned in order to keep back the crowd. Despite the presence of the constables, violence erupted. According to the *Arkansas Democrat* published later that day: "In some unaccountable manner which no one now appears to be able to explain, and during the small-sized riot that ensued, C[harles] C. Colum, one of the negro undertakers, was shot and killed and his brother, Garrett Colum, was seriously injured, and Deputy Constable Ed Lindsey was painfully cut several times." (The *Democrat* was wrong in its initial report, as it was Robert Colum, not Charles, who was killed.) The *Arkansas Gazette* contained some additional details, including the wounding of police officer Milton Lindsey, brother of the deputy constable. At some point, "half a dozen had become involved in a free-for-all fight and knives and guns were being freely displayed, although only a few were used." Shots were fired, and Colum fell dead from two bullet wounds. All of the officers present declared later that they were unable to tell from which direction the shots had been fired.

The *Democrat* and *Gazette* accounts vary in some of the specific details of the conflict (as well as in their spelling of Lindsey/Lindsay). According to the *Democrat*, the coroner had just begun the inquest into the killing of Shelby by McDonald (the latter described as a former police officer) when "a fusillade of pistol shots, followed by groans and curses, broke up the inquest and caused certain members of the jury to take refuge behind any convenient shelter." The genesis of this disturbance was the attempt by many African Americans to reach the back of the establishment where the inquest was held. Robert Colum was trying to keep the crowd at bay, and Garrett Colum "refused admission to Deputy Constable Lindsey and Ed Wright," another constable. The report held that "the negroes were very insulting and used abusive language to the officers." Suddenly, Robert Colum pulled a pistol from his pocket and picked up a knife with this other hand as a prelude to showering Lindsey with curses, and Garrett Colum attacked another man. Robert Colum allegedly pointed his gun at city attorney W. R. F. Paine and pulled the trigger, only to have the weapon misfire then and two more times. The crowd was surging back and forth, and at some point, two pistol shots rang out, with both bullets hitting Robert Colum, one in the head and one in the chest. Garrett Colum was "cut in several places during the fight and severely beaten up by a pistol in the hands of the officers" before being arrested and shipped to the city jail. Ed Lindsey, meanwhile, received a few small knife wounds, but none "deep enough to cause anything more than a slight loss of blood."[36] The *Gazette*'s coverage was lengthier. According to that paper, Milton Lindsey was stationed at the entrance of an alley at the side of the building, which was the best access point for the part of the building where the inquest was being held, a porch in the back. Reportedly, a black person attempted to pass Lindsey, and Garrett Colum protested to the officer that, as part owner of the establishment, he could determine who went in. The two began to fight, and Garrett Colum, described as "the strongest negro in Argenta," knocked Lindsey through a fence and began beating him on the head, whereupon Ed Lindsey came to his brother's aid, striking Colum on the head himself. At this point, Robert Colum rushed from the building and stabbed Ed Lindsey in the back with a knife, the blade penetrating the deputy constable's lung. Lindsey pulled a pistol from his pocket, but this was seized by Robert Colum. However, before Colum could take full possession of the firearm, Lindsey successfully "broke" it, emptying the gun of its shells, a fact which went unnoticed by Colum, who began "waving it about his head and snapping it at the men who rushed upon him, at the same time striking Lindsay [*sic*] several more blows with his knife." A number of men rushed toward Colum and Lindsey, including constable Ed Wright, deputy constable Dave Yarbrough, city attorney W. R. F. Paine, "and several members of the coroner's jury," and during the melee, the body of Wiley Shelby, "which had been placed upon the porch, was knocked to the floor and trampled upon by the men who were struggling to reach a place of safety." Two shots rang out, and Colum fell mortally wounded. His death put an end to the fighting, and the police soon dispersed the crowd. Garrett Colum, who had received several wounds, was arrested. At some point, word was sent to the Colum house that all three of the brothers had been killed, leading the three families to rush to the funeral home in a state of excitement. Milton Lindsey, upon learning that his brother had been stabbed, secured a horse and rode to the Iron Mountain railroad shops to inform other brothers of his; in fact, Ed Lindsey had been working at those same shops just the previous week before resigning to accept the position of deputy constable.[37]

Meanwhile, the original inquest into the murder of Shelby was delayed until later in the afternoon and moved to the office of justice of the peace Frank Vaugine. Coroner Vaughter's inquest ruled the killing justifiable, and after the dismissal of the jury, the hearing began before Vaugine. The first witness called, identified in the *Gazette* as Jake Mason (Pete Mason according to the *Democrat*), was a foster brother of the dead man and a fellow musician. According to his testimony, after being confronted by Shelby, Emmie Wright ran out the back, after which Shelby struck McDonald with a beer glass, to which McDonald responded by striking Shelby in the neck with his knife. Wright was put on the stand but told much the same story. Afterward, Judge Vaugine "declared that he could not hold the prisoner on the evidence introduced at either hearing and McDonald was given his liberty."

However, the *Gazette* report ends with some additional information on McDonald's own personal history—namely, that he had previously been a member of the police force "and on one occasion while off duty slapped a callboy for making remarks about himself and the Wright woman." He was arrested by a fellow officer, William Mara, but broke away from Mara on the way to jail and ran into Brod's saloon, where Mara fired at McDonald, hitting him twice. The case was tried in police court, which exonerated McDonald, though he soon gave up his position on the force. The report ends with the note that, contrary to earlier reporting, McDonald "had not been working on the freight run between here and Memphis for the past two months."[38] The *Democrat* also reported on some interesting history—namely, that this was apparently not the first scrape between Shelby and McDonald. According to testimony from Emmie Wright, about a month prior to this incident, a woman had tried to stab her at the same saloon, after which she called McDonald, who came to the saloon and ended up in a confrontation with Shelby about it.[39]

Garret Colum was charged with assault with intent to kill for his role in the later melee, but he was released on a $5,000 bond, with Mifflin W. Gibbs, John E. Bush, and Charles C. Colum as sureties. He was reported to be recovering from several injuries. Ed Lindsey continued to rest at the Levy building, attended by physicians who were reluctant to move him to the hospital for fear of opening his wounds again.[40] Meanwhile, there began an inquest into the killing of Robert Colum. As with the previous inquest, African Americans lined up around the area, eager to learn the outcome, and again the police force was deployed, though on this occasion there were no disturbances. Among the interesting testimony proffered was a statement by Paine that Milton Lindsey "had a big gun and that Deputy Constable Yarborough took it and handed it to him (Paine). After the disturbance ended Mr. Paine examined the revolver and found that one shell had been shot, evidently several days before. He then gave the revolver back to Lindsay [sic]." Yarborough himself testified that, had he not taken his fellow officer's gun, Lindsey "would have killed Garrett Colum." Lindsey himself testified that the shooting was done after he had been thrown to the ground by Colum. The jury ruled that Robert Colum had met his death "at the hands of some one unknown."[41] The *Gazette* gave a slightly different flavor to the testimony of Lindsey—to wit, that he had, while being attacked by Garrett Colum, "finally managed to reach his hand around to his pistol and had gotten it out to use when it was taken from him by one of his friends. When he regained his feet, Garrett Colum had been taken out and Robert Colum was gasping his last breath."[42]

On September 14, Garrett Colum was scheduled to appear for trial on charges of assault and battery. The *Democrat* noted that the trial was set for two o'clock but that Colum was expected to be late on account of account of accompanying his brother's body to Menifee, a predominantly black community in Conway County, for burial.[43] Colum failed to return in time, so the trial was rescheduled for September 25.[44] Meanwhile, the *Democrat* published some of the rumors surrounding the case, such as the following: "The day of the shooting Jake Miller, who was in the fight, when asked if he fired the shots that killed Colum, did not deny killing Colum but would not say that he did." In addition, an unnamed "son of the dead man" held that the fight started after "several negroes had gotten on top of the building." The officers, in response, told the people to get down, but Robert Colum replied that he owned the building and that the people could remain on the roof. This, in the view of the son, was what led to the skirmish.[45] The case against Garrett Colum was later dismissed "at the instance of Scipio Jones, the attorney for Colum, who paid a twenty-five dollar fine."[46]

The following month, the community of Argenta erupted in violence. At around a quarter to nine on the evening of October 6, 1906, a Saturday night, John B. Lindsey and son Milton were shot in downtown Argenta as they passed in front of the Colum undertaking establishment at 500 East Washington Avenue—specifically, Milton Lindsey reported that Garrett and Charles Colum had fired upon them. According to the *Gazette*, a patrol officer named Green was the first to arrive on the scene, where he was warned by Garrett Colum, "who was standing behind a flour barrel, to get away or he would be shot." Colum did fire, but the bullet missed Green, who took up a position across the street. Two other officers soon joined Green, and both were likewise fired upon, as was Robert Huddleston, a private citizen who also tried to enter the store. "Others ran to the scene," the newspaper reported, "and within a few minutes the street in the vicinity of the store was crowded with men, armed with rifles, shotguns, and pistols." By the time mayor William C. Faucette and chief of police Gabe Pratt arrived, between fifty and sixty armed men had gathered in the street; when sheriff Coburn C. Kavanaugh showed up, he deputized many of these men and placed them strategically around the building. A sergeant led some officers down the alley to see if they could draw fire from within the building, but no shots came, and the mayor led the attack on the store: "The front room of the building was broken into and lights were turned on. The door leading to the rear rooms was locked, and these rooms were dynamited, but the negroes had made their escape while the crowd was gathering in the street in front" (and had apparently locked those rear doors to create the suspicion that they still remained inside).

Their search fruitless, the posse turned its attention to the homes of the two Colums and followed up a rumor that the brothers had left via the road to Fort Smith. The Colums lived in a home at 1500 East Second Street, and when the mob of some fifty armed people showed up, they ordered the house emptied. The wives of the Colum brothers "declared that they had not seen their husbands since they left the house early in the evening." The mob turned up nothing of note in the house, but a search of the barn revealed that a wagon was missing, and some members of the posse followed tracks from the barn down Washington Avenue and then east down toward McAlmont, but the tracks eventually became impossible to follow. Meanwhile, one of the two sons of Charles Colum tried to break from the mob surrounding the house but, after being fired at, "returned and placed himself in the custody of the posse." In order to "forestall any attempt at a race riot," the mayor and sheriff ordered the saloons closed shortly after ten o'clock that night.

The *Gazette*, in an apparently early report, observed that, just past midnight, "there was no indication of a race riot" and "the streets of Argenta were quiet."[47] However, later reports document the swift emergence of vigilantism in the city. Soon after midnight, Garrett Colum's house was found on fire. Will Walker, a neighbor, told the *Democrat* that he witnessed a group of men applying coal oil to the front and rear of the residence and setting it afire. He also declared that "after the match was applied the wife of Colum, together with the children present, ran from the building, and that members of the mob forced them back in their burning home, but that later cooler heads came into control and the negroes were allowed to escape." Reportedly, a newspaperman was on the other side of the house and heard the mob attempting to force the family back into the burning home.[48] At 1.25 a.m., the Colum brothers' undertaking establishment was also found to be on fire, though "whether it was of incendiary origin or whether it was a result of the dynamiting done earlier in the night" could not be immediately ascertained. Argenta authorities called Little Rock for assistance, and a hose wagon was soon on the scene, though it was not able to stop the fire from spreading down "the entire row of frame buildings from Cypress street, on the north side of Washington avenue, to the alley between Cypress and Locust streets." These included not only the Colum building but also two grocery stores, the shoe store of Louis (or Lewis) Styles, the office of a Dr. McNeese, the Joe Baum Saloon, and a bakery. (Meanwhile, Argenta's own hose wagon was stopped after one of the horses carrying it ran into a live wire and was killed, forcing the firemen to take down the hose and drag it to the hydrant.)[49]

Other, smaller incidents also occurred during the night. Will Harding, "a painter and paper hanger" who lived in Argenta, had started toward the fire at the Colum building at 1:35 a.m. when he was "accosted by unknown persons" who inquired of his race. When he answered that he was white, "he was ordered to get back home, and he started as directed, when one in the party of unknown persons fired at him, the bullet striking him in the back." He was able to walk away, however, and was brought to

Saint Vincent's Infirmary.[50] Soon after two o'clock, the *Gazette* reported
A. L. Belding was going to the Harding residence with contractor James
Mahoney when they "discovered a fire at Sixth and pine streets, one block
from the Harding residence." To give the alarm, Mahoney fired his pistol
into the air, but as soon as he had done so, the pair "were fired at from four
different quarters by persons secreted in the darkness, who were armed
with shotguns." Mahoney was injured, but Belding escaped harm. The
house they found on fire was reported to be that of Styles, whose business
had earlier that evening been set ablaze, probably because it was right next
to the Colum establishment, though the *Gazette* reported a belief that the
house was set alight "to detract attention from the other fire."[51]

Meanwhile, an inquest was held regarding the matter of John Lindsey's
death, with the grand jury concluding that he was killed by gunshots
from Charles and Garrett Colum and Styles. Milton Lindsey described
seeing both Colum brothers, along with approximately ten other African
Americans both inside and outside the store, as he and his father walked by
the Colum establishment. Speaking to the jury, W. P. Huddleston described
seeing Garrett Colum inside the store and armed with a Winchester rifle
immediately after the shooting, while Barney Hoing reported seeing Styles,
also inside the store, firing a shot from a Winchester at someone across the
street. An examination of the body revealed eleven bullet holes.[52]

October 7 was a tense day for Argenta, and by the end of it, a white
mob had claimed the life of one Homer G. Blackman (named Blackwell in
some accounts), who operated a restaurant in the same building as Styles
and had been arrested earlier in the day. According to the *Democrat*, he
and William Hill, who was later released, were both charged with being
"implicated in the death of Mr. John B. Lindsey." Blackman reportedly
feared mob violence: "He was nervous and cringed at every footfall on
the concrete floor of the jail." Indeed, when "a number of men, masked,"
visited the jail and compelled the turnkey to produce the keys, Blackman,
"who had made no effort to go to sleep, appeared to be expecting the men"
and began pleading for his life. He was manacled and forced to walk to
the corner of Sixth and Main Streets, where a rope had been prepared
on an electric light pole: "When he had been elevated to about half the
height of the pole the free end of the rope was made fast, and those present
retired to the northwest corner of the street, where the store of Stuckey
Brothers is located." C. C. Stuckey, whose rooms were located above his
store, witnessed the murder, including the forty to fifty shots fired into

Blackman's body. Gabe Pratt, the police chief, had left the jail with other officers just a short time before Blackman was taken from the premises and was quoted in the newspaper as saying that he "had no intimation of the impending trouble." Pratt remained convinced that Blackman had been mixed up in the earlier violence, having reportedly traced the path of a shot back to Blackman's establishment, but the *Democrat* also quotes one Dr. G. W. McNiece (perhaps the same as the Dr. McNeese noted above), who insisted that Blackman had been absent nearly all week while taking care of business at the court in Chicot County and had only arrived back in town on Saturday night. Meanwhile, some "person or persons unknown" fired into a black-occupied residence and business in Argenta, though no one was injured.

The *Democrat* also reported that noted black lawyer Scipio Jones of Little Rock had, the previous day, sent "a conveyance" to the wives of Garret and Charles Colum, who were brought across the river to be housed in safety, while the family of Robert Colum remained in Argenta, save for a son, Alexander, who was also being sought by the authorities. Meanwhile, curiosity seekers were visiting Healey and Roth, the undertaking establishment where the body of Blackman was being kept during an inquest into his lynching, with the rope still around his neck.[53] In response to the violence and threat of violence, between sixty and seventy-five black women and children holed themselves up in Shorter College, where Chief Pratt visited on the night of October 8 to promise his protection and to station four officers during the night to guard them. Police were also stationed at a black schoolhouse on Military Heights and in the yards of the Rock Island Railroad to protect black workmen there. Other patrolmen were stationed throughout the city, the regular police force having "been augmented by the addition of fifteen special policemen and . . . a number of deputies." Optimism regarding the restoration of order was such that even the saloons were allowed to reopen, though close watch was kept on them. Mayor Faucette issued a proclamation announcing that only authorized persons would be allowed to carry firearms and that a thorough investigation had revealed that the Colums and Styles had fled Argenta. However, this did not stop the circulation of rumor, including a report that a particular black section of the city would be burned during the night, which led to an exodus of about three hundred African Americans from Argenta, "many of them walking out into the country" or over to Little Rock.[54] The *Democrat* reported that "as many as 500 negroes have left Argenta since the trouble

Sunday night," largely in response to rumors of "a wholesale burning of negro residences" to occur.[55]

Though quiet, October 8 proved to be busy for several people connected with the recent violence. A Pulaski County grand jury looking into the lynching was given its instructions and began deliberations, while a coroner's jury "returned a verdict to the effect that Blackman came to his death at the hands of persons unknown."[56] John Lindsey, whose body was revealed to have been hit by eleven bullets, was buried north of Argenta in a funeral that was attended by many people.[57]

As of the morning of October 9, order seemed to have been restored. The *Gazette* published a letter that morning written by Isaac Fisher, principal of Branch Normal College (now the University of Arkansas at Pine Bluff), to Gov. John Sebastian Little before the violence of the weekend. In this letter, the black educator writes on the subject of race relations in Arkansas, which he describes as "comparatively cordial," adding: "Let's have our understanding now; for no man can tell when some blind and infamous degenerate will drop a lighted match."[58] However, another one of those matches was dropped shortly before noon that same day, when Alex Champion, "a negro bartender and a member of several fraternal orders," was shot and killed at the Bridge Saloon in Argenta—quite possibly by Luther Lindsey, son of the recently buried John Lindsey.

Champion was described as "well known in Argenta and Little Rock," having worked for many years as "a barkeeper in the employ of Adolph Kahn at Fort Smith Crossing," and, at the time of his murder, he was employed by the Argenta Liquor Company. The *Democrat* had the earliest reporting on his murder. According to it, Champion had been arrested that morning "under suspicion of having a concealed weapon in his possession" and, when searched, was indeed found to have one. Around eleven o'clock, friends of his came to the jail and paid his fine, after which Champion was allowed to depart. He was found shortly thereafter at the Bridge Saloon in Argenta, where he asked where he might find D. A. Yarbrough, a bartender there. He was heading to the back of the saloon when he was shot. The *Democrat* reported that Champion was shot by one of seven other people in the establishment at that time, "all of whom escaped by the rear door, immediately after the shooting." It appeared that Champion had been followed into the saloon by these people, men whom saloon owner Joe Giles was unable to identify. Three minutes after being shot, Champion was dead. Late in the afternoon, Sheriff Kavanaugh stated that authorities suspected

Luther Lindsey of the crime.[59] Lindsey gave himself up to Chief Pratt at five o'clock. His bond was set at $3,000, which was signed by Morris Levy, after which Lindsey was released, his trial set for October 16. As the *Gazette* reported, "Lindsay refused to make a statement last evening, but through Chief of Police Pratt of Argenta, he authorized the statement that he did not deny the shooting. He also stated that he got away from the scene of the shooting as soon as possible to avoid any further trouble, but as soon as things had quieted down he gave himself up to Chief Pratt."[60]

Given the ongoing violence, yet more deputies were sworn in by the sheriff, though the night passed quietly, with very few people on the streets at all. Officers reported that the houses of many in the "negro section" were unlit, and that when police knocked on the doors of houses where lights could be seen, those lights went out immediately.[61] Local pastor S. L. Cochran of Dye Memorial Methodist Episcopal Church in Argenta was quoted as attributing all the recent violence to the saloons, complaining that they "not only violate the law by running wide open on Sunday and by running gambling places in connection with the saloon but that they keep musical instruments in the saloon with which to attract the public. . . . Every murder committed this year is directly traceable to the saloons."[62] Notorious racist and US senator Ben Tillman of South Carolina, who happened to be visiting Little Rock in the aftermath of this violence, spoke at the Central YMCA specifically on the "race question." There, he reiterated his well-known calls to end "negro domination" and preserve white supremacy, through lynch law if need be, and even referred to the recent violence in Argenta by noting that "across the river, no longer than today, race hatred is seen," adding, "The time is not far distant when the people will be compelled to come to the towns, or to form committees, Ku Klux Clans [*sic*] and shoot and kill on their own accord."[63] Meanwhile, Styles and the Colum brothers remained at large, an application to the state for reward funds to help spur the capture of the fugitives was turned down since funding had already been exhausted for the year, an inquest into the murder of Champion was held, and a grand jury began investigating the lynching of Blackman, who was buried on October 10 with only his mother, sister, and two friends in attendance.[64] The *Gazette* continued to insist upon Blackman's innocence on the basis of the impossibility of returning from Lake Village to Argenta in time to participate in the violence.[65]

John E. Bush, a prominent leader among local African Americans who was serving as the receiver of the US Land Office in Little Rock, reported fielding many inquiries from those in the black community as to whether they should sell their property and leave immediately, and he advised them all to stay, encouraging those who did stay to "attend to their own business and not jump up in arms every time some negro, who has not been attending to his own business, is taken to task for his actions."[66] Despite his advice, however, many black residents had apparently fled: "Although the city has resumed her customary quiet and no further trouble is anticipated, many negroes are leaving town, seemingly doubting the protection guaranteed them by the guardians of the peace, and the scarcity of labor resulting has caused some inconvenience to one of the railroads and a few of the contractors of the city." Many of those fleeing were reported to be heading into the country or south into Little Rock.[67] Also leaving the city was Robert R. McDonald, the man who killed Wiley Shelby and arguably set off the chain of events culminating in the Argenta riot. The police chief, acting on instructions from the mayor, ordered McDonald to leave by midnight, which he did, catching the Iron Mountain train out of town on the evening of October 11.[68]

The inquest regarding Champion's murder failed to reveal the name of the perpetrator.[69] Less than a week later, on October 16, Luther Lindsey was acquitted after a trial "consuming a little more than fifteen minutes before Justice of the Peace Vaugine."[70] And with that, the book seemed to shut on what has come to be known as the Argenta Race Riot, though one chapter remained unfinished — the whereabouts of Styles and the Colum brothers. As the *Democrat* reported, "Sheriff Kavanaugh has received no information that would lead him to the whereabouts of the three negroes and they seem to have disappeared."[71]

During the twenty-four years surveyed here, Arkansas's central county experienced a variety of lynching violence ranging from murders carried out by small, private mobs to a full-blown spectacle lynching and race riot. In addition, while most of the victims were black men and most of the perpetrators white men, there are examples of white-on-white and black-on-black violence, and one black woman was lynched. But how should this record of events be interpreted?

A comparison of Pulaski County with counties in which other southern state capitals are located might prove instructive. The Center for Studies in

Demography and Ecology's Lynching Database, which records lynchings between 1877 and 1950, has the following figures:

- Richland County, South Carolina: zero cases of lynching during the time period in question (out of 200 for the entire state).
- Wake County, North Carolina: only one in 1918 (out of 121 for the entire state), or less than 1.0 percent.
- East Baton Rouge Parish, Louisiana: only two in 1890 (out of 494 for the entire state), or less than 0.5 percent.
- Davidson County, Tennessee: one in 1884 and three in 1892, for a total of four (out of 303 for the whole state), or approximately 1.3 percent.
- Fulton County, Georgia: one in 1889 and three in 1906, for a total of four (out of 616 for the entire state), or just over 0.5 percent.
- Fayette County, Kentucky: four in 1878 and four in 1920, for a total of eight (out of 301 for the entire state), or just under 2.7 percent.
- Montgomery County, Alabama: two in 1894, one in 1896, one in 1897, one in 1910, two in 1915, three in 1919, one in 1920, one in 1925, and one in 1934, for a total of thirteen (out of 408 for the entire state), or approximately 3.1 percent.
- Hinds County, Mississippi: one in 1880, three in 1883, one in 1885, two in 1888, two in 1889, two in 1894, one in 1895, two in 1896, one in 1900, two in 1901, and one in 1906, for a total of eighteen (out of 689 for the entire state), or approximately 2.6 percent.

By comparison, Pulaski County, Arkansas, had eleven such lynchings for the whole time period covered by the database, including the 1927 lynching of John Carter (out of 317 for the entire state), or just under 3.5 percent.[72] Only the state of Alabama gets anywhere close to this percentage of lynchings in and around a state capital. Most remarkable is the comparison with those states that recorded a significantly greater number of lynchings. In Georgia, for example, which recorded 299 more lynchings than did Arkansas, only a miniscule percentage of those events occurred in Fulton County, where Atlanta is located (though this number excludes the estimated twenty-five to forty African Americans murdered in the 1906

Atlanta Race Riot).[73] Even Mississippi, which tops the chart in absolute numbers, registered nearly a full percentage point below Arkansas.

This statistical oddity might relate to what Michael Pfeifer describes as the "contradictory effects of capitalist transformation on Americans' perception of criminal justice." He writes:

> The extension of the market into rural areas illuminated class and racial tensions that heavily informed lynchings. Similarly, urbanization and industrialization created unique social spaces that raised questions about racial order and encouraged the formation of working-class white mobs. Yet capitalism also created middle classes whose distaste for public disorder led them to reform criminal justice in a manner initially unacceptable to many rural and working-class persons.[74]

Capital cities tend to be foci of such market revolutions, given that they are typically among the largest cities in their states, and the presence of state government also encourages economic development. Therefore, the higher rate of lynching in Pulaski County may well speak to its comparatively late arrival on the scene of capitalist transformation. Is there any evidence of this?

Little Rock was established in 1819 when the territorial government voted to move the state capital from Arkansas Post to its present site, though the city was not formally incorporated until 1831. The relative youth of the state, however, does not mean that its capital was younger than those of other states. For example, although Georgia was one of the original thirteen colonies, Atlanta did not exist until the 1830s, when it started as a railroad terminus, and it was not named Georgia's state capital until 1868.[75] Likewise, the town of Montgomery, Alabama, arose in 1819 from the consolidation of two smaller communities but did not become the state capital until 1846.[76] Thus Little Rock and Pulaski County do not, at first glance, seem relatively undeveloped, but their relative distance made them lacking in one significant component of industrialization— railroads. As noted, Atlanta emerged in the 1830s as an important railroad terminus, while Montgomery's designation as a state capital was based in large part on railroads already running through the community. By contrast, Arkansas's one antebellum railroad, the Memphis and Little Rock Railroad, was incomplete in 1861, with a large gap in the middle; indeed, it would be another decade before it finally connected central Arkansas with the community of Hopefield, which lay just across the Mississippi River from Memphis, Tennessee.[77]

Central Arkansas, therefore, remained a relatively rural area until long after the Civil War. In 1870, the population of Pulaski County was 32,066, of whom only 12,380 lived in Little Rock. These numbers had increased only marginally by the following census, but by 1890 the county's population had shot up to 47,329, while Little Rock's had grown to 25,874, meaning that the overwhelming majority of county population growth was concentrated in Little Rock. With this and following censuses, the Little Rock population grew at a far greater rate than the county population as a whole, so that by 1910 some 45,941 people lived in the city, or more than half of the county's 86,751.

This could well reinforce the application of Pfeifer's thesis of a market revolution and of the arrival of bourgeois values that try to tamp down "rough justice" and put in its place a less disorderly means of law enforcement and punishment. Atlanta, after all, grew at a much greater rate, increasing from 21,789 in 1870 to 154,839 by 1910, and only four lynchings were recorded for Fulton County. The capital county that comes closest to Pulaski County in the percentage of lynchings is Alabama's Montgomery County, and the city of Montgomery shows population growth similar to that in Little Rock, expanding from 10,588 in 1870 to 38,136 by 1910. Little Rock's figures thus fall in line with Montgomery more than with Atlanta, perhaps lending some credence to the Pfeifer thesis, to the extent that the increasing domination of bourgeois values can be correlated to population growth (as an indicator of economic development).

Only one lynching in this chapter happened within the capital city of Little Rock, that of Henry James. Another was described as occurring "near Little Rock," but this vague phrase cannot credibly designate it as an urban event, given the tendency of newspapers to cover large swaths of geography by locating them near some more well-known municipality. The murder of Blackman occurred just across the river in what is now North Little Rock, arguably not a rural area and certainly within the orbit of the capital. Therefore, if we include the 1927 lynching of John Carter in the total, then only three of the eleven lynchings that occurred within Pulaski County took place in the urban center; nearly three-quarters occurred in the more rural parts of the county. This lends some initial credence to the Pfeifer thesis, though much more work needs to be done in the way of comparative studies.

While the lynchings surveyed here were separated by a few years at the most, it would be nearly twenty-one years before the county experienced another case of mob violence in the lynching of John Carter. That gruesome murder of 1927 has come to be a cultural touchstone, the one lynching to which locals can still refer, as well as an academic touchstone, having been cited in numerous scholarly articles and books. However, as this chapter has shown, Pulaski County, in both its urban and rural quarters, had a deep history of violence preceding the murder of John Carter. Regarding the incidents covered here, not one person ever faced punishment for participating in a lynching, even when the governor of Arkansas himself was manhandled by a mob. This chapter, therefore, comprises not only a history of vigilante violence, but also a study of impunity, of how the failure to prosecute violence produced a worldview in which people could attack and murder the powerless without fear of punishment. That sense of impunity is the true legacy of the South's practice of "rough justice."

Stories of a Lynching

Accounts of John Carter, 1927

I n April 1927, in the panicked midst of that spring's disastrous Mississippi River flood, a young white girl named Floella McDonald disappeared on a rainy afternoon in Little Rock. When an African American janitor found her body three weeks later in a church belfry, his teenage son Lonnie Dixon was indicted for rape and murder. That night and the following, frenzied white mobs threatened law enforcement and searched area jails for young Lonnie, until the mayor appealed for them to stop and assured the city of a death sentence. On the third night, the city was calm.

But the next morning, a report reached Little Rock that a white woman and her teenage daughter had been confronted by an African American man on the outskirts of town. Peace officers and citizens hunted, found, and hanged John Carter and dragged his body to Broadway and West Ninth Streets, in the heart of Little Rock's black business district. Thousands of whites gathered and rioted around a bonfire–cum–funeral pyre for three hours until the governor dispatched the National Guard, which finally dispersed the crowd. Despite claims that law officers and city officials were negligent, if not complicit in the lynching and rioting, a grand jury disbanded after some members refused to indict them, and others resigned in protest.

Lonnie Dixon died in the electric chair less than two months later, on his birthday.

The stories of John Carter's death on May 4, 1927, and the events surrounding it, have been told in many ways, by different sources, and for different purposes. White-owned dailies in Arkansas and beyond, nationally distributed newspapers with primarily African American readers, and a Kansas journalist all published varying accounts, interpretations, and opinions. And Little Rock residents—who were children or adults in 1927—remembered and passed down information not published anywhere at the time.[1]

Considered together, the accounts paint conflicting pictures of the events, reveal holes in some documents and published reports, and raise significant questions: Was Lonnie Dixon's confession coerced? Was John Carter mentally impaired? Was Carter assaulting the women or helping them, or was his capture a case of mistaken identity? Were peace officers complicit in the death of John Carter, were they complacent while others acted, or were they overpowered by the mob gathered on that county road and later at Ninth and Broadway? This examination outlines a chronology of the main events, highlights disparities among primary sources, and considers what really might have happened and how—and why—it is remembered.

AS THE GREAT Mississippi River flood roared down the Arkansas and Mississippi rivers toward the Delta, the rushing water broke levees; washed away homes, vehicles, livestock, and people; and eventually flooded more than five million acres.[2] Everyone was tense and anxious, and the eyes of the nation were on the plight of Delta residents. On April 12 in Little Rock, eleven-year-old Floella McDonald (who also was reported as twelve or thirteen[3]) left the public library, having checked out *Mrs. Wiggs of the Cabbage Patch*, but she never arrived home. The day before, another white child, thirteen-year-old Lonnie White, had disappeared too.[4] The city mobilized a search for both children, fueled by rumors. A gas station attendant saw a girl crying in the back seat of a car with Texas plates, so a handful of deputies headed west, only to find their way blocked by high water. A woman reported a large object floating in a creek, which turned out to be a dog. Little Rock police chief Burl C. Rotenberry feared "that a fiend may have captured both children, or perhaps only one and is hiding with his victim or victims in the black Fourche [Creek] bottoms."[5]

Notices went out by telegram and radio, planes dropped leaflets bearing the children's pictures, and towns throughout the South received flyers from the Little Rock police. Troops of Boy Scouts and volunteers combed woodlands and swamps, empty barns, warehouses, and storage sheds. Reward money grew to $1,500, at a time when local department store M. M. Cohn's spring sale offered linen golf knickers for $3.50 and union suits for $1.19.[6]

When the overflowing Arkansas River reached Little Rock, six days after Floella's disappearance, news of the flood edged the missing children off the front pages. Pressed into flood relief duty, peace officers halted their search. The children were presumed dead.[7]

THREE WEEKS LATER, on Saturday, April 30, while a choir practiced and a group of Campfire Girls met in Little Rock's "fashionable" First Presbyterian Church at Eighth and Scott Streets,[8] the white church's African American janitor climbed a ladder to the belfry to investigate an odor he had noticed for several days. There he found a decomposing body and called the police. The body was identified as Floella's by her clothes, rolled stockings, and sandals. As police lowered the blanket-wrapped body out of the belfry to the waiting ambulance, crowds began to gather.[9]

Police immediately questioned Frank Dixon, the church's janitor, and then his teenage son Lonnie. Through four hours of grilling, both denied any knowledge of Floella's death.[10] The nearby *Pine Bluff Daily Graphic* reported, "A round-up of negroes was started immediately by the police" of between six and twelve African American males "known as [the Dixons'] associates."[11] A search of the church turned up blood-stained clothes in a church cabinet, identified by a cleaner's tag as Frank Dixon's.[12]

The news of Floella's discovery brought W. R. Kincheloe to police three hours later with his daughter Billie Jean—age five in one account, age eight in the others.[13] They told of an young African American man who recently had "accosted" Billie Jean near the church "two weeks or longer ago," promising little Billie Jean a toy if she returned to the church that afternoon. When the child picked Lonnie from a three-member lineup, police "tightened up on Lonnie."[14]

The next day, "it was learned" that the conversation between Billie Jean and the young man had been the same day as Floella's disappearance.[15] That afternoon—after between sixteen and twenty-four hours of questioning, most of it endured while standing and without food or legal counsel—Lonnie gave an oral confession, police announced.[16] But he did so only after "added pressure was brought on the youth by police and when he was told that his failure to tell the truth had caused his mother to be brought to jail he weakened and said that he killed Floella McDonald."[17] Lonnie was reported as fifteen, sixteen, or seventeen at the time.[18]

According to the confession, police said, Floella climbed the church steps that day to take shelter from the rain. Lonnie, across the street at the Little Rock Boy's Club, crossed the road to open the door for her, so she could go inside and get a drink. He promised her gifts (variously stated as little chairs she had admired or tickets to an "Our Gang" theater show[19]) if she would climb to the belfry with him. After she did "what he compelled," a euphemism for rape, she threatened to tell her father. He then hit her in the head with a brick, killing her.[20]

Police said Lonnie led them to an abandoned garage on Fourteenth Street where he had hidden her hat and library book.[21] An oddly prescient report in the *Democrat* two weeks earlier had theorized that, if Floella had been swept away by the flood, "the child's hat or the book which she carried might have been found." And in the following paragraph: "Another theory advanced in the girl's disappearance is that she was kidnaped by a negro fiend and held prisoner by him. He may have killed the child and carefully hidden her body."[22]

Though coroner Samuel A. Boyce had pointed out the impossibility of determining whether the girl had been "ravished," the oral confession, circumstantial and concealed evidence, and identification by the young Billie Jean Kincheloe were worth more than a written confession, said Chief Rotenberry. He charged Lonnie with criminal assault and murder.[23] The *Chicago Defender* reported to its largely African American readers that Lonnie repudiated his confession the day after his arrest.[24]

At Floella's Sunday afternoon funeral, held at the same time as police later reported that Lonnie had confessed, reverend J. O. Johnston warned, "A lynching right now, when the attention of the nation is focused on Arkansas as a result of the flood situation, would cause irreparable harm to the reputation of the state. I beseech you to leave the matter of punishment to the courts."[25]

Prosecuting attorney Boyd Cypert and a resolution by the Little Rock Bar Association both assured the city that Lonnie's age—sixteen—would not save him from execution: "In the event he pleads guilty to an assault charge, his plea may be accepted by the court and capital punishment imposed without a jury, according to local criminal lawyers."[26] And Kansas journalist Marcet Haldeman-Julius, who was in Little Rock at the time, quoted mayor Charles E. Moyer's plea to let justice take its course: "Lonnie will not escape the electric chair. We allow [sic] Lonnie's execution to be done according to law."[27]

Almost immediately after Lonnie confessed, a white mob formed outside City Hall, which had a basement jail, and grew to between three and five thousand, demanding that police turn both Dixons over to them. But Chief Rotenberry, who had faced down four previous mobs and protected prisoners under his command, instructed his officers to sneak Lonnie and his father away in separate cars, at different times, to destinations three hundred miles apart. Chief Rotenberry armed his officers with sawed-off shotguns and successfully held off the mob, who gathered for more than five hours.[28]

Southwest of the city at the "Walls," as the Arkansas State Penitentiary was commonly known, a mob of several thousand made the same demands of warden S. L. Todhunter.[29] When Todhunter insisted the Dixons were not there, a member of the mob shot through the screen door to his office, injuring no one. Todhunter demanded at gunpoint that the mob leave, then allowed them to choose a committee to search inside the prison. While the committee searched, others broke the lock on the penitentiary gate and surged inside. When the four- or five-member committee returned empty-handed, the mob broke into groups to search the premises themselves, including the warden's home. Word finally circulated that the Dixons had been taken to other jails. Frustrated and angry, as many as five hundred left in cars to search jails in the nearby communities of Benton, Hot Springs, Malvern, Pine Bluff, and Sheridan.[30]

Todhunter had requested police aid for the penitentiary from Chief Rotenberry, but officers were too busy controlling the mob at City Hall. Gov. John Martineau urged city officials to disperse the crowd, but the mayor and city council refused to use force. National Guardsmen readied tear bombs to be used if needed. The crowd hooted down a succession of local authorities who pleaded with them to leave, including Mayor Moyer, law enforcement officers, and several ministers.[31] When Rotenberry approached the edge of the crowd, "he was attacked and had to be rescued by his men." He exited City Hall in secret and called Sunday night's mob the worst he had seen, but said he never was concerned for his own safety.[32]

The *Baltimore Afro-American* reported that whites "invaded the colored section seeking Lonnie Dixon, fifteen-year-old half-breed, who confessed [to] the murder of a white child."[33]

On Monday morning, city officials breathed sighs of relief. Eighteen mob members had been arrested, but no violence resulted from Sunday night's demonstrations, though they were the largest ever in Little Rock and did not disperse until two o'clock in the morning.[34] Monday night, however, crowds again gathered and turned their frustrations on the officials who were thwarting their quest to seize the Dixons. They cut tires on police vehicles and went to the homes of Mayor Moyer, Chief Rotenberry, and the chief of detectives, Maj. James A. Pitcock, to demand the prisoners' whereabouts. By order of the mayor, Rotenberry had left town with his family.[35] At one o'clock, Pitcock, who once had dispersed a mob in Crawford County, told the City Hall crowd, "I'll give you ten minutes to get away from here, everyone [sic] of you—*and three of the ten minutes are gone.*" The crowd left.[36]

By Tuesday, May 3, three days after Floella's body was found, mob activity seemed to have stopped. A morning *Gazette* editorial praised "the authorities and the peace officers to whom it fell to handle a peculiarly difficult situation" and who averted a lynching, despite "the crime of all crimes to rouse public anger and spread, like fire in tinder, an unreasoning desire for summary and terrible vengeance." Always a moral disaster, the editorial continued, a lynching would have been "especially deplorable at this time when Arkansas is in the eyes of the nation" due to the flood.[37] Mayor Moyer praised the city's return to calm and the police chief's successful protection of Lonnie.[38]

That same morning, the Pulaski County Grand Jury indicted Lonnie Dixon for assault and first-degree murder and set a trial date two weeks later on May 19.[39] The Grand Jury warned, "We are asking aid and assistance from the outside world for our many thousands of penniless and distressed citizens. We are advertising ourselves as honest, law-abiding people and we cannot afford to do other than let the law take its course in this case."[40] And the *Democrat* editorialized, "The law requires that men must have a trial. The negro youth must be returned here to face trial. *When convicted* the legal time limit must expire before he can be executed." Mayor Moyer also chimed in: "I sincerely hope that the trial and execution of Lonnie Dixon will be allowed to proceed legally and lawfully. It is certain that he will be executed, and I sincerely hope that no further violence will be resorted to."[41] Police were prepared for mob violence Tuesday night, and were "Ordered to Resist Any Attack by Would-Be Lynchers of Negro."[42]

On Thursday, May 5, Floella's family, the McDonalds, published a "Card of Thanks" in the *Arkansas Democrat* to their "many friends for their kind words of sympathy during [their] time of trouble."[43] An adjacent column continued the front-page story of an event that appeared to be entirely different but, in the minds of the actors and the collective memory of Little Rock, never really was.

ON THE MORNING OF Wednesday, May 4, two white women — Mrs. B. E. Stewart and her seventeen-year-old daughter Glennie — had been driving a wagon toward Little Rock from the southwest with a load of eggs and butter to sell. They lived in a wooded area a mile and a half off the Twelfth Street Pike, seven miles from Little Rock.[44] At the base of a hill, they drove past an African American man walking along the road.[45] Greatly varying reports said that he asked them the location of a bridge, or whether they were going to town, or if they had any whiskey; that he ran and caught the wagon, jumped in, and grabbed the reins; that either he threatened to kill the women or he beat them with an iron bar; that Glennie fought back with a whip; that he knocked both of them out of the wagon or that they fell or jumped, and that Mrs. Stewart broke her arm; that he threw rocks at them, or chased one or both, and caught up with Glennie — or her mother — and attacked with a tree limb, and beat the mother unconscious.[46] When a passing car stopped, the man fled into the woods, and the driver picked up the women, stopped at a nearby house to phone the sheriff, and took them to the hospital, telling the news along the way.[47] These were reports in white-owned publications.

But others, particularly in the African American community, remember the story differently: a backfiring car scared the horse, the women screamed, and the man jumped up to help them control the wagon; when they protested to other whites that he was helping — not hurting — them, their pleas went unheeded.[48]

Word spread quickly. Pulaski County sheriff Mike Haynie hurried to the scene, followed almost immediately by four carloads of his own deputies, officers, and volunteers. He stationed men at regular intervals along two main roads, and the rest began combing the wooded area; runners were told to keep him informed. More volunteers arrived from Little Rock, eventually totaling as many as fifteen hundred. "Estimates vary so widely as to the number of people who were meanwhile beating the woods to drive [the man] toward one or another of these pikes that it is very difficult to come at the truth," wrote Haldeman-Julius. "Certainly the timber was alive with posses."[49]

At midday, a woman—presumably white—reported seeing a black man crouching near a road. Searchers rushed to follow his trail.[50] As the *Chicago Defender* described it, "he was walking along the highway when he heard and saw the howling mob, and fled in terror from the road, plunging into the forest. . . . His flight was the only evidence of guilt his frenzied pursuers had."[51] No one was cornered until much later in the afternoon, when a carload of officers and volunteers fired two shots at a man.[52] Within an hour, two volunteers pointed their guns at a wounded man in a tree, perhaps the same one at whom they had fired. He climbed down—or was snatched—and begged the men not to shoot.[53] They fired into the air to alert others and put him into a nearby car, while others came running.[54]

At this point, a detective reportedly recognized the captured man as John Carter, who, the previous August, had been fined $500 and sentenced to one year "on the Pulaski county farm" for entering a woman's home on East Eleventh Street and beating her with a hammer. That man had escaped from a work crew on Saturday—the day Floella's body was found—and was said to have been hiding in the woods.[55] Differing accounts would state Carter's age as twenty-two, twenty-eight, or thirty-eight.[56]

With Carter in a closed car, the gathered posse sent a messenger five miles into Little Rock to bring teenage Glennie Stewart to the scene; her mother was in the hospital. By the time the young woman arrived at close to half past five, as many as two hundred people had congregated by the car, but no senior law officers were reported to be among the gathered crowd.[57] That morning, having determined that the mob fever of the previous several nights was quelled, Governor Martineau had left town to attend a strawberry festival 125 miles away in Van Buren and planned to return that evening.[58] Mayor Moyer had ordered Chief Rotenberry out of town and had left as well, later saying he thought any crisis could be handled by men "in better mental and physical condition than the chief or myself."[59] Neither was Sheriff Haynie at the scene of the capture; he told different sources he was either two or seven miles away.[60]

While waiting for Glennie, the mob granted Carter water and a cigarette and peppered him with questions. In various reports, he denied the attack, or blamed someone else, or did not know why he did it—or all three.[61] When Glennie arrived, she identified him ("'That's the man, that's the man,' the girl cried,") and peace officers prepared to take him into town. But others seized Carter from the officers, who were described as "threatened" and "powerless" against the gathered mob.[62] "Lady," a member of the mob later told Haldeman-Julius, "there wasn't anyone in the woods that aimed to do anything but lynch that nigger from the time they started huntin' fer 'im." Asked why, he said, "Why you could jest hear people sayin' right and left, 'Rotenberry . . . ain't goin' to get away with *this* nigger like they did Lonnie Dixon.'"[63]

The *Chicago Defender* article explicitly blamed the lynching on the tenor of the city in the days after Floella McDonald's body was discovered: "Therefore the report of this latest attack was like setting a match to a gasoline torch." A week later, a letter writer agreed: "After they failed to lynch Dixon, they were determined to lynch somebody. They put out a report that a bright Race man, the color of Dixon, had attacked a white woman and lynched a real black man."[64] In published photographs, Lonnie Dixon and John Carter bear little resemblance to each other.

After Glennie identified Carter, the mob led him to a telephone pole. "Officers attempted to bluff the crowd out of its intention to lynch the negro, but they were themselves threatened and the crowd remained firm in its intentions," the *Gazette* reported.[65] Someone brought a rope, tied it to a chain, and looped a noose around Carter's neck and then over the crossbeam of the pole; a man lying in a ditch held the other end. Carter asked permission to pray: "God, here I come on this fourth day of May, 1927."[66] The mob interrupted his prayer to tell him to climb on top of a Ford roadster. When he could not, they pushed him partway up and drove the car from underneath him. He hung for two minutes before a line of between twenty-five and fifty gunmen fired two to three hundred shots into his body.[67]

The Little Rock daily papers reported that Sheriff Haynie arrived fifteen minutes after the shooting had ended. But B. E. Stewart, husband and father of the women in the wagon, told Haldeman-Julius that as he himself fired the last shot, "Sheriff Haynie was lookin' right at me."[68]

Someone suggested taking the body down, but someone else said only the coroner could do so. The mob scattered at a directive from the sheriff, who turned the still-hanging body over to Dr. Samuel Boyce, the same coroner who had been called to the scene of Floella's discovery only four days earlier. A crowd gathered again, but Boyce "could find no one who would admit having witnessed the lynching."[69] The death certificate, signed by Boyce on May 8, lists Carter's death by "Multiple gunshot wounds (killed by parties unknown in a mob)."[70]

Haynie left again, and Boyce left to call an African American undertaker. The re-assembled crowd voted to take John Carter's body to Little Rock and burn it. His body was placed on the front, or inside, of a roadster and, with dozens of cars following, was driven to the city in a procession that eventually stretched to twenty-six blocks long. Someone said the lead car carrying Carter's body drove by Sheriff Haynie, who made no move to stop it.[71]

When the chain of cars reached Fourteenth and Ringo Streets in Little Rock, the body was tied, head first, to the back of the car, and the procession continued for more than an hour, down Main Street and Markham Street, west on Broadway Street past City Hall, police headquarters, and the courthouse to Sixth, Louisiana, and Ninth Streets, finally stopping at the intersection of Ninth and Broadway, the heart of the black business district. There, they placed Carter's body at the intersection of two streetcar lines, doused it with gasoline, and set it on fire, using pews from nearby Bethel African Methodist Episcopal (AME) Church, Little Rock's largest African American church.[72] "No better spot could have been selected in order to humiliate colored people," the *Baltimore Afro-American* told its readers.[73]

Thousands of white men, women, and children, in cars and on foot, converged on Ninth and Broadway from all directions, blocking roads and sidewalks. On a corner opposite the church, women gathered on the steps of the Mosaic Templars building, national headquarters of the Mosaic Templars of America, an African American fraternal organization founded in 1883.[74]

The crowd was estimated at between four and seven thousand.[75] "Boxes, limbs, furniture, gasoline, oil, kerosene and whatever else that could be procured by the mob were thrown upon the charred body of John Carter," according to the *Democrat*, "while men and women, many with babies in their arms, danced in a circle and howled and jeered. At intervals the mob, unable to express its contempt as loudly and as vociferously as it wished, resorted to firearms."[76]

Aaron (or Aren) Christian, a young African American man who wandered onto the scene with a gun, was seized and badly beaten. When several called for lynching him, too, and tossed him toward the fire, others pulled him to safety and put him in a car. The would-be lynchers fired at the car, and a stray bullet injured Robert Love, an eighteen-year-old white man.[77] From the steps of Bethel AME Church, another young white man reasoned with the crowd, admonishing them to send the injured black man to police headquarters, "since there seem to be no policemen handy." The crowd laughed and jeered "when it was apparent to them that the police were in their own headquarters and were not abroad." They did as he suggested.[78]

Police, as the crowd obviously knew, were indeed holed up in the basement of City Hall. Heavily armed with shotguns, rifles, and thousands of rounds of ammunition, they played cards while awaiting orders to go quell the rioting. With the police chief and the mayor still out of town—and with their whereabouts and return plans apparently unknown—alderman Joe H. Bilheimer Jr. reportedly was acting mayor (but another source said Little Rock had no acting mayor that night).[79] Assistant police chief E. W. Crow was commanding the police force but would not act without direction from city council.[80] Bilheimer went to the scene at Ninth and Broadway, where someone reportedly threatened him with a pistol. At City Hall, he and the rest of city council conferred about the mood and armaments of the crowd and deemed inaction to be the best course. Major Pitcock begged permission to take fifty men and disperse the crowd. "We may lose a few," he said, "but we'll stop the riot." His request was denied, per the mayor's absentee directive that no force be used except in self-defense.[81]

"During the several hours in which the mob milled around Ninth street and Broadway and streets leading to it," the *Gazette* reported, "not a police officer in uniform was visible for several blocks around, and no plain clothes men made their presence noticeable, if they were in the vicinity."[82] However, from his hiding place in the basement of Bethel AME Church, an eyewitness saw identifiable officers; friends later advised him to keep his observations to himself, which he did.[83]

"The situation is very bad," Moyer admitted to the press the next day, "but I don't see how it could be improved by mourning today over the bodies of 250 officers and citizens such as I believe would have been the result had the police and sheriff's forces attacked the mob last night."[84] The police had received repeated pleas for aid, and each caller was told that police would soon be in control. But at nine thirty that evening, "police still were making preparations to 'get the situation in hand.'"[85]

Black Little Rock residents stayed inside and well away from the melee. As "rumor after rumor was circulated in the mob that white men had been shot by negroes" or that "negroes were mobilizing or were arming themselves," the mob scattered to search nearby neighborhoods. Alderman Bilheimer told police he saw armed white men on porches of African American homes, waiting for police.[86] But the *Chicago Defender* reported whites disbanding on the news that blacks were mobilizing.[87] Both the *Democrat* and Haldeman-Julius credited Little Rock's black population with having the "good sense and restraint" to stay inside and away from the crazed mob and avoid making the situation worse.[88]

When Governor Martineau, in Van Buren, learned of the situation, he deployed the National Guard. At ten o'clock, Capt. Harry W. Smith, Adj. Gen. J. R. Wayne, Maj. H. F. Fredeman, and Lt. Carl Scheibner led sixty Arkansas National Guardsmen of Company H, 206th Coast Artillery, armed with rifles, fixed bayonets, and tear bombs to the intersection of Ninth and Broadway Streets, converging on the site from four directions.[89] They found a chaotic scene, completely devoid of law enforcement, in which people had poked sticks into Carter's corpse and were carrying around pieces of the charred body; someone directed traffic with a burnt arm.[90]

Within ten minutes of their arrival, the National Guard had dispersed the crowd that had rioted for three hours. By ten thirty, they notified City Hall of their success in breaking up the gathering, and in another quarter hour they had sent a Dubisson and Company ambulance to police headquarters with the remains of Carter's body. The Guard blocked all access to several blocks around the intersection, including to police cars. At least one African American shop owner, who had been hiding in his business, was provided an escort home.[91]

The National Guard continued to patrol the city's streets Thursday and Friday, May 5 and 6. On Friday, police arrested a young man on Main Street who was selling photos of the lynching for fifteen cents.[92]

REACTION THE NEXT DAY was strong, swift, and mixed. In a front-page editorial, the *Arkansas Gazette* deplored the "shame of being delivered over to anarchy," calling the scene at Ninth and Broadway a "Saturnalia of savagery." Throughout America, the *Gazette* continued, "the name of Little Rock will be read with expressions of horror," and the paper demanded an accounting from "the officers who have failed us."[93] On its front page, the evening's *Democrat* printed without comment the relevant state laws addressing citizen aid to law enforcement and police duties to prevent and suppress rioting and unlawful assembly. The next day, an editorial placed blame squarely at the feet of the mayor and the aldermen, as well as the mob's leaders.[94]

Also on Thursday, Governor Martineau called a meeting of city and law enforcement authorities, but Chief Rotenberry "could not be found."[95] That same morning, the Pulaski County Grand Jury convened under the leadership of foreman Gordon N. Peay with a strongly worded charge from First Division Circuit Court judge Abner McGehee: "This community is not going to permit mob rule. You are not going to permit it, and to the limit of every faculty I possess and every power conferred by the office I hold, I am not going to permit it. . . . The most sacred institutions we possess have been endangered by this outbreak. . . . If we permit the overthrow of the law's majesty, we invite an intolerable situation in which the security of every home is threatened and the life of every innocent child is endangered."[96] Elected and appointed city staff issued statements deploring the riot and disorder, but declaring "They Acted in City's Best Interests." The unapologetic mayor said he headed back to Little Rock at 10:40 p.m., when he was notified of Carter's capture. "I have no criticism to make of the members of the council who decided against this attack," he said, "but on the other hand, want to commend them on their foresight and good judgment. As it is only one death resulted. The criminal law should be changed so that an attempted assault or attack on a woman by a man would be a capital offense." He again assured citizens that Lonnie Dixon would be executed.[97]

Sheriff Haynie called the search and lynching "orderly." The situation did not get out of hand, he said, until Carter's body was dragged to town. Saying that he was two miles away when Carter was caught, he "immediately made [his] way to the scene and when [he] arrived the negro was hanging from a telephone pole." When the coroner arrived, Haynie said, he left for his car a quarter mile away; when he returned to the scene, Carter's body was gone.[98]

Coroner Samuel Boyce denied that Carter's body had been taken from him and used Haynie's word—"orderly"—to describe the crowd. He said that when he left to find the ambulance driver, the body was removed "by persons unknown to me. Legally, I was in no way responsible for the body after I had completed the inquest."[99]

In a meeting attended by many prominent citizens, the Little Rock Chamber of Commerce adopted a seven-point resolution praising the National Guard, praising the press for its condemnation of the events, promising "any amount of money that may be necessary," and urging the Grand Jury to return indictments "against every officer shown by the facts to have been guilty of a dereliction of duty, to be followed by removal from office and by punishment under the criminal laws of the state."[100] Among those issuing statements condemning the riot were the Second Presbyterian Church and the Pulaski County chapter of the American Red Cross, which had been engaged in flood relief since mid-April.[101] A Little Rock Bar Association resolution said, "The evidence points to such weakness and cowardice on the part of our public officials charged with the preservation of the public peace as have never before been displayed in any English-speaking community."[102]

The Grand Jury requested and received from the sheriff newly deputized guards for its proceedings. By the end of the week, thirty witnesses had testified, and the jury adjourned until Tuesday.[103] One Alabama man had been arrested in Hot Springs for having participated in the lynching and burning; he was found to possess grisly souvenir body parts wrapped in a handkerchief.[104]

Sunday afternoon, May 8, a week and a day after Floella's body was discovered, police found the body of Lonnie White, who had disappeared the day before she did. They promised a full investigation into his apparent accidental drowning.[105]

On Tuesday, May 10, the Grand Jury resumed its work and heard twenty more witnesses. But by the end of the day, Peay and six others had signed a letter of resignation to Judge McGehee, citing the impossibility of securing the 75-percent vote necessary for indictments.[106] Peay wrote, "I know I have the confidence and respect of [Little Rock's] good citizens, and I feel that I cannot hold either their respect or my own if I allow this situation to be whitewashed and forgotten. I am not afraid to do my duty, and I positively refuse to concur in the inaction of this jury."[107]

Peay later told an investigator from the National Association for the Advancement of Colored People (NAACP) that he had evidence against Mayor Moyer and Sheriff Haynie and "ample proof" to indict known mob leaders. But, he said, fellow juror H. A. Cook and five others wished to indict only minor players to avoid naming officials or influential city leaders. Cook confirmed his reluctance to charge officers ("I do not think the officers in question should be indicted unless more evidence than we have heard is procured"), but blamed Peay for the breakup of the jury. It was the Grand Jury's duty to indict mob leaders and participants, he said, "if it appeared that their identities could be established."[108]

Two days later, Judge McGehee dismissed the Grand Jury without comment.[109] The *Democrat* condemned both the Grand Jury for disbanding and the court for allowing it. "If the courts permit such a fizzle, then we have no haven of protection against repetitions of mob rule—we must advise the world that the citizens of Little Rock do not disapprove of mob rule. . . . And a whitewash of the disgraceful episode would be even worse than a compromise."[110] In a sharp turn from his strong charge convening the Grand Jury, McGehee did not call a special jury, as some had anticipated, but said he would delay the investigation to the next Grand Jury, scheduled for nearly four months later. The subsequent NAACP investigative report cites McGehee as later seeing "no reason why the subject of the burning and lynching should come before this Jury or, in fact, ever be brought up again."[111] Prosecuting attorney Boyd Cypert also told the NAACP he thought it best to let the matter drop, as did Chief Rotenberry, Major Fredeman of the National Guard, and numerous others who refused further comment. Cypert said, according to the report, "If indictments were brought the sympathy of the majority would be on the wrong side, acquittal would be certain, and the lasting impression would be that the action against white persons in such a matter was an outrage and race hatred would be strengthened." The NAACP investigator found that "the better class of white people, including those whose indignation had been highest last summer," agreed with Cypert. He also said the well-known local African American attorney Scipio Jones "advised [him] to see very few colored people as it was, he thought, likely to injure them if it became known, and they could give [him] very little help."[112]

ON LOCAL EDITORIAL PAGES in the days immediately after the lynching, letter writers alternately praised and condemned city officials, officers, and the newspapers' stances. They debated whether a show of force would have prevented the lynching and riot or, as Mayor Moyer had postulated, would have escalated the violence.[113] Before it stopped accepting unsigned letters, the *Gazette* printed one that read, "There are times when it is necessary to make an example of a negro to protect our girls."[114] In mid-June, the *Chicago Defender* printed a letter from a white man who signed himself, "A Citizen for 35 Years, Little Rock, Ark." He said, "The Ku Klux elected the city officials and those officials who were not in the mob were hidden away, so that everything was done in an orderly way." He called Little Rock "a Ku Klux town" and "hell on earth." Indeed, Mayor Moyer and Sheriff Haynie previously had been members of—or had been endorsed by—the local Klan.[115]

POLICE HAD HIDDEN Lonnie Dixon in a jail in Texarkana. On Monday, May 16, he was brought back to the "Walls" state penitentiary and kept under the heavy armament of the same National Guard unit that had so effectively quelled the rioting. The next day, Lonnie, without counsel present, entered a "not guilty" plea in Floella McDonald's death.[116] His first court-appointed lawyer had announced he would be out of town the day of the trial and thus could not serve. On Tuesday afternoon before the trial on Thursday, with Judge McGehee's consent, the Pulaski County Bar Association appointed new attorneys—Ector Johnson and J. F. Willis—using slips of paper drawn out of a hat. That afternoon, only two days before the trial, Lonnie's new capital defense team had "not yet mapped out a defense," nor had they seen a copy of the indictment.[117]

Jury selection took most of Thursday morning, May 19, with the courthouse surrounded by National Guardsmen and 150 special deputy sheriffs.[118] When testimony began, Lonnie's attorneys positioned him as an accessory to the crime committed by Eugene Hudson, age sixteen, who had been arrested earlier in the week in anticipation of his being named.[119] Floella's father and sister testified, as did motorcycle patrolman Homer R. Barrett (the first officer to have arrived at First Presbyterian Church), Chief Rotenberry, and other officials. The sole witness in his own defense, Lonnie said he had only made the oral confession because he needed food and sleep and had wanted his mother released from custody. Cross-examination by prosecuting attorney Boyd Cypert did not shake Lonnie's account.[120]

The jury received the case at 6:05 p.m. and returned to the courtroom, having found Lonnie guilty, in only seven (or ten, or twelve) minutes.

Waiving his right to a two-day waiting period, Lonnie was given the sentence of death in the electric chair on June 24, his seventeenth (or eighteenth) birthday.[121]

On June 22, Lonnie's mother visited him for the last time. At her urging, he signed a new confession that implicated Eugene Hudson, as he had testified at the trial.[122] But in the early morning of June 24, a few hours before his death, Lonnie dictated yet another confession to assistant prosecuting attorney Carl E. Bailey and warden S. L. Todhunter, after they "had remained in the death house for two hours after midnight, stressing the advisability of a confession," and after Bailey had lectured Lonnie on the sin of lying and the pending injustice to Hudson. Bailey and Todhunter said the confession, which Bailey typed and which was witnessed by ministers M. V. Hudson of Alexander and O. A. Perry of Plumerville, was "given willingly with the horrible details and with no attempt to introduce mitigating circumstances or a color of pathos."[123] This confession corroborated little Billie Jean Kincheloe's story that he had stopped her, too. New details included that Lonnie had assaulted Floella in the church basement and choked her, forced her to climb the ladder to the belfry, saying he would let her out there. When he told her he was going to kill her, she asked to go see her parents and promised to return the next day so he could kill her then. He hit her in the head with a brick, climbed back down and changed shirts and then, hearing her moan, returned to the belfry and slit her throat. He blamed two Texarkana jail mates for his having implicated Eugene Hudson to try to save his own life and apologized to his mother for lying to her.[124]

He repeated his acknowledgement of guilt a few hours later in the electric chair. More than twelve hundred people had applied to witness the execution; thirty were admitted.[125] He died in either eight or twelve minutes, longer than some reports of the time the jury took to condemn him.[126]

THE LYNCHING OF John Carter and the riot that followed were reported by the Associated Press, and in newspapers as far away as Chicago, New York, and Washington, DC.[127] Some sources described it as the first recorded mob violence in Pulaski County for thirty-six years, though this was in error.[128] (See chapter 7 for accounts of the 1892 lynching of Henry James in Little Rock and the 1906 race riot in Argenta.) Because of the flood, all eyes were on this region of the country, where levees were breaking and residents were being forced from their homes.[129] Little Rock leaders immediately recognized the potential damage that a lynching could do to the region's reputation at a time of great need. Even before the mob began the search that resulted in John Carter's death, Rev. Johnston's remarks at Floella's funeral, an editorial in the *Gazette*, and the Grand Jury that indicted Lonnie Dixon all emphasized that the state desperately needed national sympathy and aid for flood relief. In other words, a lynching would look very, very bad. The morning after the lynching, the *Gazette* editorialized that, across the country, "the name of Little Rock will be read with expressions of horror."[130] Research into whether or to what extent the violence may have impacted flood aid would be revealing.

The 1920s press, dependent on advertisers and subscribers, largely reflected the attitudes of its readers. Headlines and articles about Floella McDonald, Lonnie Dixon, and John Carter were no exception, using condemnatory language prior to any specific suspicions of guilt. During the extended search for the missing children, police chief Burl Rotenberry's suggestion that they may have been "kidnapped by a 'fiend'" was inflammatory enough, as well as unfounded, in the midst of the raging flood, and then he suggested they were captive in an African American section of town.[131]

After Floella's body was found, though the coroner pronounced it "impossible to tell if the girl had been ravished," the same article reported, "Before folding the sheet over the form, [funeral home employee Neil] Smith picked up a silk undergarment that lay beside it, telling the tragic story of the horrible ordeal that apparently preceded Floella's death."[132] Lonnie's final, dictated confession said he assaulted her in the church basement. Why would he have carried her underwear to the belfry, unless she held onto it herself while climbing the ladder? Or if she put it back on in the basement, did one of them remove it again in the belfry?

Publicized as happening at the same time as Floella's funeral,[133] Lonnie's first, oral confession was variously placed at 2:00, 2:30, 4:00, or even 4:30 p.m. and took place under circumstances that were questionable, at the least, and today would be called coercive. Still a minor by all accounts of his age, Lonnie had been denied rest, food, and legal counsel for between sixteen and twenty-four hours.[134] "He consistently denied all knowledge of the crime until late [Sunday] when Chief Rotenberry took his turn at questioning," the *Gazette* wrote. "No promise of escape or lenience was made to the negro boy as an inducement for him to confess. He was told, according to the police and the assistant prosecuting attorney, that the best he could expect would be a speedy execution and that the worst a torturing death at the hands of a mob."[135] No doubt he knew that crowds were gathering, that he and his father already had been announced as suspects, and that little Billie Jean had identified him the previous day. "You know, if you had a mob out there and you're a child, you would admit to anything as well," one of Lonnie's nieces pointed out.[136] Newspapers reported that he "held out until he was told that his mother had been arrested and was being detained in jail" because he had not yet told the truth.[137] But whose version of the truth—his, or what Little Rock officials wanted to hear?

"There was much speculation about the force used to get the confession," Clifford E. Minton, an eyewitness to the spectacle at Ninth and Broadway Streets, reported in *America's Black Trap*. "The proceedings involving the sheriff, prosecutor and the court left important unanswered questions. With 'expedited due process' . . . Lonnie Dixon was convicted and electrocuted."[138] Another of Lonnie's nieces described conversations in her family: "After I listened to some people, it was like it was a set-up. You listen to other family members and he actually did it. . . . I have questions about it, but I know he admitted he did it. But after being questioned, and I'm sure abused, for so long, you admit anything for people to leave you alone."[139]

Lonnie recanted this oral confession the next day, according to the *Chicago Defender*, something Chief Rotenberry had predicted: "Sufficient corroborative evidence was obtained by the police to convict the janitor's son," the *Democrat* reported on May 2, "even though he should repudiate his confession, according to Chief Rotenberry."[140] Did the circumstances of the confession lead Rotenberry to assume he would recant?

On the witness stand at his trial, Lonnie said he had only confessed because he wanted food and rest, and wanted his mother to be released, and then said he was not guilty. A month later, facing death in a few hours, he reverted to an enhanced version of the same confession Rotenberry had first reported. But that came only after an extended session with Bailey and Todhunter. Why did the *Democrat* feel a necessity to make explicit that the final dictated and signed confession was "given willingly"?[141] To emphasize his guilt to eager readers, or to reassure them about a possibly questionable situation?

The entire scenario would have played well to conditioned white cultural assumptions that black males were dangerous to white females. The initial "round-up" of suspects, including janitor Frank Dixon and his son, apparently included no whites at all. One white woman, who was a Little Rock child of Floella's age in 1927, noted that arresting only African American suspects "threw the white fellow in the clear, if it was a white fellow, you know, because they blamed it on the black. . . . That just cleared the case." She went on to say, "It was many times when the blacks were accused and, you know . . . I don't think they were guilty. . . . Just to get, get it moved away from the real one who did it, you know. Closed it up."[142]

Some speculated about a romantic relationship between Floella and Lonnie, and here the conflicting reports of their ages become important. Floella was generally reported as eleven or twelve, though by the time of Lonnie's execution she was listed as thirteen. The death certificate says twelve.[143] One source reported Lonnie as fifteen when he was arrested, but elsewhere he was reported as sixteen or seventeen. According to his family, he was sixteen when arrested and died on his seventeenth birthday.[144] If Floella was eleven and Lonnie eighteen when he died, even a friendship would have been less likely than if they were at the other extremes—thirteen and fifteen. In her memoir, Edith McClinton tells of knowing Lonnie Dixon because he "dated a friend of mine and was from a very good family." As McClinton had heard it, "It was rumored that the girl was seeing Lonnie at the same time she was going steady with a white boy. When the white boyfriend found out, allegedly, he killed her and framed Lonnie for the crime."[145] In 1929, Simon and Schuster published a novel, *Violence*, by Marcet Haldeman-Julius (the Kansas journalist) and her husband, Emanuel, based on the Little Rock story and promoted as "A Novel of Love and Justice in the Central South." They wrote of interracial friendships, a lynching, and an execution, predating Richard Wright's *Native Son* by eleven years and Lillian Smith's *Strange Fruit* by fifteen.[146]

Local news reports described Lonnie as a "half-breed" and "polyglot," based on his skin color, and his mother as "mullato" [sic].[147] "I could see where, if one thought he was white, then it is very possible that he could have had a relationship with another white person," acknowledged his niece, who said people often thought her mother (Lonnie's sister) was white.[148] As another niece remembers, "I do realize that was rumored. . . . I heard my mom and my dad say that is what the case was, and it basically just got out of hand."[149] The Dixon family, which remained in Little Rock, never again learned the whereabouts of Lonnie's father, Frank Dixon, nor regained contact with him, despite a newspaper report that he was released from custody and immediately left the state.[150]

On the notion of Lonnie being framed, Marcet Haldeman-Julius pointed out that the entire city had been thoroughly combed during the search for the missing children: "It is during this time that I think it not in the least improbable that the little girl's book and hat may have been found."[151] On April 17, only five days after Floella disappeared, the *Democrat* had reported the theory that, if Floella had drowned, "the child's hat or the book which she carried might have been found." Also: "Another theory advanced in the girl's disappearance is that she was kidnaped by a negro fiend and held prisoner by him. He may have killed the child and carefully hidden her body."[152] So someone expected that her body and her possessions might be found in two different places. That circumstances seemed to bear out this speculation at least raises questions about what some officers already may have known nearly two weeks before finding her body.

The day of Floella's funeral, the *Democrat* reminded its readers, "Every vacant house in the city was searched thoroughly for traces of the children and not a single clue was found."[153] The circumstances of Lonnie's several confessions, the possibility that the hat and glove might previously have been discovered, and the city's frenzy following the discovery of Floella's body should have poked holes in what officials presented as an airtight case against him. As Haldeman-Julius wrote to NAACP president Walter White, "of course it is in just such a case as this that a trial is necessary. But Lonnie is not going to get a trial. The best, the very best that he can hope for is a legalized lynching, and he will only get that because governor John Martineau is ashamed for the good name of Arkansas, of the recent disgraceful unchecked trampling upon law and order."[154]

City officials already had assured their constituents either of Lonnie's guilt or that his age would not save him from the electric chair. In an apparent attempt to absolve Lonnie's lawyers from blame for defending him, Judge McGehee emphasized that they had been randomly chosen. Jurors, hardly comprised of his peers, took only a very few minutes to decide on death for the young man with conflicting confessions, no other witnesses in his defense, and appointed lawyers who had a single day to prepare.[155] A nephew of Floella's, an attorney himself, agreed: "He was lynched, too."[156]

AS IN MOST LYNCHINGS, guilt of a capital crime—in addition to the question of vigilante "justice"—hardly was determined in John Carter's death, either. Although white-owned newspapers reported that he had attacked the Stewart mother and daughter, that account was not universal. Reporting from Little Rock on May 6, *Chicago Defender* writer Lewis J. Walker wrote, "Somewhere in the vicinity, after hours of searching, [the mob] sighted Carter." He was walking down the road when he "saw the howling mob, and fled in terror from the road, plunging into the forest." His flight, the *Defender* pointed out, was "the only evidence of guilt his frenzied pursuers had." When they caught him, Carter "steadfastly denied the charge," even when mob members hit him with a revolver, kicked him in the knees, and demanded, "Say you did it! Say you did it! You ———." The reporter based his article on "stories of the capture as related later by members of the mob."[157] For "telling the truth about the reign of savagery that has gripped Arkansas' chief city," the *Defender* was barred from distributing in Little Rock for two weeks. And "because he had bared their fiendishness," a mob drove Theodore Holmes, the associate editor of the African American *Little Rock Survey*, "from his home . . . and [he was] forced to flee to St. Louis."[158]

In *Scars From a Lynching*, Edith McClinton wrote that the mob had decided to choose "any black man and lynch him in Lonnie's place." After the entire day, she wrote,

> The mob chose its innocent victim and came down the street yelling like a pack of wild dogs. All the commotion excited a horse that was carrying a white woman and her daughter. The horse ran wildly down the street and a black man named John Carter was on his way home when he saw the runaway horse. He leaped into the wagon and stopped the horse. The angry mob . . . misconstrued the incident. . . . The men grabbed John Carter and drug him away.
>
> The woman screamed, "No! No! He was helping us. Don't hurt 'em [*sic*], please! Please don't hurt 'em!" She kept screaming as they drug him out of sight.[159]

McClinton's version compresses and reorders events that were reported differently virtually everywhere else. Such a conflation is not uncommon in complicated situations, and the Little Rock case is no exception.[160] Nor would it be unusual that memories of African Americans differ from those of whites. "I heard some stories about what had happened, how it had happened," said a lifelong Little Rock resident who is African American, "but not one of those stories ever said that John Carter was guilty of anything other than trying to help someone." Clifford Minton also did not trust the published version of events. "There was more than one version of what happened on May 4, 1927," he wrote. "These versions of the story came from Whites. All of the pieces did not appear to fit in the guarded press reports. Blacks expressed the opinion that the daily papers wrote both facts and fiction."[161]

The white-owned dailies had written that the women were taken to Research Hospital for treatment. But the NAACP report had this to say: "[Grand Jury foreman Gordon N.] Peay said one of the leaders of the procession and burning was Dr. L. L. Marshall, head of the Research Hospital on West 14th Street, to which the two women were taken after the attack of the Negro. Dr. Marshall is (Mr. Peay said) a man with a criminal record, having served two penitentiary sentences for criminal operations. His hospital has a shady reputation and he is considered a person of very poor standing in the community."[162] The hospital's reputation and the involvement of its director could cast doubt on the reported injuries for which the women were treated.

JOHN CARTER'S AGE was variously listed as twenty-two, twenty-eight, and thirty-eight. Little Rock's 1926 City Directory included eight individuals named John Carter in Little Rock and North Little Rock; by 1928, there were only four.[163] On Carter's death certificate, coroner Samuel Boyce wrote that he was "about 38," with no other known information.[164] But a detective was said to have recognized Carter as an escaped prisoner, raising the question of whether more records would have been available regarding a previously convicted man. Two published photographs, one of a man sitting in a car, labeled "Ten Minutes Later He Was Lynched,"[165] and a head-and-shoulders image labeled "John Carter,"[166] portray a man who appears much closer to twenty-two than to thirty-eight.

The family of one of the Little Rock area's John Carters says their John Carter was never incarcerated, that he vanished one day on his way home from work. He very well could have been the man captured on the road, but of course they were not called, as Glennie Stewart was, to identify him, and the published photographs do not seem to match the family's own.[167] So whose photo was in the newspapers, and what happened to their relative, if this was not him?

Carter was widely reported to have been mentally disabled. "There seems to be no question in anyone's mind that he was a moronic type,"

Haldeman-Julius said.[168] The *Democrat* took the events at hand as proof because "the fact that he attacked the women on a main traveled highway at a time of day when vehicles were almost constantly passing strengthens the belief that his actions were the result of insanity."[169] Even the NAACP report said he was "known to be insane and feeble-minded."[170] But no substantial evidence, other than bad judgment, is offered anywhere.

In light of so many inconsistencies, we may ask how anyone could have been certain of the identity of the man lynched that day on the Twelfth Street Pike, what might really have happened between him and the two women, and whether, in a less charged atmosphere, he might not have paid for the encounter with his life.

THE DIVIDED REACTION among Little Rock's white residents to police protection of the Dixons and to the lynching and riot illustrates the inherent conflict between the region's need to be seen as law-abiding, and therefore worthy of flood relief, and the southern white societal dictate to protect white females from the perceived threat posed by African American males. Several whites were questioned about thirteen-year-old Lonnie White's disappearance and dismissed.[171] But even before Floella's body had been discovered, Chief Rotenberry blamed African Americans for her absence, and, as soon as she was found, no whites were reported to have been "rounded up." During the search for Floella, "police feared that the child might had [sic] been grabbed up by a negro."[172]

That Lonnie was charged at all was based on his identification by a five- or eight-year-old white female, whose word was given primacy over that of an African American male twice her age. "I do not . . . put any stock into the little girl who said, 'Well, just last week or two weeks ago or last month he approached me, too,'" said Floella's nephew. "I don't believe that. . . . She probably just wanted to be part of it, part of the deal," he said, wondering whether she may have had help picking Lonnie out of the line-up.[173] When Frank Dixon was pointed out to her, she said no, and then she picked out Lonnie. Why was the elder Dixon specifically identified to her first, especially when the newspaper noted that father and son looked very much alike?[174]

Accost was most often the word of choice to describe what otherwise sounded like simply a conversation between Billie Jean Kincheloe and "a negro who tried to talk to her as she passed the church two weeks or longer ago." Her parents "thought nothing of it at the time," possibly because, until Floella's body was found, the child had omitted that the young man was African American.[175] "When Billie Jean heard that the body of the McDonald child had been found in the belfry of the church, she told her parents she believed "'that negro' did it."[176] Several weeks after the incident that ultimately would doom Lonnie, the child added the race of the teenager. And the day she pointed to Lonnie, her parents did not recall when she had told them the story; but the next day, they remembered exactly, and that sealed Lonnie's fate: "Definitely determining that date that Billy [sic] Jean Kincheloe, aged five was accosted by Lonnie Dixon, but not harmed, as April 12, the day when Floella disappeared, caused police Sunday to center their accusations against the son of the janitor." With her accusation against him, police "turned their entire attention on him with the result that one of the most brutal murders in the history of the state was solved."[177]

Perhaps little Billie Jean told exactly what happened. But the sequence raises questions.

An unsigned letter to the *Gazette* on May 7 says John Carter's lynching was necessary to "protect our girls."[178] The girls on everyone's minds were Floella McDonald, Billie Jean Kincheloe, and seventeen-year-old Glennie Stewart. The letter, therefore, already shows a melding of the Lonnie Dixon and John Carter stories. The Saturday morning *Gazette* would have been printed only two nights after the National Guard dispersed the rioting mob.

Floella, Billie Jean, and Glennie all would have known, to varying degrees based on their ages, what 1920s southern society expected of white females and assumed about black males.[179] In an editorial that differed in numerous respects from the white Little Rock press, the *Chicago Defender* said "even the woman said to have been attacked was not there to identify Carter."[180] This may have been a reference to Mrs. Stewart, who reportedly was in Research Hospital at the time. But Glennie was the one brought to face the man they had caught. Whether or not he was the same man she had seen that morning, and whether that man had been helping the women control their horse, seeking directions, or trying to harm them, the roused white mob of hundreds of Glennie's neighbors, law enforcement, and Little Rock residents all believed that they had caught a guilty party. They expected her positive identification, and, just like little Billie Jean Kincheloe, that is what she gave them.

In the aftermath of all that happened, some African Americans moved away from Little Rock. "As a result of the trial [of Lonnie Dixon] and the lynching of John Carter, thousands of our people left Little Rock," the *Chicago Defender* reported, citing record ticket sales by Missouri Pacific Railroad officials, including $2,000 worth "to members of our Race" the day after the lynching and riot.[181] African Americans in Little Rock did not forget what had happened, nor its inherent danger. Thirty years later in 1957, as the Little Rock Nine prepared to desegregate Little Rock Central High School, Mrs. Birdie Eckford feared for her daughter Elizabeth. She told NAACP state president Daisy Bates, "When I was a little girl, my mother and I saw a lynch mob dragging the body of a Negro man through the streets of Little Rock. . . . Mrs. Bates, do you think this will happen again?" And at a 2013 public presentation in Little Rock about the 1927 events, an audience member recalled that when she graduated from high school in in the late 1970s, twenty years after desegregation, her mother was afraid: "The fear was that someone would come into our house and take me away." She traced this fear to the community's continued awareness of the lynching.[182]

THE MEMORIES OF MANY Little Rock residents soon followed the lead of the *Gazette* letter writer: that the mob had caught and lynched the man who murdered the little girl. "Carter and Lonnie Dixon, they were all mixed into one," said a Little Rock area gentleman born in the early 1930s; "To me, Lonnie Dixon was the one who was drug." Floella's nephew said, "I knew the story but I would hear stories that John Carter was the one who murdered Floella McDonald." A niece of Lonnie's had this analysis: "What I think happened was, and from what I was told, when these gangs of people—the whites—did not find Lonnie nor Frank, they branched out. They searched everything that they could and . . . someone told them that John Carter was Lonnie Dixon. Now that is the way I heard it. They were looking for Lonnie, and poor John Carter got in the way."[183]

With the mental substitution of one African American man for another already firmly in place by the time the lynch mob on the county road had caught John Carter, the long-standing conflation in Little Rock's common memory is not surprising.

In light of so many inconsistencies—in news accounts, in statements by public officials, and in the memories of eyewitnesses and other primary sources — what do we really know about the whole story, ninety years later? That a child, a teenager, and a man were all brutally killed in 1927, and that the three deaths were inextricably intertwined. Much analysis remains to be done. In 1998, a white man who was fifteen in 1927 encapsulated the situation. Some of his memories conflict with memories of others and with published reports. But the atmosphere of the times — laden as it was with racially charged fears, assumptions, and expectations — is abundantly evident: "But you know, they caught that colored guy, bunch of white guys, and they was transferring that colored guy from one place to another, and they got that colored guy . . . who committed the rape and everything on this little white girl. They took him up on the Main Street Bridge in Little Rock, or Broadway Bridge in Little Rock. Burnt him up! Everything except his heart. They couldn't burn his heart up. Do you know for the next four or five years after that there wasn't a rape in Little Rock?"[184]

"Working Slowly but Surely and Quietly"

The Arkansas Council of the Association of Southern Women for the Prevention of Lynching, 1930–1941

In 1930, Americans witnessed an upsurge of lynching and mob violence that plagued the southern states and shamed the entire nation. Lynching, of course, was not a new or novel occurrence. Neither was the activism to bring about its end. Organizations such as the National Association for the Advancement of Colored People (NAACP) and the Commission on Interracial Cooperation (CIC) had been founded in 1909 and 1919, respectively, to foster improved race relations and economic conditions among southern blacks and whites and to end lynching and other forms of racial violence. Lynching could not be eradicated merely by cross-racial communications, however. Reformers also challenged the racial violence meted out on black bodies and the ways in which it reinforced attitudes about sex, gender, and white supremacist ideologies. Black women reformers and organizations like Ida B. Wells-Barnett, the National Association of Colored Women, and the NAACP's antilynching crusaders had long engaged in this work and advanced this rhetoric. Wells-Barnett, in particular, had written about lynching in the South and had demystified it as a necessary punishment for black men who had allegedly raped white women, by arguing instead that it was a ruse to control African Americans' aspirations.[1] Additionally, black women and their organizations had informed the public about lynchings' deleterious impact on African American families and communities and, by extension,

American democratic ideals. They had also solicited white women's assistance—often to no avail.

Some southern white women, however, influenced by this early anti-lynching activism and its rhetoric, challenged patriarchal rationales for mob violence because they understood that they were deeply entrenched in paradigms that falsely positioned them as paragons of racial purity—which, in turn, reinforced white male hegemony over black people and white women alike. To this end, in 1930, Jessie Daniel Ames and a group of southern white women founded the Association of Southern Women for the Prevention of Lynching (ASWPL). This chapter unearths middle-class white women's activism and the organizations with which they affiliated as they engaged antilynching reform, as members of the Arkansas council of the Association of Southern Women for the Prevention of Lynching (AC-ASWPL).

The ASWPL's primary objective was to use white women's moral and social leverage to educate and persuade southern whites to end lynching in rural communities.[2] Southern white women's antilynching activism transgressed gender and racial conventions. Their activism was subversive, yet it occurred within a conservative framework that employed class and racial privilege to subtly undermine racist and sexist norms. Yet, white women's "cloak of privilege,"[3] leadership positions, and class advantages more often than not protected them from the harshest reactions to their activism, a tactic Ames and Arkansas women understood well.

Ames, also a member of the CIC and its director of women's work, sought to create an independent network of middle-class white and typically evangelical Christian women's organizations. ASWPL founders were not interested in creating yet another women's organization. Instead, they sought to harness the skills and social connections of women who were already members of myriad organizations to construct a movement broad enough to include white women throughout the South.[4] In Arkansas, such women's organizations as the Arkansas Democratic Women's Clubs and the Arkansas Federation of Women's Clubs endorsed the ASWPL's activities. When Ames issued a call to meet in Atlanta, Georgia, on November 1, 1930, twenty-six white women from six southeastern states answered. A similar meeting was held several days later on November 6 in Dallas, Texas,[5] where Ames met with white women from Texas, Louisiana, Oklahoma, and Arkansas. By April 1931, there were antilynching associations in all of the southern states save Florida, which later founded a state council.[6]

According to the lynching records kept by the Tuskegee Institute in Alabama, Arkansas did not actually have any incidents of mob violence in 1930.[7] However, like other state councils, the AC-ASWPL obtained literature and facilitated its reform activities through Jessie Daniel Ames and the national body in Atlanta, Georgia. When the ASWPL first organized, Little Rock's Susan Streepey, president of the Little Rock Federation of Women's Clubs and chairperson of its Arkansas council, was among the southern white women who endorsed the following statement confirming their dedication to antilynching reform in their home state: "We pledge ourselves to arouse public opinion to the menace of the crime of lynching by educating the youth of our own communities to an understanding of the consequences of such lawless acts, and by calling upon press, pulpit, schools, and every patriotic citizen to join us in a campaign against such violations of law and civilization and the teachings of religion."[8]

This was issued to the Associated Press and the Negro Associated Press. In addition to Streepey, other Little Rock women leaders endorsed this press statement.[9] Lillian McDermott, Arkansas's first certified social worker, did so enthusiastically: "I shall be glad to render any assistance to the Organization for the Prevention of Lynching, and shall be glad to have my name placed on your mailing list and to have it used in the statement to the press."[10] White women from Arkansas who did not attend the founding meeting in Dallas participated in a leadership school sponsored by the Methodist Episcopal Church, South (MECS) at Mount Sequoyah, located in the Ozark Mountains in Fayetteville, Arkansas, where they discussed the impact of lynching and mob violence on southern race relations. While there, they signed a resolution to condemn lynching and educate their communities about lynching.[11] They also rejected lynching as an excuse to protect white womanhood: "We recognize that all lynching will be defended so long as the public generally accepts the assumption that it is for the protection of white women. We hold that we owe it not only to our own times but to posterity to repudiate acts of mobs and lynchers and declare that if our constitution, our laws, our courts cannot protect women, then our civilization is a travesty and our religion a mockery."[12]

Earlier in 1931, the AC-ASWPL issued its own statement, which said in part, "Be it resolved that the women here assembled heartily endorse the southwide movement of women to educate for the prevention of lynching; that they unanimously condemn lynching as a substitute for the order processes of law and pledge themselves to use their utmost efforts and influences to put a stop to this evil."[13] It was also in 1931 that the AC-ASWPL was credited with preventing, through their intervention, one African American from being lynched in Arkansas. Their activism further attracted notice; by April 1931, thirty-seven Arkansans in four counties had endorsed the AC-ASWPL's antilynching educational program.[14]

Arkansas women certainly must have experienced some trepidation because of the dangerous nature of their activism. They were essentially rejecting lynching as a form of chivalry designed to protect and control them.[15] Early AC-ASWPL executive committee members included women from Little Rock, Batesville, Augusta, and Texarkana.[16] In 1931, the Arkansas Federation of Women's Clubs, the Arkansas Congress of Parents and Teachers, and other white women's organizations resolved that they would, in cooperation with the AC-ASWPL, contact the Arkansas Bar Association and urge it to use its influence to encourage the state legislature to revise the state's criminal codes to abolish criminal trial delays due to technicalities.[17]

Arkansas women wasted little time making plans to share antilynching information with their local organizations. In 1931, for instance, Katherine Smith of the Arkansas Federation of Women's Clubs wrote Jessie Daniel Ames informing her of AC-ASWPL's plans to present information at the next city and state Federation of Women's Clubs meetings. She intimated to Ames her hopes that club women would embrace antilynching reform. Smith was further optimistic that Erle Chambers—because of her connections to Arkansas politics, women's organizations, and the Arkansas Tuberculosis Association—was the right person for the job: "With one like Miss Chambers working slowly but surely and quietly—the movement against lynching will be launched in due time—as you would wish it. It has to grow."[18]

In November 1931, the ASWPL's central council held its first meeting in Atlanta, Georgia. The records do not bear the names of any Arkansas women who attended this first meeting, although there was much discussion about doing so in correspondence with Jessie Daniel Ames. Indeed, Susan Streepey wrote Ames expressing her regret that she was unable to attend the meeting but lending her support to the antilynching cause: "Every effort of ours to either go or send a delegate has been thwarted and to our great disappointment, Arkansas will not be represented. You may be sure that we are in heartiest sympathy with the great task to which you have set your hands and will be doing what we can to further the cause."[19] Della Reaves, the AC-ASWPL chairperson, attended the meeting in 1932, by which time fifty-one Arkansas women from seven counties and eight towns had signed antilynching pledges. She and other central council members pledged their dedication to "A lynchless south in 1933." This effort involved encouraging sheriffs to sign pledges agreeing to help end lynching and reminding them of their responsibility to uphold the law.[20] Reaves's attendance at the 1932 meeting was timely. Earlier in the year, on September 15, 1932, Frank Tucker, a twenty-five-year-old African American male, was lynched by a white mob across the street from his father's home in Crossett, Arkansas, for allegedly stealing ten dollars from a local bank and slashing a marshal's throat.[21] Tucker's lynching may have been the result of a labor dispute. The list of names of those in the mob included the general manager of the Crossett Lumber Company.[22]

Many white women did not understand their antilynching activism as a racial issue but rather as a moral concern that blighted their state and the South's reputation. The Little Rock conference of the MECS, the Little Rock conference of the Women's Missionary Society of the MECS, and the north Arkansas conference of the MECS all dedicated themselves to antilynching educational programs in the state. At times, individual members of these groups provided financial support. In 1935, for instance, Sallie M. Bacon, treasurer of the Women's Missionary Society of the north Arkansas conference of the MECS, and a resident of Booneville in Logan County, sent a five-dollar donation to the ASWPL. In her note, she affirmed her support of the organization's activism: "It is small but carries with it the efforts of women of this conference to help in the great work you are carrying on."[23]

Women's connections were particularly important in the rural South, where informal and, at times, familial contacts with local officials were often the best means by which to encourage them to uphold the law and to keep the community from being stigmatized by a lynching.[24]

The ASWPL had no true constituency but rather an organizational structure that consisted of an executive director, a central council, an executive committee, and thirteen state councils comprised of women leaders of state organizations that were often already involved in antilynching activism.[25] The central council was the clearinghouse for the thirteen state councils' antilynching activism.[26] Central council meeting delegates were chosen from among southern white women who accepted responsibility for disseminating information about the ASWPL and its activities in their home state.[27]

Most Arkansas women who served on the central council of the ASWPL lived in Little Rock and were state or national leaders in their own right.[28] For example, one ASWPL member, Pulaski County's Erle Rutherford Chambers, was executive secretary of the Arkansas Public Health Association[29] and executive secretary of the Arkansas Tuberculosis Association.[30] In 1922, she was the first woman elected to the Arkansas state legislature. In addition to serving on the ASWPL central council, Lillian McDermott, also from Pulaski County, was also appointed a state chairperson responsible for assisting Pres. Franklin D. Roosevelt's "reemployment" drive.[31] Adolphine Fletcher Terry—public education advocate, cofounder of the Little Rock branch of the American Association of University Women, wife of US Rep. David Terry, and someone who was later known for helping to establish the Women's Emergency Committee during the 1957 Little Rock Central High School crisis—also served on the ASWPL's central council in from 1932 until approximately 1937.[32] These three women, who had also served together on the Arkansas State Interracial Committee in the 1920s, were connected by their activism and through their employment with the Pulaski County Juvenile Court. Erle Chambers and Lillian McDermott had both served as probation officers because of Terry's urging and endorsement.[33]

Other AC-ASWPL members included Addie Flenniken, Arkansas state president of the Woman's Missionary Commission (an auxiliary of the Southern Baptist Convention), and Ruth Thorpe, also from Little Rock, who was in 1934 elected one of the vice presidents of the National Parent Teacher Congress.[34] Because the congress also had a race relations committee, Jessie Daniel Ames asked Thorpe to use her influence in the organization in hopes of securing the organization's endorsement for the ASWPL's antilynching program.[35]

The flurry of correspondence between Jessie Daniel Ames and Arkansas women attests to the latter's dedication to eradicating lynching in Arkansas. By 1933, ASWPL state councils had been established throughout the South. Little Rock's Susan Streepey was a vice chairperson on the organization's central council in 1933. Jessie Daniel Ames maintained constant and voluminous correspondence with vice chairpersons, impressing upon them the importance of obtaining signatures from women's organizations that supported educating the public to end lynching.[36] Della Reaves was state council chairperson in 1933, the year during which 226 Arkansas women and three men had signed antilynching pledges.[37] It was during this year that Arkansas made the honor roll along with Florida, Kentucky, Ohio, and Virginia for having a lynchless year.[38]

In 1934, the AC-ASWPL reported that no lynchings had occurred in the state and that the actions of local women had, in fact, prevented the lynching of African Americans in Stuttgart, Blytheville, Osceola, and Hot Springs by encouraging law officials to uphold the law and stave off mob violence. In three of the cases, the accused had been taken out of town for their protection. In Blytheville, the accused was kept in Mississippi County, but the number of guards responsible for his protection was increased.[39] Also by 1934, 592 Arkansas women had signed antilynching pledges, as had fifty-three men and three law officials.[40] To be clear, not all southern women who signed the pledges were associated with the AC-ASWPL even if they supported its work. Rather, the ASWPL filed away their names and contact information so that women who lived nearby could be contacted to investigate a lynching or the threat thereof.[41] This was the case with the aforementioned Sallie M. Bacon's letter and donation in 1935. Jessie Daniel Ames responded to her letter and check: "It was spontaneous and it gave me heart, for I believe that when things like this happen, it indicates that we are making progress on a sane and convincing line. I have put your name on our mailing list and from time to time you will receive literature."[42] Clearly, many of these women tackled or at least discussed lynching in their own organizations. Women who served on the state council of the AC-ASWPL provided them with information, literature, and guidance as they sought to understand and end lynchings by harnessing the moral authority of their own groups.[43]

The AC-ASWPL was dedicated to eradicating lynching in the South but adamantly opposed federal interference to do so. They chose instead to employ moral suasion to compel to officials to follow the letter of the law. In 1934, the ASWPL central council met in Atlanta, Georgia, where they adopted a resolution calling upon Pres. Franklin D. Roosevelt, southern governors, and congressmen to "work out a cooperative plan between the federal government and state government in eradicating the evil of lynching" as state and local authorities had regularly failed to bring lynch mob participants to justice even when—or perhaps because—their identities were known. Jessie Daniel Ames impressed upon southern women the importance of writing their state governors, particularly in light of the Costigan-Wagner federal antilynching bill, which had been drafted by the NAACP and introduced to Congress in January 1934. The bill proposed federal trials for members of mobs, fines or jail time for officials who inadequately discharged their duties, and a fine of $2,000 to $10,000 to the county where a lynching had occurred, with the money going to lynching victims' families.[44] (See chapter 10 for more on Arkansas and antilynching legislation.)

ASWPL members and Jessie Daniel Ames, for that matter, were particularly concerned about the implications of this bill if it passed. Ames argued that "if we are going to contend for state's rights in the handling of this crime, it is high time the state's officials take action on it."[45] Women in Arkansas called upon their governor to speak against lynching in the state, a task that proved difficult for Della Reaves. After considerable effort, she procured a statement from Gov. Junius M. Futrell in which he claimed, "There should be no lynching is not a debatable proposition. With a properly constituted and organized State Police Force in this State, I feel almost certain that another lynching will never occur."[46]

The ASWPL did not endorse federal antilynching legislation; neither did the AC-ASWPL or Arkansas officials.[47] Indeed, Ames, like many southern women, sought to effect change from within the South and typically eschewed federal intervention as an affront to state rights and southern identity and sensibilities.[48] Among the women who attended the meeting and may have voiced similar concerns about and objections to the Costigan-Wagner bill was Ruth Thorpe, the state council representative from Little Rock.[49] Della Reaves actually went to Washington, DC, to observe the Costigan-Wagner bill hearings and to meet with Arkansas's governor and attorney general, a move which Jessie Daniel Ames quipped would leave her with her "hopes still unfulfilled."[50] Ames, like many ASWPL members, deferred to states' rights to handle mob violence and contended that the bill, if passed, would almost certainly be unenforceable.

The central council further outlined a new plan to immediately investigate, report, and collect lynching statistics, tactics previously honed by African American antilynching activist Ida B. Wells-Barnett, the NAACP, and the Tuskegee Institute in Alabama.[51] This information was then published in ASWPL pamphlets and released to the press in order to expedite bringing the guilty parties to justice.[52]

ASWPL state councils had been established throughout the South by 1935, and by 1936 approximately thirty thousand women had signed anti-lynching pledges.[53] The ASWPL congratulated itself for collecting these signatures and for the growing number of white women's organizations that endorsed the ASWPL's activities. In fact, Jessie Daniel Ames, who had made plans to visit Arkansas in March 1936, cancelled her plans because the AC-ASWPL had not reported any lynchings in 1935. She made plans to visit at a later date but had clearly decided that her services were required elsewhere when she said, "I will be back through Arkansas some other time and I am sure we can arrange another meeting, but when Arkansas just does not lynch, it cannot get the attention that these wicked states do."[54] Ames's optimism and the AC-ASWPL's accomplishments unfortunately were sullied by the 1936 lynching of Willie Kees.

On April 29, 1936, nineteen-year-old Willie Kees was killed near Lepanto, in Poinsett County, for allegedly attempting to assault a white woman. Kees was arrested and jailed by city marshal Jay May. May intercepted a mob bent on murdering Kees and convinced them to allow the justice system to run its course. He did the very thing that would have garnered him positive acknowledgement by the ASWPL in local Arkansas and regional southern newspapers. May was also unusual in that he offered to release Kees if he promised to leave Poinsett County and not return. It is possible that Kees failed to appreciate the precariousness of his situation because he allegedly was found in a house just outside of Lepanto, where he was re-arrested by May on April 29.[55] A masked white mob, perhaps incensed by the bravado of Kees's decision to remain in town, wrested him from May's protection and absconded with him in a car. He was found murdered two hours later. His hands were tied behind his back, and he had been shot three times. According to an inquest by justice of the peace W. T. Thurman, Kees's death was "from gunshot wounds at the hands of parties unknown," a popular refrain in the lynching investigations of countless African Americans.[56]

Willie Kees's lynching is noteworthy because it was the first recorded in Poinsett County and the last in Arkansas. The AC-ASWPL had prided itself on how its educational program had positively impacted white Arkansans. In 1937, Della Reaves, the AC-ASWPL chairman reported, "We have converted many women to our way of thinking. We have made our state and county officials realize where we stand and I am sure we have been a big help. Unfortunately, this past year in Arkansas we had a lynching, the first in three years."[57] Reaves wrote Poinsett County sheriff J. D. DuBard and Governor Futrell demanding that they investigate the incident. Her demand was couched in terms that relayed her concern for how such an atrocity might negatively impact Arkansas's reputation as a relatively progressive and racially moderate state when she exclaimed in her letter, "The Arkansas Council of the Association of Southern Women for the Prevention of Lynching deeply deplores the mob murder of Negro Willie Kees at Lepanto and we implore you to demand an investigation of their crime and blot upon the fair name of our beloved state of Arkansas." When she did not hear back from the governor, Reaves sent a copy of the letter to the *Arkansas Gazette*. He then wrote her and enclosed the letter he had sent to the Poinsett County sheriff. Reaves subsequently forwarded that reply to the *Arkansas Gazette* and also wrote the sheriff and the county's prosecuting attorney. Both failed to respond.[58] Although Arkansas had not experienced any lynchings in the previous three years—Ames's reason for not visiting AC-ASWPL in 1936—Willie Kees's murder had made national news and underscored the need for ongoing antilynching education in the state. Reaves understood this as well and wrote Ames, telling her, "I think you had better place Arkansas on your 'visiting list' again."[59]

Reaves's letter to Arkansas's governor was particularly urgent because the local newspaper in which it was printed, the Blytheville *Courier News*, and other state newspapers echoed the similar sentiments about the senselessness of mob violence and its poor reflection on the state.[60] An article in the *Arkansas Gazette* particularly lamented the lynching as "lawless violence" and the unfortunate circumstance that it had occurred "in the year when Arkansas invites the whole nation to join in celebration of its centennial."[61] Like members of the AC-ASWPL, the writer believed that Willie Kees's lynching had projected a negative image of the state and its residents.

The lynching of Kees and two other African Americans in Georgia led to renewed calls for a vote on the Costigan-Wagner bill that had first been proposed in January 1934. The bill was soundly repudiated by southern politicians, including Arkansas's own Hattie Caraway, the first woman elected to the US Senate in 1932.[62] In 1938, in an address before the Senate, Caraway claimed she "never approved or condoned lynchings" and that she has always been "sick at heart when [she] read of anyone being executed without a trial in the courts."[63] However, she believed the

Costigan-Wagner and, later, the Wagner-Van Nuys bill were unconstitutional and would be a "gratuitous insult to the south," thereby assuming a position in favor of states' rights that won her widespread praise among her male colleagues.[64] Caraway, who was not an AC-ASWPL member, resisted federal intervention to eradicate southern mob violence even as she must have certainly been aware of the group's activism.

The AC-ASWPL continued its slow but sure and quiet work of antilynching education among white Arkansans. Like councils around the South, their activities were reported in the ASWPL's bulletins. The ASWPL held its annual meeting in Atlanta, Georgia, in January 1938, the outcome of which was a report titled, "With Quietness They Work: Report of the Activities of Southern Women in Education Against Lynching During 1937." While the memory of the Willie Kees lynching must have been fresh in her mind, Arkansas council chairperson Della Reaves, who was unable to attend the annual meeting, reported that twenty-five representatives from ten state organizations attended a one-day institute on "Education Against Lynching" held in Little Rock in March 1937. The ASWPL central council had decided in 1935 that holding these institutes was necessary in cities where lynchings had recently occurred.[65] Jessie Daniel Ames also visited Little Rock in 1937, and there she met with the AC-ASWPL and high school and college students. Subsequent antilynching education programs were sponsored by the AC-ASWPL and such organizations with religious affiliations as the Little Rock conference of the Methodist Episcopal Church, South, and the Woman's Missionary Union of the Arkansas Baptist Convention. Leaders of secular groups like the Business and Professional Women's Club and the Arkansas branch of the American Association of University Women encouraged their members to endorse an antilynching program in 1937 after reviewing copies of ASWPL's publication "Southern Women and Lynching."[66] Embracing the cause of ecumenicalism, Della Reaves also reached out to the local affiliate of the National Council of Jewish Women (NCJW), which was scheduled to meet in Little Rock the following week, although her efforts were to no avail. Nationally, Jewish council leaders supported the ASWPL.[67] However, southern Jewish women were more cautious. Reaves quite likely did not understand that Jewish women were hesitant to risk their own precarious situation among southern whites—and often eschewed overt antilynching activism—when she reported to Ames that "Jewish women do not endorse unpopular measures."[68]

The AC-ASWPL also continued to impress upon law officials the importance of their role in controlling mobs and preventing racial violence. During 1937, sheriffs throughout Arkansas utilized educational posters on lynchings to enlighten their officers and local whites and to discourage mob violence; they also received approximately one thousand pieces of antilynching literature from the AC-ASWPL. Additionally, women sent law officials letters and managed to secure forty-eight signatures on anti-lynching pledges. According to Reaves, no lynchings occurred in Arkansas in 1937. Indeed, another report recorded that lynchings had actually been prevented in Ouachita and Miller counties because of AC-ASWPL educational programs and the cooperation of women's organizations and law officials.[69]

The AC-ASWPL was convinced that education was the best means to inform whites about the dangers of mob violence—namely, that their town could be blighted by a lynching and the failure of jurisprudence. They did not support antilynching legislation and believed that their "program of education of public opinion" was "bearing fruit." They also were exceedingly confident that "[their] Arkansas officers [were] wide awake to their responsibilities and making every effort for a lynchless state."[70] Their confidence quite likely stemmed from their recording of the 776 women, fifty-three men, three officers, and residents of fifty-one towns in twenty-nine counties who signed pledges to end lynching in Arkansas; too, in a 1938 report, the AC-ASWPL heralded the intercession of local women and the quick action of sheriffs that had prevented the lynching of three black men in Crittenden and Lafayette Counties.[71]

In 1937, the number of leaders from Arkansas women's organizations that endorsed the AC-ASWPL increased as well. Such leaders included, for example, Lila Ashby, a credit manager for the C. J. Lincoln Company (a pharmaceutical company) who was also a member of the Arkansas Business and Professional Women's Club, which had been founded in 1919.[72] Ashby was the treasurer of the Little Rock Association of Credit Men in the 1920s and was one of the organization's founders. Additionally, she was the corresponding secretary of the National Federation of Business and Professional Women's Clubs and was the vice president of the Arkansas club. Ashby served on the board of the Little Rock Young Women's Christian Association, whose Christian tenets may have influenced her decision to become involved with the AC-ASWPL.[73] AC-ASWPL members also included Jennie Dodge, a former Little Rock public school educator and probation officer, who was chairperson of the Arkansas State Hospital Board in Little Rock (she resigned in 1937) and later a member of the National Probation Association.[74] Dodge had worked with both Adolphine Fletcher Terry and Erle Chambers assisting delinquent children and was part of a woman's organizational network that certainly must have influenced her decision to become involved in the AC-ASWPL's work.[75]

Although most of the women on the Arkansas council were centrally located in Little Rock, the geographic diversity of its membership is telling. Members hailed from Batesville, Fayetteville, Augusta, Magazine, and Texarkana. It is striking however, that save Augusta and Texarkana, most resided in areas with relatively few African Americans. Most of these women were leaders in such organizations as the Arkansas Democratic Women's Clubs, the North Arkansas Women's Society of Christian Service, Women's Missionary Society, the Arkansas Parent-Teacher Association, the Arkansas Federation of Women's Clubs, and, by 1938, the Arkansas branch of the American Association of University Women—organizations that, like the AC-ASWPL and the ASWPL, did not welcome African American women's membership.[76] There seems to have been some limited local interracial activism, however. In 1937, Della Reaves participated in a leadership school for black women, perhaps to inform them about the AC-ASWPL's work.[77] Interracial interactions were more likely to occur among national black and white women leaders. In 1938, for instance, the ASWPL central council and the Special Committee of Negro Women of the Commission on Interracial Cooperation met at the Tuskegee Institute in Alabama to discuss the feasibility of the ASWPL remaining an all-white organization. Little Rock's Ruth Thorpe attended this meeting on the AC-ASWPL's behalf, and there she almost certainly interacted with such African American women leaders as CIC representatives Mary McCleod Bethune (founder of the Daytona Normal and Industrial Institute in Florida, which later became Bethune-Cookman University) and Jennie Moton (wife of R. R. Moton, Booker T. Washington's successor at the Tuskegee Institute in Alabama).[78]

By 1939, only three lynchings were reported in ASWPL literature. In none of the three cases had the victims been accused of crimes against white women. In Arkansas, twenty-eight-year-old Walter Lee Frazier's bullet-riddled body was found on a back road in El Dorado, Arkansas.[79] After his death was reported to the NAACP, Jessie Daniel Ames wrote

Della Reaves and asked her to use her connections to ascertain what had
actually occurred. Reaves responded with a letter from Violette McKinney,
vice president of the Little Rock conference of the Women's Missionary
Society, claiming that Frazier had in fact not been lynched by a mob, but
rather he had been shot by the party he had allegedly attempted to rob.[80]
Reaves also reported that an attempted lynching had been thwarted in
Jefferson County after Sylvester Williams, a twenty-year-old black male,
had been charged with assaulting and murdering a nineteen-year-old white
woman near Altheimer in May 1939. After a crowd gathered in front of the
county jail intent upon lynching Williams, deputy sheriffs spirited him
away to Little Rock for his protection. Three weeks later, he was tried and
given the death penalty. The jury had only deliberated his case for a minute.[81] Because the young man had not, in fact, been lynched or subjected to
mob violence, the AC-ASWPL commended the local sheriff, the National
Guard, and the state police for their lifesaving actions.[82]

By 1940, lynchings had declined throughout the South, perhaps due
in small part to the ASWPL's antilynching program, but more likely due
to the democratic and moral rhetoric of World War II, which made racial
violence increasingly unpopular. When the ASWPL Central Council met
in 1941, Jessie Daniel Ames questioned whether or not the organization
should continue its activism. Although lynchings had not abated, murdering black men for the alleged crime of raping and sexually assaulting white
women had become indefensible. Consequently, leaders felt the ASWPL
had achieved its goals. The central council meeting in February 1941 was
its last.[83]

The AC-ASWPL continued to request antilynching materials from the
national body, which were then distributed to local sheriffs. Jessie Daniel
Ames applauded Arkansas women for their successful and influential antilynching program. She rejoiced that no lynchings had occurred over the
previous twelve months and commented that "the sheriffs of Arkansas
are to be especially commended for their efforts to prevent mob violence,
which have brought about such splendid results."[84] Its members did not
report any additional lynchings or mob violence in Arkansas. Rather, in
1940, the AC-ASWPL reported that, due to its efforts, local authorities
had prevented the lynchings of black men in Hempstead, Drew, and
Woodruff Counties in August and September of that year by moving them
to out-of-town locations.[85]

The AC-ASWPL disbanded in 1941, but its activism attests to its connection to white women throughout the South who, as Gail Murray has argued, by "throwing off the cloak of privilege," challenged the racial ideology that resulted in mob violence that terrorized black communities under the guise of protecting white women's honor and virtue.[86] The AC-ASWPL's efforts may not have eradicated lynching in Arkansas, but they utilized antilynching education in southern white communities to discourage racial violence and employed their organizational, personal, and community contacts as conduits for their activism. By doing so "slowly but surely and quietly," they clearly informed public opinion in ways that led to the eventual demise of lynchings and mob violence throughout the South.

Holding the Line

The Arkansas Congressional Delegation and the Fight over a Federal Antilynching Law

On June 13, 2005, the United States Senate adopted a resolution apologizing for its consistent failure, over numerous decades, to enact a federal antilynching law.[1] In the voice vote that took place more than a century after the introduction of the first federal antilynching measure, the voices of Arkansas's senators, Mark Pryor and Blanche Lincoln, both of whom co-sponsored the resolution, should arguably have been among the loudest.[2] Indeed, notwithstanding the Founding Fathers' intent that the House and Senate would be bodies of equals, individuals representing the distinctive interests of their constituents against the backdrop of a broader union, Arkansas's congressional delegation, especially its senators, played an outsized historical role in the decades-long effort to prevent the enactment of any federal antilynching legislation.

There is no denying that the effort to prevent the enactment of any antilynching legislation was part of the broader southern resistance to any and all federal civil rights legislation, and support of that obstructionist effort was often central to political survival in the South during this period. But in many ways, the antilynching efforts were the first major battleground, the issue that first focused a spotlight on the complex interrelationship between race, the lines of jurisdiction in a constitutionally based federal system, and the simple but often stark realities that characterized politics, especially racial politics in twentieth-century America. When viewed against this background, a look at how the Arkansas delegation navigated this politically charged path offers important lessons about power and influence in the Congress, especially in the Senate, as well as vivid examples of the way Arkansas's representatives wielded the influence they possessed. And, in the end, a study of these events makes clear that, among the constitutionally directed factors that distinguish the House and the Senate, not to mention the personalities at play, it was the actions — or inaction — of its senators that accounted for Arkansas's greatest culpability.

All of this stems, of course, from the fact that, in the long and tangled history of race relations in the United States, few issues have generated more emotional heat than lynching. At the same time, few issues have more fully illustrated the distinctive political landscape that characterized the South following the Civil War. Indeed, central to southern politics, in the aftermath of Reconstruction and well into the twentieth century, was the maintenance of a social system dedicated to black subservience and white supremacy on a daily basis. Fueled by a war-induced resentment, if not outright hatred, of the Republican Party, politics in the South was a Democratic Party enterprise, and through the adroit and often heavy-handed use of poll taxes, literacy tests, and white primaries, the Democrats narrowed it even further, making it a white man's enterprise. While there was no shortage of intraparty battles among the Democrats, the realities of the region's one-party system, wholly rooted in the fault lines that had led to the Civil War, allowed southern legislators to retain and consolidate power in ways that their northern counterparts, faced with true interparty competition, could not. That, in turn, allowed southern legislators to accumulate congressional seniority at a time when office tenure, more than any recognized expertise or knowledge, was the basis of congressional power. As a result, with its members holding the reins of some of the most important committees in both the House and the Senate, at the peak of its power the South achieved a bit of a stranglehold on the legislative process, a fact that made both bodies, but especially the Senate, bunkers against federal efforts to change the southern way of life. Adding to their seniority-based power was the ability of the southern senators to bring the Senate to a standstill through the use of the filibuster, a weapon they employed on numerous occasions to bend the body to their will.[3]

In addition to the distinctive political landscape that both characterized the South and also made possible its outsized influence in Congress at large, and the Senate in particular, some of the Supreme Court's early interpretations of the Fourteenth Amendment only encouraged a continuation of the "states' rights" mentality that had existed before the war. First came the Supreme Court's rulings in the *Slaughterhouse Cases* (1873), wherein a majority of the justices reduced the reach of the Privileges or Immunities Clause, limiting the federal government's ability to protect the rights of the freedmen from state action.[4] This was coupled with the rulings in the *Civil Rights Cases* (1883), wherein the court not only invalidated the major anti-discrimination provisions of the post–Civil War civil rights acts, but also narrowly interpreted the Fourteenth Amendment so as to limit the federal government's power to protect individual rights, maintaining instead that aggrieved citizens should look to the states for protection.[5] These rulings not only reinforced, but even legitimized, the South's natural preference to see lynching—along with poll taxes, white primaries, and literacy requirements—as matters best left to the states and localities, and not subjects with which the federal government should interfere.

However, despite this rather forbidding political and legal climate, when, in 1901, a federal antilynching law was proposed for the first time, the issue suddenly assumed a place in the forefront of the slowly developing debate on civil rights in the United States—a debate that, among many things, highlighted the divide between federal power and states' rights. As lawmakers began addressing the crime, their efforts laid bare the distinctive interactions between human behavior and governmental policy, between political realities and political ambitions, and between the distinctive historical traditions of the South and the realities of representative politics.

In fact, the legislative efforts to enact a federal antilynching law in the first half of the twentieth century offer textbook lessons in the realities of the seniority-based power structure that existed in Congress at the time. The treatment accorded lynching offers vivid examples of the way the system operated. Indeed, opposition to antilynching legislation was often played as a trump card by southern power brokers who seldom evinced the slightest bit of hesitation at holding other legislation—be it the president's or a colleague's—hostage in the effort to prevent the enactment of any federal antilynching legislation. It was also an issue that served to illustrate the gaps between law and justice in the South while shining a light on why federal intervention would ultimately be necessary to secure justice.

While the states had been dealing—or not—with the problem of lynching for almost the whole of the post-Reconstruction era, the issue did not really get onto the congressional radar until 1901. At that time, after years of southern indifference both to the lynchings and the ongoing

examples of white-on-black violence that came to characterize life in
the post-Reconstruction South, northern legislators finally resolved to
address the situation. Although unsure of exactly how to proceed, in 1901,
Massachusetts senator George F. Hoar introduced a bill calling for a federal
ban on lynching. Buttressed by research conducted by his friend Albert E.
Pillsbury, the former attorney general of Massachusetts, Hoar submitted
a proposal, based on the Fourteenth Amendment's equal protection pro-
vision, that would "protect citizens of the United States against lynching
in default of protection by the States."[6] The law was similar to many of
the existing, but unenforced, state laws, but perhaps most importantly,
it provided for trials by a federal jury—which, it was believed, would
increase the likelihood of achieving convictions. The initial reaction to the
proposal was mixed, with many in the northern media offering support
while anticipating southern opposition.[7] African American organizations,
not surprisingly, were particularly supportive.[8] However, before too long,
opposition, much of it centered in southern newspapers, did emerge, and
while the bill was based in the Fourteenth Amendment, many of the opponents vigorously attacked the proposal on constitutional grounds, arguing
that it represented a gross encroachment by the federal government on
state authority.[9] In the end, the bill failed to garner any real support, and in
May 1902, the Senate Judiciary Committee, chaired by Hoar (whose own
confidence in the bill's constitutionality had been shaken by the onslaught
of opposition), accepted this argument, determining that the federal government, in fact, had no authority to intervene in state matters of this type.
The bill was set aside.[10]

There the issue remained until 1918 when Leonidas Dyer, a Republican
congressman from Saint Louis, Missouri, introduced his antilynching bill,
a proposal that became known as the Dyer bill. The legislation, very similar to the 1901 bill introduced by Senator Hoar, defined a mob as three
or more persons acting without authority of law. It held them liable for
prosecution in federal court as a capital crime. In addition, officials who
allowed lynchings to occur were also subject to prosecution resulting in
substantial fines and imprisonment.[11] The bill gained little attention in
the early going. Indeed, the National Association for the Advancement of
Colored People (NAACP), which would spearhead antilynching efforts
in the upcoming decades, did not support the bill until 1919. In fact, the
group had originally withheld support because Moorfield Storey, an attorney and the first president of the NAACP, expressed his belief that the law

was unconstitutional. However, upon further review, he changed his mind, and, abandoning its opposition, the NAACP threw its support behind the bill, initiating a new chapter in the developing effort.[12]

Arkansas's congressional delegation watched these developments with a wary eye. While the state was not immune to lynchings, it was not the hot-bed that Mississippi, Georgia, Texas, and Louisiana were. And yet, like all their southern brethren, elites in Arkansas had concerns about the extension of federal power, especially in the area of race, that were not limited simply to antilynching laws but rather extended to any incursions by the federal government into state affairs. With consistent representation on the House Judiciary Committee, the portal through which all prospective bills of this kind passed, the state's political power brokers were able to keep abreast of any threat. While none of their members achieved major influence, Arkansas's congressional delegation enjoyed almost continuous membership on the House Judiciary Committee, a fact that allowed them to keep a close eye on the almost two hundred antilynching measures that were introduced from 1882 to 1968.[13] The line began in 1885 with the Third District's John Rogers, who served on the committee until 1891. He was followed by the Fourth District's William Terry, who occupied a seat on the panel from 1893 until 1901. After another one-term hiatus, the state again gained a seat on the committee when John S. Little, having been redistricted from the Second to the Fourth District, assumed a seat, which he held from 1903 to 1907. At that point, Charles Chester Reid of the Fifth District took up the state's banner, serving until 1911. Third District representative John C. Floyd assumed a seat in 1911 and served until 1915, when former prosecutor and First District congressman Thaddeus Caraway came aboard, beginning a stint that would run until 1921 when he moved on to the Senate. Caraway was followed by the Third District's John N. Tillman, whose tenure ran from 1921 to 1929.[14] Second District representative John Miller, whose political fortunes had been boosted when, as chief prosecutor, he effectively navigated the political and racial minefield that was left in the wake of the infamous Elaine Massacre of 1919, was a Judiciary Committee member for three terms, serving from 1933 until 1938.[15] He was followed by William Fadjo Cravens, who represented the Fourth District and occupied a committee seat from 1941 to the end of 1948, when he was followed by his successor in the Fourth District, Boyd Tackett, who vigilantly guarded the state's interests as a committee member from 1949 to 1951.[16]

The NAACP's newfound but enthusiastic support came at an important moment, serving as a valuable complement to the additional public support that had emerged in the aftermath of the turbulent and violent summer of 1919. In fact, that summer, the first following World War I, would prove to be something of a milestone in the battle to secure equal rights in the United States. With both the white and the black soldiers who had fought to "make the world safe for democracy" struggling to find their place in an economy that was having difficulty finding its postwar footing, as well as in a home front democracy whose reality still fell short of its promise, there was a feeling of national uneasiness.[17] Unhappily, those tensions erupted in a series of race riots in cities including San Francisco, California; Omaha, Nebraska; Chicago, Illinois; Knoxville, Tennessee; Wilmington, Delaware; and Washington, DC.[18] Arkansas was not spared the racially based turmoil that characterized the volatile summer. In fact, by the time the dust had settled, the series of events in Phillips County, commonly referred to as the Elaine Massacre, was recognized as one of the more infamous incidents, one that would ultimately have major ramifications in the ongoing debates about antilynching laws. In addition, the US Army's involvement, coupled with later involvement by the federal courts, raised anew issues of federal versus state authority, an issue that directly touched on the lynching debate.

The Elaine Massacre began on the night of September 30, 1919, when white agitators apparently tried to break up a meeting in which blacks, primarily sharecroppers, were discussing the possibility of unionizing by joining the local chapter of the Progressive Farmers and Household Union of America. The attack escalated into a melee, and violence broke out, beginning a multi-day episode that may have resulted in as many as two hundred deaths, although the exact body count remains debated to this day.[19] As the violence continued, Gov. Charles Brough got permission from the War Department to use federal troops to restore order. However, by some accounts, the troops also engaged in similar indiscriminate violence against African Americans, a fact conveniently seized upon by officials who sought to deflect and minimize the charges of critics who characterized the incident as essentially a wholesale lynching party.[20]

Historians continue to try to sort out the charges and counter-charges, and the body count itself remains uncertain.[21] What is clear is that over four hundred African Americans were taken into custody, well over one hundred local African Americans were charged with crimes allegedly stemming from the incident, and twelve African Americans were charged and convicted of murder for their role in the event, which was described in the white press as an attempted insurrection.[22] But in the end, the murder convictions ultimately were all overturned, and by the time the United States Supreme Court had spoken, life had returned to "normal" in a region whose economic instability was matched by a similarly unsteady racial situation.[23]

And yet the Elaine Massacre's impact would endure, for while the riot would ultimately fade in people's memories, *Moore v. Dempsey*, the 1923 decision by the US Supreme Court in the case that arose from the riots, would have long-term legal ramifications. Indeed, in ruling that the proceedings that had resulted in the convictions and death sentences for six African Americans were a violation of their federal due process rights, the court offered, however unintentionally, a powerful reminder of what could happen when the federal government got involved in local matters, especially on the racial front.[24]

The summer's turmoil served both as a backdrop and an impetus for Dyer's continuing efforts, and in fact, when the Saint Louis congressman re-introduced his bill in 1920, he was not alone in his pursuit of a law whose need had seemingly been heightened by the events of the summer of 1919. Rather, on January 29, 1920, the House Judiciary Committee opened hearings on three federal antilynching bills.[25] The hearings themselves were an important historical and symbolic event, offering an unprecedented opportunity for groups, led by the NAACP, to outline grievances and offer ideas about how to combat them. The committee, chaired by Minnesota's Arthur Volstead of Prohibition renown, considered three distinct measures, for in addition to Representative Dyer's bill (a revised version of his 1918 proposal), bills had also been introduced by Rep. Frederick Dallinger of Boston, Massachusetts, and Rep. Merrill Moores of Indianapolis, Indiana.[26]

The opposition to the historic presentation was swift and pointed. Led by Arkansas committee member and former prosecutor Thaddeus Caraway, a group of congressmen attacked the bill on constitutional grounds, asserting that the Founding Fathers had been clear in opposing the intervention by the federal government in state and local affairs.[27] It was a not atypical line of attack, as the constitutional arguments represented the political high ground for a new generation of legislators who sought to avoid the racially heated rhetoric that had characterized some of their predecessors in the late nineteenth century. At the same time, later that year when the NAACP offered a report supporting Dyer's bill, Caraway countered with a two-page response that termed the NAACP's document "merely a reprint of a brief filed with the committee by a society domiciled in New York which has for its sole object, not the securing of justice for Negros charged with a crime, but immunity from punishment for their crimes."[28] In fact, Caraway's opposition was not a surprise, for following the infamous Elaine Massacre, he had minimized the action of white citizens, defending his constituents while instead placing the responsibility, if not the blame, at the feet of the military.[29] Declaring that "the killing of Negroes that followed [the insurrection] was not a lynching and not the result of a mob, but was done very largely by soldiers of the United States under the command of their officers and in obedience to orders issued by the War Department," Caraway made clear that the events of the summer of 1919, especially those that had taken place in Arkansas, should have no bearing on congressional consideration of the antilynching proposal.[30] In the end, the energetic and two-pronged attack served its purpose. The Dyer bill was defeated.[31]

Dyer tried again in 1922, and this time he had the backing of the president when Warren G. Harding expressed his strong support for a federal statute to address the issue.[32] Indeed, the "Party of Lincoln" contingent expressed its solid support for the legislation on January 26, 1922, when the House passed the Dyer bill by a vote of 231 to 119.[33] However, when it reached the Senate, Arkansas's Thaddeus Caraway, having been elected to the upper house in 1920, was there to greet it. When the Senate Judiciary Committee voted the bill out of committee by a two-vote margin, a predominantly party-line vote (deserting the Republican ranks was the ever-independent William G. Borah), the Democrats, and especially their southern leaders, were ready for action.[34] Interestingly, regional differences were initially minimized, for in noting the partisan lines on which the committee had voted, they couched their opposition in political terms. Arkansas's Caraway spoke for many of his Democratic colleagues when he derisively noted that the Republican-sponsored measure was in fact "never intended to be passed [but] . . . was only a bid to induce the negro to continue to vote the Republican ticket."[35]

In the end, House passage of the Dyer bill moved the Senate's southern contingent to action, and they responded with what one reporter termed "one of the most efficiently conducted filibusters in the history of the senate."[36] Caraway served as one of the leaders of an effort that brought the regular flow of business to a standstill, and he minced no words as he attacked both the bill and its supporters. Speaking on the Senate floor, Arkansas's junior senator declared, "Here is the truth of the matter: I am sure, although I have no way to substantiate it, that a society known as the society for the protection of the rights of the colored people wrote this bill and handed it to the proponents of it. These people had but one idea in view, and that was to make rape permissible."[37] Forcefully denouncing the bill, Caraway argued that Dyer's proposal would serve only to "encourage a negro to believe that the strong arm of the Federal Government was going to . . . protect him and save him from punishment, however infamous his crime might be."[38] In addition, he charged that the real intent of the NAACP in sponsoring the antilynching legislation was not only to make rape acceptable, but also to "allow the guilty to go unpunished if that rape should be committed by a Negro on a white woman in the South."[39] In that effort, Caraway and his allies achieved a major victory, for with over a thousand presidential appointments, including the Supreme Court nomination of Pierce Butler, awaiting action, the Republican majority agreed to table the bill in order to allow necessary business to be completed before the impending adjournment.[40] Indeed, so effective was the 1922 filibuster that the Republicans, recognizing the enduring political realities that had dictated the fate of the Dyer bill in the Senate, would never again mount a substantive effort on behalf of an antilynching bill. Instead, it would fall to the northern and western wings of the Democratic Party to revive the effort—but not for another decade. At the same time, this lack of effort by the Republicans, while arguably little more than an acknowledgement of the political realities of the time, would ultimately provide an opening which, by the end of the New Deal, allowed the Democrats to reverse the longstanding loyalty of the nation's African Americans to the "Party of Lincoln."[41]

In the meantime, the Democratic Party was experiencing a change in its Senate leadership, one that had no small impact on Arkansas's political fortunes. While Thaddeus Caraway had played a more public role in the battle over the Dyer bill, his senior colleague, Joseph T. Robinson, was equally opposed to the measure, asserting that it was little more than an election-year effort by Republicans intended to appeal to the black vote.[42] And yet, while Caraway was leading the charge against the Dyer bill, Senator Robinson was strengthening his own political position, an effort that would ultimately have a major impact on future antilynching law battles. In late 1922, Alabama senator Oscar Underwood announced that he would step down as Democratic leader. Robinson quickly organized a campaign that preempted the field, and while Furnifold Simmons of North Carolina had been the early favorite, by the time the party met to vote, Robinson faced no opposition and was elected by acclaim.[43] From that position, one which ultimately made him the veritable gatekeeper for all legislation—race-related and otherwise—he was able to protect the state's interests on a range of issues, none more important than antilynching legislation. Indeed, over the next decade and a half, no legislator would wield more power in the debates and maneuverings that characterized the next round of efforts to enact an antilynching law than would Democratic Senate leader Joseph T. Robinson.

Robinson's ascension to the position of Democratic Senate leader represented the culmination of a determined climb. Born in 1872, he received his early education in a one-room schoolhouse before embarking on a successful legal career. Trading upon his developing courtroom reputation, he was elected to Congress in 1902 at the age of thirty. In a quick succession of events, Robinson, after representing the Sixth District for a decade, was elected governor in 1912, but only days after he had assumed the governorship, the state's junior senator, Jeff Davis, died of a sudden heart attack. Using his considerable influence as governor, Robinson persuaded the legislature to choose him to succeed Davis, making him the last Arkansas senator to be chosen by the state legislature. He soon established himself as the consummate Senate insider, party loyalist, and workhorse.[44] Unhappily for Robinson, he came to power as the leader of a party that was most definitely in the minority. However, at least on the issue of lynching, that minority status was not necessarily a bad thing for Robinson, for the dynamics of the fight over the Dyer bill led the pragmatic leaders of the Republican majority to the apparent conclusion that it was not an issue that could likely be pursued with any great success.[45] In addition, historians have speculated that the close call on the Dyer bill was a spur to the many antilynching state laws (albeit weak ones) that were passed in the aftermath of the efforts.[46] Whether the hope that taking care of business at home would fend off federal interference in this area—an incursion that could open the door to more intrusive federal legislation in areas of even greater concern—was a realistic one or not, congressional efforts to pursue an antilynching bill were all but invisible for the remainder of the 1920s, and the number of lynchings themselves appeared also to diminish, reducing the pressure for federal intervention.[47]

But lynching was not an issue that would go away, and the disproportionate representation the South enjoyed in the Senate compared to the House, coupled with the filibuster option, made the Senate the logical place for the southerners to make their stand. Consequently, as Senate minority leader from 1923 to 1933 and then majority leader from 1933 until his death in the summer of 1937, Arkansas's Robinson was at command central as both sides again tried to navigate the labyrinth of the legislative process. Robinson limited the opportunities for the antilynching forces to have their efforts impact an increasingly disparate Democratic coalition. Indeed, the very nature of the antilynching efforts had changed over the course of Robinson's stewardship. Originally, he had been fending off what could be dismissed as partisan, Republican-sponsored efforts, but the challenges he encountered as majority leader originated within his own party from northern and western Democrats.

Ultimately, however, it was a southern concern, one that forced Robinson to balance his regional and state loyalties and responsibilities with those that came with his party leadership. While many southern senators approached lynching in an ideological way, scoring points with constituents back home through demagogic speeches that trumpeted southern virtue, Robinson, while no stranger to the power of Senate oratory, chose to serve as a manager and gatekeeper for the opponents of the antilynching laws. Effectively utilizing his power as Democratic floor leader, Robinson simply prevented the bills from seeing the light of day. Although he was both a loyal Democrat and a faithful servant of the president, a man whose unstinting loyalty to Pres. Franklin D. Roosevelt would, in the view of many, ultimately kill him, Robinson was fundamentally opposed to any federal antilynching legislation. Consequently, so long as the president offered no direct support of the antilynching bills, Robinson was happy and able to keep them bottled up. This frustrated the bills' backers, while also affording his fellow southerners the luxury of not even having to make the effort to engage in a filibuster, the likes of which had so often been necessary to defeat legislation that had overwhelmingly passed the House.

This was never clearer than with the Costigan-Wagner bill, first introduced in 1934 by Colorado senator Edward Costigan and his colleague Robert Wagner of New York. The proposed legislation included no direct federal action against those who actually engaged in the act of lynching. Rather, it was aimed at local law enforcement officials who had long turned a blind eye to the actions of local mobs and, in doing so, had failed to "assure to persons within [the] jurisdiction of every State the equal protection of the laws."[48] The bill received a favorable report in March from the sub-committee chaired by Indiana senator Frederick Van Nuys, but Robinson blocked all efforts to bring it to the Senate floor.[49] This was certainly no sur-prise given that a preliminary headcount by the NAACP of likely votes on the measure had both Robinson and his Arkansas colleague Hattie Caraway among the twenty-three definitely opposed.[50] Indeed, in a further example of both Robinson's opposition and his influence, later that spring, when NAACP executive director Walter White sought President Roosevelt's sup-port in the effort to bring the Costigan-Wagner antilynching bill to a vote, the president reportedly told White that Joe Robinson had said the bill was unconstitutional.[51] Despite White's extensive and well-researched rebuttal, the president would not concede. In addition, later in that same conver-sation, Roosevelt made clear to White just how much influence Robinson and his colleagues had, admitting that were he to come out in support of an antilynching bill, the southerners—Robinson, Vice Pres. John Nance Garner of Texas, and numerous committee chairs—would block every-thing he proposed. With the nation still mired in the Depression, the pres-ident matter-of-factly declared, "I just can't take that risk."[52]

However, events forced Congress's hand, and after the summer of 1934 saw an upturn in racial violence, in April 1935 Costigan announced his intention to push for consideration of his bill on the Senate floor. The announcement was greeted with dismay because no one expected anything but opposition from the southern contingent, opposition that would take the form of a filibuster that would put on hold a raft of other important pending legislation, including the Social Security Act.

It was a challenging situation for the majority leader, and Robinson quickly found himself forced to lead an effort to fend off this latest attempt to enact an antilynching law. However, in this case, that effort was made more difficult by the fact that the opposition was less united than usual—at least, as far as their strategy was concerned. Sen. Pat Harrison of Mississippi, one of the leaders with Thaddeus Caraway of the 1922 filibuster that had derailed the Dyer bill, announced that he was open to allowing the Senate to vote and take up the law, although he added that he would then immediately enter a motion to set it aside.[53] Other Senate opponents had no patience for even considering the proposal, maintaining that such legislation deserved no consideration by Congress.[54] When the Costigan-Wagner antilynching bill was sent back to committee on April 24, Costigan proposed instead that it be brought to the floor. That proposed move was met with loud opposition by southern members, and the result was the start of a discussion of the bill's fundamental intent and purpose.[55] As the deliberations proceeded, Robinson was worried both about the progress of the bill and its impact on ongoing important legislation. Given his concerns, he sought initially to table the bill, but his first effort to do so on April 26 was defeated by one vote, and debate on the proposal continued.[56] As the calendar turned to May, Robinson was determined to rid the Senate of the nuisance but was struggling to keep his troops in line.[57] Reasserting his authority and stressing the importance of completing the president's program to lift the nation from the jaws of the continuing economic depression, Robinson regained control of his disparate majority. Adroitly holding the threat of a filibuster by his southern colleagues in reserve, the majority leader kept substituting other bills—additional pieces of the New Deal program—for the Costigan-Wagner measure and, in the end, was able to further the president's interests while also preventing any further consideration of the Costigan-Wagner proposal.[58]

In the spring of 1937, in the aftermath of both Roosevelt's landslide reelection victory, one that swept into office ever greater Democratic majorities, and a pair of highly publicized daylight murders in Mississippi, the House acted on the latest antilynching proposal, the Gavagan bill (named for Joseph Andrew Gavagan, US representative from New York). Although southerners had expressed outrage over the Mississippi incidents, demanding swift local justice (a call cynical observers believed was intended only to forestall federal action), they were no more supportive of the Gavagan measure and its companion in the Senate, the Wagner-Van Nuys bill (Costigan had retired from the Senate after the 1936 election, finally succumbing to ill health, but Van Nuys, a long-time Judiciary Committee member, was ready to step in and take up Costigan's cause).[59] Both measures were comparable to previous versions but had been revised to reflect changes in the social landscape.[60] The new bills, unlike earlier versions, did not include violence involving gangsters or racketeers nor riots that occurred in the course of labor disputes. They also sought to expand the reach of the Lindbergh Kidnapping Act in an effort to include some of the more egregious cases like the 1934 lynching of Claude Neal in Florida, which had shocked the nation's sensibilities.[61] However, for the most part, the thrust of the bills remained the same, and with public opinion polls showing support for such legislation running at 70 percent, with even southerners supporting a federal act by a 30-percent margin, supporters were far more optimistic than they had been at any time since the original introduction of the Dyer bill.[62] At the same time, the opposition among the southern delegation remained strong. Typical was the position of Arkansas's congressman John McClellan, who not only joined many of his colleagues in opposition, but more pointedly asserted that the law was not only unconstitutional but that the whole effort was little more than an anti-South gambit aimed at embarrassing the region.[63] Meanwhile, his fellow Arkansas representative, John E. Miller, attacked the NAACP's role in the effort, declaring, "I know the heat has been applied to you [supporters of the bill] by the greatest racketeering organization in the United States today, an organization that is preying upon the credulity of the colored race."[64] When the bill came to a vote, the region did not have enough firepower to block the effort, and in April, by a 277–120 vote, the House passed the Gavagan measure and sent it on to the Senate, which, having already begun to wrestle with their version, the Wagner-Van Nuys bill, was less than welcoming.[65]

In fact, even a cursory glance at Senate history would have left the most casual observer fully aware of the reality that, the 1936 election results notwithstanding, the Senate remained a place where southern power made passage of an antilynching law highly unlikely. And as if that history were not enough, prospects for passage were further complicated by the fact that the antilynching bill reached the upper house at as bad a time as could possibly be imagined—right in the midst of the body's consideration of President Roosevelt's controversial "court reform" bill. Indeed, the infamous "court-packing" plan was already proving to be one of the most fractious and divisive pieces of legislation the Senate had ever addressed, and as a result, the self-styled "world's greatest deliberative body" was torn in numerous, and in some cases previously unimaginable, ways.

Such was the political reality when, in June 1937, in the midst of its deliberations and study of the president's court bill, the Senate Judiciary Committee gave the Wagner-Van Nuys bill a favorable report, setting the stage for another round of what could have been called legislative hide-and-seek.[66] More than ever, the president needed southern support if he was to get his court bill passed, and the southern senators knew it. In addition, the situation was further complicated by the fact that Roosevelt had implied that Robinson's reward for years of service, and more specifically, for passage of the court bill, would be a career-crowning appointment to the nation's highest court—although such rumors resulted in vocal opposition from liberal activists and civil rights groups.[67] The convergence of these factors only added to the majority leader's burden. Court opponents would welcome an antilynching filibuster, while antilynching advocates now felt pressure to support the court bill in the hope that the reward for their support would be the elusive, but long sought, White House backing of their cause.[68] In the middle of all of these machinations was Robinson, the political wheeler-dealer who, true to his reputation for legislative balancing, had been able to fend off the effort in April to bring the Wagner-Van Nuys bill to the floor while the court bill took center stage. However, the stress of the battle became too much, and on the morning of July 14, Joseph Robinson was found dead on the floor of his apartment, an apparent victim of a massive heart attack.[69] His death effectively killed the court bill as well, although a change in the Supreme Court's approach, coupled with the retirement of conservative justice Willis Van Devanter, rendered the issue moot.[70]

The new Senate majority leader, Alben Barkley of Kentucky, Roosevelt's choice in the hard-fought contest for Robinson's successor, was no less determined than Robinson had been to prevent consideration of the Wagner-Van Nuys proposal, but the bill's supporters were not easily denied.[71] They tried first to attach it as an amendment to a railroad bill, and then they tried a parliamentary maneuver that also failed.[72] After those defeats, another parliamentary gambit offered a postmortem lesson in the extent of Joe Robinson's control of the Senate calendar, and thus his critical role in limiting consideration of antilynching legislation in the Senate.[73]

Seeking to repair the fissures that had developed in the course of the Senate's consideration of Roosevelt's effort to "reform" the Supreme Court, soon after Barkley's ascension to the position of majority leader, the Senate Democrats held a dinner aimed at reuniting the disparate elements of the majority. The evening went well, and a spirit of harmony seemed to be restored. However, the next day, on the Senate floor, in a surprise move, Senator Wagner sought to have his antilynching bill put to a vote. Barkley objected, arguing that the leadership had agreed to consider other legislation first. When that assertion was not accepted by the presiding officer, Vice President Garner, Barkley made a motion to adjourn, an action that would have overridden Wagner's motion and ended the threat. In response, a group of maverick Democrats teamed with the Republicans to defeat the adjournment motion. Asked by a Democrat how to vote, Barkley, in utter frustration, declared, "I don't know! Ask [Republican leader Charles] McNary! He's the only real leader round here. That was a hell of a harmony dinner we had last night."[74] To Barkley's relief, the ever-present threat of a filibuster allowed him to persuade Wagner to withdraw his bill so as to allow other business to go forward. But in gaining this concession, Barkley had to promise to take it up in the following session.[75] In fact, however, a southern filibuster blocked that effort as well, and while the stalemate would continue through 1938 and 1939, by that time the pressure for action had lessened significantly.[76] Indeed, with only three reported lynchings in 1939, public support slipped from the 1937 high of 70 percent to 55 percent in 1940.[77]

Although Joe Robinson had occupied center stage as majority leader, his Senate colleague was herself a national figure who might well have impacted the antilynching debates had she been so inclined. Hattie Caraway had been appointed in 1931 to replace her husband, Thaddeus, when he died suddenly from complications following surgery.[78] Initially viewed as an historical footnote, another senatorial wife appointed to hold a seat until the political powers in the state could organize their campaigns to win a lengthier stay, in 1932 Caraway defied all expectations and beat the odds in turning back a multi-candidate field that included some of the state's leading political heavyweights. Not only did she win election in her own right, she became the first woman in history to do so. Six years later, she did it again, defeating Rep. John L. McClellan to win a second term.[79] Throughout this time, Caraway was a dutiful guardian of her state's interests, and her stand on lynching typified that approach. Reflecting the complex balance between humanity and politics, Senator Caraway made clear that she abhorred the practice of lynching. At the same time, however, she was no less clear about her opposition to federal legislation designed to curb it. Indeed, in January 1938, "Silent Hattie," as she was known, took to the Senate floor to express her thoughts on the issue. In that forum, she acknowledged that race relations should be improved, adding that she despised law enforcement without due process. At the same time, Caraway expressed clearly her opposition to any federal antilynching bill, believing that it targeted the southern states, and especially her home state. She added that the bill then under consideration was not needed in Arkansas, noting that not only had the state not had a lynching in a year, but that a recent case occurred in Crittenden County where the law was carried out despite rumors that a lynching was in the works.[80] In an assertion that belied her image as a silent observer of the Senate's deliberations, she called the antilynching measure a "gratuitous insult to the South," adding that "certain groups want to destroy the South not only as a political entity but as a business threat in competition with other sections."[81] She never wavered in her views, and later, in an interview during World War II, at a time when the incidence of lynching had dropped to almost none, Caraway reiterated her long-expressed stance, telling a reporter that while she was opposed to brutality, she also opposed any federal antilynching efforts. She said, "I am against lynching. Don't see any reason for a law now, because there is not any more lynching going on now. Since it is on decline I don't see how a federal bill will help."[82] In addition, in a remark reminiscent of her late husband's comments in opposition to the Dyer bill, she told the African American interviewer, "You know how some of you all are—apt to take advantage of everything. An anti-lynching bill might cause trouble. People might get out of hand, maybe."[83]

In the end, Senator Caraway was steadfast in her opposition to a federal antilynching law despite the fact that some certainly expected that her gender might make her more sympathetic to the inhumane nature of the act and thus more open to a legislative response. At the same time, her gender was also a factor on another level as people debated an act that was often defended as a legitimate response to crimes against southern womanhood. All of these factors complicated the equation for Hattie Caraway, as did the existence of a vocal and influential group called the Association of Southern Women for the Prevention of Lynching (whose history is covered in the previous chapter). Founded in 1930 under the leadership of Texas suffragist advocate Jessie Daniel Ames, the organization sought to end lynching while also debunking the argument that lynching was a legitimate defense of the virtue of southern women.[84] Fighting the battle at the local level by educating people on the realities of the act and its motivation, the group sought pledges from local sheriffs and police officers to uphold the law and prevent lynchings.[85] In 1938, the organization issued a pamphlet that documented both an overall drop in lynching and an increase in the number of cases in which local officials, apparently honoring the pledge, took action and prevented lynchings.[86] All of this provided cover for those who opposed the antilynching legislation because such efforts made the whole issue seem increasingly superfluous. The women's group, which disbanded in 1942, at a time when lynchings had declined to almost nothing, also provided political cover for the Senate's most prominent woman. Like Caraway's opposition, the association's opposition to lynching was matched by an opposition to federal antilynching legislation, which they believed would undermine their local efforts.[87] For Caraway, it was a convenient and helpful approach by a group whose very nature could have caused political trouble for the quiet but cagey office holder. Indeed, no number of learned lawyers echoing Caraway's belief that a federal statue was unconstitutional had the impact that the region's major female-led antilynching organization had by sharing—and thus supporting—her view that it was a problem best handled at the local level.

The onset of World War II and the major decrease in the number of lynchings taking place across the South resulted in the issue taking a back seat to more pressing legislative business into the mid-1940s.[88] However, the return to a segregated home by African American soldiers who had just fought for the cause of freedom and democracy not only brought racial issues back into play but, in many ways, heightened their urgency.[89] In addition, the debate over the inclusion of calls for anti–poll tax and anti-lynching legislation in the Democratic Party's 1948 campaign platform led to a party split, resulting in the creation of the States' Rights Democratic Party (the Dixiecrats), as well as another round of antilynching law politics.[90] Indeed, Arkansas's senior senator, John McClellan, found himself caught in the middle, for as a candidate for reelection in 1948, McClellan was in the awkward position of running on a platform which he did not support, especially its antilynching and anti–poll tax planks, as well as with a standard bearer, Pres. Harry Truman, whose renomination he had originally opposed. In the end, McClellan split the difference, declaring himself an independent Democrat, one who refused to support the national ticket formally but who also steered clear of the infamous Dixiecrats, whose early strength in the state dissipated as the election neared. The politically nimble McClellan castigated Truman's leftward turn on civil rights while also trumpeting his own efforts on behalf of the state. It was a successful approach. He met with no opposition in the primary, and he dispatched his cursory November opponent by more than 200,000 votes of the just over 230,000 cast.[91]

Nationally, however, after Truman's stunning reelection victory, the Congress that convened in 1949 found itself addressing the latest in the long line of antilynching proposals. Indeed, in the aftermath of Truman's civil rights–fueled 1948 victory, there were predictions in the black press that passage of an antilynching bill, as well as other civil rights initiatives, might finally be achievable.[92] However, the realities of the filibuster and the difficulty of achieving cloture remained. Nevertheless, Sen. Hubert Humphrey of Minnesota and Sen. Wayne Morse of Oregon teamed with veteran Robert Wagner and introduced a bill in March 1949. In April, the White House, as well as one of Arkansas's own representatives, Brooks Hays, followed suit, offering additional proposals.[93] While Hays's sponsorship did reflect a crack in the South's previously solid opposition to any federal intervention, it was no less a reflection of his moderate, church-based approach to racial issues, one that in the end called for basic legal protections for blacks but in a still segregated society.[94] Ultimately, all three proposals were little more than weaker versions of the efforts previously defeated during the New Deal.[95] On the surface, though, the addition of the White House sponsorship that had been so coveted during the Roosevelt years, as well as the sponsorship of such a measure by a southern member, offered some hope that change was in the air. But there was no change in the way the proposals were met by the southern legislators who still held sway in Congress. In fact, even though the practice of lynching had essentially ceased, arguably making the legislation moot and no real threat to the South, from the beginning, southerners had seen a federal antilynching law as less about lynching itself and more about the intrusion by the federal government into state affairs (no small paradox given the increasing number of federal dollars the region was happy to accept[96]) especially as they related to racial matters. Consequently, the battle continued. Arkansas's own Boyd Tackett, a vigilant member of the House Judiciary Committee, reaffirmed the continuing opposition to antilynching law efforts and offered a telling counterpoint to Hays's proposal in testimony before the committee in 1950. Sharing his own distinctive and personalized historical interpretation, Tackett claimed (contrary to the historical record) that there had, in fact, been more lynchings of whites than blacks in his lifetime, while also asserting that there had been only a single black lynching in Arkansas in the past thirty-eight years.[97] Tackett further reminded the Judiciary Committee of his record as a prosecuting attorney, offering his work in that arena as evidence of his anti-discriminatory beliefs. Finally, he asserted that "every time this Congress meets up here and uses some of this political demagoguery, to stir up the feelings between the white and the colored people, they are not doing but one thing, and that is holding back the colored people within my section."[98] It was an interesting performance by a man whose own Democratic Party would leave him without a congressional district of his own after the 1950 census resulted in the state losing a seat.[99]

Not surprisingly, a federal antilynching law found no more support from Arkansas's senators. Indeed, as the 1950s got underway, both J. William Fulbright and John McClellan were solidly ensconced in the Senate seats they would hold until well into the 1970s, positions from which they would become titans of the postwar body, exercising power and influence on a range of issues—but not civil rights. On that issue, they were the good soldiers, falling in line behind the region's consistent obstructionist efforts. McClellan had shown how to achieve the balance as he deftly walked the tightrope that was Democratic Party politics in 1948, handily winning reelection. Meanwhile, Fulbright's expansive leadership in the foreign arena was balanced by a willingness to fall into line on anything related to civil rights. That had been made clear in 1950, when he led the effort to rebuff an attempt by the antilynching law forces to attach their proposal as an amendment to an oleomargarine tax bill that he was shepherding through to passage.[100] Fulbright adroitly dispatched the threat, but not before reminding observers that, had he wanted to be, the erudite, scholarly former president of the University of Arkansas could have been a leader in the fight for civil rights. Sid McMath, who as governor had sought unsuccessfully to have Arkansas enact a statewide antilynching measure, was particularly disappointed by Fulbright's failure.[101] And yet their contrasting electoral records may well offer the clearest evidence of the political realities of Arkansas at that time.[102] Indeed, beyond the realities of McMath's record at the polls, the defeat of his statewide antilynching proposal, while perhaps undermining the federalism arguments of the Washington delegation that maintained that the effort should be handled at home—though clearly that was not happening—was arguably a telling reminder of the states' political stance on the issue, one that the politically astute Fulbright and McClellan could not—and would not—ignore.

In fact, over the next decade and a half, in response to the emergence of a full-scale civil rights movement, one whose focus extended well beyond lynching, Fulbright and McClellan toed the southern Democratic Party line. They signed the Southern Manifesto in defiance of *Brown v. Board of Education*, and they supported the actions of their southern brethren whose determined efforts to prevent the enactment of federal civil rights legislation harkened back to tactics Thaddeus Caraway and Joe Robinson had employed in derailing the antilynching law proposals of the 1920s and 1930s.[103] While Fulbright and McClellan were not the leaders of the effort that their Arkansas predecessors had been, they nevertheless faithfully protected their white electoral base, supporting the southern cause in ways that kept them politically secure so they could be leaders in the areas like foreign policy and labor union corruption that made their national reputations. In so doing, they made clear that they would not risk their careers or jeopardize their power by making even symbolic sacrifices for an issue that, right up until the passage of the Civil Rights Act and the Voting Rights Act in 1964 and 1965, was a litmus test of regional loyalty.

Ultimately, it was wholly appropriate that Arkansas's members were among the leaders of the Senate's 2005 effort to make amends and apologize for that body's failure to pass antilynching legislation for so many years. Indeed, it was the least they could do, for while every senator who opposed those proposals carried some share of both the guilt and the responsibility, at the height of the efforts to pass a federal antilynching law, arguably no state could claim a greater role in its prevention than Arkansas. In the end, however, no legislative apology, no matter how well intentioned, could erase that legacy.

CONTRIBUTORS

RICHARD BUCKELEW wrote his doctoral dissertation (University of Arkansas) on lynching in Arkansas and has continued to research, write, and present papers on this topic. He currently serves as associate professor of history at Bethune-Cookman University.

RANDY FINLEY is a professor of history at Georgia Perimeter College and author of *From Slavery to Uncertain Freedom: The Freedman's Bureau in Arkansas* (1996). In addition, he has published book chapters in *The Freedmen's Bureau and Reconstruction: Reconsiderations* (1999), *The Southern Elite and Social Change: Essays in Honor of Willard B. Gatewood, Jr.* (2002), and *Arsnick: The Student Nonviolent Coordinating Committee in Arkansas* (2011).

NANCY SNELL GRIFFITH is a graduate of Dickinson College (Carlisle, Pennsylvania) and Syracuse University. She is the author of numerous works on local history, including dozens of entries on racial violence for the online *Encyclopedia of Arkansas History and Culture*, and she recently retired as the Archives and Special Collections librarian at Presbyterian College in Clinton, South Carolina.

STEPHANIE HARP holds an MA in history from the University of Maine and has written and presented widely on the 1927 lynching of John Carter in Little Rock, Arkansas. She was the organizer, lead presenter, and grant writer of "Project 1927," which was held at the Mosaic Templars Cultural Center in Little Rock in 2013. She also presented at "Without Sanctuary: A Conference on Lynching and the American South," held at the University of North Carolina–Charlotte in 2012.

KELLY HOUSTON JONES holds a PhD in history from the University of Arkansas and is an assistant professor of history at Austin Peay University. She has published articles in the *Arkansas Historical Quarterly* and *Agricultural History*, as well as book chapters in *Race and Ethnicity in Arkansas: New Perspectives* (2014), *Competing Memories: The Legacy of Arkansas's Civil War* (2016), and *Arkansas Women: Their Lives and Times* (forthcoming).

CHERISSE JONES-BRANCH holds a PhD in history from the University of South Carolina and currently serves as associate professor of history at Arkansas State University. She is the author of *Crossing the Line: Women's Interracial Activism in South*

Carolina during and after World War II (2014), which received the Letitia Woods Brown Book Award from the Association of Black Women Historians. She is also coeditor of *Arkansas Women: Their Lives and Times* (forthcoming).

GUY LANCASTER holds a PhD in Heritage Studies from Arkansas State University and serves as the editor of the online *Encyclopedia of Arkansas History and Culture*, a project of the Butler Center for Arkansas Studies at the Central Arkansas Library System. He is author of *Racial Cleansing in Arkansas, 1883–1924: Politics, Land, Labor, and Criminality* (2014), which won the J. G. Ragsdale Award for Best Book-Length Study in Arkansas History, as well as the John William Graves Book Award, both from the Arkansas Historical Association; it also received the Booker Worthen Literary Prize. He is also coeditor of *To Can the Kaiser: Arkansas and the Great War* (2015).

TODD E. LEWIS studied under the supervision of Willard B. Gatewood Jr. at the University of Arkansas, receiving his MA in history in 1989 (thesis title: "Ben Bogard and the Crusade Against Rum, Romanism, and Evolution in Arkansas, 1926–1928") and his PhD in history in 1995 (dissertation title: "Race Relations in Arkansas, 1910–1929"). He is the author of "Mob Justice in the 'American Congo': 'Judge Lynch' in Arkansas During the Decade After World War I," which appeared in the Summer 1993 issue of the *Arkansas Historical Quarterly*, as well as several other articles on topics related to religion, politics, and race relations in Arkansas. He is currently Lead Processing Archivist in the Special Collections Department of the University of Arkansas Libraries.

WILLIAM H. PRUDEN III is currently the Director of Civic Engagement and a college counselor at Ravenscroft School in Raleigh, North Carolina. A history major at Princeton University, he earned a JD from Case Western Reserve University, as well as master's degrees from Wesleyan University and Indiana University. An educator for over thirty years, he has taught American history and government at both the collegiate and secondary levels and has also published articles on a wide range of historical, political, and college admission topics.

VINCENT VINIKAS has served on the faculty of the University of Arkansas at Little Rock since he completed his PhD in history at Columbia University in 1983. His monograph on the development and influence of national advertising appeared as *Soft Soap Hard Sell: American Hygiene in an Age of Advertisement* (Iowa State, 1992). He has written for the *American Historical Review, Journal of American History, Journal of Southern History*, the *Historian, Business History Review, Journal of Social History, Journal of Economic History, Technology and Culture, Arkansas Historical Quarterly, American Studies, Mississippi Historical Quarterly*, and the journal of the *Social History of Medicine*. Vinikas is currently engaged in an investigation of the propaganda of World War II. His study of lynching first appeared in the August 1999 issue of the *Journal of Southern History* and is reprinted here with permission.

NOTES

Introduction

1. Ernest Dumas, "Racism: More than Cops," *Arkansas Times*, December 11, 2014, http://www.arktimes.com/arkansas/racism-more-than-cops/Content?oid =3575452 (accessed January 23, 2016).
2. State News, *Arkansas Gazette*, March 11, 1892, p. 1. For more information about the Coy lynching, see Larry LeMaster, "Ed Coy (Lynching of)," *Encyclopedia of Arkansas History and Culture*, http://www.encyclopediaofarkansas.net /encyclopedia/entry-detail.aspx?entryID=7035 (accessed January 23, 2016).
3. Local Paragraphs, *Arkansas Gazette*, May 30, 1882, p. 4.
4. Richard Buckelew, "Racial Violence in Arkansas: Lynchings and Mob Rule, 1860–1930" (PhD diss., University of Arkansas, 1999).
5. *Lynching in America: Confronting the Legacy of Racial Terror* (Montgomery, AL: Equal Justice Initiative, 2014), http://www.eji.org/files/EJI%20Lynching%20 in%20America%20SUMMARY.pdf (accessed January 9, 2016); Grif Stockley, *Blood in Their Eyes: The Elaine Race Massacres of 1919* (Fayetteville: University of Arkansas Press, 2001); Grif Stockley and Jeannie M. Whayne, "Federal Troops and the Elaine Massacres: A Colloquy," *Arkansas Historical Quarterly* 61 (Autumn 2002), 272–83.
6. Christopher Waldrep, *The Many Faces of Judge Lynch: Extralegal Violence and Punishment in America* (New York: Palgrave Macmillan, 2002), 72.
7. Ibid, 84.
8. Ibid, 134–45.
9. Ibid, 182.
10. Jens Meierhenrich, ed., *Genocide: A Reader* (New York: Oxford University Press, 2014), 17–18.
11. Paul Dumouchel, *The Barren Sacrifice: An Essay on Political Violence* (East Lansing: Michigan State University Press, 2015), xi.
12. Ibid., xvii.
13. Stathis N. Kalyvas explores this dynamic in his *The Logic of Violence in Civil War* (New York: Cambridge University Press, 2006).
14. Robert R. Mackey, "Bushwackers, Provosts, and Tories: The Guerrilla War in Arkansas," in *Guerrillas, Unionists, and Violence on the Confederate Home Front*, edited by Daniel E. Sutherland (Fayetteville: University of Arkansas Press, 1999), 172.

15. Quoted in Mark K. Christ, "Who Wrote the Poison Spring Letter?" in *"All Cut to Pieces and Gone to Hell": The Civil War, Race Relations, and the Battle of Poison Spring*, edited by Mark K. Christ (Little Rock: August House, 2003), 100.

16. Gregory J. W. Urwin, "Poison Spring and Jenkins' Ferry: Racial Atrocities during the Camden Expedition," in Christ, *"All Cut to Pieces"*, 125.

17. Daniel Kato, *Liberalizing Lynching: Building a New Racialized State* (New York: Oxford University Press, 2015), 35.

18. Ibid, 39.

19. Dumouchel, *Barren Sacrifice*, 90.

20. Randy Finley, *From Slavery to Uncertain Freedom: The Freedmen's Bureau in Arkansas, 1865–1869* (Fayetteville: University of Arkansas Press, 1996), 144.

21. Ibid, 145–146.

22. Ibid, 147.

23. Cal Ledbettter Jr., "The Constitution of 1868: Conqueror's Constitution or Constitutional Continuity?" *Arkansas Historical Quarterly* 44 (Spring 1985), 16–41.

24. William B. Darrow, "The Killing of Congressman James Hinds," *Arkansas Historical Quarterly* 74 (Spring 2015), 18–55.

25. Charles J. Rector, "D. P. Upham, Woodruff County Carpetbagger," *Arkansas Historical Quarterly* 59 (Spring 2000), 59–75.

26. Alan W. Trelease, *White Terror: The Ku Klux Klan Conspiracy and Southern Reconstruction* (New York: Harper & Row, 1971), 174.

27. Kathleen Bell, "Pope County Militia War," *Encyclopedia of Arkansas History and Culture*, http://www.encyclopediaofarkansas.net/encyclopedia/entry-detail.aspx?entryID=2277 (accessed June 30, 2016).

28. Earl F. Woodward, "The Brooks and Baxter War in Arkansas, 1872–1874," *Arkansas Historical Quarterly* 30 (Winter 1971), 315–36.

29. Walter Nunn, "The Constitutional Convention of 1874," *Arkansas Historical Quarterly* 27 (Autumn 1968), 177–204.

30. Carl H. Moneyhon, *Arkansas and the New South, 1874–1927* (Fayetteville: University of Arkansas Press, 1997), 18.

31. William Gibson, *Burning Chrome* (New York: Eos, 2003), 199.

32. Moneyhon, *Arkansas and the New South*, 39.

33. Kato, *Liberalizing Lynching*, 108.

34. For an exploration of Unionist sentiment and activity during the Civil War, see Rebecca Howard, "Civil War Unionists and Their Legacy in the Arkansas Ozarks" (PhD diss., University of Arkansas, 2015).

35. Bruce E. Baker, *This Mob Will Surely Take My Life: Lynchings in the Carolinas, 1871–1947* (New York: Continuum, 2008), 48–49.

36. Brent M. S. Campney, *This Is Not Dixie: Racist Violence in Kansas, 1861–1927* (Urbana: University of Illinois Press, 2015), 203.

Chapter 1, "Doubtless Guilty"

1. Two helpful broad discussions of slave lynching occur in Christopher Waldrep, *Lynching in America: A History in Documents* (New York: New York University Press, 2006) and Michael J. Pfeifer, *The Roots of Rough Justice: Origins of American Lynching* (Urbana: University of Illinois Press, 2010).

2. Orville W. Taylor, *Negro Slavery in Arkansas*, (repr., Fayetteville: University of Arkansas Press, 2000), 235–36; Pfeifer, *Roots of Rough Justice*, 32.

3. *Chillicothe (OH) Scioto Gazette*, August 19, 1846; *History of Benton, Washington, Carroll, Madison, Crawford, Franklin, and Sebastian Counties, Arkansas* (Chicago: Goodspeed Publishing Co., 1889), 189–90. Although the men that the slave worked with were technically deputized at the last minute and were therefore working for the sheriff, no one bothered going through the trouble to arrest or try Work.

4. Michael J. Pfeifer's discussion of the cotton frontier includes Texas and Missouri with little mention of Arkansas as part of that context. Only five of the fifty-six slave lynchings he examines occurred in Arkansas. Pfeifer, *Roots of Rough Justice*, 34, 93–94; Edward Ayers, *Promise of the New South: Life after Reconstruction*, fifteenth anniversary edition (New York: Oxford University Press, 2007), 156–57.

5. *Arkansas Gazette*, April 7, 1835.

6. Ibid.

7. Waldrep, *Lynching in America*, xviii, 70.

8. Ibid, xix; Pfeifer, *Roots of Rough Justice*, 39. In each incident presented in this chapter, I do not venture to determine the guilt of enslaved people—only to describe the events as alleged and analyze the fate of the accused. It is important for the reader to remember that sources for these occurrences are exclusively from the point of view of white society and never include the direct voices of the accused bondspeople.

9. Untitled, *The Liberator* (Boston, Massachussetts), December 14, 1849, p. 200; "More Murder and Lynching in Arkansas," *The Liberator* (Boston, Massachussetts), January 18, 1850, p. 12.

10. Karen Ryder, "'To Realize Money Facilities': Slave Life Insurance, the Slave Trade, and Credit in the Old South," in, *New Directions in Slavery Studies: Commodification, Community, and Comparison*, edited by Jeff Forret and Christine Sears (Baton Rouge: Louisiana State University Press, 2015), 53–61; Pfeifer, *Roots of Rough Justice*, 35–36.

11. Taylor, *Negro Slavery in Arkansas*, 108.

12. *History of Northwest Arkansas*, 191–192. Because it was written so long after the events, this account as a sole source should be read with caution. However, the same entry includes other antebellum incidents that are remarkably faithful to contemporary newspaper coverage. Therefore, I find it reasonable to trust that the basic facts in this story are similar to those that whites believed to be true when the events occurred.

13. Pfeifer, *Roots of Rough Justice*, 33.

14. "From Washington County—Fayetteville 9th May, 1860," *Arkansas Gazette*, May 18, 1860; Washington County Tax Records, 1856, 1859, microfilm, Washington County Courthouse, Fayetteville, Arkansas; U.S. Bureau of the Census, Manuscript Census Returns, Seventh and Eighth Censuses of the United States, 1850 and 1860, Population Schedules, Washington County, AR; *History of Benton, Washington, Carroll, Madison, Crawford, Franklin, and Sebastian Counties*, 192.

15. "From Washington County—Fayetteville 9th May, 1860," *Arkansas Gazette*, May 18, 1860.

16. Ibid.

17. "Mob and Murder in Saline County," *Arkansas Gazette*, October 27, 1854; Pulaski County Indictment Book B, pp. 281, 290, 304–8, microfilm, Arkansas State Archives (formerly the Arkansas History Commission), Little Rock, Arkansas.

18. "Mob and Murder in Saline County," *Arkansas Gazette*, October 27, 1854.

19. Ibid.

20. Kelly Houston Jones, "The Peculiar Institution on the Periphery: Slavery in Arkansas," PhD diss. (University of Arkansas, 2014), 24–25, 29–37.

21. "Mob Violence," *Arkansas Democrat*, July 17, 1846; Carl H. Moneyhon, "Slavery," *Encyclopedia of Arkansas History and Culture*, http://www.encyclo pediaofarkansas.net/encyclopedia/entry-detail.aspx?entryID=1275 (accessed September 15, 2016).

22. Waldrep, *Lynching in America*, 68.

23. Herbert Aptheker, *Nat Turner's Slave Rebellion, Including the 1831 "Confessions"* (repr., New York: Dover Publications, 2006), 75–83; *Laws of Arkansas Territory*, 521–25.

24. Josiah Gould, *A Digest of the Statutes of Arkansas; Embracing All Laws of a General and Permanent Character, in Force at the Close of the Session of the General Assembly of 1856* (Little Rock: Johnson & Yerkes, State Printers, 1858), 257–58, 272; Chris M. Branam, "Slave Codes," *Encyclopedia of Arkansas History and Culture*, http://www.encyclopediaofarkansas.net/encyclopedia /entry-detail.aspx?entryID=5054 (accessed January 1, 2016).

25. *Hervy v. Armstrong* (1854), 15 Ark., 164.

26. Sally E Hadden, *Slave Patrols: Law and Violence in Virginia and the Carolinas* (Cambridge, MA: Harvard University Press, 2001), 72–77.

27. *Austin, a Slave v. the State* (1854), 14 Ark. 555; George E. Lankford, "Austin's Secret: An Arkansas Slave at the Supreme Court," *Arkansas Historical Quarterly* 74 (Spring 2015), 56–73; Gould, *Digest of the Statutes of Arkansas*, 822–23, 1027–29.

28. John Hope Franklin and Loren Schweninger, *Runaway Slaves: Rebels on the Plantation* (New York: Oxford University Press, 1999), 79, 150–56.

29. "Horrible Murder," *Arkansas Gazette*, August 16, 1849; "Lynching in Arkansas," *The Liberator* (Boston, Massachussetts), November 9, 1849.

30. Ibid. Alph's story is included in Kelly Houston Jones, "'A Rough, Saucy Set of Hands to Manage': Slave Resistance in Arkansas," *Arkansas Historical Quarterly* 71 (Spring 2012), 18, without the additional details found in the *Liberator*'s report.

31. "Shocking Murder and Speedy Administration of Justice," *Arkansas Gazette*, December 9, 1840.

32. "Runaway Negro Killed," *Arkansas Gazette*, February 2, 1836.

33. "Negro Man Shot," *Arkansas Gazette*, March 23, 1842.

34. Waldrep, *Lynching in America*, 22, 69.

35. Ibid., 68.

36. Jones, "A Rough, Saucy Set of Hands to Manage," 17–19.

37. "Atrocious Murder," *Arkansas Gazette*, February 1, 1849.

38. Taylor, *Negro Slavery in Arkansas*, 235; Bertram Wyatt-Brown, *Southern Honor: Ethics and Behavior in the Old South*, twenty-fifth anniversary ed. (Oxford University Press, 2007), 389. These secondary sources hold that the event occurred in Chicot County. However, the diary of one Corydon E. Fuller, who was traveling through the area at the time, places the lynching in Ashley County. See Nancy Snell Griffith, "Ashley County Lynching of 1857," *Encyclopedia of Arkansas History and Culture*, http://www.encyclopediaofarkansas.net/encyclo pedia/entry-detail.aspx?entryID=7993 (accessed October 14, 2016).

39. Diane Miller Sommerville, *Rape and Race in the Nineteenth-Century South* (Chapel Hill: University of North Carolina Press, 2004), 4.

40. *Dennis v. The State*, 5 Ark., 230–234; *Joe Sullivant v. The State*, 8 Ark., 400–406; *Pleasant v. The State*, 13 Ark., 360–79.

41. Crawford County Tax Records, 1842, microfilm, roll 22, Arkansas State Archives, Little Rock, Arkansas.

42. 5 Ark. 231.

43. Ibid.

44. Ibid., 233–34.

45. Sommerville, *Rape and Race*, 84.

46. Tax Rolls Dallas County, Arkansas, 1846, roll 45, Arkansas State Archives, Little Rock, Arkansas.

47. .8 Ark. 401.

48. Ibid., 402–3.

49. 11 Ark. 392.

50. US Bureau of the Census, Seventh Census of the United States, 1850, Population Schedule, Hempstead County, AR.

51. 11 Ark., 392.

52. Ibid., 393–94.

53. Ibid., 394.

54. Ibid., 392.
55. Hempstead County Tax Records, 1850, microfilm, Arkansas State Archives, Little Rock, Arkansas.
56. 11 Ark., 395–396.
57. Ibid., 410.
58. There is evidence that mob violence connected to rape allegations occurred more frequently in other parts of the antebellum South. 13 Ark., 363–65, 372, 379; Pfeifer, *Roots of Rough Justice*, 37, 41.
59. Pfeifer, *Roots of Rough Justice*, 32.
60. George Lankford, ed, Bearing Witness: Memories of Arkansas Slavery: *Narratives from the 1930s WPA Collections*, 2nd ed. (Fayetteville: University of Arkansas Press, 2006), 54.

Chapter 2, "At the Hands of a Person or Persons Unknown"

1. Story L. Matkin-Rawn, "'We Fight for the Rights of Our Race': Black Arkansans in the Era of Jim Crow" (PhD diss., University of Wisconsin Madison, 2009), 28.
2. Karlos Hill, "Resisting Lynching: Black Grassroots Responses to Lynching in the Mississippi and Arkansas Deltas, 1882–1938" (PhD diss., University of Illinois at Urbana-Champaign, 2009), 39.
3. Matkin-Rawn, "'We Fight,'" 28.
4. Ibid., 14.
5. Ibid., 67.
6. Finnegan, Terence, *A Deed So Accursed: Lynching in Mississippi and South Carolina, 1881–1940* (Charlottesville: University of Virginia Press, 2013), 74.
7. Hill, "Resisting Lynching," 70–74.
8. Richard A. Buckelew, "Racial Violence in Arkansas: Lynchings and Mob Rule, 1860–1930" (PhD diss., University of Arkansas, 1999).
9. Equal Justice Initiative, *Lynching in America: Confronting the Legacy of Racial Terror* (Montgomery, AL: Equal Justice Initiative, 2015), 40, 43.
10. W. Fitzhugh Brundage. *Lynching in the New South: Georgia and Virginia, 1880–1930* (Urbana: University of Illinois Press, 1993)
11. See Finnegan, *A Deed So Accursed*.
12. Brundage, *Lynching in the New South*, 26.
13. "A Diabolical Crime," *Arkansas Gazette*, June 8, 1887, p. 8.
14. "President's Speech in City Park a Notable Deliverance," *Arkansas Gazette*, October 26, 1905, p. 3.
15. "A Lynch Law Not a Preventative," *Mena Star*, December 21, 1900, p. 2.
16. "Retribution," *Arkansas Gazette*, July 2, 1875, p. 4.
17. "Arkansas Mob Imitates Ohio," *Public Ledger* (Memphis, Tennessee), September 24, 1877, p. 2.

18. "Summary Vengeance," *Ottawa Free Trader* (Ottawa, Illinois), June 3, 1882, p. 2.

19. Untitled, *Ottawa Free Trader* (Ottowa, Illinois) February 16, 1884, p. 3.

20. "A Negro Outrager Hanged," *Lancaster Daily Intelligencer* (Lancaster, Pennsylvania), September 9, 1884, p. 3.

21. "Judge Lynch's Work," *Daily Alta California*, October 8, 1885, p. 5, online at http://cdnc.ucr.edu/cgi-bin/cdnc?a=d&d=DAC18851008.2.57.1# (accessed December 12, 2015). "Would-Be Ravisher Hunted Down by Citizens of Jackson County and Summarily Disposed Of," *Arkansas Gazette*, October 8, 1885, p. 3.

22. "Dewitt's Tragedy," *Arkansas Gazette*, December 24, 1891, p. 4; Untitled, *Deseret Evening News* (Salt Lake City, Utah), December 22, 1891, p. 4.

23. "England Killings," *Arkansas Gazette*, February 12, 1892, p. 6; "Three Negroes Killed." *Arkansas Democrat*, February. 9, 1892, p. 1.

24. "Bullets and Fire: A Negro Murdered and His Body Burned by a Mob of His Own Race," *Arkansas Gazette*, November 15, 1893, pp. 1, 5; "The Varner Lynchers," *Arkansas Gazette*, November 18, 1893, p. 6.

25. "Mob of Eight Men Lynches a Negro in an Arkansas Town," *Salt Lake Herald*, February 21, 1901, p. 1.

26. "Three Negroes Lynched by Mob," *Richmond Planet* (Richmond, Virginia), October 13, 1906, p. 8.

27. "Negro Is Shot to Death by a Mob at Helena," *Arkansas Gazette*, November 19, 1921, p. 1; *St. Louis Argus* quoted in Ashraf H. A. Rushdy, *The End of American Lynching* (New Brunswick, NJ: Rutgers University Press, 2012), 198.

28. "Masked Men Kill Negro," *Bisbee Daily Review* (Bisbee, Arizona), February. 4, 1922, p. 1; "Negro Killed by Unknown Persons," *Arkansas Gazette*, February 5, 1922, p. 8.

29. "Masked Men Kill Negro," *Bisbee Daily Review* (Bisbee, Arizona), February 4, 1922, p. 1; "Negro Killed by Unknown Persons," *Arkansas Gazette*, February 5, 1922, p. 8.

30. "Young Negro Lynched at Lepanto," *Arkansas Gazette*, April 30, 1936, p. 1.

31. "A Negro Hanged," *Arizona Republican* (Phoenix), June 24, 1891, p.1; "General Notes," *Chariton (IA) Patriot*, July 1, 1891, p. 2.

32. "An Unnatural Father Lynched by His Colored Brethren," *Arkansas Gazette*, July 25, 1885, p. 1.

33. "Negro White Caps," *Arkansas Gazette*, January 15, 1889, p. 1.

34. "Bullets and Fire: A Negro Murdered and his Body Burned by a Mob of his Own Race," *Arkansas Gazette*, November 15, 1893, pp. 1, 5; "The Varner Lynchers," *Arkansas Gazette*, November 18, 1893, p. 6.

35. "News in Brief." *Hutchinson (KS) Gazette*, December 26, 1895, p. 6; "Negro Lynched by Negroes," *Roanoke (VA) Daily Times*, December 22, 1895, p. 8.

36. "Negroes Lynch a Negro," *Arkansas Gazette*, April 21, 1905, p. 2.

37. "Wiping out the Negroes," *Indianapolis Journal*, October 2, 1891, p. 1; William F. Holmes, "The Arkansas Cotton Pickers Strike of 1891 and the Demise of the Colored Farmers' Alliance," *Arkansas Historical Quarterly* 32 (Summer 1973), 107–19. However, applying the label of "lynching" to this collective set of murders poses some challenges that are explored in greater detail in chapter 5 of the present volume. Buckelew's dissertation lists only nine victims for this particular mob action, while the Center for Studies in Demography and Ecology's Lynching Database (http://lynching.csde .washington.edu) lists only Ben Patterson's murder as a lynching.

38. "Negro Hanged for Stealing," *New York Times*, May 15, 1897, p. 7.

39. "Lynched for Hog Stealing," *Atlanta Constitution*, January 2, 1898, p. 3.

40. Michael W. Fitzgerald, "The Ku Klux Klan: Property Crime and the Plantation System in Reconstruction," *Agricultural History* 71 (Spring 1997), 186–206.

41. "Drunken Mob Makes an Attack on a Negro Normal School in Arkansas," *Arizona Republican*, June 30, 1897, p. 8; "General News," *Nebraska Advertiser*, September 24, 1897, p. 2; "Mob Beats a Colored Preacher," *Naugatuck (CT) Daily News*, June 24, 1897, p. 1.

42. "Two Negroes Were Lynched by Enraged Citizens," *Arkansas Gazette*, June 15, 1898, p. 2.

43. Matkin-Rawn, "'We Fight,'" 95.

44. "Arkansas Scene of a Bloody Race War," *Tombstone Prospector* (Tombstone, Arizona), November 13, 1896, p. 1. "Race War," *Record-Union* (Sacramento, California), November 14, 1896, p. 1.

45. "Negroes Massacred," *Saint Paul Globe* (Minnesota), December 8, 1896, p. 5.

46. "Arkansas' Race War," *Wichita Daily Eagle*, December 26, 1896, p. 1.

47. "Arkansas Mill Hands Fired on by Mob and Twelve of Them Wounded," *Kansas City Daily Journal*, December 18, 1896, p. 2.

48. "Arkansas Mill Hands," *Kansas City Daily Journal*; "Negroes Shot Down," *Daily Huronite* (Huron, South Dakota), December 19, 1896, p. 1.

49. "Outlaws Indicted," *Idaho Daily Statesman*, July 26, 1897, p. 2; "Race Riot in Arkansas," *New York Times*, July 26, 1897, p. 1; "Whites vs. Blacks," *Arkansas Gazette*, July 25, 1897, p. 2.

50. "A Race War is Imminent in Arkansas," *Salt Lake Herald*, August 7, 1896, p. 6; "Race War in Arkansas. Three Negroes Killed, Eight Wounded, Others Banished," *New York Times*, August 10, 1896, p. 1.

51. "Allies of Huns Lynch Farm Hand," *Chicago Defender*, June 22, 1918, quoted in the Equal Justice Initiative's *Lynching in America*, 39; "Negro Is Lynched by Mob," *Daily Free Press* (Carbondale, Illinois), June 14, 1918, p. 2.

52. Robert Thomas Kerlin, *The Voice of the Negro 1919* (New York: E. P. Dutton, 1920), online at https://archive.org/details/voiceofnegro191900kerl (accessed December 12, 2015); "Negro Lynched by Mob at Star City," *Arkansas Gazette*, June 15, 1919, p. 6.

53. "Prof. Gibson, Arkansas Teacher Shot to Death," *Dallas Express*, January 15, 1921, p. 1, online at http://texashistory.unt.edu/ark:/67531/metapth278336 /m1/1/ (accessed December 12, 2015).

54. "Arkansas Mob Kills Negro Soldier," *Philadelphia Evening Public Ledger*, September 3, 1919, p. 21.

55. "Hempstead Mob Lynches Negro near Guernsey," *Arkansas Gazette*, July 29, 1922, p. 1.

56. Brundage, *Lynching in the New South*, 19–20.

57. In some studies, including Finnegan's, Delta counties are equated with those counties having the highest concentration of African Americans. This does not hold true in Arkansas. Some of Arkansas's northern Delta counties were slow to develop, and counties that were not in the Delta had economies based on cotton. In 1900, traditional Delta counties like Arkansas, Clay, Craighead, Cross, Greene, Mississippi and Poinsett were fewer than 50 percent African American. Other non-Delta counties, like Lafayette, Ouachita, and Ashley, were majority African American. For purposes of this study, I have used data from the 1900 federal census, which lists the populations as follows: Chicot (87.1 percent), Crittenden (84.6 percent), Desha (81.7 percent), Phillips (78.6 percent), Lee (77.8 percent), Jefferson (72.8 percent), Monroe (65.4 percent), Saint Francis (64.1 percent), Lincoln (63.1 percent), Lafayette (61.2 percent), Woodruff (61.0 percent), Ouachita (55.7 percent), Ashley (53.7 percent), Drew (52.9 percent).

58. Hill, "Resisting Lynching," 8.

59. Brundage, *Lynching in the New South*, 19.

60. "Bloody Race War," *Richmond Dispatch*, September 21, 1892, p. 8; "Urged on by White Men," *New York Sun*, September 21, 1892, p. 1.

61. "Swung Him Up," *Arkansas Gazette*, July 15, 1892, p. 1.

62. "He's Gone: No Longer Will the Lecherous Beast Indulge His Lust upon Earth," *Arkansas Gazette*, May 14, 1892, p. 1; "A Night's Work," *Arkansas Gazette*, May 15, 1892, pp. 1, 5; "Some Questions." *Saint Paul (MN) Appeal*, May 21, 1892, p. 2.

63. "An Arkansas Lynching," *Houston Daily Post*, November 15, 1897, p. 5; "Fled from a Murderous Sheriff," *New York Sun*, December 7, 1897, p. 1; "Murder Most Foul," *Osceola Times*, November 13, 1897, p. 4; "To the People of Mississippi County," *Osceola Times*, December 4, 1897, p. 4; "Strung Up, According to Programme," *Osceola Times*, November 20, 1897, p. 4; Untitled, *Osceola Times*, December 18, 1897, p. 1.

64. "Lynchings in Arkansas," *Sacramento Daily Union*, January 9, 1898, p. 1; "Mob's Work: Four Negroes Lynched near Bearden," *Arkansas Gazette*, January 8, 1898, p. 1; "Five Southern Lynchings," *New York Times*, January 9, 1898, p. 10.

65. "Posse Lynches Negro," *Washington (DC) Herald*, February 11, 1917, p. 11.

66. "Negro Burned to Death by Arkansas Mob," *Bisbee (AZ) Daily Review*, January 27, 1921, p. 1.

67. "Governor Irate at Lynching of Negro," *Arkansas Gazette*, January 27, 1921, p. 1.

68. "With Officers Making No Attempt at Restraint, Mob Burns Negro Body and Creates a Reign of Terror," *Arkansas Gazette*, May 5, 1927, pp. 1, 13; "Law and Order Betrayed (An Editorial)," *Arkansas Gazette*, May 5, 1927, p. 1.

69. "Negro Slayer Is Killed by Posse," *Arkansas Gazette*, June 9, 1927, p. 5. "Prominent Race Man Is Victim of Mob," *Pittsburgh Courier*, June 18, 1927, pp. 1, 8.

70. "Negro Is Lynched by Mob at Wilmot," *Arkansas Gazette*, August 26, 1927, p. 1.

71. Brundage, *Lynching in the New South*, 262.

72. Ibid., 21.

73. Ibid., 33.

74. Ibid., 19.

75. Finnegan, *A Deed So Accursed*, 155.

76. Grace Elizabeth Hale, *Making Whiteness: The Culture of Segregation in the South, 1890–1940* (New York: Vintage, 1999); Amy Louise Wood, *Lynching and Spectacle: Witnessing Racial Violence in America, 1890–1940* (Chapel Hill: University of North Carolina Press, 2011).

77. Brundage, *Lynching in the New South*, 37.

78. James H. Cone, *The Cross and the Lynching Tree* (Maryknoll, NY: Orbis Books, 2011), 10.

79. Untitled, *Decatur (IL) Daily Republican*, March 12, 1881, p. 2.

80. "At the Stake," *Arkansas Gazette*, February 21, 1892, p. 1; Rev. D. A. Graham, "Some Facts about Southern Lynchings," *Indianapolis Recorder*, June 10, 1899.

81. "Two Brutal Murderers Lynched Sunday Night at Pine Bluff," *Arkansas Gazette*, February 16, 1892, p. 1.

82. "Two Lynched," *Arkansas Gazette*, July 16, 1895, p. 1.

83. "'Hang Him!' Shouted an Angry Mob at Texarkana," *Arkansas Gazette*, June 4, 1898, p. 3.

84. "Lynchers of Women," *Wichita Daily Eagle*, August 11, 1898, p. 6.

85. "Mob at Conway Lynched Negro," *Arkansas Gazette*, September 23, 1905, p. 1.

86. "Lynch Negro Slayer," *Washington (DC) Evening Star*, March 24, 1912, p. 20.

87. "Negro Lynched," *Daily Missoulian* (Missoula, Montana), June 20, 1913, p. 1.

88. "Negro Is Lynched at Hot Springs, Ark.," *Salt Lake Tribune*, June 20, 1913, p. 2.

89. "Negro Lynched near Little Rock," *Tulsa (OK) Star*, June 26, 1915, p. 2.

90. "Lynch Negro," *Tacoma (WA) Times*, December 3, 1915, p. 1.

91. "Lynch Negro," *Canfield (OH) Mahoning Dispatch*, October. 13, 1916, p. 4.

92. "Negro Slayer Is Burned at Stake," *Arkansas Gazette*, January 27, 1921, p. 1. William Pickens, "The American Congo—Burning of Henry Lowry," *The*

Nation, March 23, 1921, p. 427, online at http://www.unz.org/Pub/Nation -1921mar23-00426 (accessed December 12, 2015).

93. "Civilization or Barbarism — Which?" *Dallas (TX) Express*, February 19, 1921, p. 4.

94. "Negro Chained to Log and Burned Alive," *Hayti (MO) Herald*, February 3, 1921, p. 1.

95. Lee A. Dew, "The Lynching of 'Boll Weevil,'" *Midwest Quarterly* 12 (1971), 145–53; "Negro Slayer of Policeman Hanged," *Arkansas Gazette*, December 27, 1920, p. 1.

96. "Negro Hanged for Attack on White Woman," *Arkansas Gazette*, March 16, 1921, p. 1.

97. "2 Negroes Lynched by Mobs in South," *New York Times*, August 2, 1922, p. 19; "Gilbert Harris Hanged on Como Triangle Today," *Hot Springs New Era*, Extra edition, August 1, 1922, p. 1; "Negro Lynched by Hot Springs Mob," *Arkansas Gazette*, August 2, 1922, p. 1.

98. "An Arkansaw Lynching. The Murderers of Merchant Patton Disposed Of," *Austin (TX) Weekly Statesman*, September 27, 1894, p. 5; "Foully Murdered," *Arkansas Gazette*, September. 22, 1894, p. 1.

99. "Negro Burned Alive by a Mob near El Dorado," *Arkansas Gazette*, May 22, 1919, p. 1.

100. "Summary of News," *Weston (WV) Democrat*, December. 21, 1874, p. 4.

101. "The Varner Sensation," *Arkansas Gazette*, December 29, 1882, p. 4.

102. "His Black Neck Broken by a Mob Composed Entirely of Three Hundred Negroes," *Arkansas Gazette*, July 1, 1892, p. 1.

103. "Swung Him Up: Lynching of a Black Ravisher in Desha County," *Arkansas Gazette*, July 15, 1892, p. 1.

104. "Killed a Liberia Boomer." *New York Sun*, December 10, 1892, p. 1.

105. "Lightfoot's Death." *Arkansas Gazette*, December 14, 1892, p. 4.

106. Brundage, *Lynching in the New South*, 36.

107. Finnegan, *A Deed So Accursed*, 4.

108. Ibid., 149.

109. Brundage, *Lynching in the New South*, 28.

110. Ibid., 19–20.

111. Finnegan, *A Deed So Accursed*, 149.

112. Brundage, *Lynching in the New South*, 36–37.

113. Ibid., 67.

114. Finegan, *A Deed So Accursed*, 51.

115. Hill, "Resisting Lynching," 89.

Chapter 3, A Lynching State

1. James H. Cone, *The Cross and the Lynching Tree* (Mary Knoll, NY: Orbis Books, 2011), xv, 9; Malcolm Argyle quoted in Grif Stockley, *Ruled by Race:*

Black/White Relations in Arkansas from Slavery to the Present (Fayetteville: University of Arkansas Press, 2009), 127.

2. Richard A. Buckelew, "Violence in Arkansas: Lynchings and Mob Rule, 1860–1930" (PhD diss., University of Arkansas, 1999), 224–42.

3. Ibid.

4. Ida B. Wells-Barnett, "The Red Record: Tabulated Statistics and Alleged Causes of Lynching in the United States" (1895), online at http://www.gutenberg.org /files/14977/14977-h/14977-h.htm (accessed December 5, 2016).

5. Robert W. Thurston, *Lynching: American Mob Murder in Global Perspective* (Burlington, VT: Ashgate Publishing Company, 2011), 66; Amy Louise Wood, *Lynching and Spectacle: Racial Violence in America, 1890–1940* (Chapel Hill: University of North Carolina Press, 2009), 5; Raymond Arsenault, *The Wild Ass of the Ozarks: Jeff Davis and the Social Basis of Southern Politics* (Philadelphia, PA: Temple University Press, 1984), 12; John McDaniel Wheeler, "The People's Party in Arkansas, 1891–1896," (PhD diss., Tulane University, 1975), 49, 1. Bruce E. Baker, *This Mob Will Surely Take My Life: Lynchings in the Carolinas* (London: Continuum Press, 2008), 71.

6. Kenneth C. Barnes, *Who Killed John Clayton? Political Violence and the Emergence of the New South, 1861–1893* (Durham, NC: Duke University Press, 1998), 5; *Arkansas Gazette*, October 22, 1895, p. 1, and October 30, 1897, p. 4.

7. John William Graves, *Town and Country: Race Relations in Urban-Rural Context, Arkansas, 1865–1905* (Fayetteville: University of Arkansas Press, 1990), 138; Lawrence Goodwyn, *Democratic Promise: The Populist Movement in America* (New York: Oxford University Press, 1976), vii.

8. Graves, *Town and Country*, 210, 201; Wheeler, "The People's Party," 272–73.

9. Barnes, *Who Killed John Clayton?*, 23–29; Fon Louise Gordon, *Caste and Class: The Black Experience in Arkansas, 1880–1920* (Athens: University of Georgia Press, 1995), 23–29; Arsenault, *Wild Ass of the Ozarks*, 41; *Arkansas Gazette*, November 11, 1897, p. 3. For an argument that local county politics critically affected racial participation after the secret ballot and poll tax laws, see Chris N. Branam, "Another Look at Disfranchisement in Arkansas, 1888–1894," *Arkansas Historical Quarterly* 69 (Autumn 2010), 245–262.

10. *Arkansas Gazette*, August 8, 1897, p. 4; December 3, 1897, p. 2; March 17, 1899, p. 1; January 9,1898, p. 1; January 12, 1898, p. 1; January 27, 1898, p. 1; January 28, 1898, p. 1; November 16, 1897, p. 6.

11. Quoted in Graves, *Town and Country*, 189, 147; Guy Lancaster, *Racial Cleansing in Arkansas, 1883–1924: Politics, Land, Labor, and Criminality* (Lanham, MD: Lexington Books, 2014), 32, 51, 88; *Arkansas Gazette*, February 12, 1898, p. 8.

12. Quoted in Christopher Waldrep, *The Many Faces of Judge Lynch: Extralegal Violence and Punishment in America* (New York: Macmillan, 2002), 4–5; Michael Ayers Trotti, "What Counts: Trends in Racial Violence in the Postbellum South," *Journal of American History* 100 (September 2013), 377.

13. Buckelew, "Racial Violence in Arkansas," 3.
14. *Arkansas Gazette*, July 16, 1897, p. 6; July 21, 1897, p. 1; July 24, 1897, p. 1; February 10, 1894, p. 1; Bruce Baker, "Under the Rope: Lynching and Memory in Laurens County, South Carolina," 319–46, in *Where the Memories Grow: History, Memory, and Southern Identity* (Chapel Hill: University of North Carolina Press, 2000); Lisa Arellano, *Vigilantes and Lynch Mobs: Narratives of Community and Nation* (Philadelphia, PA: Temple University Press, 2012), 1–3, 138; Richard M. Perloff, "The Press and Lynchings of African Americans." *Journal of Black Studies* 30 (January 2006), 327.
15. *Arkansas Gazette*, July 22, 1897, p. 4; August 22, 1895, p. 1; August 27, 1895, p. 1; June 4, 1898, p. 2; February 9, 1898, p. 1.
16. Thomas P. Clark, *The Southern Country Editor* (Gloucester, MA, 1964), 233; *Atlanta Constitution*, June 10, 1899, p. 6; June 6, 1892, p. 4; Waldrep, *Many Faces*, 112.
17. *Arkansas Gazette*, October 24, 1897, p. 1; November 12, 1895, p. 1; August 25, 1897, p. 1; February 24, 1898, p. 5; *Atlanta Constitution*, May 30, 1896, p. 1; Waldrep, *Many Faces*, 212.
18. Waldrep, *Many Faces*, 12; Michael J. Pfeifer, "At the Hands of Parties Unknown? The State of the Field of Lynching Scholarship." *Journal of American History* 101 (December 2014), 838; Amy Kate Bailey and Stewart E. Tolnay, *Lynched: The Victims of Southern Mob Violence* (Chapel Hill: University of North Carolina Press), 3; Thurston, *Lynching*, 1–4; Stewart E. Tolnay and E. M. Beck. *A Festival of Violence: An Analysis of Southern Lynchings, 1882–1930* (Urbana: University of Illinois Press, 1992), 18–33, 56. For the slippery slope Cliometricians climb on when defining and counting lynchings, see Trotti, "What Counts," 375–400.
19. *Arkansas Gazette*, December 11, 1897, p. 1; February 24, 1898, p. 5; January 27, 1899, p. 1; *Atlanta Constitution*, October 18, 1897, p. 2; *New York Times*, November 6, 1890, p. 1; August 9, 1898, p. 12.
20. *Arkansas Gazette*, January 8, 9, 15, 27, 28; February 9, 24, 25; March 3, 11; June 4, 15, and 17, 1898; November 12, 1895, p. 1; *Arkansas Gazette*, July 9, 1891, p. 1; January 6, 1899, p. 1; February 1, 1898, p.1.
21. *Arkansas Gazette*, June 12, 1890, p. 1, June 23, 1891, p. 1, and August 25, 1897, p. 1 (hung from a tree); October 15, 1897, p. 1 (railroad trestle); July 9, 1891, p. 1, February 18, 1892, p. 1 (telephone pole); February 15, 1890, p. 1 (bridge); February 14, 1890, p. 1; April 19, 1899, p. 2; August 24, 1897, p. 1; May 14, 1892, p. 1; November 15, 1893, p. 1; June 4, 1898, p. 1; July 15, 1898, p. 1; November 5, 1895, p. 1; October 2, 1891, p. 1; February 21, 1892, p. 1; June 4, 1894, p. 3.
22. *Arkansas Gazette*, February 15, 1890, p. 1; July 21, 1891, p. 1; April 19, 1899, p. 2; February 16, 1892, p. 1.
23. *Arkansas Gazette*, July 16, 1897, p. 6.

24. *Arkansas Gazette*, January 8, 1898, p. 1; January 9, 1898, p. 1; December 12, 1897, p. 1.

25. *Arkansas Gazette*, February 9, 1892, p. 1; June 23, 1891, p. 1; February 28, 1899, p. 1.

26. Daniel Joseph Singal, *The War Within: From Victorian to Modernist Thought in the South, 1919–1945* (Chapel Hill: University of North Carolina Press, 1982), 32–33.

27. Joel Williamson, *The Crucible of Race: Black/White Relations in the American South Since Emancipation* (New York: Oxford University Press, 1984), 307; Susan Jean, "'Warranted' Lynchings: Narratives of Mob Violence in White Southern Newspapers, 1880–1940," *American Nineteenth Century History* 6 (November 2005), 367; Pfeifer, "At the Hands of Parties Unknown," 834; Gail Bederman, *Manliness and Civilization: A Cultural History of Gender and Race in the United States, 1880–1917* (Chicago: University of Chicago Press, 1995), 11, 121–169.

28. *Arkansas Gazette*, March 2, 1899, p. 1; June 15, 1898, p. 2; November 12, 1895, p. 1; July 8, 1891, p. 1; August 24, 1897, p. 1.

29. *Arkansas Gazette*, December 17, 1897, p. 1; June 4, 1898, p. 2; October 6, 1895, p. 1; October 8, 1895, p. 3.

30. *Arkansas Gazette*, June 22, 1894, p. 1; August 7, 1897, p. 1; July 26, 1891, p. 1.

31. *Arkansas Gazette*, December 12, 1897, p. 1; June 4, 1898, p. 3; May 14, 1892, p. 1; June 15, 1898, p.2.

32. *Arkansas Gazette*, January 8, 1898, p. 1.

33. *New York Times*, February 23, 1892, p. 4; *New York Times*, November 5, 1895, p. 4; February 24, 1893, p. 9.

34. *Arkansas Gazette*, July 20, 1891, p. 2; July 19, 1895, p. 3; August 25, 1897, p. 1; July 9, 1891, p. 1; July 22, 1897, p. 1; March 2, 1899, p. 1.

35. *Arkansas Gazette*, January 8, 1898, p. 1; April 19, 1899, p. 2; December 22, 1891, p. 1.

36. Fred W. Allsopp, *Little Adventures in Newspaperdom.* (Little Rock: Arkansas Writers Publishing Company, 1922), 129–130.

37. *Arkansas Gazette*, May 14, 1892, p. 1.

38. *Arkansas Gazette*, February 21, 1892, p. 1.

39. *Arkansas Gazette*, June 4, 1898, p. 3.

40. *Arkansas Gazette,* August 27, 1897, p.4; September 17, 1897, p. 4; January 3, 1898, p. 4; June 23, 1891, p. 1.

41. *New York Times,* July 31, 1899, p. 3; Quoted in *New York Times*, August 12, 1899, p. 6.

42. *New York* Times, December 7, 1897, p.3; Arkansas *Gazette*, February 28, 1894, p. 1.

43. *Arkansas Gazette*, February 28, 1894, p. 1; September 23, 1897, p. 2; February 28, 1899, p. 1; *Atlanta Constitution*, August 23, 1895, p. 1.

44. *Arkansas Gazette*, February 24, 1898, p.5; February 25, 1898, p.1; February 26, 1898, p.1; February 16, 1892, p. 1; *New York Times*, August 9, 1898, p. 12.

45. *Arkansas Gazette*, January 15, 1898, p. 1; January 3, 1899, p. 4; *Atlanta Constitution*, November 9, 1895, p. 3; *New York Times*, November 23, 1894, p. 5.

46. Kidada E. Williams, *They Left Great Marks on Me: African American Testimonies of Racial Violence From Emancipation to World War I* (New York: New York University Press, 2012), 111; Waldrep, *Many Faces*, 109; *Philadelphia Christian Recorder*, March 24, 1892. Found in Herbert Aptheker, ed., *A Documentary History of the Negro People in the United States*, Vol. 2 (New York: The Citadel Press, 1970), 793–794; *Arkansas Gazette*, December 5, 1897, p. 1. For an overview of the *Christian Recorder*, see Gilbert Anthony Williams, *The Christian Recorder, Newspaper of the African Methodist Episcopal Church: History of a Forum for Ideas, 1854–1902* (Jefferson, NC: McFarland and Co., 1996).

47. *Arkansas Gazette*, September 12, 1897, p. 10; February 5, 1899, p. 14.

48. E. M. Beck and Stewart E. Tolnay, "When Race Didn't Matter: Black and White Mob Violence against Their Own Color," in *Under Sentence of Death: Lynching in the South*, edited by W. Fitzhugh Brundage (Chapel Hill: University of North Carolina Press, 1997), 142; *Arkansas Gazette*, September 23, 1894, p. 1; November 15, 1893, p. 1; January 26, 1899, p. 4; *New York Times*, July 20, 1891, p. 2; August 11, 1898, p. 5.

49. *Christian Recorder*, March 24, 1892; Kenneth C. Barnes, *Journey of Hope: The Back-to-Africa Movement in Arkansas in the Late 1800s* (Chapel Hill: University of North Carolina Press, 2004), 85–89.

50. *Arkansas Gazette*, June 15, 1891, p. 2; W. Fitzhugh Brundage, "Black Resistance and White Violence in the American South, 1880–1940," in Brundage, *Under Sentence of Death*, 271–272.

51. William F. Holmes, "The Arkansas Cotton Pickers Strike of 1891 and the Demise of the Colored Farmer's Alliance," *Arkansas Historical Quarterly* 32 (Summer 1973), 111–17. See also Carl H. Moneyhon, *Arkansas and the New South, 1874–1929* (Fayetteville: University of Arkansas Press, 1997), 73; Graves, *Town and Country*, 205. Buckelew's dissertation counts only nine victims of lynching resulting from the Lee County strike, while the Center for Studies in Demography and Ecology's Lynching Database (http://lynching.csde .washington.edu) only lists Ben Patterson for this particular event.

52. Holmes, "Arkansas Cotton Pickers Strike," 117; *Arkansas Gazette*, October 2, 1891, p. 1.

53. *Arkansas Gazette*, March 18, 1899, p. 2; F. I. Stockton Letter to W. H. Hemphill, March 29, 1899, transcribed by owner of the letters, Matt Hemphill.

54. *Arkansas Gazette*, March 22, 1899, p. 1.

55. *Arkansas Gazette*, March 23, 1899, p. 1; March 24, 1899, p. 1 and 2; March 25, 1899, p. 2.

56. *Nebraska State Journal*, March 24, 1899, quoted in Nancy Snell Griffith,

"Little River County Race War of 1899," *Encyclopedia of Arkansas History and Culture*, http://www.encyclopediaofarkansas.net/encyclopedia/entry-detail .aspx?entryID=7062 (accessed July 27, 2016); *Houston Daily Post*, March 23, 1899, p. 6, quoted in Griffith, "Little River"; *New York Times*, March 24, 1899, p. 2; *Chicago Tribune*, March 24, 1899; *Texarkana Gazette*, March 26, 1899, p. 1; *San Francisco Call*, March 24, 1899, p. 1, quoted in Griffith, "Little River"; *Texarkana Gazette*, March 19, 1899, p. 1 and March 24, 1899, p. 1; *Arkansas Gazette*, March 25, 1899, p. 1; *Texarkana Gazette*, March 16, 1899, p. 1.

57. Buckelew, "Violence in Arkansas," 241.

58. Trotti, "What Counts," 398; Baker, *This Mob*, 143. For the most recent foray into Cliometricians using statistics effectively and creatively to prove that, in many cases, those lynched were newly arrived and marginal members of the community, see Bailey and Tolnay, *Lynched*, 211. But what context made a community most fearful of these "marginal" members? Were there certain contexts that made the "marginal" appear more dangerous to the community than at other times? The irrational seems to vex historians and sociologists who want everything countable.

Chapter 4, The Clarendon Lynching of 1898

1. W. R. Mayo, "Clarendon (Monroe County)," *Encyclopedia of Arkansas History and Culture*, http://www.encyclopediaofarkansas.net/encyclopedia/entry-detail .aspx?entryID=942 (accessed November 9, 2015); Jo Claire English, *Clarendon Arkansas History*, http://www.argenweb.net/monroe/history/hisclare.htm (accessed November 9, 2015); "Big Lynching Bee in Ark.," *Oshkosh (WI) Daily Northwestern*, August 10, 1898.

2. "Clarendon Assassination," *Brinkley (AR) Argus*, August 4, 1898. Note on sources: due to the lack of extant sources on this murder and subsequent lynching, this chapter relies heavily on a very wide variety of contemporary newspaper accounts, focusing primarily on those from Clarendon or Monroe County, Arkansas.

3. "John Tunnell Orr: Overview," Ancestry.com (accessed November 9, 2015).

4. "Her Unhappy Life," *Milwaukee Weekly Wisconsin*, August, 20, 1898.

5. English, *Clarendon Arkansas History*; Carl H. Moneyhon, *Arkansas and the New South, 1874–1929* (Fayetteville: University of Arkansas Press, 1997), 40.

6. "Family Group Sheet: John Tunnell Orr," Ancestry.com (accessed November 9, 2015).

7. "Clarendon Assassination."

8. "Four Dead, Bold Work of the Clarendon Mob," *Arkansas Gazette*, August 11, 1898.

9. "Her Unhappy Life," *Weekly Wisconsin* (Milwaukee), August 20, 1898.

10. "Four Dead."
11. Barbara Welter, "The Cult of True Womanhood: 1820–1860," *American Quarterly* 18.2, part 1 (1966), 152.
12. "Her Unhappy Life"; "Five Lynched," *Kansas City Journal* (Kansas City, Missouri), August 10, 1898.
13. "Lynching of the Orr Murderers," *Sacramento Record-Union* (Sacramento, California), August 11, 1898.
14. "Four Dead."
15. Ibid.
16. "She Thought of Home," *Wisconsin Weekly Advocate* (Milwaukee), August 13, 1898.
17. "Clarendon Assassination."
18. "Mob Avenges Orr's Death," *New York Times*, August 11, 1898.
19. A coroner's inquest is a "quasi-judicial proceeding" that is used to determine the manner of death in cases deemed suspicious or difficult to determine. See Paul MacMahon, "The Inquest and the Virtues of Soft Adjudication," *Yale Law and Policy Review* 33 (2015), 276.
20. "Orr's Murder Is Avenged," *Brinkley (AR) Argus*, August 11, 1898.
21. "Four Dead"
22. Ibid.
23. "Four Dead"; "Orr's Murder Is Avenged."
24. "Four Dead"
25. "She Thought of Home."
26. Ibid.
27. "Orr's Murder Is Avenged."
28. "Four Dead."
29. "Orr's Murder Is Avenged."
30. "Lynching of the Orr Murderers."
31. "Four Dead."
32. "To Stop Lynching," *Arkansas Democrat*, August 12, 1898.
33. "Four Dead."
34. "Four Dead"; "About Clarendon's Trouble," *Brinkley (AR) Argus*, August 18, 1898; "Horrible Work of an Arkansas Mob," *New Orleans Daily Picayune*, August 11, 1898.; Walter B. Stevens, *Centennial History of Missouri (The Center State): One Hundred Years in the Union, 1820–1921*, vol. 2 (Saint Louis: S. J. Clarke Publishing Company, 1921); AccessGenealogy.com, https://www.access genealogy.com/missouri/centennial-history-of-missouri.htm (accessed October 14, 2015).
35. "She Thought of Home"; "Seeks to Excuse Her," *Wisconsin Weekly Advocate* (Milwaukee), August 13, 1898.
36. "She Thought of Home"; "Miss Morris in Jail," *Waukesha (WI) Freeman*, August 18, 1898.

37. Crystal N. Feimster, *Southern Horrors: Women and the Politics of Rape and Lynching* (Cambridge, MA: Harvard University Press, 2009).
38. Elizabeth Hines and Eliza Steelwater, "Project HAL: Historical American Lynching Data Collection Project," http://people.uncw.edu/hinese/HAL /HAL%20Web%20Page.htm (accessed December 20, 2015); Stewart E. Tolnay and E. M. Beck, *Festival of Violence: An Analysis of Southern Lynchings, 1882–1930* (Urbana: University of Illinois Press, 1992); Richard A. Buckelew, "Racial Violence in Arkansas: Lynchings and Mob Rule, 1860–1930" (PhD diss., University of Arkansas, 1999).
39. "True Womanhood." See also Beverly Schwartzberg, "Lots of Them Did That: Desertion, Bigamy, and Marital Fluidity in Late Nineteenth-Century America," *Journal of Social History* 37 (Spring 2004), 573–600; Nancy F. Cott, *Public Vows: A History of Marriage and the Nation* (Cambridge, MA: Harvard University Press, 2000); and Nancy F. Cott, "Giving Character to Our Whole Civil Polity: Marriage and the New Public Order in the Late Nineteenth-Century," in *U.S. History as Women's History: New Feminist Essays*, edited by Linda K. Kerber, Alice Kessler-Harris, and Kathryn Kish Sklar (Chapel Hill: University of North Carolina Press, 1995).
40. Martha H. Patterson, *Beyond the Gibson Girl: Reimagining the America New Woman, 1895–1915*. (Urbana: University of Illinois Press, 2008).
41. Peter W. Bardaglio, *Reconstructing the Household: Families, Sex, and the Law in the Nineteenth-Century South* (Chapel Hill: University of North Carolina Press, 1995); Robert L. Griswold, "Law, Sex, Cruelty, and Divorce in Victorian America, 1840–1900," *American Quarterly* 38 (Winter 1986), 721–45; Elizabeth Pleck, *Domestic Tyranny: The Making of American Social Policy Against Family Violence from Colonial Times to the Present* (Oxford: Oxford University Press, 1987); David Peterson Del Mar, *What Trouble I Have Seen: A History of Violence against Wives* (Cambridge, MA: Harvard University Press, 1997); Elizabeth B. Clark, "Matrimonial Bonds: Slavery and Divorce in Nineteenth-Century America," *Law and History Review* 8 (Spring 1990), 25–54.

Chapter 5, Thirteen Dead at Saint Charles

1. *Biographical and Historical Memoirs of Eastern Arkansas* (Chicago: Goodspeed Publishing Co., 1890), 646. In 1900, of 12,973 people who lived in Arkansas County, in which Saint Charles is located, 4,058 residents were black. See "13 Negroes Were Slain: Wholesale Killing Occurred in Arkansas Co. Race War Last Week," *Arkansas Democrat*, March 29, 1904, p. 5.
2. "Eleven Negroes Victims of Mob," *Arkansas Gazette*, March 27, 1904, pp. 1, 3.
3. Ibid.
4. Ibid., 4. However, whites were not necessarily spared the extraordinary brutality of southern lynch mobs. For examples of atrocities committed on white victims,

see the discussion of "White Brutality" in E. M. Beck and Stewart E. Tolnay, "When Race Didn't Matter: Black and White Mob Violence against Their Own Color," in W. Fitzhugh Brundage, ed., *Under Sentence of Death: Lynching in the South* (Chapel Hill: University of North Carolina Press, 1997), 148. The three examples that Beck and Tolnay cite are from Arkansas.

5. George Allan England, "Rural Locutions of Maine and Northern New Hampshire," *Dialect Notes* 4 (1914), 71.

6. J. G. Randall, "The Blundering Generation," *Mississippi Valley Historical Review* 27 (June 1940), 3–28.

7. Ibid., 7 (first and last quotations of the paragraph) and 9–13. An account of the W. R. Barksdale camp, the United Confederate Veterans' resolve can be found in an editorial from the Memphis *Scimitar* reprinted as "Stop Those Lynchings," in the Marianna, Arkansas, *Lee County Courier*, April 2, 1904, p. 1. Agreeing with the opposition of the veterans to "the burning of negroes," the article notes that this "is not the vaporing of theorizing Northern sentimental- ists" and that "it is not remembered that any representative body in the South has ever before come out so strongly for the right on this subject of negro burn- ings." Another newspaper account of this development appears in a collection of newspaper reports compiled by Ralph Ginzburg, ed., "Confederate Veterans Deplore Lynching Except for Rape," *100 Years of Lynchings* (1962; rpt., Balti- more, MD: Black Classics Press, 1988), 67–68. The scholarly utility of this anthology of newspaper accounts is seriously compromised because, although the reports collected in this volume are presented as verbatim reprints, the compiler warns in his "Foreword" that some "have been drastically rewritten" (p. 5).

8. Randall, "Blundering Generation," 11. Roberta Senechal de la Roche might object strongly to the conclusion that lynchings were unpredictable; she insists that "southern whites seldom lynched capriciously." Rather than confining her use of the term *lynching* to a category of event whose outcome is death, her pri- mary qualification instead depends upon the motive of the lynchers, which she postulates must be to punish. Her theory hinges upon a definitional insistence that any given lynching must be characterized by "a logic of individual liability" for a deviant act that would make the procedure predictable. She contends that, according to this definition, beatings would constitute what she calls "a mild form of lynching." Thus her effort to make the term *lynch* operational leaves us with a definition that, narrow in one sense, is too broad in another. She con- cedes that "no data have yet been systematically gathered" to sustain her the- ory. See Roberta Senechal de la Roche, "The Sociogenesis of Lynching," in Brundage, ed., *Under Sentence of Death*, 48, 50, and 53.

9. Randall, "Blundering Generation," 9 (two quoted words in text).

10. The "History of the History of Lynching" that Joel Williamson conveyed in a "round table" in the *Journal of American History* takes some very odd turns.

In the discussion of why "historians didn't or couldn't see lynching," as David W. Blight posed the question, or as David Levering Lewis put it, "why the phenomenon has been forgotten or untreated," the scholars who participated in this forum tended to neglect the nature of the evidence. See David Thelen, ed., "What We See and Can't See in the Past," *Journal of American History* 83 (March 1997), 1217–72. For quotations, see Williamson, 1242; Blight, 1256; and Lewis, 1263. The forum is composed of an essay entitled "Wounds Not Scars: Lynching, the National Conscience, and the American Historian" by Joel Williamson; six referees' reports by Blight, Lewis, Edward L. Ayers, George M. Fredrickson, Robin D. G. Kelley, and Steven M. Stowe; and a later comment by Jacquelyn Dowd Hall.

11. The exact difficulty in tabulating the number of lynchings can be illustrated by reference to "Appendix A: The Creation of a New Inventory of Southern Lynchings," in Stewart E. Tolnay and E. M. Beck, *A Festival of Violence: An Analysis of Southern Lynchings, 1882–1930* (Urbana: University of Illinois Press, 1995), 260. They report that in Arkansas, for the period 1882 to 1930, there were 241 "confirmed lynch victims" and another 27 possible victims. One must be advised, however, that all of their elegant computations of the occurrence of lynching in America hang upon a pretense. One of the four tests in their stringent definition of the phenomenon is that "the group [of murderers] must have acted under the pretext of service to justice or tradition." Tolnay and Beck do not identify the historical point at which lynching itself became the sort of tradition that might serve this qualification that they impose upon their data. See also Robert L. Zangrando, *The NAACP Crusade against Lynching, 1909–1950* (Philadelphia: Temple University Press, 1980), 5.

12. Rev. E. Malcolm Argyle, letter dated March 14, 1892, to the Philadelphia *Christian Recorder*, March 24, 1892, reprinted as "Report from Arkansas, 1892" in Herbert Aptheker, ed., *A Documentary History of the Negro People in the United States*, vol. 2: *From the Reconstruction Era to 1910* (New York: Citadel Press, 1951), 792–94 (quotations on p. 793).

13. James Elbert Cutler, *Lynch-Law; An Investigation into the History of Lynching in the United States* (New York: Longmans, Green, and Co., 1905), 188 and 179–80.

14. Walter White, *Rope and Faggot: A Biography of Judge Lynch* (New York: A. A. Knopf, 1929), 234 and 227; and Zangrando, *NAACP Crusade Against Lynching*, 5.

15. Tolnay and Beck, *Festival of Violence*, ix, 17.

16. *Lynching Goes Underground* (1940), reprinted in Gunnar Myrdal, with the assistance of Richard Sterner and Arnold Rose, *An American Dilemma: The Negro Problem and Modern Democracy* (New York: Harper and Bros., 1944), 1350n40 (quotation).

17. Marion Hughes, *Three Years in Arkansaw: Beats All Books You Ever Saw* (Chicago: M. A. Donahue & Co., 1904), 85–86. Hughes's work is placed in a humorous literary context on p. 128 of Lee A. Dew, "'On a Slow Train Through

Arkansaw'—The Negative Image of Arkansas in the Early Twentieth Century," *Arkansas Historical Quarterly* 39 (Summer 1980), 125–35.

18. "Five Negroes Lynched: Make Nine Killed by Whites in a Week in One . . . County," *New York Times*, March 26, 1904, p. 1; "War on Negroes for Simple Brawl," *New York Times*, April 3, 1904, p. 1, which cites thirteen fatalities at Saint Charles. As Zangrando concludes, *NAACP Crusade*, 4, "one can merely guess how widespread the phenomenon actually was." See White, *Rope and Faggot*, 228–30. Cutler compiled his figures, long regarded as definitive, by comparing files from numerous periodicals including the *Chicago Tribune*, the *New York Times*, the *New York Tribune*, and many magazines. Cutler, *Lynch-Law*, 280–81 contains a complete list of the periodicals he used. The National Association for the Advancement of Colored People (NAACP), when compiling *Thirty Years of Lynching in the United States, 1889–1918* (New York, 1919), relied largely upon the newspaper files of the Library of Congress. Although the NAACP computed thirteen total dead at Saint Charles, the time period that they cited for all of the killings—one day, March 26—is incomplete (p. 50). It was not a one-day event. Also see Tolnay and Beck's discussion in "Appendix B: Types of Errors and Other Problems in Existing Inventories," *Festival of Violence*, 265–67. The statistical dimensions of lynching, as Michael Ayers Trotti observes, "force scholars to confront challenges on at least three levels: definition, evidence, and interpretation." See "What Counts: Trends in Racial Violence in the Postbellum South," *Journal of American History* 100 (September 2013), 375.

19. On "revolution and anarchy," see James Weldon Johnson's testimony to a US Senate Judiciary Committee hearing, quoted in White, *Rope and Faggot*, 212; and Albert Bushnell Hart, "Lynching," in Andrew C. McLaughlin and Albert Bushnell Hart, eds., *Cyclopedia of American Government*, 2nd ed., vol. 2 (New York, 1930), 381.

20. Howard Smead, *Blood Justice: The Lynching of Mack Charles Parker* (New York: Oxford University Press, 1986), x. Opponents of federal antilynching legislation, by equating lynchings with simple acts of homicide, could then insist that the crime fell entirely within the jurisdiction of the states.

21. See the discussion in Jessie Parkhurst Guzman et al., *1952 Negro Year Book: A Review of Events Affecting Negro Life* (New York: Wm. H. Wise & Co., 1952), 275–76.

22. Cutler, *Lynch-Law*, 186.

23. See "Appendix II: Chronological List of Persons Lynched in United States, 1889 to 1918, Inclusive, Arranged by States," *Thirty Years of Lynching*, 43–105.

24. Richard Maxwell Brown, *Strain of Violence: Historical Studies of American Violence and Vigilantism* (New York: Oxford University Press, 1975), 216.

25. "Table 2-I. The Five Worst Incidents of Lynchings with Black Victims," in Tolnay and Beck, *Festival of Violence*, 31.

26. John William Graves, *Town and Country: Race Relations in an Urban-Rural Context, Arkansas, 1865–1905* (Fayetteville: University of Arkansas Press, 1990); Fon Louise Gordon, *Caste and Class: The Black Experience in Arkansas, 1880–1920* (Athens: University of Georgia Press, 1995); and Benjamin Travis Laney III, "The History Highlights of Saint Charles, Arkansas" (MA thesis, Arkansas State Teachers College, 1961).

27. "Masked Mob Whips Prisoner: Cows Missouri Sheriff and Releases Man Held for Highway Robbery," *New York Times*, March 26, 1904, p. 1.

28. W. Fitzhugh Brundage, *Lynching in the New South: Georgia and Virginia, 1880–1930* (Urbana: University of Illinois Press, 1993), 294 and 293; "War on Negroes for Simple Brawl," *New York Times*, April 3, 1904, p. 1. For an analysis of the reliability of newspaper accounts of lynching, see also Bruce E. Baker, *This Mob Will Surely Take My Life: Lynching in the Carolinas, 1871–1947* (New York: Continuum, 2008), 121–43.

29. Mary Church Terrell, "Lynching from a Negro's Point of View," *North American Review* 178 (June 1904), 853–68 (quotation on p. 853, where Terrell also mentions that in the first three months of 1904, fifteen blacks were lynched in Arkansas). A search of the *Colored American Magazine* revealed that it did not carry news of Saint Charles, although articles did appear on lynching. See "Homicidal Mania in the Southern States," *Colored American Magazine* 7 (July 1904), 467–69. Also see *Analytical Guide and Indexes to the Colored American Magazine 1900–1909* (2 vols.; Westport, CT: Greenwood Press, 1974). A search of the national edition of the *Baltimore Afro-American* for 1904 revealed that it, too, neglected to report the affair. The *Voice of the Negro*, however, did relay details of what it described as a "carnival of murder in Arkansas." "Thirteen Lynched in Arkansas," *Voice of the Negro* 1 (May 1904). African American newspapers are tracked in Vilma Raskin Potter, *A Reference Guide to Afro-American Publications and Editors, 1827–1946* (Ames: Iowa State University Press, 1993). Also see Amanda Saar, "Black Arkansas Newspapers, 1869–1975: A Checklist," 1976, typescript, Center for Arkansas History and Culture, University of Arkansas at Little Rock; "African American Research Resources at the Arkansas State Archives," http://cdm16790.contentdm.oclc.org/cdm/singleitem/collection/p16790coll13/id/287/rec/1 (accessed October 15, 2016). For a survey of several lynchings in 1904, see Ray Stannard Baker, *Following the Color Line: American Negro Citizenship in the Progressive Era* (New York: Harper, 1964; orig. pub. with different subtitle in 1908), 175–215.

30. "Eleven Negroes Victims of Mob," *Arkansas Gazette*, March 27, 1904, p. 1. The word *riot* had a different connotation than it has today, according to Hugh Davis Graham and Ted Robert Gurr, *Violence in America: Historical and Comparative Perspectives*, vol. 2 (Washington, DC: Sage Publications, 1969), 304. As they put it, "Interracial riots in the early years of the century were essentially pogroms in which the Negroes were victims of white aggression."

31. "Eleven Negroes Victims of Mob," *Arkansas Gazette*, March 27, 1904, p. 1. In this article, both *who* and *that* are used when referring to blacks. A previous article, "Five Negroes Shot to Death by Mob," *Arkansas Gazette*, March 26, 1904, p. 1, reports that "a few days ago," the Griffins and a white man named Searcy had "a difficulty," during which one of the Griffins threatened Searcy with a beer bottle. Then, on Monday, the Griffins ran into Searcy and his brother at Woolfork and Norsworthy, a store. "Without warning," one of the Griffins knocked both Searcys unconscious, "fracturing their skulls," perhaps fatally. Then the Griffins attacked the deputy sheriff who tried to arrest them. This version of events on Monday may be apocryphal; since the Searcys are otherwise unmentioned in the published record of this week in east Arkansas, one suspects that their alleged injuries may have been less severe than reported here.

32. The full text of Davis's speech appears in "President's Speech in City Park a Notable Deliverance," *Arkansas Gazette*, October 26, 1905, p. 3. Roosevelt's reply appears in the same article on pp. 1 and 3. Also see "Cheering Crowds Greet President Roosevelt," *Arkansas Gazette*, October 26, 1905, p. 1.

33. "President's Speech in City Park a Notable Deliverance," p. 3. Roosevelt countered Davis's remarks by likening the behavior of lynchers to the bestiality of rapists. On the Roosevelt/Davis exchange in 1905 see also L. S. (Sharpe) Dunaway, *What a Preacher Saw Through a Key-Hole in Arkansas* (Little Rock: Parke-Harper Publishing Company, 1925), 63–64.

34. Willard B. Gatewood Jr., "Theodore Roosevelt and Arkansas, 1901–1912," *Arkansas Historical Quarterly* 32 (Spring 1973), 19; Raymond Arsenault, *The Wild Ass of the Ozarks: Jeff Davis and the Social Bases of Southern Politics* (Philadelphia: Temple University Press, 1984), 212. Also see Robert W. Meriwether, "The Faulkner County Lynching (1905)," *Faulkner Facts and Fiddlings* 33 (Fall/Winter 1991), 1–2, who calls Davis's speech "the most famous defense of lynching"; Cal Ledbetter Jr., "Jeff Davis and the Politics of Combat," *Arkansas Historical Quarterly* 33 (Spring 1974), 16–37; and Gordon, *Caste and Class*, 50–51. Also see J. V. Bourland, "Introductory," in L. S. Dunaway, *Jeff Davis, Governor and United States Senator: His Life and Speeches* (Little Rock: Democrat Print. and Litho. Co., 1913), 8.

35. Gordon, *Caste and Class*, 45, 37.

36. On the pardon, see text of "Governor Davis's Speech at Eureka Springs," in Dunaway, *Jeff Davis*, 78; and Arsenault, *Wild Ass*, 188.

37. Davis is quoted in Arsenault, *Wild Ass*, 214; Richard L. Niswonger, "A Study in Southern Demagoguery: Jeff Davis of Arkansas," *Arkansas Historical Quarterly* 39 (Summer 1980), quotations from 123 and 124; Richard L. Niswonger, *Arkansas Democratic Politics, 1896–1920* (Fayetteville: University of Arkansas Press, 1990), 100–101. In his memoir of the lynching in Saint Charles, J. M. Henderson Jr. refers to the political legacy of "the Carpet-Baggers." Henderson

explains, "The Campaign of 1896 was a heated one in Arkansas County, and some leading Republicans made a strenuous effort to control and corral the Negro vote. . . . This was true as to the campaign of 1900. At any rate there developed a very discourteous attitude on the part of some negroes toward the white people." He drew no connection between Davis or more contemporary political campaigns and the killings. J. M. Henderson Jr., "St. Charles Massacre," in *Brief Stories of St. Charles in Romance & Tragedy* (privately printed, n.d.), 10 (copy in Center for Arkansas History and Culture, University of Arkansas at Little Rock). Henderson was in his twenties at the time of the lynching and presumably had firsthand knowledge.

38. Niswonger, *Arkansas Democratic Politics*, 100.

39. Henderson, "St. Charles Massacre," 10. On Henderson's background see Fred W. Allsopp, *History of the Arkansas Press for a Hundred Years and More* (Little Rock: Park Harper Publishing, 1922), 50; and Clio Harper, *History of the Arkansas Press Association* (Little Rock: Arkansas Press Association, 1930), 64. Antipathy between lower-class whites and blacks, which this member of the local elite alleged, cannot be assumed. For an intriguing analysis of the interaction of racial, class, and commercial forces in the cultural construction of southern race relations in the early twentieth century, see Stephen H. Norwood, "Bogalusa Burning: The War Against Biracial Unionism in the Deep South, 1919," *Journal of Southern History* 63 (August 1997), 591–628. Also see Carl H. Moneyhon, *Arkansas and the New South, 1874–1929* (Fayetteville: University of Arkansas Press, 1997), 106, who notes that heightened competition for land led white tenants to try to drive black tenants out of Lonoke County in 1905.

40. Henderson, "St. Charles Massacre," 10. Despite its detail, this source contains inconsistencies: in Henderson's account, the name of "Aaron Hinton" is assigned to the part played by Griffin in all other accounts, which identify Hinton as the man killed later, on Thursday afternoon. Also see Boyd W. Johnson, "Historic Saint Charles," *Grand Prairie Historical Bulletin* 6 (July 1963), 44.

41. Brown, *Strain of Violence*, 217.

42. "Eleven Negroes Victims of Mob," *Arkansas Gazette*, March 27, 1904, p. 1. DeWitt was the sole county seat at the time, but later in the 1920s the community of Stuttgart was designated a dual county seat.

43. Myrdal, *American Dilemma*, 560. Ida B. Wells-Barnett, an outspoken crusader against lynching, urged blacks to arm themselves, insisting that "a Winchester rifle should have a place of honor in every home." She believed that "when the white man . . . knows he runs as great a risk of biting the dust every time his Afro-American victim does, he will have greater respect for Afro-American life." Wells-Barnett is quoted in Paula Giddings, *When and Where I Enter: The Impact of Black Women on Race and Sex in America* (New York: William Morrow, 1984), 20.

44. Myrdal, *American Dilemma*, 561 (first quotation), 563 (second quotation),

and 564; White, *Rope and Faggot*, 9 (third quotation), and also see 197–98.
According to a study of fourteen southern states over the course of thirty years,
the rate of lynchings bore a close inverse relationship to the population of a
given county—the fewer people, the higher the incidence of lynchings. See
Erle Fiske Young, "The Relation of Lynching to the Size of Political Areas:
A Note on the Sociology of Popular Justice," *Sociology and Social Research* 12
(March/April 1928), 348–53. The population of Arkansas County, where Saint
Charles is located, was 12,973 in 1900; it increased by 24.1 percent to 16,103 in
1910. Data do not suggest the sort of dramatic demographic shift that would
trigger the social instability that Dennis B. Downey and Raymond M. Hyser
found operating in their study of a northern lynching in 1911. See Downey
and Hyser, *No Crooked Death: Coatesville, Pennsylvania, and the Lynching of
Zachariah Walker* (Urbana: University of Illinois Press, 1991).

45. "Midnight's Musings. Some Awful Incidents Connected With Burning a
Woman at the Stake," *Afro-American Ledger*, March 5, 1904, p. 1. Also see Paul
A. Gilje, *Rioting in America* (Bloomington: Indiana University Press, 1996),
102. Gilje reports that before this black couple was burned to death, the sadists
"poked out an eyeball with a stick." Richard Hofstadter and Michael Wallace,
eds., *American Violence: A Documentary History* (New York: Knopf, 1970), 469.

46. "Eleven Negroes Victims of Mob," *Arkansas Gazette*, March 27, 1904, p. 1.
Other towns that were represented in the crowd included Roe, Ethel, and
Clarendon. "Five Negroes Shot to Death by Mob," *Arkansas Gazette*,
March 26, 1904, p. 1.

47. "Eleven Negroes Victims of Mob," *Arkansas Gazette*, March 27, 1904, p. 1.

48. J. E. Cutler, "Race Riots and Lynch Law—A Northern Professor's View,"
Outlook 85 (February 2, 1907), 267; and Arthur F. Raper, *The Tragedy of
Lynching* (Chapel Hill: University of North Carolina Press, 1933), 13 (second and third quotations). A case study of one hundred lynchings committed
between 1929 and 1940 reveals that police officers actually participated in at
least half of them, and in the overwhelming majority of the remaining cases,
they either condoned or tacitly approved of the violence. Myrdal, *American
Dilemma*, 562, 1346n1, and 1347n17. There were of course exceptions. Sheriff
Richard W. Bandy of Jackson County, Arkansas, made news around the turn of
the century by repelling a lynch mob bent on killing a man whom he believed
to be wrongly accused of crime. See Harry Lee Williams, "'Uncle Dick' Bandy,
Early Jackson County Sheriff, Holds Off Mob, Wins Wide Acclaim," *Stream
of History* 23 (Summer 1986), 18–19.

49. Johnson, "Historic St. Charles," 44; and J. M. Henderson Jr., "Vigilantees
[sic]," in *Grand Prairie Historical Bulletin* 8 (July 1965), 17 on M. A. Baker
as sheriff. In its only editorial comment on the thirteen homicides in Saint
Charles, the *Arkansas Democrat* opined that "the new sheriff of that county
appears to have his hands full." *Arkansas Democrat*, March 29, 1904, p. 4.

50. "Eleven Negroes Victims of Mob," *Arkansas Gazette*, March 27, 1904, p. 1.

51. Ibid. This listing, however, was not complete. Two more would be murdered thereafter.

52. "Five Negroes Shot to Death," *Memphis Commercial Appeal*, March 26, 1904, p. 1; in its version of "Five Negroes Shot to Death by Mob," the Saturday *Arkansas Gazette* reported that "the Griffin boys" were apprehended: "if so, it probably means that two more will be killed." The Sunday *Arkansas Gazette*, which cites eleven dead by name, does not mention them. In its last words on the terror, an editorial on the following Tuesday, it merely states that "thirteen" had been killed. The researcher must assume that two of the thirteen were the Griffins. See "In Arkansas County," *Arkansas Gazette*. In "Thirteen Negroes Killed in the St. Charles Riot," *Memphis Commercial Appeal*, March 29, 1904, p. 1, it was reported that the Griffins "were killed" on Saturday. The other statewide newspaper to cover the events was the *Arkansas Democrat* in "Nine Negroes Shot to Death," in its issue of March 27, 1904, p. 1.

53. White, *Rope and Faggot*, 8. Henderson, "St. Charles Massacre," 11, reports that a grand jury "was unable to find out who the members of the mob were." When deciphering a document, the historian must be sensitive not only to what it says; to comprehend what it means, he or she must also be attuned to what is left unsaid. One must be aware of the "negative evidence" that in this case reveals that an official investigation was not high on the agenda.

54. Myrdal, *American Dilemma*, 559 and 564; Smead, *Blood Justice*, x; as Zangrando summed it up, *NAACP Crusade*, 8, lynchers "expected and enjoyed immunity from the law."

55. Jacquelyn Dowd Hall, *Revolt against Chivalry: Jessie Daniel Ames and the Women's Campaign against Lynching* (New York: Columbia University Press, 1979), 142.

56. Ibid. What was true of lynchings in general was applicable to this specific example. See "In Arkansas County," *Arkansas Gazette*, March 29, 1904, p. 4, which asserts that "the negroes threw down the gauntlet." This editorial noted that whenever blacks believed "that their weight of numbers gives them the right or the power to do as they please, a conflict between the two races is inevitable." The Memphis paper reported that in Saint Charles, blacks outnumbered whites, "and trouble has been brewing for a long time, as the negroes for the past two years have been getting insolent and belligerent." See "Thirteen Negroes Killed in the St. Charles Riot," *Memphis Commercial Appeal*, March 28, 1904, p. 1.

57. Johnson, "Historic St. Charles," 44.

58. L. Scott Stafford, "Slavery and the Arkansas Supreme Court," *University of Arkansas at Little Rock Law Journal* 19 (Spring 1997), 413–64.

59. George M. Fredrickson, *The Black Image in the White Mind: The Debate on Afro-American Character and Destiny, 1817–1914* (New York: Harper & Row, 1971), 276 and 282.

60. Henderson, "St. Charles Massacre," 10–11; Johnson, "Historic St. Charles," 44. Also see "Tenth Negro Killed in the St. Charles Race Riot," *Memphis Commercial Appeal*, March 27, 1904, p. 12, concerning the Thursday night killings (that the article reports as having occurred on Wednesday). Noting only that "a white man was shot in the abdomen by one of the guards as he did not stay in the place assigned him," the newspaper does not explain what transpired.

61. White, *Rope and Faggot*, 245, and 248–49 for "Table VI: States by Number of Persons Lynched, by Population, by Church Membership, and by Denominations." Of the "Total Church Population" in Arkansas, 79.5 percent were Methodist or Baptist. Cutler, *Lynch-Law*, 186–89, could find no clear correlation between the incidence of lynching and the percentage of blacks in the population, nor the percentage of foreign-born people, nor the percentage of illiterate people.

62. Myrdal, *American Dilemma*, 563; White, *Rope and Faggot*, 9, and 245–46; and Raper, *Tragedy of Lynching*, 21–23 (quotation on p. 22).

63. One must piece together the controversy that attended Bishop Brown's remarks in Massachusetts. See "Negroes Growing Worse, Says Bishop Brown of Arkansas," *Boston Evening Record*, February 8, 1904; "Bishop Brown Claims Misrepresentation, But Still Maintains That Southern Negroes Have Deteriorated," *Boston Evening Record*, February 16, 1904; untitled editorial comment, *Boston Evening Record*, February 27, 1904; and "Cambridge Protests," *Cambridge (MA) Tribune*, February 27, 1904. Also see a pamphlet by Edward Abbott titled "'A Great Problem'; Rev. Dr. Abbott Takes Up the Negro Question, as Suggested by Bishop Brown's Utterances" (Little Rock: n.d. [1904]), particularly 5–6; "Bishop Brown on Negroes," *Arkansas Democrat*, February 18, 1904, p. 2; J. E. Bush, "Reply to Bishop Brown," *Arkansas Gazette*, February 21, 1904; and Arsenault, *Wild Ass*, 212 and 315n31. On Brown's career, see Ronald Carden, *William Montgomery Brown (1855–1937): The Southern Episcopal Bishop who Became a Communist* (Lewiston, NY: Edwin Mellen Press, 2007). Also see Rt. Rev. William Montgomery Brown, D.D., Bishop of Arkansas, *The Crucial Race Question; or, Where and How Shall the Color Line Be Drawn* (Little Rock: The Arkansas Churchman's Publishing Co., 1907).

64. "In Arkansas County," *Arkansas Gazette*, March 29, 1904, p. 4.

65. "Five Negroes Lynched," *New York Times*, March 26, 1904, p. 1; and "Arkansas State News: Nine Negroes Killed," *Atkins (AR) Chronicle*, April 1, 1904, p. 1.

66. "Arkansas State News: Nine Negroes Killed," *Atkins (AR) Chronicle*, April 1, 1904, p. 1; "Negroes Slain in Arkansas Co.," *Arkansas Democrat*, March 25, 1904, p. 1; "13 Negroes Were Slain," *Arkansas Democrat*, March 29, 1904, p. 5; and "Five Negroes Shot to Death by Mob," *Arkansas Gazette*, March 26, 1904, p. 1; "Eleven Negroes Victims of Mob," *Arkansas Gazette*, March 27, 1904, p. 1.

67. "Tenth Negro Killed in the St. Charles Race Riot," *Memphis Commercial Appeal*, March 27, 1904, p. 12.

68. Henderson, "St. Charles Massacre," 10–11; and Johnson, "Historic St. Charles," 44.

69. Ibid.

70. Ibid.

71. Brundage, *Lynching in the New South*, especially "Mobs and Ritual," 17–48.

72. Tolnay and Beck, *Festival of Violence*, 21. See the discussion in Brundage, "'To Draw the Line': Crimes and Victims," in *Lynching in the New South*, 49–85, although as Brundage cautions, "it was not essential to mob members that their victims be actually guilty of a crime" (p. 49).

73. "Five Negroes Lynched," *New York Times*, March 26, 1904, p. 1. Most of the killings in the printed record occurred in the passive voice: that is, whites did not kill, but rather blacks were killed.

74. "Eleven Negroes Victims of Mob," *Arkansas Gazette*, March 27, 1904, p. 1. The difficulty over details, stated the Memphis paper, was "owing to the remoteness of St. Charles, and to the fact that news of the result of the riot is not given out freely," in "13 Negroes Were Slain," *Memphis Commercial Appeal*, March 29, 1904, p. 5.

75. The immediate response to the horror by the blacks of Saint Charles was described briefly in "Thirteen Negroes Were Slain in the St. Charles Race Riot," *Memphis Commercial Appeal*, March 28, 1904, p. 1. It noted that Saturday was an election day, and usually the village was "crowded with negroes, but during the entire day only two negroes were seen." The article concluded that "the negroes are quiet and are attending strictly to their work."

76. "Eleven Negroes Victims of Mob," *Arkansas Gazette*, March 27, 1904, p. 1. The *Arkansas Democrat* quotation appeared on the following Tuesday in "13 Negroes Were Slain," *Arkansas Democrat*, March 29, 1904, p. 5.

77. For a survey of the evolution of legal structures designed to substitute for chattel slavery by constituting wage slavery, see Douglas A. Blackmon, *Slavery by Another Name: The Re-Enslavement of Black Americans from the Civil War to World War II* (New York: Doubleday, 2008).

78. *Williams vs. Mississippi*, 1898.

79. For insightful analysis of communal bonds forged through lynchings, see Amy Louise Wood, *Lynching and Spectacle: Witnessing Racial Violence in America, 1890–1940* (Chapel Hill: University of North Carolina Press, 2009).

80. For a fuller consideration of lynching as punishment, see Michael J. Pfeifer, *Rough Justice: Lynching and American Society, 1874–1947* (Urbana: University of Illinois Press, 2004).

81. An example of the limitations of this approach might be the discussion of the torching of Ricelor Cleodas Watson in Dominic J. Capeci Jr., *The Lynching of Cleo Wright* (Lexington: University Press of Kentucky, 1998). After dragging

the victim through town chained to the back of an automobile, the lynchers doused him in gasoline and set him ablaze for a crowd of hundreds who witnessed his death agony, his screams interrupting Sunday church services that were running past noon. "In short," concludes Capeci on p. 167, "Wright beckoned his own destroyers, and they complied."

82. See, for instance, the souvenir postcard photo of the hanging charred torso of Jesse Washington, and the message handwritten on the back: "This is the barbiecue [sic] we had last night. My picture is to the left with a cross over it[.] your son Joe." Author unknown, reproduced in James Allen, Hilton Als, Congressman John Lewis, and Leon F. Litwack, *Without Sanctuary: Lynching Photography in America* (Santa Fe: Twin Palms, 2000), plates 25–26. As James Allen commented in his "Notes on the Plates," pp. 174–75, "Repeated references to eating are found in lynching-related correspondence, such as *"coon cooking,"* *"barbecue,"* and *"main fare."* Emphasis his.

83. Tolnay and Beck, *Festival of Violence*, in particular "Table 2-5. The Reasons Given for Black Lynchings."

Chapter 6, "Through Death, Hell and the Grave"

1. *Arkansas Gazette*, February 21, 1901, p. 1.

2. *Arkansas Democrat*, May 4, 1927, p. 1; *Arkansas Gazette*, May 5, 1927, p. 1; *Crisis* 34 (July 1927), 168. See also the Harmon L. Remmel scrapbook, which contains numerous press clippings on the lynching; labeled Scrapbook, Item 5, hereafter referred to as Remmel Scrapbook 5, it is located in Republican Party, Arkansas, State Committee Records, 1882–1956, Special Collections Department, Mullins Library, University of Arkansas Libraries, Fayetteville. A printed account of the lynching is Marcet Haldeman-Julius, "The Story of a Lynching: An Exploration of Southern Psychology," *Little Blue Book* No. 1260, (Girard, KS: Haldeman-Julius Publications, no date), in the Haldeman-Julius Collection, Special Collections Department, Mullins Library, University of Arkansas Libraries, Fayetteville.

3. For methods of execution of lynching victims in Arkansas during the period 1910–29, see Todd E. Lewis, "Race Relations in Arkansas, 1910–1929" (PhD diss., University of Arkansas, 1995), 485–88.

4. In several cases during the period 1910–27, lynch mobs numbered in the hundreds and even the thousands. See Lewis, "Race Relations in Arkansas."

5. See Lewis, "Race Relations in Arkansas," for details of the ritualized nature of lynching. The author's dissertation includes two chapters addressing lynching in Arkansas from 1910 to 1929. These represent an expansion of his article "Mob Justice in the 'American Congo': 'Judge Lynch' in Arkansas during the Decade after World War I," *Arkansas Historical Quarter* 52 (Summer 1993), 156–84; the discussion in this article is limited to the period 1919–29.

6. Tuskegee Institute and the National Association for the Advancement of Colored People (NAACP) kept statistics on lynching in the United States. Unfortunately, no definitive list exists as the lists do not agree on the exact number of lynchings. Nevertheless, the two lists have an approximate annual and overall agreement. In 1889–1918, the Tuskegee Institute recorded 3,133 persons lynched, 645 white and 2,488 black, while the NAACP recorded 3,224 persons lynched, 702 white and 2,522 black. See National Association for the Advancement of Colored People, *Thirty Years of Lynching*, (New York: Arno Press and the New York Times, 1969); and Tuskegee Institute Department of Records and Research, "Lynchings by State and Race, 1882–1959," n.d.. This document appears to be a printed version of lynching statistics from ca. 1960 published on annually by the institute in the *Negro Year Book*.

7. Examples emphasizing the role of non-southern antilynching efforts include Christopher Waldrep, *African Americans Confront Lynching: Strategies of Resistance from the Civil War to the Civil Rights Era* (New York: Rowman and Littlefield, 2009); and Robert L. Zangrando, *The NAACP Crusade against Lynching, 1909–1950* (Philadelphia: Temple University Press, 1980). With regards to lynching in Arkansas, neither Nan Elizabeth Woodruff nor Karlos Hill discuss the antilynching efforts of conservative whites and African Americans. See Nan Elizabeth Woodruff, *American Congo: The African American Freedom Struggle in the Delta* (Cambridge, MA: Harvard University Press, 2003); and Karlos Hill, "Resisting Lynching: Black Grassroots Responses to Lynching in the Mississippi and Arkansas Deltas, 1882–1938" (PhD diss., University of Illinois at Urbana-Champaign, 2009).

8. W. Fitzhugh Brundage includes discussions of the antilynching efforts of southern white conservatives in Virginia and Georgia. See Brundage, *Lynching in the New South: Georgia and Virginia, 1880–1930* (Urbana: University of Illinois Press, 1993), 188–89, 216–25, 234–38.

9. James Elbert Cutler, *Lynch-Law* (New York: Longmans, Green, and Company, 1905), 157. See also *Thirty Years of Lynching* and "Lynchings by State and Race, 1882–1959."

10. *Thirty Years of Lynching*, 31–32, 52.

11. "Lynchings by State and Race, 1882–1959." Other states with worse records than Arkansas were Mississippi, Georgia, Texas, Louisiana, and Alabama. The Tuskegee Institute did not record any lynchings in Arkansas after 1936.

12. *Thirty Years of Lynching*, 34–35. Available evidence does not confirm seven of these events as lynchings. One case, that of the "unnamed Negro" lynched for robbery on October 8, 1917, could not be corroborated. In four cases, those of Charley Lewis (see *Arkansas Democrat*, October 18, 1911, p. 1), Jacob Bowers (see *Arkansas Gazette*, September 13, 1915, pp. 1, 2, 3), the white "unnamed highwayman" in Vandervoort (actually George Banks, see *Arkansas Gazette*, January 22, 1916, p. 2, and January 23, 1916, p. 19), and Allen Mitchell (see

Memphis Commercial Appeal, June 14, 1918, p. 1), the victim may have been lynched, but the press accounts indicate that each was shot while resisting arrest. The account of the murder of Frederick Wagner of Garland County, a man who had made pro-German remarks, resembles an assassination more than a lynching; working in the field among his children, Wagner was shot from a distance by two men (see *Arkansas Gazette,* August 29, 1918, p. 8). Finally, Lee Simms was the first black man executed in the state's electric chair; he was not lynched, contrary to what the NAACP claimed (see *Arkansas Gazette,* September 5, 1913, p. 1; September 6, 1913, p. 12).

13. *Thirty Years of Lynching,* 51.
14. For the period 1910–29, see Lewis, "Race Relations in Arkansas," 485–88.
15. Richard Buckelew, "Racial Violence in Arkansas: Lynchings and Mob Rule, 1860–1930" (PhD diss., University of Arkansas, 1999), 242–54; his list of lynchings includes data from the 1860s to 1936.
16. Ibid.
17. For more information on nightriders and their actions related to driving African Americans off land or away from certain jobs, see Guy Lancaster, *Racial Cleansing in Arkansas, 1883–1924: Politics, Land, Labor, and Criminality* (Lanham, MD: Lexington Books, 2014).
18. Ryan Poe, "Race Riots," *Encyclopedia of Arkansas History and Culture,* http://www.encyclopediaofarkansas.net/encyclopedia/entry-detail.aspx?entryID =5170 (accessed January 16, 2016).
19. Secondary sources detailing these conditions include James Harris Fain, "Political Disfranchisement of the Negro in Arkansas" (Master's thesis, University of Arkansas, 1961); Fon Louise Gordon, *Caste and Class: The Black Experience in Arkansas, 1880–1920* (Athens: University of Georgia Press, 1995); John William Graves, *Town and Country: Race Relations in an Urban-Rural Context, Arkansas, 1865–1905* (Fayetteville: University of Arkansas Press, 1990); Carl H. Moneyhon, "Black Politics in Arkansas During the Gilded Age, 1876–1900," *Arkansas Historical Quarterly* 44 (Autumn 1985), 222–45. In addition to *Town and Country,* Graves has written several additional articles published in the *Arkansas Historical Quarterly* and *Journal of Southern History.*
20. See Lewis, "Race Relations in Arkansas," 26–66.
21. E. M. Woods, *Blue Book of Little Rock and Argenta, Arkansas* (Little Rock: Central Printing Company, 1907). Argenta was the contemporary name of North Little Rock.
22. Sources on Bush include A. E. Bush and P. L. Dorman, eds., *History of the Mosaic Templars of America: Its Founders and Officials* (Little Rock: Central Printing Co., 1924); and C. Calvin Smith, "John E. Bush: The Politician and the Man, 1880–1916," *Arkansas Historical Quarterly* 54 (Summer 1995), 115–33.
23. Woods, *Blue Book,* 145.

24. Ibid., 144.

25. Ibid., 147.

26. Ibid., 146.

27. Ibid., 151.

28. Ibid., 144.

29. Ibid., 151.

30. Ibid., 144.

31. Ibid., 149.

32. Ibid., 148.

33. Ibid., 148.

34. For a discussion of the life of Washington, see *Up from Slavery: An Autobiography* (Garden City, NY: Doubleday, Page and Company, 1924). For a detailed discussion of the relationship between Booker T. Washington and black Arkansans, see Lewis, "Race Relations in Arkansas, 1910–1929," 78–97. One notable exception was Joseph Carter Corbin, the Reconstruction era state superintendent of public instruction. For information on Corbin, see Izola Preston, "Joseph Carter Corbin," *Encyclopedia of Arkansas History and Culture*, http://www.encyclopediaofarkansas.net/encyclopedia/entry-detail.aspx ?entryID=1624 (accessed October 4, 2016).

35. "The Standard Printed Version of the Atlanta Exposition Address, Atlanta, Georgia, September 18, 1895," in *Booker T. Washington Papers*, edited by Louis R. Harlan, vol. 3 (Urbana: University of Illinois Press, 1974), 584.

36. For information on Morris, see Todd E. Lewis, "Elias Camp Morris," *Encyclopedia of Arkansas History and Culture*, http://www.encyclopediaofarkansas.net /encyclopedia/entry-detail.aspx?entryID=433 (accessed January 21, 2016).

37. "An Account of the Twenty-Fifth Anniversary of Tuskegee Institute by Jesse Max Barber, May 1906," in *Booker T. Washington Papers*, vol. 9, 15; "To Theodore Roosevelt, Tuskegee, Alabama, September 19, 1907," in *Booker T. Washington Papers*, vol. 9, 337.

38. "To Fred Warner Carpenter, Tuskegee Institute, Alabama, September 12, 1908," in *Booker T. Washington Papers*, vol. 9, 623; "Reports of Pinkerton Detective F. E. Miller," in *Booker T. Washington Papers*, vol. 9, 645–46.

39. "An Account of Washington's Tour of Texas by Horace D. Slatter, Tuskegee, Alabama, October 14, 1911," in *Booker T. Washington Papers*, vol. 11, 331–32.

40. For a discussion of Roosevelt's relationship with Arkansas, see Willard B. Gatewood, "Theodore Roosevelt and Arkansas, 1901–1912," *Arkansas Historical Quarterly* 32 (Spring 1973), 3–24.

41. Untitled speech beginning "Your Excellency," 1905, Jeff Davis Papers, Special Collections, University of Arkansas Libraries, Fayetteville, Arkansas, Box 10, File 1.

42. John E. Bush to Emmett J. Scott, September 5, 1905, Booker T. Washington Papers, February 2, 1902–September 20, 1915, Film 650, Mullins Library, University of Arkansas, Fayetteville, Arkansas.

43. Press account of these events include *Arkansas Gazette*, March 24, 1904, p. 1; March 26, 1904, p. 1; and March 27, 1904, pp. 1, 2. See also Vincent Vinikas, "Specters in the Past: The Saint Charles, Arkansas, Lynching of 1904 and the Limits of Historical Inquiry," *Journal of Southern History* 65 (August 1999), 535–64 (reprinted in modified form as chapter 5 of this volume).

44. *Arkansas Gazette*, March 29, 1904, p. 4.

45. *Chicago Tribune*, April 3, 1904, pp. 1, 2.

46. *Arkansas Gazette*, April 6, 1904, p. 4.

47. *Arkansas Gazette*, January 15, 1909, p. 11. Donaghey's inaugural address outlined a thoroughly Progressive program, advocating reforms in education, conservation of resources, increasing the power of the railroad commission, eliminating the convict lease system and the abuse of prisoners, the need for banking regulations, election reforms including the adoption of the initiative and referendum, and laws protecting the interests of labor. See *Arkansas Gazette*, January 15, 1909, pp. 1, 10–12.

48. *Arkansas Gazette*, April 8, 1909, p. 3

49. T. D. Crawford and Hamilton Moses, *A Digest of the Statutes of Arkansas Embracing All Laws of a General Nature in Force at the Close of the General and Special Sessions of General Assembly of 1919* (Little Rock: Democrat Printing and Lithographing Company, 1919), 736–37.

50. *Arkansas Gazette*, May 12, 1909, p. 3; May 13, 1909, p. 3

51. *Arkansas Gazette*, March 30, 1909, p. 1; April 2, 1909.

52. *Arkansas Gazette*, March 30, 1909, p. 1.

53. *Arkansas Gazette*, April 2, 1909.

54. *Arkansas Gazette*, May 24, 1909, p. 2.

55. *Arkansas Gazette*, May 25, 1909, p. 1.

56. *Arkansas Gazette*, May 26, 1909, p. 1.

57. *Arkansas Gazette*, May 28, 1909, p. 1.

58. *Arkansas Gazette*, May 29, 1909.

59. Theo Bond and Dan A. Rudd, *From Slavery to Wealth: The Life of Scott Bond*, edited by Willard B. Gatewood (Fayetteville, AR: Phoenix International, 2008), 13.

60. *Arkansas Gazette*, November 15, 1915, p. 15.

61. Minutes of the University Commission on Race, n.p., n.d., 5. This item was donated to the University of Arkansas by Brough and is available in the main stacks.

62. Ibid., 16–17; 28–30.

63. Ibid., 7.

64. Ibid., 45.

65. Ibid., 46.

66. Ibid., 72–73.

67. For details on the Washington, DC, session, see ibid., 18–23.

68. Charles Hillman Brough Speech, December 1914, p. 6, Charles Hillman

Brough Papers, Special Collections, University of Arkansas Libraries, Fayetteville, Arkansas.

69. Ibid., 29.

70. Ibid., 30.

71. Ibid., 29.

72. Ibid., 7.

73. Ibid., 9.

74. For information on Jones, see Tom W. Dillard, "Scipio A. Jones," *Arkansas Historical Quarterly* 31 (Autumn 1971), 201–19.

75. E. C. Morris to Brough, March 31, 1916, Charles Hillman Brough Papers, Box 2, File 21.

76. Scipio A. Jones to Brough, November 14, 1916, Charles Hillman Brough Papers, Box 3, File 36.

77. For a discussion of the struggle between Lily White and black Republicans in Arkansas, see Tom W. Dillard, "To the Back of the Elephant: Racial Conflict in the Arkansas Republican Party," *Arkansas Historical Quarterly* 33 (Spring 1974), 3–15. This author has discussed this conflict in "Race Relations in Arkansas, 1910–1929," 126–85, 366–449, and in "'Caesars Are Too Many': Harmon Liveright Remmel and the Republican Party of Arkansas, 1913–1927," *Arkansas Historical Quarterly* 56 (Spring 1997), 1–25. For a discussion of the Arkansas Republican Party during the late nineteenth and early twentieth centuries, see Marvin Frank Russell, "The Republican Party of Arkansas, 1874–1913" (PhD diss., University of Arkansas, 1985).

78. Lewis, "Race Relations in Arkansas, 1910–1929," 486–87

79. The Elaine riot was front-page news for several days in several newspapers including the *Arkansas Democrat*, *Arkansas Gazette*, and *Helena (AR) World*. I discuss the Elaine riot in "Race Relations in Arkansas, 1910–1929," 219–73. Important secondary accounts of these events include O. A. Rogers Jr., "The Elaine Riots of 1919," *Arkansas Historical Quarterly* 19 (Summer 1960), 142–50; J. W. Butts and Dorothy James, "The Underlying Causes of the Riot of 1919," *Arkansas Historical Quarterly* 20 (Spring 1961), 95–104; Arthur L. Waskow, *From Race-Riot to Sit-In, 1919 and the 1960s: A Study in the Connections Between Conflict and Violence* (Garden City, NY: Doubleday and Company, 1966), 121–42; B. Boren McCool, *Union, Reaction, and Riot* (Memphis: Bureau of Social Research, 1970); Richard C. Cortner, *A Mob Intent on Death: The NAACP and the Arkansas Riot Cases* (Middletown, CT: Wesleyan University Press, 1988); Grif Stockley, *Blood in Their Eyes: The Elaine Massacres of 1919* (Fayetteville: University of Arkansas Press, 2001); and Jeannie M. Whayne, "Low Villains and Wickedness in High Places: Race and Class in the Elaine Riots," *Arkansas Historical Quarterly* 58 (Autumn 1999), 285–313.

80. For a list of the disposition of the cases, see Lewis, "Race Relations in Arkansas, 1910–1929," 481–84.

81. For information on the appeals of these twelve men, see The Arkansas Cases, September 1, 1923, all in Miscellaneous Correspondence, 1917–25, 1928–32, National Association for the Advancement of Colored People, Film 651, Mullins Library, University of Arkansas Libraries, Fayetteville, Arkansas. The main focus in Cortner, *A Mob Intent on Death*, is these cases.

82. *Crisis* 21 (December 1920), 66.

83. *Fayetteville Democrat*, 10 October 1919, p. 2.

84. See the individual "Lynching Records" for 1922–27 in the Lynching File, Tuskegee Institute Archives, Tuskegee, text-film. *Negro Year Book, 1937–1938*, 157, gives a list of annual lynching statistics featuring lynchings and attempted lynchings for 1914–1937.

85. Prisoners taken from officers included Wilson, Jameson, Lowery, Turner, Harris/Harrison, "George," Blade/Blazes, and Pounds. Those taken from jails included Robinson, McIntyre, Thomas, Tuggle, Slater, Owen, and Harris. See Lewis, "Race Relations in Arkansas, 1910–1929," 485–88, for details on the lynchings.

86. *Arkansas Democrat*, October 4, 1919, p. 4.

87. *Arkansas Democrat*, October 7, 1919, p. 4. Actually, the Phillips County record on lynching was not as clean as contemporary white Arkansans believed. Chapter 1 of the present volume recounts two slaves being lynched there in 1849. Dan Reynolds was lynched in 1888, followed by a man (unnamed by sources) in 1889. According to an NAACP source, a black man had been lynched in the county in 1890, and Henry Phillips was lynched in 1897. See *Thirty Years of Lynching*, 48; Brent E. Riffel, "Lynching," *Encyclopedia of Arkansas History and Culture*, http://www.encyclopediaofarkansas.net /encyclopedia/entry-detail.aspx?entryID=346 (accessed October 11, 2016). Furthermore, in November 1921, two other African Americans were lynched: Will Turner and Dallas Knickerson. Turner's body was burned in front of the court house in Helena. *Arkansas Gazette*, November 19, 1921, p. 1; November 26, 1919, p. 1. One other African American, Owen Flemming, was lynched in Phillips County as the alleged murderer of a white overseer on June 8, 1927.

88. Ida B. Wells-Barnett, "The Arkansas Race Riot" (Chicago, n.d.), in Governor Charles Hillman Brough Scrapbooks, Film 272, Audio-Visual Department, Mullins Library, University of Arkansas, Fayetteville, Arkansas.

89. Walter White, "'Massacring Whites' in Arkansas," *Nation* 109 (December 6, 1919), 715–16; "The Real Causes of Two Race Riots," *Crisis* 19 (December 1919), 56–62.

90. *Arkansas Gazette*, December 27, 1920, p. 1; December 28, 1920, p. 6; *Memphis Commercial Appeal*, December 27, 1920, p. 1; Lee A. Dew, "The Lynching of 'Boll Weevil,'" *Midwest Quarterly* 12 (January 1971), 145–53.

91. *Arkansas Democrat*, December 27, 1920, p. 1; *Arkansas Gazette*, December 26, 1920, p. 1; *Memphis Commercial Appeal*, December 26, 1920, p. 1; *Pine Bluff*

Daily Graphic, December 26, 1920, p. 1; Pickens, "The American Congo," 426–27. Lowery's name was alternatively spelled as "Lowry," and press accounts also called him "Henry Lyons," "Will Johnson," and "Charley Giles." See *Arkansas Gazette*, December 29, 1920, p. 1; *Memphis Commercial Appeal*, December 27, 1920, p. 8; *Pine Bluff Daily Graphic*, December 28, 1920, p. 1.

92. *Arkansas Democrat*, January 26, 1921, p. 1; *Arkansas Gazette*, January 27, 1921, p. 9; *Memphis Press*, in *An American Lynching* (New York: The National Association for the Advancement of Colored People, 1921), 4. *An American Lynching* consists entirely of press clippings on the Lowery lynching.

93. *Arkansas Democrat*, January 26, 1921, p. 1; *Memphis Press*, January 26, 1921, p. 1, in *An American Lynching*, 5.

94. *Arkansas Democrat*, January 26, 1921, p. 1.

95. *Memphis Press*, January 27, 1921, p. 1, in *An American Lynching*, 3, 4. Roddy's account served as the source of information for accounts published in other newspapers such as the *Arkansas Democrat* and *Arkansas Gazette*.

96. *Arkansas Democrat*, January 27, 1921, p. 1; *Arkansas Gazette*, January 27, 1921, p. l.

97. National Association for the Advancement of Colored People, Minutes of the Meeting of the Board of Directors, February 14, 1921, 3; and April 11, 1921, 1–2, both in National Association for the Advancement of Colored People, Minutes of the Meetings of the Board of Directors, 1909–29, Mullins Library, University of Arkansas, Fayetteville, Arkansas, text-film. "The American Congo" by Pickens was the NAACP account published in the *Nation*, while "An American Lynching" was the NAACP pamphlet appearing in Congress. For reaction to the lynching outside of Arkansas, see also *Chicago Defender*, February 5, 1921; *New York Globe*, January 28, 1921; and Laredo *Times*, January 27, 1921, all in the Lynching Files, Reel 221, Tuskegee Institute Archives, Tuskegee, text-film; see also the *New York World*, January 28, 1921, p. 12.

98. *Arkansas Democrat*, January 28, 1921, p. 6; *Arkansas Gazette*, January 28, 1921, p. 6; *Arkansas Methodist*, February 3, 1921, p. 1.

99. *Arkansas Democrat*, January 27, 1921, p. 1; *Arkansas Gazette*, January 27, 1921, p. 1.

100. R. P. Stewart to David Y. Thomas, February 17, 1921, David Yancey Thomas Papers, Special Collections, University of Arkansas Libraries, Fayetteville, Arkansas, Box 2, Series 2 File 4, Folder 1.

101. *Arkansas Gazette*, March 13, 1921, pp. 1, 10.

102. *Arkansas Democrat*, March 17, 1921, p. 1; March 18, 1921, p. 1, 18; March 19, 1921, p. 1; *Arkansas Gazette*, March 18, 1921, pp. 1, 10.

103. *Arkansas Democrat*, March 18, 1921, p. 1; March 22, 1921, p. 1; March 19, 1921, p. 1.

104. Ibid., March 19, 1921, p. 8.

105. Ibid., March 25, 1921, p. 9; March 26, 1921, p. 8; March 29, 1921, p. 6.

106. Ibid., March 19, 1921, p. 6.

107. *Arkansas Gazette*, April 13, 1921, p. 6.

108. *Arkansas Democrat*, April 9, 1921, p. 4.

109. Ibid., April 9, 1921, p. 1.

110. *Arkansas Gazette*, April 11, 1921, p. 1.

111. Ibid., July 21, 1921, p. 1.

112. Ibid., January 17, 1923, p. 1. For additional accounts of the Gregor lynching, see Brooks R. Blevins, "The Strike and the Still: Anti-Radical Violence and the Ku Klux Klan in the Ozarks," *Arkansas Historical Quarterly* 52 (Winter 1993), 417–19; J. K. Farris, *The Harrison Riot or the Reign of the Mob on the Missouri and North Arkansas Railroad* (Wynne, AR: Rev. J. K. Farris, 1924), 90–101; and Orville Thrasher Gooden, *The Missouri and North Arkansas Railroad Strike* (New York: Columbia University Press, 1926), 131–35.

113. *Arkansas Gazette*, August 12, 1923, p. 1. According to the press account, the lynching occurred in "Murphyville" in Union County, although contemporary maps do not indicate such a place; it may have been an oil-drilling camp. A local from Smackover remembered that a "negro" who had "made an insulting remark to a white woman" had been "strung up . . . in the field" and that "oil-field workers [were] supposed to have done the lynching." See Boyce House, *Oil Boom: The Story of Spindletop, Burkburnett, Mexia, Smackover, Desdemona, and Ranger* (Caldwell, ID: The Caxton Printers, Ltd., 1941), 161.

114. *Arkansas Gazette*, May 30, 1925, p. 1.

115. "Lynchings by State and Race, 1882–1959."

116. For accounts of the origins and debate of the Dyer antilynching bill, see the numerous entries in US Congress, 1921–1922, The Dyer Bill Debate, 67th Cong., 2nd Sess., *Congressional Record*, vol. 62, parts 1 and 2; Charles Flint Kellogg, *NAACP: A History of the National Association for the Advancement of Colored People, 1909–1920* (Baltimore: Johns Hopkins University Press, 1967), 209–46; George C. Rable, "The South and the Politics of Antilynching Legislation, 1920–1940," *Journal of Southern History* 51 (May 1985), 201–20; and Zangrando, *NAACP Crusade*, 51–71.

117. Zangrando, *NAACP Crusade*, 51–64.

118. Ibid., 64–71.

119. "Address of Senator Robinson Before Ohio State Bar Association, Akron, Ohio, Jan. 27, 1922," Joseph Taylor Robinson Papers, Special Collections, University of Arkansas, Fayetteville, Arkansas. This speech was also printed in the *Arkansas Gazette*, January 28, 1922, p. 5.

120. See US Congress, 1922, The Dyer Bill Debate, 67th Cong., 3rd Sess., *Congressional Record*, vol. 63, part 1, 335–37, 398–409.

121. Ibid., 1011.

122. Ibid., 1010.

123. Ibid., 1011.

124. US Congress, 1922, The Dyer Bill Debate, 67th Cong., 2nd Sess., *Congressional Record*, vol. 62, part 2, 1707.

125. Ibid., 1703.

126. Ibid.

127. Ibid., 1705.

128. US Congress, 1922, The Dyer Bill Debate, 67th Cong., 3rd Sess., *Congressional Record*, vol. 63, part 1, 400. Caraway probably meant the NAACP when he referred to the "society for the protection of the rights of colored people."

129. For examples of the *Gazette*'s editorial campaign against the Dyer bill, see *Arkansas Gazette*, November 2, 1921, p. 6; December 25, 1921, section II, p. 4; December 28, 1921, p. 6; January 6, 1922, p. 6; January 27, 1922, p. 6; January 28, 1922, p. 6; March 2, 1922, p. 6; June 14, 1922, p. 6; July 2, 1922, section II, p. 4; July 8, 1922, p. 6.

130. *Arkansas Gazette*, November 2, 1921, p. 6.; January 27, 1922, p. 6.

131. *Arkansas Gazette*, December 25, 1921, section II, p. 4.

132. For additional comments on Chicago, see *Arkansas Gazette*, December 28, 1921, p. 6; and January 6, 1922, p. 6.

133. *Arkansas Gazette*, March 2, 1922, p. 6.

134. *Arkansas Gazette*, November 2, 1921, p. 6.

135. See Rable, "South and the Politics," 201–20.

136. Amanda Saar has produced an extensive list of black newspapers that have existed in Arkansas. Unfortunately, for the time period in question, only a very few fragments exist for 1901–35, and those fragments do not include discussions of lynching.

137. *Pine Bluff Daily Graphic*, March 24, 1921, p. 4.

138. Ibid., September 30, 1919, p. 4; October 9, 1919, p. 4; March 24, 1921, p. 4.

139. *Arkansas Methodist*, October 2, 1919, p. 1.

140. For examples of antilynching editorials, see *Arkansas Democrat*, October 3, 1919, p. 4; October 4, 1919, p. 4; January 28, 1919, p. 6; May 4, 1927, p. 10; May 6, 1927, p. 16; May 17, 1927, p. 8; *Arkansas Gazette*, January 28, 1921, p. 6; March 19, 1921, p. 6; March 24, 1921, p. 6; February 24, 1922, p. 6; May 21, 1922, section II, p. 4; May 25, 1922, p. 6; May 26, 1922, p. 6; June 17, 1922, p. 6; August 3, 1922, p. 6; August 6, 1922, section II, p. 4; August 16, 1922, p. 6; Harmon Remmel Scrapbook 5.

141. *Arkansas Gazette*, August 16, 1922, p. 6.

142. See "Law and Order Betrayed," *Arkansas Gazette*, May 5, 1927; and "Law or Mobocracy?" *Arkansas Democrat*, May 5, 1927, both in Remmel Scrapbook 5.

143. *Arkansas Democrat*, May 6, 1927, p. 8; May 7, 1927, p. 1; May 8, 1927, p. 3.

144. *Arkansas Democrat*, May 7, 1927, p. 1; May 8, 1927, p. 3.

145. "Minutes of the Meeting on After the War Cooperation Held at the Georgian Terrace Hotel, Atlanta, Georgia, March 17, 1919," in the Commission on Interracial Cooperation Papers, Reel 20, Series II, File 1, text-film.

146. "Conference of Inter-Racial Secretaries, June 25, 1920," 16; "Minutes of Inter-Racial Commission, June 25, 1920," Commission on Interracial Cooperation Papers, Reel 20, Series II, File 3, text-film.

147. "Minutes of Inter-racial Commission Held November 17, 1920, Atlanta, Georgia," 18a–18b; Commission on Interracial Cooperation Papers, Reel 20, Series II, File 31, text-film.

148. J. H. Reynolds to D. Y. Thomas, November 4, 1919, and December 24, 1919, in David Yancey Thomas Papers, Special Collections Department, Fayetteville, Arkansas, Box 2, Series 2, File 4, Folder 1. The exact relationship of these state organizations to the Arkansas Commission on Interracial Cooperation chapter remains unclear.

149. "Conference of Inter-Racial Secretaries, June 25, 1920," 16; in the Commission on Interracial Cooperation Papers, Reel 20, Series II, File 3, text-film.

150. A. C. Millar to D. Y. Thomas, December 23, 1919; David Yancey Thomas Papers, Special Collections Department, Fayetteville, Arkansas, Series 1, Subseries 1, File 1, Folder 2.

151. "Interracial Committee Meeting February 17, 1920," Commission on Interracial Cooperation Papers, Reel 20, Series II, File 3, 4, text-film.

152. D. Y. Thomas to J. H. Reynolds, November 10, 1919; David Yancey Thomas Papers, Special Collections Department, Fayetteville, Arkansas, Box 2, Series 2, File 4, Folder 1.

153. Thomas S. Staples to A. R. Elliott, January 26, 1921; David Yancey Thomas Papers, Special Collections Department, Fayetteville, Arkansas, Box 2, Series 2, File 4, Folder 1.

154. A. C. Millar to D. Y. Thomas, December 23, 1919; David Yancey Thomas Papers, Special Collections Department, Fayetteville, Arkansas, Box 1, Series 1, Subseries 1, File 1, Folder 2.

155. See T. J. Woofter Jr. and Isaac Fisher, eds., *Cooperation in Southern Communities: Suggested Activities for County and City Inter-racial Committees* (Atlanta: Commission on Interracial Cooperation, n.d.), 15–18. Educated at the Tuskegee Institute, Fisher was a protégé of Booker T. Washington. His appointment as head of Branch Normal College was opposed by Joseph Carter Corbin—who, as part of the state's Republican government during Reconstruction, had served as head of public instruction—as well as by other African Americans who rejected the Tuskegee program. See Elizabeth L. Wheeler, "Isaac Fisher: The Frustrations of a Negro Educator at Branch Normal College, 1902–1911," *Arkansas Historical Quarterly* 41 (Spring 1982), 3–50. His activities with the commission included serving on the board of the Tennessee chapter and editing publications.

156. Woofter and Fisher, *Cooperation in Southern Communities*, 15.

157. *The Mob Still Rides: A Review of the Lynching Record, 1931–1936* (Atlanta: Commission on Interracial Cooperation, n.d.).

158. "Statement as of October First of the Work for 1922 of the Commission on Interracial Cooperation," Commission on Interracial Cooperation Papers, Reel 4, Series I, File 48, 18, text-film.

159. *Southern White Women on Lynching and Mob Violence* (Atlanta: Commission on Interracial Cooperation, n.d.), 3.

160. "The Interracial Front: Annual Report Commission on Interracial Cooperation 1933," Commission on Interracial Cooperation Papers, Reel 4, Series I, File 58, 10, text-film.

161. Erle Chambers to Jessie Daniel Ames, October 20, 1936, Association of Southern Women for the Prevention of Lynching Papers, Reel 5, File 98, text-film.

162. "Pronouncement, Arkansas Association of Women for the Prevention of Lynching," February 20, 1931, Association of Southern Women for the Prevention of Lynching Papers, Reel 5, File 98, text-film.

163. Monroe N. Work, ed., *Negro Year Book, 1937–1938* (Tuskegee, AL: Tuskegee Institute, 1937), 157.

164. John Shelton Reed, "A Note on the Control of Lynching," *Public Opinion Quarterly* 33 (Summer 1969), 268–71.

165. US Congress, 1922, The Dyer Bill Debate, 67th Cong., 2d Sess., *Congressional Record*, vol. 62, part 2, 1773–96. George B. Tindall, *The Emergence of the New South* (Baton Rouge: Louisiana State University Press, 1967), 174; Walter White, *Rope and Faggot*, 176–81.

166. Jessie Daniel Ames to Mrs. B. J. Reaves, June 19, 1939, Association of Southern Women for the Prevention of Lynching Papers, Reel 5, File 98, text-film.

167. See clippings from several newspapers including the *Arkansas Democrat*, the *Baltimore Sun*, and the *Tampa Bay Bulletin*, May 8–June 3, 1939, in Association of Southern Women for the Prevention of Lynching Papers, Reel 3, File 48, text-film.

168. *Arkansas Democrat*, May 25, 1939, 1–2, in Association of Southern Women for the Prevention of Lynching Papers, Reel 3, File 48, text-film.

169. Michael J. Pfeifer, *Rough Justice: Lynching and American Society, 1874–1947* (Urbana: University of Illinois Press, 2004), 123.

170. Jessie Daniel Ames to the Sheriffs of Arkansas, May 28, 1940, Association of Southern Women for the Prevention of Lynching Papers, Reel 5, File 98, text-film.

Chapter 7, Before John Carter

1. James Reed Eison, "Dead, but She Was in a Good Place, a Church," *Pulaski County Historical Review* 30 (Summer 1982), 30–42; Brian D. Greer, "The Last Lynching: A New Look at Little Rock's Last Episode of Deadly Mob Justice," *Arkansas Times*, August 4, 2000, pp. 12–19; Todd Lewis, "Mob Justice in the

'American Congo': 'Judge Lynch' in Arkansas during the Decade after World War I," *Arkansas Historical Quarterly* 52 (Summer 1993), 156–84.

2. Jay Jennings, *Carry the Rock: Race, Football, and the Soul of an American City* (New York: Rodale, 2010), 37–50. In addition, a public program exploring the lynching, "Project 1927: The Lynching of John Carter," held at the Mosaic Templars Cultural Center in Little Rock on February 15, 2013, attracted a large crowd, with many in the audience offering their own family recollections regarding the event.

3. Amy Louise Wood, *Lynching and Spectacle: Witnessing Racial Violence in America, 1890–1940* (Chapel Hill: University of North Carolina Press, 2009), 42–43, 190–93.

4. Richard Buckelew, "Racial Violence in Arkansas: Lynchings and Mob Rule, 1860–1930" (PhD diss., University of Arkansas, 1999). Buckelew lists as occurring in Pulaski County the 1884 lynching of one Mat Orton, but Orton was actually lynched in Arkansas City for the crime of arson; see "Swift Retribution," *Arkansas Gazette*, September 10, 1884, p. 1.

5. Interestingly, although the Arkansas State Archives (formerly the Arkansas History Commission) in Little Rock has on microfilm copies of inquest records from Pulaski County between 1865 and 1904, these records contain no inquests relating to the lynchings presented in this chapter, despite the fact that, for some of these, news accounts do report the holding of an inquest.

6. Local Paragraphs, *Arkansas Gazette*, May 30, 1882, p. 4. There is one person listed in Pulaski County by the name of James Sanders who might fit the description of a "colored youth," a resident of Badgett Township to the east of Little Rock, born in 1872. If this is the person, he would have been approximately ten years old at the time of his death—which does not, unfortunately, exist outside the realm of possibility. Nancy C. Carr shows up on the census as a resident of Union Township, having been born in 1861 and working as a domestic.

7. "Summary Vengeance," *Ottawa (IL) Free Trader*, June 3, 1882, p. 2; "Criminal," *Rock Island (IL) Argus*, May 31, 1882, p. 1. The *Argus* identifies the victim as "Minnie Carr."

8. "Bad and Baseless Rumors," *Arkansas Gazette*, June 6, 1882, p. 4.

9. Local Paragraphs, *Arkansas Gazette*, June 9, 1882, p. 4.

10. "Sheriff Oliver," *Arkansas Gazette*, June 20, 1882, p. 4.

11. "Important Events," *Highland Weekly News* (Highland County, Ohio), August 30, 1882, p. 2.

12. "Telegraphic Twistings," *National Republican*, August 25, 1882, p. 1.

13. "Four Highwaymen Lynched," *Indianapolis Journal*, December 18, 1889, p. 3.

14. W. Fitzhugh Brundage, *Lynching in the New South: Georgia and Virginia, 1880–1920* (Urbana: University of Illinois Press, 1993), 19.

15. "The Vengeance of the Mob," *Arkansas Gazette*, May 15, 1892, p. 5.

16. Brundage, *Lynching in the New South*, 18.

17. "D., S. THUD," *Arkansas Gazette*, May 14, 1892, p. 1. The absence of senior law enforcement officials was common during some lynchings, especially those that were widely anticipated. Regarding the title of the *Gazette*'s article, "D., S. Thud" was apparently an abbreviation for "dull, sickening thud" employed during the era, usually to describe the sound of someone being hanged, but sometimes also figuratively in connection with falling stock prices or the like; one example of the term being employed in a sports context is: "Dull, Sickening Thud," *Chicago Tribune*, September 8, 1889, p. 12.

18. "He's Gone," *Arkansas Gazette*, May 14, 1892, p. 1.

19. Wood, *Lynching and Spectacle*, 39, 62.

20. "He's Gone," *Arkansas Gazette*, May 14, 1892, p. 1.

21. "A Night's Work," *Arkansas Gazette*, May 15, 1892, pp. 1, 3.

22. "Stretched and Riddled," *Wichita Daily Eagle*, May 15, 1892, p. 2.

23. "Gov. Eagle Beaten by Mob," *Seattle Post-Intelligencer*, May 15, 1892, p. 2; "The Little Rock Lynching," *Los Angeles Herald*, May 15, 1892, p. 1; "A Black Brute Hanged by a Mob," *Salt Lake Herald*, May 15, 1892, p. 2; "Hanged High," *Arkansas Democrat*, May 14, 1892, p. 1.

24. "Some Questions," *Saint Paul (MN) Appeal*, May 21, 1892, p. 2. *Lex talionis* is the Latin term for the law of retaliation, or more commonly the "eye for an eye" form of justice.

25. "He's Gone," *Arkansas Democrat-Gazette*, May 14, 1892, p. 1.

26. "D., S. THUD," *Arkansas Gazette*, May 14, 1892, p. 1.

27. *Arkansas Reports: Cases Determined in the Supreme Court of Arkansas*, vol. 29 (Little Rock, 1876), 116–21; online at http://opinions.aoc.arkansas.gov/weblink8/o/doc/128488/Electronic.aspx (accessed May 15, 2015).

28. *Arkansas Reports: Cases Determined in the Supreme Court of Arkansas*, vol. 50 (Little Rock, 1888), 330–38; online at http://opinions.aoc.arkansas.gov/web link8/o/doc/156319/Page2.aspx (accessed May 15, 2015). See also Hawley, John Gardner, *American Criminal Reports*, vol. 7 (Chicago: Callahan and Company, 1889), 585–93.

29. Sandels, L. P., and Joseph M. Hill, *A Digest of the Statutes of Arkansas* (Columbia, MO: Press of E. W. Stephens, 1894), 572. Another digest of criminal laws published that same year observes that "rape may be committed on a female under the age of puberty or one so young as not to be capable of giving her consent." See Roberts and Hamiter, *The Criminal Laws of Arkansas* (Little Rock: Brown Printing Company, 1894), 201.

30. "A Ghastly Find," *Arkansas Gazette*, March 12, 1894, p. 1; "Suspended from the Limb of a Tree," *Salt Lake Herald*, March 12, 1894, p. 1.

31. "News in Brief," *Hutchinson (KS) Gazette*, December 26, 1895, p. 6; "News in Sunday's Journal," *Indianapolis Journal*, December 23, 1895, p. 6.

32. Ann V. Collins, *All Hell Broke Loose: American Race Riots from the Progressive Era through World War II* (Santa Barbara: Praeger, 2012), xvi.

33. Ibid., 5.
34. Larry LeMasters, "Feuds," *Encyclopedia of Arkansas History and Culture*, http://www.encyclopediaofarkansas.net/encyclopedia/entry-detail.aspx?entry ID=6468 (accessed June 11, 2015).
35. "White Man Cut Negro's Throat," *Arkansas Gazette*, September 12, 1906, p. 7. According to the *Arkansas Democrat*, Wiley and Pete Shelby entered the establishment at the same time; that newspaper also states explicitly that Wiley Shelby and McDonald were "engaged in a quarrel over the woman" and that Shelby did, in fact, pull a knife from his pocket. See "Negro Undertaker Killed at an Inquest in Argenta Today," *Arkansas Democrat*, September 12, 1906, p. 1.
36. "Negro Undertaker Killed at an Inquest in Argenta Today," *Arkansas Democrat*, September 12, 1906, p. 1.
37. "Negro Killed in Desperate Fight," *Arkansas Gazette*, September 13, 1906, p. 10. The *Democrat*, in a follow-up, acknowledged that Ed Lindsey had been wounded more seriously than originally reported in its pages. The coroner later made a public statement that Shelby's body had not been disturbed during the melee and that he had attempted to resume the inquest once order was restored but was unable to continue due to the absence of witnesses; see "Who Killed Robert Colum?" *Arkansas Democrat*, September 13, 1906, p. 6.
38. "M'Donald Exonerated of Charge of Murder," *Arkansas Gazette*, September 13, 1906, p. 10.
39. "In the City of Argenta," *Arkansas Democrat*, September 13, 1906, p. 5.
40. Ibid.; "In the City of Argenta," *Arkansas Democrat*, September 14, 1906, p. 5.
41. "Who Killed Robert Colum?" *Arkansas Democrat*, September 13, 1906, p. 6.
42. "No Blame Fixed for Colum Killing," *Arkansas Gazette*, September 14, 1906, p. 10.
43. "The Colum Trial This Afternoon," *Arkansas Democrat*, September 14, 1906, p. 6; Larry Taylor, "Menifee (Conway County)," *Encyclopedia of Arkansas History and Culture*, http://www.encyclopediaofarkansas.net/encyclopedia /entry-detail.aspx?entryID=6344 (accessed June 4, 2015).
44. "In the City of Argenta," *Arkansas Democrat*, September 15, 1906, p. 2.
45. "The Colum Trial This Afternoon," *Arkansas Democrat*, September 14, 1906, p. 6.
46. "In the City of Argenta," *Arkansas Democrat*, September 18, 1906, p. 5.
47. "John B. Lindsay Slain by Fusillade from Store of Negroes in Argenta," *Arkansas Gazette*, October 7, 1906, pp. 1, 14.
48. "John Lindsey Dead at Hands of Assassins, Blackwell Lynched by Determined Men," *Arkansas Democrat*, October 8, 1906, p. 1.
49. "Colum Building Burned to Ground," *Arkansas Gazette*, October 7, 1906, p. 1.
50. "Will Harding Shot by Unknown Person," *Arkansas Gazette*, October 7, 1906, p. 1.
51. "Fired on Men Who Gave Fire Alarm in Argenta," *Arkansas Gazette*, October 7, 1906, p. 1.

52. "John Lindsey Dead at Hands of Assassins, Blackwell Lynched by Determined Men," *Arkansas Democrat*, October 8, 1906, p. 3.

53. "John Lindsey Dead at Hands of Assassins, Blackwell Lynched by Determined Men," *Arkansas Democrat*, October 8, 1906, pp. 5, 6. The *Gazette* later offered some evidence backing up the contention of Blackman that he could not have participated in the murder of John Lindsay, finding witnesses who swore that he was on the train from Lake Village the night of the murder, and while the train had been scheduled to arrive in Little Rock at 6:50 p.m., in fact it was running significantly late, arriving at the Valley Station at the foot of Rock Street in Little Rock at 8:20 p.m. This would have left Blackman between ten and twenty-five minutes to depart the station, cross the river, and arrive at the Colum establishment before participating in the shooting of Lindsay. See "Blackman in Lake Village Saturday," *Arkansas Gazette*, October 9, 1906, p. 1.

54. "Every Section of Argenta Guarded," *Arkansas Gazette*, October 9, 1906, pp. 1, 9.

55. "All Is Quiet in Argenta," *Arkansas Democrat*, October 9, 1906, p. 2.

56. "Instructs Grand Jury on Lynching," *Arkansas Gazette*, October 9, 1906, p. 7; "No Blame Fixed for Lynching of Negro," *Arkansas Gazette*, October 9, 1906, p. 12.

57. "11 Bullet Holes in Lindsay's Body," *Arkansas Gazette*, October 9, 1906, p. 9; "Jno. B. Lindsay Was Buried Yesterday," *Arkansas Gazette*, October 9, 1906, p. 12.

58. "Negro Educator on Race Clashes," *Arkansas Gazette*, October 9, 1906, p. 9.

59. "Alex Champion Killed in Bridge Saloon at Noon," *Arkansas Democrat*, October 9, 1906, p. 1; "Luther Lindsey Is Suspected," *Arkansas Democrat*, October 9, 1906, p. 7.

60. "Alex Champion, Negro, Killed," *Arkansas Gazette*, October 10, 1906, p. 1.

61. "Extra Guards on Duty in Argenta," *Arkansas Gazette*, October 10, 1906, p. 1.

62. "In the City of Argenta," *Arkansas Democrat*, October 10, 1906, p. 3. Blaming the violence on establishments serving alcohol proved popular, as an ordinance abolishing "winerooms" was introduced in the city council. This ordinance provided for "the immediate closing of all wine rooms adjoining, in or near saloons." See "Argenta News and Notes," *Arkansas Gazette*, October 14, 1906, p. 15; "Argenta News and Notes," *Arkansas Gazette*, October 16, 1906, p. 13. The Reverend W. F. Andres, another Methodist minister, publicly opined that "the turmoil and uneasiness among both whites and blacks lately had been the result of licensing the sale of liquor by irresponsible and reckless saloon men." See "Minister Talks of Argenta Trouble," *Arkansas Gazette*, October 16, 1906, p. 7.

63. "A Crisis Is Now Appearing Says Senator Benj. Tillman," *Arkansas Democrat*, October 10, 1906, pp. 1, 3.

64. "Champion Inquest Was Held Today," *Arkansas Democrat*, October 10, 1906,

p. 6; "Will Bury Body of Blackman Today," *Arkansas Gazette*, October 10, 1906, p. 10; "No Reward for Colum Bros.," *Arkansas Democrat*, October 11, 1906, p. 1; "To Take up Lynching of Negro Tomorrow," *Arkansas Gazette*, October 11, 1906, p. 9; ; "Blackman's Body Buried," *Arkansas Gazette*, October 11, 1906, p. 12; "Grand Jury Is Investigating Lynching of Argenta Negro," *Arkansas Democrat*, October 12, 1906, p. 1.

65. "Mob Lynched an Innocent Negro," *Arkansas Gazette*, October 11, 1906, p. 10.

66. "Advises Negroes to Remain Here," *Arkansas Gazette*, October 11, 1906, p. 10.

67. "Argenta Is Back to Usual Conditions," *Arkansas Gazette*, October 11, 1905, p. 12; "No More Trouble Feared in City," *Arkansas Gazette*, October 12, 1906, p. 10.

68. "M'Donald Must Leave Argenta," *Arkansas Gazette*, October 12, 1906, p. 5; "McDonald Leaves City 'By Request,'" *Arkansas Democrat*, October 12, 1906, p. 3. A later report indicated that Emmie Wright, who was at the center of the original fight, also departed the city; see "Argenta News and Notes," *Arkansas Gazette*, October 13, 1906, p. 10.

69. "No Blame Fixed for the Killing," *Arkansas Gazette*, October 11, 1905, p. 12.

70. "Argenta News and Notes," *Arkansas Gazette*, October 17, 1906, p. 12.

71. "The Day in Courts," *Arkansas Democrat*, October 16, 1906, p. 6.

72. CSDE Lynching Database, http://lynching.csde.washington.edu/#/home (accessed May 17, 2016).

73. Gregory Mixon, "Atlanta Race Riot of 1906," *New Georgia Encyclopedia*, http://www.georgiaencyclopedia.org/articles/history-archaeology/atlanta-race-riot-1906 (accessed May 18, 2016).

74. Michael J. Pfeifer, *Rough Justice: Lynching and American Society, 1874–1947* (Urbana: University of Illinois Press, 2004), 10–11.

75. Andy Ambrose, "Atlanta," *New Georgia Encyclopedia*, http://www.georgia encyclopedia.org/articles/counties-cities-neighborhoods/atlanta (accessed May 18, 2016).

76. Mary Anne Oglesby Neely, "Montgomery," *Encyclopedia of Alabama*, http://www.encyclopediaofalabama.org/article/h-1833 (accessed May 18, 2016).

77. Van Zbinden, "Memphis and Little Rock Railroad (M&LR)," *Encyclopedia of Arkansas History and Culture*, http://www.encyclopediaofarkansas.net/encyclopedia/entry-detail.aspx?entryID=2304 (accessed May 18, 2016).

Chapter 8, Stories of a Lynching

1. The following recounting of events is drawn from April–June 1927 articles in the *Arkansas Democrat*, *Arkansas Gazette*, and the *Chicago Defender*, and from Marcet Haldeman-Julius, *The Story of a Lynching: An Exploration of Southern Psychology*, Little Blue Book 1260, ed. E. Haldeman-Julius (Girard, KS: Haldeman-Julius Publications, 1927), which first appeared as "The Story of

a Lynching: An Exploration of Southern Psychology," *Haldeman-Julius Monthly* 6.3 (August 1927), 3–32, 97–103. Hereinafter Haldeman-Julius refers to Little Blue Book 1260, unless otherwise noted. Discrepancies among these and other sources will be addressed below.

2. Pete Daniel, *Deep'n As It Come: The 1927 Mississippi River Flood* (Fayetteville: University of Arkansas Press, 1996), 7; John M. Barry, *Rising Tide: The Great Mississippi Flood of 1927 and How It Changed America* (New York: Simon and Schuster, 1997); Frederick Simpich, "The Great Mississippi Flood of 1927," *National Geographic* 52 (September 1927), 243–89. The magnitude of the flood's human toll is fictionalized in William Faulkner, "Old Man," in *Three Famous Short Novels* (New York: Vintage Books, 1961), 77–184; Richard Wright, "Down By the Riverside," in *Uncle Tom's Children* (New York: Harper & Row, Publishers, 1938), 54–102; and Richard Wright, "The Man Who Saw the Flood," in *Eight Men* (New York: HarperPerennial, 1996), 102–8.

3. "Patrolmen Aid in Search for Girl," *Arkansas Gazette*, April 13, 1927; "Officers Hunt Two Children Who Vanished," *Arkansas Gazette*, April 14, 1927; "Martineau Demands Order at Dixon's Trial," *Arkansas Democrat*, May 15, 1927.

4. "Young Negro Slayer Rushed from State," *Arkansas Democrat*, May 2, 1927; "Parents Fear Son Has Been Kidnapped," *Arkansas Gazette*, April 13, 1927.

5. "Search for Missing Children Is Broadened," *Arkansas Democrat*, April 14, 1927; "Still No Clue to Missing Children," *Arkansas Gazette*, April 16, 1927; "Missing Girl May Be Flood Victim," *Arkansas Gazette*, April 17, 1927; "Officers Hunt," *Arkansas Gazette*, April 14, 1927.

6. "Still No Clue," *Arkansas Gazette*, April 16, 1927; "No Trace Found of Missing Children After Four Days' Hunt," *Arkansas Democrat*, April 17, 1927; "Hunt for Missing Children Futile," *Arkansas Democrat*, April 24, 1927; Advertisement, *Arkansas Gazette*, May 1, 1927.

7. "Missing Children Believed Drowned," *Arkansas Gazette*, April 20, 1927; "Flood Relief Halts Search for Children," *Arkansas Democrat*, April 20, 1927; "Hunt for Missing Children Delayed," *Arkansas Gazette*, April 21, 1927.

8. Peg Smith, interview by the author, Springdale, Arkansas, April 15, 2000; "Death Sentence Dealt to Negro," *Harrison Daily Times*, May 20, 1927.

9. "Eight Negroes Arrested in Murder of Floella McDonald; Janitor Is Center of Probe," *Arkansas Democrat*, May 1, 1927; "Missing Girl's Body Found in Church Belfry," *Arkansas Gazette*, May 1, 1927; Haldeman-Julius, 17.

10. "Eight Negroes," *Arkansas Democrat*, May 1, 1927.

11. "Corpse of Little Rock Girl, Missing Three Weeks, Found in Church Belfry," *Pine Bluff Daily Graphic*, May 1, 1927.

12. "Eight Negroes," *Arkansas Democrat*, May 1, 1927; Haldeman-Julius, 17; "Missing Girl's Body," *Arkansas Gazette*, May 1, 1927.

13. "Young Negro Slayer," *Arkansas Democrat*, May 2, 1927; "Eight Negroes,"

Arkansas Democrat, May 1, 1927; "Missing Girl's Body," *Arkansas Gazette*, May 1, 1927; Haldeman-Julius, 17.

14. "Missing Girl's Body," *Arkansas Gazette*, May 1, 1927; "Young Negro Slayer," *Arkansas Democrat*, May 2, 1927; "Negro Youth Confesses to Brutal Crime," *Arkansas Gazette*, May 2, 1927; "Little Girl's Testimony Is Cause of Confession," *Arkansas Gazette*, May 2, 1927; "Eight Negroes," *Arkansas Democrat*, May 1, 1927; Haldeman-Julius, 17.

15. "Young Negro Slayer," *Arkansas Democrat*, May 2, 1927.

16. Haldeman-Julius, 9–10; "Negro Youth Confesses," *Arkansas Democrat*, May 2, 1927; "Lonnie Dixon to Die at Sunrise," *Arkansas Gazette*, June 24, 1927; "Girl's Murderer Sentenced to Die," *Arkansas Gazette*, May 20, 1927.

17. Haldeman-Julius, 9; "Young Negro Slayer," *Arkansas Democrat*, May 2, 1927.

18. Haldeman-Julius, 64; Maudella Morehead-Parham, interview by the author, Little Rock, Arkansas, February 16, 2013; "Young Negro Slayer," *Arkansas Democrat*, May 2, 1927; "Takes Full Blame for Crime Before Going to 'Chair,'" *Little Rock Daily News*, June 24, 1927; "Dixon Assumes All Blame for Killing," *Arkansas Gazette*, May 25, 1927.

19. Haldeman-Julius, 10; "Takes Full Blame," *Little Rock Daily News*, June 24, 1927.

20. Haldeman-Julius, 6, 10; "Young Negro Slayer," *Arkansas Democrat*, May 2, 1927; "Negro Youth Confesses," *Arkansas Gazette*, May 2, 1927.

21. "Young Negro Slayer," *Arkansas Democrat*, May 2, 1927.

22. "No Trace Found," *Arkansas Democrat*, April 17, 1927.

23. "Young Negro Slayer," *Arkansas Democrat*, May 2, 1927; Haldeman-Julius, 10–11.

24. "Flee Little Rock after Lynching Bee," *Chicago Defender*, May 28, 1927.

25. "Negro Youth Confesses," *Arkansas Gazette*, May 2, 1927.

26. Haldeman-Julius, 22; "Young Negro Slayer," *Arkansas Democrat*, May 2, 1927; "Boy Fiend Liable to Death Penalty," *Arkansas Gazette*, May 3, 1927.

27. "The Story of a Lynching," *Haldeman-Julius Monthly*, 3; Haldeman-Julius, 12.

28. Haldeman-Julius, 19; "Early Trial for Killer Is Planned," *Pine Bluff Daily Graphic*, May 2, 1927; Haldeman-Julius, 11, 18; "Young Negro Slayer," *Arkansas Democrat*, May 2, 1927.

29. "Prison History and Events, 2011–1838," Arkansas Department of Correction, http://adc.arkansas.gov/about/Pages/PrisonHistoryPage2.aspx (accessed October 26, 2015).

30. Haldeman-Julius, 21–22; "Young Negro Slayer," *Arkansas Democrat*, May 2, 1927; "Negro Youth Confesses," *Arkansas Gazette*, May 2, 1927; "Lynching Pyre Is Taken from Bethel Church," *Baltimore Afro-American*, May 14, 1927.

31. "Young Negro Slayer," *Arkansas Democrat*, May 2, 1927; Haldeman-Julius, 19–20.

32. "Young Negro Slayer," *Arkansas Democrat*, May 2, 1927; Haldeman-Julius, 20, 23; "Crowds Gather to Lynch Young Negro," *Arkansas Gazette*, May 2, 1927.

33. "Lynching Pyre," *Baltimore Afro-American*, May 14, 1927.

34. Haldeman-Julius, 20, 23; "Young Negro Slayer," *Arkansas Democrat*, May 2, 1927.

35. "Good Time Is Had by All of Desperate 'Avengers,'" *Arkansas Gazette*, May 3, 1927; "Slayer Still Is Hunted by Mobs," *Arkansas Gazette*, May 3, 1927; "Police Prepared for Mob Violence," *Arkansas Gazette*, May 4, 1927.

36. Haldeman-Julius, 24, 25 (emphasis in original).

37. Editorial, "A Moral Disaster Little Rock Escaped," *Arkansas Gazette*, May 3, 1927.

38. Haldeman-Julius, 26.

39. "Lonnie Dixon Trial May 19," *Arkansas Democrat*, May 4, 1927; "Lonnie Dixon Case Is Set for May 19," *Arkansas Gazette*, May 5, 1927.

40. "Child's Slayer Quickly Indicted," *Arkansas Democrat*, May 3, 1927.

41. Editorial, "The Test of Citizenship," *Arkansas Democrat*, May 4, 1927 (emphasis added); "City Officials Deplore Riot and Disorder," *Arkansas Democrat*, May 5, 1927.

42. "Police Prepared," *Arkansas Gazette*, May 4, 1927.

43. "Card of Thanks," *Arkansas Democrat*, May 5, 1927.

44. Haldeman-Julius, 31; "Two Women in Wagon Beaten by Negro Man," *Arkansas Democrat*, May 4, 1927; "Mob's Lynching of Negro Brute Starts Trouble," *Arkansas Gazette*, May 5, 1927.

45. Haldeman-Julius, 31.

46. Haldeman-Julius, 31–32; "Mob's Lynching," *Arkansas Gazette*, May 5, 1927; "Two Women," *Arkansas Democrat*, May 4, 1927; "Hanged to Phone Pole; Is Riddled with 250 Bullets," *Little Rock Daily News*, May 4, 1927.

47. "Two Women," *Arkansas Democrat*, May 4, 1927; Haldeman-Julius, 32–33.

48. Edith W. McClinton, *Scars From a Lynching*, rev. ed., ed. Stacey James McAdoo and Christie Ellison-Thompson (Little Rock: Backyard Enterprises, 2000), 53; Greg Bryant, interview by the author, Little Rock, Arkansas, February 15, 2013.

49. Haldeman-Julius, 35, 37.

50. Haldeman-Julius, 36; "Mob's Lynching," *Arkansas Gazette*, May 5, 1927.

51. "Arkansas Mob Sets Record for Savagery," *Chicago Defender*, May 7, 1927.

52. "Mob's Lynching," *Arkansas Gazette*, May 5, 1927; "Mob Lynches Negro after He Confesses," *Arkansas Democrat*, May 5, 1927.

53. "Mob's Lynching," *Arkansas Gazette*, May 5, 1927; Haldeman-Julius, 36; "Arkansas Mob," *Chicago Defender*, May 7, 1927.

54. "Mob's Lynching," *Arkansas Gazette*, May 5, 1927; Haldeman-Julius, 36.

55. "Mob Lynches," *Arkansas Democrat*, May 5, 1927; Haldeman-Julius, 33–34.

56. "Little Rock Mob Lynches a Negro," *New York Times*, May 5, 1927; "Negro Killed by Angry Mob," *Harrison Daily Times*, May 5, 1927; "Hanged to Phone Pole," *Little Rock Daily News*, May 4, 1927; "Mob Lynches," *Arkansas*

Democrat, May 5, 1927; Clifford E. Minton, *America's Black Trap*, advance ed. (Gary, IN: Alpha Book Co., 2001), 91.

57. "Mob Lynches Negro," *Arkansas Democrat*, May 5, 1927; "Mob's Lynching," *Arkansas Gazette*, May 5, 1927.

58. "Around the City," *Arkansas Democrat*, May 4, 1927.

59. Haldeman-Julius, 35–36.

60. Haldeman-Julius, 36–37; "Mob Lynches," *Arkansas Democrat*, May 5, 1927.

61. "Mob's Lynching," *Arkansas Gazette*, May 5, 1927; Haldeman-Julius, 37–38; "Mob Lynches," *Arkansas Democrat*, May 5, 1927; "Arkansas Mob," *Chicago Defender*, May 7, 1927.

62. "Mob's Lynching," *Arkansas Gazette*, May 5, 1927; Haldeman-Julius, 38–40; "Mob Lynches," *Arkansas Democrat*, May 5, 1927.

63. Haldeman-Julius, 39 (emphasis in original).

64. "Arkansas Mob," *Chicago Defender*, May 7, 1927; "The Way of American Mob Justice," *Chicago Defender*, May 14, 1927 (this letter is signed "An Old Citizen Here for 35 Years. Little Rock, Ark.").

65. "Mob's Lynching," *Arkansas Gazette*, May 5, 1927; "Mob Lynches," *Arkansas Democrat*, May 5, 1927.

66. "Mob's Lynching," *Arkansas Gazette*, May 5, 1927; "Mob Lynches," *Arkansas Democrat*, May 5, 1927; Haldeman-Julius, 40.

67. Haldeman-Julius, 41–42; "Mob's Lynching," *Arkansas Gazette*, May 5, 1927; "Mob Lynches," *Arkansas Democrat*, May 5, 1927; "Arkansas Mob," *Chicago Defender*, May 7, 1927.

68. "Mob Lynches," *Arkansas Democrat*, May 5, 1927; "Mob's Lynching," *Arkansas Gazette*, May 5, 1927; Haldeman-Julius, 42.

69. "Mob Lynches," *Arkansas Democrat*, May 5, 1927; "Mob's Lynching," *Arkansas Gazette*, May 5, 1927; Haldeman-Julius, 46.

70. Arkansas State Board of Health, Bureau of Vital Statistics, Certificate of Death, File No. 658, John Carter, filed May 5, 1927.

71. Haldeman-Julius, 48–50; "Mob's Lynching," *Arkansas Gazette*, May 5, 1927; "Mob Lynches," *Arkansas Democrat*, May 5, 1927.

72. Haldeman-Julius, 50–51; "Mob's Lynching," *Arkansas Gazette*, May 5, 1927; "State Troops Guard against New Disorder," *Arkansas Democrat*, May 5, 1927; McClinton, *Scars*, 54.

73. "Lynching Pyre," *Baltimore Afro-American*, May 14, 1927.

74. "Mob's Lynching," *Arkansas Gazette*, May 5, 1927; "About the Museum," Mosaic Templars Cultural Center, http://www.mosaictemplarscenter.com /About/about-the-museum (accessed November 3, 2015); "Lynching Pyre," *Baltimore Afro-American*, May 14, 1927.

75. "State Troops," *Arkansas Democrat*, May 5, 1927; "Arkansas Mob," *Chicago Defender*, May 7, 1927.

76. "State Troops," *Arkansas Democrat*, May 5, 1927.

77. "Arkansas Mob," *Chicago Defender*, May 7, 1927; "Mob's Lynching," *Arkansas Gazette*, May 5, 1927; "State Troops," *Arkansas Democrat*, May 5, 1927.

78. Haldeman-Julius, 51; "State Troops," Arkansas Democrat, May 5, 1927.

79. Haldeman-Julius, 52; "Body Dragged through Main Street of City," *Arkansas Gazette*, May 5, 1927.

80. "Mob's Lynching," *Arkansas Gazette*, May 5, 1927; "State Troops," *Arkansas Democrat*, May 5, 1927; "City Officials," *Arkansas Democrat*, May 5, 1927; Haldeman-Julius, 52; "Body Dragged," *Arkansas Gazette*, May 5, 1927.

81. Haldeman-Julius, 52–53.

82. "Order Quickly Is Restored by Guard," *Arkansas Gazette*, May 5, 1927.

83. Minton, *America's Black Trap*, 91–92.

84. "City Officials," *Arkansas Democrat*, May 5, 1927; Haldeman-Julius, 54.

85. "State Troops," *Arkansas Democrat*, May 5, 1927.

86. "State Troops," *Arkansas Democrat*, May 5, 1927, "Mob's Lynching," *Arkansas Gazette*, May 5, 1927.

87. "Arkansas Mob," *Chicago Defender*, May 7, 1927.

88. Haldeman-Julius, 56; "State Troops," *Arkansas Democrat*, May 5, 1927.

89. "State Troops," *Arkansas Democrat*, May 5, 1927; "Order," *Arkansas Gazette*, May 5, 1927.

90. "Governor Expected Here Early Today," *Arkansas Gazette*, May 5, 1927; "Mob's Lynching," *Arkansas Gazette*, May 5, 1927; "State Troops," *Arkansas Democrat*, May 5, 1927; Greg Bryant, interview, February 15, 2013.

91. "Order," *Arkansas Gazette*, May 5, 1927.

92. "Order," *Arkansas Gazette*, May 5, 1927; "Civil Authorities Again in Charge," *Arkansas Gazette*, May 7, 1927.

93. Editorial, "Law and Order Betrayed," *Arkansas Gazette*, May 5, 1927.

94. "State Laws Providing for Law Enforcement," *Arkansas Democrat*, May 5, 1927; Editorial, "The City Officials Deplore," *Arkansas Democrat*, May 6, 1927.

95. "Moyer, Haynie and Others at State Capitol," *Arkansas Democrat*, May 5, 1927.

96. "Moyer, Haynie," *Arkansas Democrat*, May 5, 1927; "Circuit Judge's Charges to Pulaski County Grand Jury," *Arkansas Democrat*, May 6, 1927.

97. "City Officials," *Arkansas Democrat*, May 5, 1927.

98. "Hanging Was Orderly, Says Sheriff Haynie," *Arkansas Democrat*, May 5, 1927. He said he immediately went to the scene from two miles away but allegedly arrived after Glennie Stewart, whom someone had traveled to Little Rock to bring back, a reported distance of five miles; "Mob Lynches Negro," *Arkansas Democrat*, May 5, 1927; "Mob's Lynching," *Arkansas Gazette*, May 5, 1927.

99. "Coroner Boyce Issues Statement," *Arkansas Democrat*, May 5, 1927.

100. "Resolutions Adopted by Chamber of Commerce," *Arkansas Gazette*, May 6, 1927; "Business and Professional Men Demand Action against Authorities Found Derelict," *Arkansas Democrat*, May 6, 1927.

101. "Grand Jury Investigation of Mob Disorders Is Halted until Tuesday,"

Arkansas Democrat, May 8, 1927; "20 Witnesses Heard Tuesday by Grand Jury," *Arkansas Democrat*, May 10, 1927.

102. "Bar Pledges Full Aid to Prosecutors," *Arkansas Democrat*, May 6, 1927.

103. "Grand Jury," *Arkansas Democrat*, May 8, 1927.

104. "Man with Gruesome Lynching Souvenir Held at Hot Springs," *Arkansas Democrat*, May 8, 1927.

105. "Death of Boy Investigated by Officers," *Arkansas Democrat*, May 9, 1927.

106. "No Decision upon Request of the Grand Jury," *Arkansas Democrat*, May 11, 1927.

107. "Special Investigation of the John Carter Lynching, Little Rock, Ark.," National Association for the Advancement of Colored People (NAACP) Papers, Manuscript Division, Library of Congress, Washington, DC, Group I, Series C: Container 349: Folder "Sub-File—Lynching-Little Rock, Ark. 1918–1927, 8; "No Decision," *Arkansas Democrat*, May 11, 1927.

108. "Special Investigation," NAACP, 6–8; "No Decision," *Arkansas Democrat*, May 11, 1927.

109. "Grand Jurors Discharged by Circuit Judge," *Arkansas Democrat*, May 12, 1927.

110. Editorial, "Will It End in a Fizzle?" *Arkansas Democrat*, May 11, 1927.

111. "Special Investigation," NAACP, 9–10 (underlining in original). The NAACP report is undated but cites the August 1927 issue of the *Haldeman-Julius Monthly*, so the investigation took place at least after that publication and includes several references to "this winter" and "last summer."

112. "Special Investigation," NAACP, 10–14.

113. "From the People," *Arkansas Gazette*, May 7–10, 1927; "Our Readers' Views," *Arkansas Democrat*, May 8–9, 1927.

114. "From the People, Gazette Reader Believes That Police Used Good Judgment," *Arkansas Gazette*, May 7, 1927.

115. Letter to the editor, "Hell in Little Rock," *Chicago Defender*, June 4, 1927. While a full treatment of the Klan's power in Little Rock and Pulaski County is beyond the scope of this essay, this letter writer's characterization was accurate. The Klan had opposed governor John Martineau in 1926, but mayor Charles Moyer was endorsed by the Klan in the election of 1924. In 1928, sheriff Mike Haynie was a member of the Mystic Knights of Arkansas, an organization formed after the dissolution of the Arkansas Klan, and is described as a "former Klansman." See Charles Alexander's "Defeat, Decline, Disintegration: The Ku Klux Klan in Arkansas, 1924 and After," *Arkansas Historical Quarterly* 22 (Winter 1963), 309–31. "In 1922, a slate of Klan-endorsed candidates gained control of Pulaski County politics," according to "Ku Klux Klan (after 1900)," Encyclopedia of Arkansas History and Culture, http://www.encyclopediaof arkansas.net/encyclopedia/entry-detail.aspx?search=1&entryID=2755 (accessed August 15, 2016). The national Women of the Ku Klux Klan was

chartered in Little Rock in 1923, an event reported on the front page of the *Arkansas Gazette*, and was active in charity work as late as the spring of 1927. Kathleen M. Blee, *Women of the Klan: Racism and Gender in the 1920s* (Berkeley: University of California Press, 1991), 27–28; Alexander, "Defeat, Decline, Disintegration," 326; and "Women of the Ku Klux Klan (WKKK)," Encyclopedia of Arkansas History and Culture, http://www.encyclopedia ofarkansas.net/encyclopedia/entry-detail.aspx?search=1&entryID=4220 (accessed August 15, 2016). For more on the Klan's influence in Arkansas in the 1920s, see also Carl H. Moneyhon, *Arkansas and the New South, 1874–1929* (Fayetteville: University of Arkansas Press, 1997), 138–44.

116. "Lonnie Dixon Is Brought to 'Walls,'" *Arkansas Gazette*, May 17, 1927; "Dixon Enters Not Guilty Plea in Court," *Arkansas Democrat*, May 17, 1927.

117. "Lonnie Dixon to Implicate Second Youth," *Arkansas Democrat*, May 18, 1927; "Negro's Lawyers Selected by Lot," *Arkansas Gazette*, May 18, 1927.

118. "Defense and State Outline Cases to Jury," *Arkansas Democrat*, May 19, 1927.

119. "Lonnie Dixon to Implicate," *Arkansas Democrat*, May 8, 1927; "Defense and State," *Arkansas Democrat*, May 19, 1927.

120. "Lonnie Dixon Is Resigned to His Fate," *Arkansas Democrat*, May 20, 1927.

121. "Girl's Murderer," *Arkansas Gazette*, May 20, 1927; "Lonnie Dixon to Die in Chair June 24," *Pine Bluff Daily Graphic*, May 20, 1927; Haldeman-Julius, 63; Maudella Morehead-Parham, interview, February 16, 2013; "Lonnie Dixon Is Resigned," *Arkansas Democrat*, May 20, 1927.

122. "Mother Visits Doomed Negro," *Arkansas Democrat*, June 22, 1927; "Slayer's Mother in Farewell Visit," *Arkansas Gazette*, June 22, 1927; "Dixon Assumes All Blame for Killing," *Arkansas Gazette*, June 25, 1927.

123. "'Captain, I've Lied to You,' Lonnie Dixon Says to Prison Warden Shortly Before Death," *Arkansas Democrat*, June 24, 1927; "Dixon Admits Full Guilt Before Execution," *Arkansas Democrat*, June 24, 1927.

124. "Dixon Admits," *Arkansas Democrat*, June 24, 1927.

125. "Mother Visits," *Arkansas Democrat*, May 22, 1927; "Dixon Admits," *Arkansas Democrat*, June 24, 1927.

126. "Dixon Assumes," *Arkansas Gazette*, June 25, 1927; "Takes Full Blame," *Little Rock Daily News*, June 24, 1927.

127. May 5, 1927: "Negro is Hanged and Body Burned," *Atlanta Constitution*; "Guardsmen Patrolling Little Rock Streets Following Disorders," *Atlanta Journal*; "Negro Lynched after Attack on Mother, Girl, 17," *Chicago Tribune*; "Negro Club Wielder Is Strung Up on Pole," *Memphis Commercial Appeal*; "Negro Hanged, Body Bullet Riddled and Burned in Arkansas," *Montgomery (AL) Advertiser*; "Lynchers Burn Negro's Body on Funeral Pyre," *New York Sun and Globe*; "Little Rock Mob Lynches a Negro," *New York Times*; "Mob Burns Man's Body in Little Rock Street," *Washington Post*. May 6, 1927: "Officials Blamed for Lynching Riot," *New York World*; "City Accused after

Lynching," *New York Mail and Evening Telegram*; "Little Rock Mob Kills Negro and Shoots Up Town," *The Daily Worker*; "Youth Lynched in Ark. by Mob of 1000 Whites," *St. Louis Argus*; "Lynching," *Baltimore Afro-American*, May 7, 1927; "Little Rock Mob Lynches Youth," *New York Amsterdam News*, May 11, 1927; "Lynching Pyre Is Taken from Bethel Church," *Baltimore Afro-American*, May 14, 1927; "Editorial Paragraphs," *The Nation*, May 25, 1927.

128. "Mob's Lynching," *Arkansas Gazette*, May 5, 1927.

129. Barry, *Rising Tide*; Daniel, *Deep'n as It Come*; Simpich, "The Great Mississippi Flood of 1927."

130. "Negro Youth Confesses," *Arkansas Gazette*, May 2, 1927; Editorial, "A Moral Disaster," *Arkansas Gazette*, May 3, 1927; "Child's Slayer," *Arkansas Democrat*, May 3, 1927; Editorial, "Law and Order Betrayed," *Arkansas Gazette*, May 5, 1927.

131. "Officers Hunt," *Arkansas Gazette*, April 14, 1927.

132. "Eight Negroes," *Arkansas Democrat*, May 1, 1927.

133. "Takes Full Blame," *Little Rock Daily News*, June 24, 1927; "Young Negro Slayer," *Arkansas Democrat*, May 2, 1927.

134. "Girl's Murderer," *Arkansas Gazette*, May 20, 1927.

135. "Negro Youth Confesses," *Arkansas Gazette*, May 2, 1927.

136. Clai Morehead Hall, interview by the author, Little Rock, Arkansas, February 16, 2013.

137. "Negro Youth Confesses," *Arkansas Gazette*, May 2, 1927; "Young Negro Slayer," *Arkansas Democrat*, May 2, 1927.

138. Minton, *America's Black Trap*, 92–93.

139. Maudella Morehead-Parham, interview, February 16, 2013.

140. "Flee Little Rock," *Chicago Defender*, May 28, 1927; "Negro Youth," *Arkansas Gazette*, May 2, 1927.

141. "Captain, I've Lied," *Arkansas Democrat*, June 24, 1927; "Dixon Admits," *Arkansas Democrat*, June 24, 1927.

142. Othel Brodie, interview by the author, Little Rock, Arkansas, May 16, 1998.

143. "Martineau Demands Order," *Arkansas Democrat*, May 15, 1927; Arkansas State Board of Health, Bureau of Vital Statistics, Certificate of Death, File No. 856, Floella McDonald, filed May 1, 1927.

144. Maudella Morehead-Parham, interview, February 16, 2013.

145. McClinton, *Scars*, 51–52.

146. Marcet and E. Haldeman-Julius, *Violence* (New York: Simon and Schuster, 1929); "Radical Responses to the Great Depression Images," Special Collections Library, University of Michigan, http://quod.lib.umich.edu/cgi/i/image/image-idx?c=sclradic;subview=detail;view=entry;cc=sclradic;entryid=x-sce00621;viewid=SCE00621.TIF (accessed August 17, 2016); Richard Wright, *Native Son* (New York: Harper and Row, Publishers, 1966), orig. pub. 1940; Lillian Smith, *Strange Fruit* (New York: Harcourt Brace and Co., 1992), orig. pub. 1944.

147. "Lonnie Dixon Unmoved as Fate Is Sealed in Court," *Arkansas Gazette*, May 20, 1927; "Young Negro Slayer," *Arkansas Democrat*, May 2, 1927.

148. Clai Morehead Hall, interview, February 16, 2013.

149. Maudella Morehead-Parham, interview, February 16, 2013.

150. Maudella Morehead-Parham, interview, February 16, 2013; "Lonnie Dixon Is Resigned," *Arkansas Gazette*, May 20, 1927.

151. Haldeman-Julius, 16.

152. "No Trace Found," *Arkansas Democrat*, April 17, 1927.

153. "Cases of Two Children Have No Connection," *Arkansas Democrat*, May 1, 1927.

154. Marcet Haldeman-Julius to Walter White, May 10, 1927, "Special Investigation," NAACP.

155. "Girl's Murderer," *Arkansas Gazette*, May 20, 1927; "Lonnie Dixon to Die," *Pine Bluff Daily Graphic*, May 20, 1927; Haldeman-Julius, 63.

156. Greg Bryant, "Project 1927" (presentation), Mosaic Templars Cultural Center, Little Rock, Arkansas, February 15, 2013.

157. "Arkansas Mob," *Chicago Defender*, May 7, 1927.

158. "Mob Drives Editor out of Arkansas," *Chicago Defender*, May 21, 1927.

159. McClinton, *Scars*, 53–54.

160. Bruce E. Baker, "Under the Rope: Lynching and Memory in Laurens County, South Carolina," in W. Fitzhugh Brundage, ed., *Where These Memories Grow: History, Memory, and Southern Identity* (Chapel Hill: University of North Carolina Press, 2000).

161. Audience member, "Project 1927" (presentation), Mosaic Templars Cultural Center, Little Rock, Arkansas, February 15, 2013; Minton, *America's Black Trap*, 92.

162. "Special Investigation," NAACP, 6.

163. *Polk's Little Rock and North Little Rock Directory, 1926* (Little Rock: R. L. Polk and Co., Publishers, 1926); *Polk's Little Rock (Arkansas) City Directory, 1928, Including North Little Rock and Park Hill* (Kansas City, MO.: R. L. Polk and Co., Publishers, 1928). Apparently, no Little Rock or North Little Rock directory was published in 1927.

164. Certificate of Death, John Carter.

165. "10 Minutes Later He Was Lynched," *Harrison Daily Times*, May 10, 1927; "10 Minutes Later He Was Lynched," *Pine Bluff Daily Graphic*, May 17, 1927; "The Story of a Lynching," *Haldeman-Julius Monthly*, 2.

166. "John Carter," *Arkansas Gazette*, May 5, 1927.

167. George Fulton Sr., "Project 1927" (presentation), Mosaic Templars Cultural Center, Little Rock, Arkansas, February 15, 2013.

168. Haldeman-Julius, 33.

169. "Two Women," *Arkansas Democrat*, May 4, 1927.

170. "Special Investigation," NAACP, 2.

171. "Rotenberry Again Questions Youth," *Arkansas Democrat*, April 22, 1927; "Worthless Clue in Hunt for Children," *Arkansas Democrat*, April 25, 1927; "Missing Boy's Case Probed," *Arkansas Democrat*, April 28, 1927.

172. "Cases of Two Children," *Arkansas Democrat*, May 1, 1927.

173. Greg Bryant, interview, February 15, 2013.

174. "Eight Negroes," *Arkansas Democrat*, May 1, 1927.

175. "Negro Youth Confesses," *Arkansas Gazette*, May 2, 1927; "Little Girl's Testimony," *Arkansas Gazette*, May 2, 1927; "Eight Negroes," *Arkansas Democrat*, May 1, 1927.

176. "Little Girl's Testimony," *Arkansas Gazette*, May 2, 1927.

177. "Young Negro Slayer," *Arkansas Democrat*, May 2, 1927 (this article lists her age as five); "Little Girl's Testimony," *Arkansas Gazette*, May 2, 1927.

178. "From the People, Gazette Reader Believes," *Arkansas Gazette*, May 7, 1927.

179. See Nancy MacLean, *Behind the Mask of Chivalry: The Making of the Second Ku Klux Klan* (New York: Oxford University Press, 1994) and Anne Firor Scott, *The Southern Lady: From Pedestal to Politics, 1830–1930*, Twenty-Fifth Anniversary Edition (Charlottesville: University of Virginia Press, 1995).

180. Editorial, "Arkansas," *Chicago Defender*, May 14, 1927.

181. McClinton, *Scars*, 56; "Flee Little Rock," *Chicago Defender*, May 28, 1927.

182. Daisy Bates, *The Long Shadow of Little Rock* (Fayetteville: University of Arkansas Press, 1987), 4, 62; Audience member, "Project 1927" (presentation), Mosaic Templars Cultural Center, Little Rock, Arkansas, February 15, 2013. For more memories by Little Rock residents, see Jay Jennings, *Carry the Rock: Race, Football, and the Soul of an American City* (New York: Rodale Inc., 2010), 30–50; James Reed Eison, "Dead But She Was In a Good Place, a Church," *Pulaski County Historical Review* 30 (Summer 1982), 30–42.

183. Curtis Sykes, interview by the author, Little Rock, Arkansas, April 9, 2000; Greg Bryant, "Project 1927," February 15, 2015; Maudella Morehead-Parham, "Project 1927" (presentation), Mosaic Templars Cultural Center, Little Rock, Arkansas, February 15, 2013.

184. Raymond Meyers, interview by the author, Little Rock, Arkansas, May 16, 1998.

Chapter 9, "Working Slowly but Surely and Quietly"

1. Jordynn Jack and Lucy Massagee, "Ladies and Lynching: Southern Women, Civil Rights, and the Rhetoric of Interracial Cooperation," *Rhetoric & Public Affairs* 14, no. 3 (2011), 495–96.

2. Jacquelyn Dowd Hall, *Revolt against Chivalry: Jessie Daniel Ames and the Women's Campaign Against Lynching* (New York: Columbia University Press, 1993), 159.

3. I appropriated this term from Gail Murray's *Throwing off the Cloak of Privilege:*

White Southern Women Activists in the Civil Rights Era (Gainesville: University Press of Florida, 2004).

4. Henry E. Barber, "The Association of Southern Women for the Prevention of Lynching, 1930–1942," *Phylon* 34, no. 4 (1973), 380.

5. "History of Movement," Association of Southern Women for the Prevention of Lynching Papers (hereinafter called ASWPL Papers), reel 1.

6. Barber, "Association," 379–380.

7. "No Lynchings in Arkansas," *Blytheville (AR) Courier News*, January 2, 1931, p. 4.

8. "Association of Women of the South for the Prevention of Lynching," January–April 30, 1931, "Report Mrs. Ames," May 1932, Commission on Interracial Cooperation Papers, series VI, reel 45; Katherine B. Smith to Jessie Daniel Ames, February 4, 1931, ASWPL Papers, reel 5.

9. "Those Representing State Ass'ns. Cont.," 1931, ASWPL Papers, reel 1.

10. Lillian McDermott to Jessie Daniel Ames, October 16, 1931, ASWPL Papers, reel 1.

11. Erle Chambers to Jessie Daniel Ames, August 6, 1931, ASWPL Papers, reel 5.

12. "Methodist Women to Begin Campaign Against Lynching," *Monroe (LA) News-Star*, July 10, 1931, p. 12; Mrs. J. M. Hughey (Marianna), Miss Nellie P. Denton (Fort Smith), Mrs. J. C. Green (Little Rock), Mrs. R. G. Cox (Little Rock), Mrs. C. B. Nelson (Little Rock), and Mrs. Ira A. Brumley (North Little Rock), Mrs. John W. Bell (Greenwood), and Mrs. W. F. Woodard (Pine Bluff), all signed the resolution; "Petition Deploring Lynching Signed: Forty Women in Leadership School Sign Paper Friday," *Hope (AR) Star*, July 10, 1931, p. 1; see Secretary to Mrs. Ames to Else Chambers, August 6, 1931, ASWPL Papers, reel 5.

13. "Statements Issue to the Press by States upon Organization, Arkansas, February 20, 1931," and "Pronouncement, Arkansas Association of Women for the Prevention of Lynching," passed February 20, 1931, ASWPL Papers, reel 5.

14. "Lynching Statistics for the First Six Months, 1922–1931 Inclusive," and "Association of Women of the South for the Prevention of Lynching, January–April 30, 1931," ASWPL Papers, reel 5.

15. Philip Dray, *At the Hands of Persons Unknown: The Lynching of Black America* (New York: Modern Library, 2002), 330.

16. ASWPL Executive Committee, Commission on Interracial Cooperation Papers, series VII, reel 45. This list also contains the "selected" names from the ASWPL's list of Arkansas women's signatures.

17. "Statements Issued to the Press by States Upon Organization, Arkansas, February 20, 1931," and "Pronouncement, Arkansas Association of Women for the Prevention of Lynching," passed February 20, 1931, ASWPL Papers, reel 5. The following women were signatories to this pronouncement: Mrs. John P. Streepey, Mrs. Raymond Gesell, Mrs. C. E. Witt, Mrs. J. S. Ligon,

Mrs. J. H. Riggin, Mrs. A. H. Hammann, Mrs. Frank F. Fuller, Miss Lurline
Moody, Mrs. Carl Erickson, Mrs. Laura P. Eshe, Mrs. E. Ellenbogen, Mrs.
Clio Harper, Mrs. O. D. Tucker Sr., Mrs. H. C. Gibson, Mrs. Sam M. Taylor,
Alma L. Keys, Mrs. T. J. Newman, Mrs. David D. Terry, Erle Chambers,
Lillian McDermott, Mrs. B. J. Reaves, Mrs. Curtis Stoute, Mrs. Percy R.
Smith, Mrs. William, McCombs, Lula B. Chase, Mrs. W. Moody, Mrs. J. R.
McAllister, Mrs. J. K. Smith, Blanche Martin, Mrs. E. A. Sherblom, and
Pearle Davis.

18. Katherine B. Smith to Jessie Daniel Ames, January 19, 1931, ASWPL Papers,
reel 5.

19. Mrs. John P. Streepey to Jessie Daniel Ames, November 18, 1931, ASWPL
Papers, reel 1.

20. "7000 Women Represented at Two-Day Meeting Here, Pledge Vigilant Effort
for Lynchless South in 1933," *Atlanta Constitution*, November 20, 1932, p. A19;
Progress of Association of Southern Women for the Prevention of Lynching,
July 1, 1932, ASWPL Paper, reel 5.

21. T. S. Walker to Walter White, May 6, 1933, Papers of the NAACP, Antilynching, Series A: Investigative Files, 1912–1953; "Crossett Mob Lynches
Negro," *Courier News* (Blytheville, Arkansas), September 16, 1932, p. 1.

22. Ibid.

23. Sallie M. Bacon to ASWPL, December 28, 1935, ASWPL Papers, reel 5.

24. Dray, *At the Hands*, 331.

25. Barber, "Association," 380.

26. "Points to Emphasize in Presenting the Movement against the Crime of
Lynching," ASWPL Papers, reel 1.

27. Hall, *Revolt*, 172.

28. "This Business of Lynching," ASWPL Bulletin No. 4, January 1935

29. Erle Chambers, "Two Years of Seed Sowing: Being the Report of the Executive
Secretary of the Arkansas Public Health Association May 25, 1919" (N.p.:
Jordan-Foster Print. Co., 1919).

30. "Miss Erle Chambers, Arkansas, Craighead, Pulaski," *Jonesboro (AR) Daily
Tribune*, June 27, 1922, p. 3.

31. Lillian McDermott to Jessie Daniel Ames, October 16, 1931, ASWPL Papers,
reel 5; "Mrs. Lillian McDermott State Reemployment Head," *Blytheville
(AR) Courier News*, August 18, 1933, p. 1; Stephanie Bayless, *Obliged to Help:
Adolphine Fletcher Terry and the Progressive South* (Little Rock: Butler Center
Books, 2011), 54.

32. "Funeral Scheduled for Adolphine Terry," *Northwest Arkansas Times*
(Fayetteville), July 26, 1976, p. 11; Peggy Harris, "Adolphine Fletcher Terry,"
Encyclopedia of Arkansas History and Culture, http://www.encyclopediaof
arkansas.net/encyclopedia/entry-detail.aspx?entryID=1779 (accessed
September 12, 2015).

33. Bayless, *Obliged to Help*, 54; Women Members Arkansas State Inter-Racial Committee, Little Rock, Arkansas, April 14, 1922, ASWPL Papers, reel 5.

34. "Dr. Truett Will Speak at W.M.U. Opening Session," *Anniston (AL) Star*, May 10, 1931, p. 10; "Parent Teacher Congress Installs New President," *Blytheville (AR) Courier News*, May 18, 1934, p. 1.

35. Jessie Daniel Ames to Mrs. C. H. Thorpe, February 6, 1935, ASWPL Papers, reel 5.

36. Jessie Daniel Ames to central council ASWPL, March 16, 1933, ASWPL Papers, reel 1.

37. Annual Bulletin, ASWPL, January 1933, ASWPL Papers, reel 1.

38. "Arkansas on Honor Roll of States Without Lynchings," newspaper clipping from unknown paper, probably the *Arkansas Gazette*, 1934, in the ASWPL Papers, reel 5.

39. "This Business of Lynching," ASWPL Bulletin No. 4, January, 1935, p. 6.

40. Ibid., 19.

41. Dray, *At the Hands*, 330.

42. Jessie Daniel Ames to Mrs. W. T. Bacon, January 10, 1936, ASWPL Papers, reel 5.

43. Barber, "Association," 381.

44. "Lynching Is Hit by Southern White Women: Resolution Passed at Meeting," *Atlanta Daily World*, January 10, 1934, p. 1; Hall, "Revolt," 238; Dray, *At the Hands*, 341.

45. Jessie Daniel Ames to Mrs. C.H. Thorpe, May 9, 1935, ASWPL Papers, reel 5.

46. J. M. Futrell to Mrs. B. J. Reaves, January 8, 1935, ASWPL Papers, reel 5.

47. Mary Jane Brown, *Eradicating This Evil: Women in the American Anti-Lynching Movement, 1892–1940* (New York: Garland Publishing, Inc., 2000), 183.

48. Anne Stefani, *Unlikely Dissenters: White Southern Women in the Fight for Racial Justice, 1920–1970* (Gainesville: University Press of Florida, 2015), 79.

49. "Lynching Is Hit by Southern White Women: Resolution Passed at Meeting," *Atlanta Daily World*, January 10, 1934, p. 1.

50. Jessie Daniel Ames to Mrs. B. J. Reaves, March 6, 1935, ASWPL Papers, reel 5.

51. Crystal N. Feimster, *Southern Horrors: Women and the Politics of Rape and Lynching* (Cambridge: Harvard University Press, 2009), 231.

52. "Lynching Is Hit by Southern White Women: Resolution Passed at Meeting," *Atlanta Daily World*, January 10, 1934, p. 1.

53. Dray, *At the Hands*, 331.

54. Jessie Daniel Ames to Mrs. B. J. Reaves, March 9, 1936, ASWPL Papers, reel 5.

55. Nancy Snell Griffith, "Lynching of Willie Kees," *Encyclopedia of Arkansas History and Culture*, http://www.encyclopediaofarkansas.net/encyclopedia/entry-detail.aspx?search=1&entryID=7855 (accessed September 8, 2015).

56. "South Stirred by Lynchings: 2 Negros Lynched by Mobs, Another Threatened," *Deadwood (SD) Pioneer-Times*, May 1, 1939, p. 1.

57. *Southern Women Look at Lynching* (Atlanta: ASWPL, 1937), 14.

58. Ibid., 15.

59. Della Reaves to Jessie Daniel Ames, May 1, 1936, ASWPL Papers, reel 5.

60. "Women Demand Inquiry into Lepanto Lynching," *Blytheville (AR) Courier News*, May 5, 1936, p. 1.

61. "After All Those Years without a Lynching," *Blytheville (AR) Courier News*, May 1, 1936, p. 4.

62. Nancy Hendricks, *Senator Hattie Caraway: An Arkansas Legacy* (Charleston: The History Press, 2013), 61.

63. "The Anti-Lynching Bill Speech of Hon. Hattie W. Caraway of Arkansas in the Senate of the United States, January 13, 1938," courtesy of the Old State House Museum Collection, Little Rock, Arkansas.

64. Ibid.; "Woman Aids Lynch Bill Fight: Mrs. Hattie Caraway of Arkansas Joins Filibusterers," *Orangeburg (SC) Times and Democrat*, January 14, 1938, p. 1.

65. Jessie Daniel Ames to Mrs. B. J. Reaves, May 18, 1936, ASWPL Papers, reel 5.

66. "With Quietness They Work: Report of the Activities of Southern Women in Education Against Lynching during 1937" (Atlanta: ASWPL, February 1938); Della Reaves to Jessie Daniel Ames, April 12, 1937; Secretary to Mrs. Ames to Mrs. B. J. Reaves, April 19, 1937, ASWPL Papers, reel 5.

67. Hall, "Revolt," 178.

68. Della Reaves to Jessie Daniel Ames, April 12, 1937, ASWPL Papers, reel 5.

69. Ibid.; "Feeling Is Tense," ASWPL Bulletin No. 8, February 1938.

70. Ibid.

71. Ibid.; "Prevented Lynchings," January–July 1, 1938, ASWPL Papers, reel 5. The sheriff increased the number of guards protecting the men in Crittenden County. In Lafayette County, the sheriff whisked the man out of town.

72. "This Credit Manager Does Not Find the Duties Monotonous," *Indianapolis News*, August 25, 1923, p. 20.

73. Ibid.

74. Bayless, *Obliged to Help*, 54; "Board Chairman in Clash with Kolb," *Hope (AR) Star*, February 22, 1937, p. 1; "Capitol Settles Down," *Gentry (AR) Journal-Advance*, December 9, 1937, p. 4; "The Court That Puts Popcorn before Prison," *Lincoln (NE) Star*, March 9, 1941, p. 44.

75. Bayless, *Obliged to Help*, 54.

76. "Report of Activities," 1938, ASWPL Papers, reel 5.

77. Della Reaves to Jessie Daniel Ames, August 23, 1937, ASWPL Papers, reel 5.

78. Hall, *Revolt*, xxx.

79. "Start Probe in Arkansas Lynching: Lynching off Ark Record," *New York Amsterdam News*, February 11, 1939, p. 1.

80. Jessie Daniel Ames to Mrs. B. J. Reaves, June 19, 1939; Mrs. A. R. McKinney to Mrs. B. J. Reaves, July 17, 1939, ASWPL Papers, reel 5.

81. "Jury Deliberates One Minute, Sends Negro to Chair," *Hope (AR) Star*, May 25, 1939, p. 1.

82. Della Reaves to Jessie Daniel Ames, May 26, 1939; "Lynchings Prevented,"

January–July 1939, ASWPL Papers, reel 5; "Lynching Averted as Officers Take Negro from Mob," *Hope (AR) Star*, May 6, 1939, p. 1.

83. Barber, "Association," 387.

84. Jessie Daniel Ames to "Sheriffs of Arkansas," May 28, 1940, ASWPL Papers, reel 5.

85. "Report on Instances in Which Mob Violence or Lynchings Were Prevented, 1940," ASWPL Papers, reel 5.

86. See Murray, *Throwing Off the Cloak of Privilege*.

Chapter 10, Holding the Line

1. "Senate Apologizes for Not Enacting Anti-Lynching Law," ABC News, June 13, 2005, http://abcnews.go.com/WNT/story?id=845713 (accessed December 12, 2015).

2. "S.Res. 39 (109th): Lynching Victims Senate Apology Resolution," online at https://www.govtrack.us/congress/bills/109/sres39 (accessed December 12, 2015).

3. V. O. Key Jr., *Southern Politics in State and Nation*, new ed. (Knoxville: University of Tennessee Press, 1984). Over half a century after its original publication, this work remains the single best treatment of the distinctive world of southern politics, especially the one-party system that was so central to its operations until things began to change in the nineteen sixties. Key illuminates the variety of ways that southerners maintained their power, as well as its impact on both the local and national political scene.

4. *Slaughterhouse Cases*, 83 U.S. 36 (1873).

5. *Civil Rights Cases*, 109 U.S. 3 (1883).

6. Quoted in Adam Burns, "Without Due Process: Albert Pillsbury and the Hoar Anti-lynching Bill," *American Nineteenth Century History* 11.2 (2010), 237, online at http://www.tandfonline.com/eprint/DK54dArGPDxTDsSMwgmS/full (accessed December 12, 2015).

7. Burns, "Without Due Process," 239.

8. Ibid.

9. Ibid., 239–240.

10. Ibid., 241.

11. Robert L. Zangrando, *The NAACP Crusade Against Lynching, 1909–1950* (Philadelphia: Temple University Press, 1980), 43.

12. Zangrando, *NAACP Crusade*, 44.

13. "Senate Apologizes for Not Enacting Anti-Lynching Law," ABC News.

14. "Appendix No. 5 — Membership of the Committee on the Judiciary from the 13th through the 97th," *A History of the Committee on the Judiciary, 1813–2006*, online at http://www.gpo.gov/fdsys/pkg/GPO-CDOC-109hdoc153/pdf/GPO-CDOC-109hdoc153-5-5-12.pdf (accessed December 12, 2015).

15. Robert Whitaker, *On the Laps of Gods: The Red Summer of 1919 and the Struggle for Justice That Remade a Nation* (New York: Crown Publishers, 2008), 164–66.

16. "Appendix No. 5—Membership of the Committee on the Judiciary from the 13th through the 97th," *A History of the Committee on the Judiciary, 1813–2006*. Tackett would prove to be the last of the long line of Arkansas representatives who served on the Judiciary Committee while legislation relating to lynching in particular, and civil rights generally, was in the forefront of the committee's responsibilities. However, it was not an issue for Arkansas or the South, for it would still be another decade before the committee's increasingly liberal cast would be able to overcome the still solid opposition to all civil rights legislation presented by the southern Senate bloc, whose members included Arkansas's John McClellan and J. William Fulbright.

17. Cameron McWhirter, *Red Summer: The Summer of 1919 and the Awakening of Black America* (New York: St. Martin's Griffin, 2012), 12–14, 17.

18. "Anti-Lynching Law Legislation Renewed," US House of Representatives History, Art & Archives, http://history.house.gov/Exhibitions-and-Publications/BAIC/Historical-Essays/Temporary-Farewell/Anti-Lynching-Legislation/; McWhirter, *Red Summer*, map opposite p. 1.

19. McWhirter, *Red Summer*, 225.

20. Ibid., 219.

21. Ibid., 225.

22. Ibid., 226–27.

23. Ibid., 259.

24. *Moore v. Dempsey*, 261 U.S. 86 (1923); Zangrando, *NAACP Crusade*, 85–86.

25. McWhirter, *Red Summer*, 246; Jeffrey A. Jenkins, Justin Peck, and Vesla M. Weaver, "Between Reconstructions: Congressional Action on Civil Rights, 1891–1940," May 14, 2009, 25, online at http://faculty.virginia.edu/jajenkins/Jenkins-Peck-Weaver.pdf (accessed December 12, 2015).

26. Jenkins, Peck, and Weaver, 25; McWhirter, *Red Summer*, 247.

27. McWhirter, *Red Summer*, 247.

28. Ibid., 250.

29. Whitaker, *On the Laps of Gods*, 218.

30. Ibid.

31. Jenkins, Peck, and Weaver, "Between Reconstructions," 24; McWhirter, *Red Summer*, 250.

32. Keith Finley, "Southern Opposition to Civil Rights in the United States Senate: A Tactical and Ideological Analysis, 1938–1965" (PhD diss., Louisiana State University, 2003), 20, online at http://etd.lsu.edu/docs/available/etd-0702103-151627/unrestricted/Finley_dis.pdf (accessed December 12, 2015); Zangrando, *NAACP Crusade*, 57.

33. Zangrando, *NAACP Crusade*, 64.

34. Ibid., 66.

35. Daniel S. Holt, ed., *Debates on the Federal Judiciary: A Documentary History*, vol. 2, *1875–1939*, 193, online at http://www.fjc.gov/public/pdf.nsf/lookup /debates-federal-judiciary-vol-ii.pdf/$file/debates-federal-judiciary-vol-ii.pdf (accessed December 12, 2015).

36. "G.O.P., Whipped by Filibuster, Kills Dyer Bill," *Chicago Tribune*, December 3, 1922, p. 5, online at http://archives.chicagotribune.com/1922/12/03/page/5 /article/g-o-p-whipped-by-filibuster-kills-dyer-bill (accessed December 12, 2015).

37. Barbara Holden-Smith, "Lynching, Federalism, and the Intersection of Race and Gender in the Progressive Era," *Yale Journal of Law and Feminism* 8.2 (1996), 59, online at http://www.soc.umn.edu/~samaha/cases/smith_lynching _feminism.html (accessed December 12, 2015).

38. Ibid, 59.

39. Justin Tackett, "Stanford Historian Examines the Politics of Sexual Violence," *Stanford Report*, September 11, 2013, online at http://news.stanford.edu /news/2013/september/politics-sexual-violence-091113.html (accessed December 12, 2015).

40. "Lynch Law Held Up By Filibuster," *Milwaukee Sentinel*, November 30, 1922, p. 2, online at https://news.google.com/newspapers?nid=1368&dat=19221130 &id=iv5PAAAAIBAJ&sjid=vgoEAAAAIBAJ&pg=7068,5693840&hl=en; "G.O.P., Whipped by Filibuster, Kills Dyer Bill," *Chicago Tribune*; "Filibuster Kills Anti-Lynching Bill," *New York Times*, December 3, 1922, online at: http://query.nytimes.com/mem/archive-free/pdf?res=950CE1D7153AEF33 A25750C0A9649D946395D6CF (accessed December 12, 2015).

41. Jenkins, Peck, and Weaver, "Between Reconstructions," 39–40.

42. Cecil Edward Weller Jr., *Joe T. Robinson: Always a Loyal Democrat* (Fayetteville: University of Arkansas Press, 1998), 95.

43. Ibid., 95–96.

44. For the most complete treatment of Robinson's career, see Weller, *Joe T. Robinson*.

45. Jenkins, Peck, and Weaver, "Between Reconstructions," 37–38.

46. Holden-Smith, "Lynching," 39.

47. Ibid., 39; Zangrando, *NAACP Crusade*, 99.

48. Zangrando, *NAACP Crusade*, 114–15.

49. Nancy J. Weiss, *Farewell to the Party of Lincoln: Black Politics in the Age of FDR* (Princeton, NJ: Princeton University Press, 1983), 103.

50. "Poll of United States Senate on the Wagner-Costigan Anti-Lynching Bill," NAACP Papers, Library of Congress, Washington, DC, online at NAACP'S Anti-Lynching Campaign in the 1930s, Documents to Accompany Investigative Journalism Game, http://edsitement.neh.gov/sites/edsitement.neh.gov/files /worksheets/combined.pdf (accessed December 12, 2015).

51. Weiss, *Farewell*, 105.

52. Ibid., 106.

53. "Anti-Lynching Bill Engages Senate in Lengthy Filibuster," *Vassar Miscellany News*, May 1, 1935, p. 1, online at http://newspaperarchives.vassar.edu /cgi-bin/vassar?a=d&d=miscellany19350501-01.2.7 (accessed December 12, 2015).

54. Ibid.

55. Jenkins, Peck, and Weaver, "Between Reconstructions," 47.

56. Ibid., 48; "Anti-Lynching," *Vassar Miscellany*.

57. "Anti-Lynching," *Vassar Miscellany*.

58. Jenkins, Peck, and Weaver, "Between Reconstructions," 48; Isabelle Whelan, "The Politics of Federal Anti-lynching Legislation in the New Deal Era" (MA thesis, Institute for the Study of the Americas, 2007), 22, online at http:// sas-space.sas.ac.uk/1569/1/Whelan_Isabelle%20Dissertation%20complete .pdf (accessed December 12, 2015).

59. Ibid.

60. Ibid., 241.

61. Ibid.

62. Weiss, *Farewell*, 241–42.

63. Robin Bernice Balthrope, "Lawlessness and the New Deal: Congress and Antilynching Legislation, 1934–1938," (PhD diss., Ohio State University, 1995), 188, online at https://etd.ohiolink.edu/rws_etd/document/get/osu 1269368027/inline (accessed December 12, 2015).

64. Zangrando, *NAACP Crusade*, 143.

65. Ibid.

66. Ibid., 144.

67. Jeff Sheshol, *Supreme Power: Franklin Roosevelt vs. the Supreme Court* (New York: W. W. Norton & Company, Inc., 2010), 449–50.

68. Weiss, *Farewell*, 243.

69. Weller, *Joe T. Robinson*, 167.

70. Zangrando, *NAACP Crusade*, 145; Weller, *Joe T. Robinson*, 167.

71. Weiss, *Farewell*, 244.

72. Ibid.; Zangrando, *NAACP Crusade*, 145.

73. Balthrope, "Lawlessness," 192.

74. Donald A. Ritchie, "Alben W. Barkley: The President's Man," in Richard A. Baker and Roger H. Davidson, eds., *First among Equals: Outstanding Senate Leaders of the Twentieth Century* (Washington, DC: Congressional Quarterly, Inc., 1991), 133–34.

75. Ibid., 134.

76. "Filibuster Ended as Senate Shelves Anti-Lynch Bill," *New York Times*, February 22, 1938, online at http://partners.nytimes.com/library/national/race /022238race-ra.html (accessed December 12, 2015); Whelan, "Politics," 27.

77. Weiss, *Farewell*, 248–49.

78. "Hattie Wyatt Caraway," US House of Representatives, History, Art & Archives, online at http://history.house.gov/People/Listing/C/CARAWAY ,-Hattie-Wyatt-(Cooo138)/ (accessed December 12, 2015); Nancy Hendricks, *Senator Hattie Caraway: An Arkansas Legacy* (Charleston, SC: The History Press, 2013).

79. "Hattie Wyatt Caraway," US House of Representatives.

80. "Bill, Anti-Lynching—Hattie Caraway Speech, January 13, 1938," Old State House Museum Collection, online at http://www.collections.oldstatehouse .com/emuseum40/view/objects/asitem/106/8/title-asc;jsessionid=CAA2520 CE5ECA97EA85DA5CD206DC3DC?t:state:flow=foc93fe2-9885-494f-a9d6 -5aa2988747c0 (accessed December 12, 2015).

81. "Anti-Lynching Bill Is Denounced in Senate by Its Only Woman Member," *Lawrence (KS) Daily Journal-World*, January 13, 1938, p. 1, online at https:// news.google.com/newspapers?nid=2199&dat=19380113&id=UmZeAAAA IBAJ&sjid=F2ENAAAAIBAJ&pg=4469,3137538&hl=en (accessed December 12, 2015).

82. Michael Carter, "Senator Hattie Caraway Is a Reactionary Southerner," *Baltimore Afro-American*, November 6, 1943, p. 5, online at https://news.google .com/newspapers?nid=2205&dat=19431102&id=a2BGAAAAIBAJ&sjid =huUMAAAAIBAJ&pg=1050,4146672&hl=en (accessed December 12, 2015).

83. Carter, "Senator Hattie Caraway," 5.

84. "Jessie Daniel Ames," *The Rise and Fall of Jim Crow*, Public Broadcasting Service, http://www.pbs.org/wnet/jimcrow/stories_people_ames.html (accessed December 12, 2015).

85. Rhae Lynn Barnes, "A Man Was Lynched Yesterday: Jessie Daniel Ames and the Association of Southern Women for the Prevention of Lynching, 1930–1942," U.S. History Scene, http://ushistoryscene.com/article/aswpl/ (accessed December 12, 2015).

86. "Feeling Is Tense," Pamphlet issued by the Association of Southern Women for the Prevention of Lynching, February 1938, online at http://ia802705.us .archive.org/28/items/FeelingIsTense/ASPL.pdf (accessed December 12, 2015).

87. Whelan, "Politics," 7–8.

88. Weiss, *Farewell*, 248–49.

89. Robert Shogan, *Harry Truman and the Struggle for Racial Justice* (Lawrence: University Press of Kansas, 2013), 1–2.

90. Ibid., 119–26.

91. Sherry Laymon, *Fearless: John L. McClellan, United States Senator* (Mustang, OK: Tate Publishing & Enterprises, LLC, 2011), 99–101.

92. Zangrando, *NAACP Crusade*, 201.

93. Balthrope, "Lawlessness," 231.

94. John Kyle Day, "Lawrence Brooks Hays," *Encyclopedia of Arkansas History*

and Culture, http://www.encyclopediaofarkansas.net/encyclopedia/entry-detail
.aspx?entryID=506 (accessed December 12, 2015).

95. Balthrope, 231–32.

96. Zangrando, *NAACP Crusade*, 117.

97. "Antilynching and Protection of Civil Rights," Hearing Before Subcommittee
No. 3 of the Committee on the Judiciary House of Representatives, Eighty-
First Congress, First and Second Sessions: Testimony of Hon. Boyd Tackett, a
Representative in Congress from the State of Arkansas, June 29, 1949, 221–23,
online at https://babel.hathitrust.org/cgi/pt?id=umn.31951d03669262m;view
=1up;seq=157 (accessed July 26, 2016).

98. Ibid.

99. William H. Pruden III, "Boyd Anderson Tackett," *Encyclopedia of Arkansas
History and Culture*, http://www.encyclopediaofarkansas.net/encyclopedia
/entry-detail.aspx?entryID=4657 (accessed December 12, 2015); Sidney S.
McMath, *Promises Kept* (Fayetteville: University of Arkansas Press, 2003),
285–87.

100. Oleomargarine Tax Repeal, *CQ Almanac*, 1950, online at https://library.cqpress
.com/cqalmanac/document.php?id=cqal50-1376743 (accessed December 12,
2015).

101. "Oral History Interview with Sidney S. McMath, September 8, 1990,"
Southern Oral History Program, University of North Carolina at Chapel Hill,
http://dc.lib.unc.edu/cdm/compoundobject/collection/sohp/id/8635/rec
/1 (accessed December 12, 2015).

102. Ibid. McMath was elected governor in 1948 after opposing the Dixiecrat effort
to take over the state party. He was reelected in 1950 but was defeated in his bid
for third term in 1952. An effort to defeat John McClellan for a US Senate seat
in 1954 was also unsuccessful, as was a final attempt to regain the governorship
against incumbent Orval Faubus in 1962. In contrast, after serving one term in
the House of Representatives, Fulbright unseated incumbent Hattie Caraway
and then was reelected on four occasions before being defeated for a sixth term
in 1974 by David Pryor. See McMath, *Promises Kept* and Randall Bennett
Woods, *Fulbright: A Biography* (New York: Cambridge University Press, 1995)
for fuller treatments of their respective careers.

103. Laymon, *Fearless*, 249–50; Woods, *Fulbright*, 209–11.

INDEX

Abbott, Charles, 143–44
Abbott, F. M., 143–44
Adams, Dave, 171
African Americans: and the interracial cooperation movement, 159–62, 164–66; as members of lynch mobs, 36–37, 55–56, 57–59; as middle class, 135–37; pseudoscientific depictions of, 147; as railroad and industry workers, 43–45; as Union soldiers, 8; during slavery, 17–34; migration into Arkansas, 36
African Colonization Society, 81. *See also* Back-to-Africa movement.
Aiken, Ned, 78–79
Alabama, 5, 31, 67, 70, 138, 190–92, 208, 225, 230, 235, 248
Alexander, Arkansas, 211
Allen, Henry J., 150
Allsopp, Fred W., 75
Alph (slave), 27–28
Altheimer, Arkansas, 236
American Association of University Women, 228, 233, 235
American Citizen, 82
American Legion, 152–53
American Red Cross, 159, 208
Ames, Jessie Daniel, 162, 166, 224–26, 228–33, 235–36, 255
Anderson, James, 27
Anderson, Roy, 48
Antilynching legislation, 13, 229–30, 239–59. *See also* Costigan-Wagner antilynching bill; Dyer antilynching bill; Gavagan antilynching bill; Senate

bill 88; Wagner-Van Nuys antilynching bill
Appeal, 47, 176–77
Appeal-Avalanche, 82
Apperson, S. M., 47, 172
Archer, Arthur O., 97–98
Arellano, Lisa, 67
Argenta, Arkansas, 40, 167, 178–89, 211. *See also* North Little Rock, Arkansas
Argyle, Malcolm, 61, 80
Arkadelphia Siftings, 64–65
Arkansas Baptist College, 136, 137
Arkansas Baptist Convention, 233
Arkansas Bar Association, 162, 226
Arkansas Business and Professional Women's Club, 234
Arkansas Congress of Parents and Teachers, 226
Arkansas County, Arkansas, 38, 54, 117, 140–41, 146. *See also* Arkansas Post, Arkansas; DeWitt, Arkansas; Saint Charles, Arkansas; Stuttgart, Arkansas
Arkansas Delta, 36, 81–82, 87, 135
Arkansas Democrat, 38, 84, 97, 122, 125, 150, 152, 154, 159, 175, 176, 179, 181–82, 184–85, 186–87, 189, 198, 200–1, 204, 206–7, 209, 213, 215, 218
Arkansas Democrat (antebellum), 25
Arkansas Democratic Women's Clubs, 224, 235
Arkansas Digest of Statutes, 177
Arkansas Federation of Women's Clubs, 224, 226, 235